Jorie Graham

CONTEMPORARY NORTH AMERICAN POETRY

Alan Golding, Adalaide Morris, and Lynn Keller
Series Editors

Jorie Graham

Essays on the Poetry

edited by Thomas Gardner

THE UNIVERSITY OF WISCONSIN PRESS

The University of Wisconsin Press
1930 Monroe Street
Madison, Wisconsin 53711

www.wisc.edu/wisconsinpress/

3 Henrietta Street
London WC2E 8LU, England

Copyright © 2005
The Board of Regents of the University of Wisconsin System
All rights reserved

5 4 3 2 1

Printed in the United States of America

Library of Congress Cataloging-in-Publication Data
Jorie Graham : essays on the poetry / edited by Thomas Gardner.
p. cm. — (Contemporary North American poetry)
Includes bibliographical references and index.
ISBN 0-299-20320-4 (hardcover : alk. paper) — ISBN 0-299-20324-7
(pbk. : alk. paper)
1. Graham, Jorie, 1951—Criticism and interpretation.
I. Gardner, Thomas, 1952– II. Series.
PS3557.R214J67 2005
811'.54—dc22
2004012821

Contents

Acknowledgments   vii

Introduction
THOMAS GARDNER   3

1. Jorie Graham: Art and Erosion (1992)
   BONNIE COSTELLO   13

2. *from* Countering Culture: Review of *Materialism* (1994)
   ELISABETH FROST   34

3. *from* Postlyrically Yours: Review of *Materialism* (1994)
   CALVIN BEDIENT   38

4. Jorie Graham: The Moment of Excess (1995)
   HELEN VENDLER   42

5. Iconoclasm in the Poetry of Jorie Graham (1995)
   ANNE SHIFRER   60

6. Listening for a Divine Word: Review of *The Errancy* (1997)
   FORREST GANDER   75

7. Jorie Graham's Big Hunger (1997)
   JAMES LONGENBACH   82

8. *from* Exquisite Disjunctions, Exquisite Arrangements: Jorie Graham's "Strangeness of Strategy" (1998)
   BRIAN HENRY   102

9. *from* Jorie Graham's Incandescence (1999)
   THOMAS GARDNER   113

10. *from* Breaking and Making: Review of *Swarm* (2000)
    STEPHEN YENSER   147

11. To Feel an Idea: Review of *Swarm* (2001)
    JOANNA KLINK   156

12. Indigo, Cyanine, Beryl: Review of *Never* (2003)
    HELEN VENDLER   170

13. Jorie Graham's _____s (2003)
    THOMAS J. OTTEN   185

14. The Place of Jorie Graham
    JAMES LONGENBACH   206

15. Jorie Graham Listening
    WILLARD SPIEGELMAN   219

16. The Speaking Subject In / Me: Gender and Ethical Subjectivity in the Poetry of Jorie Graham
    CYNTHIA HOGUE   238

17. "Tell Them *No*": Jorie Graham's Poems of Adolescence
    STEPHEN BURT   257

18. Toward a Jorie Graham Lexicon
    CALVIN BEDIENT   275

Contributors   293

Index of Graham's Works   297

Index of Names   301

Acknowledgments

Thanks to Lynn Keller, Dee Morris, and Alan Golding for their support of this work.

Calvin Bedient's "Postlyrically Yours" originally appeared in *The Threepenny Review* (Summer 1994). Reprinted by permission of the author.

Bonnie Costello's "Jorie Graham: Art and Erosion" originally appeared in *Contemporary Literature* 33 (2) (1992). Reprinted by permission of the Board of Regents of the University of Wisconsin System.

Elisabeth Frost's "Countering Culture" originally appeared in *The Women's Review of Books* 11 (6) (1994). Reprinted by permission of the author.

Forrest Gander's "Listening for a Divine Word" originally appeared in *The Boston Book Review* (Summer 1997). Reprinted by permission of the publisher.

Thomas Gardner's "Jorie Graham's Incandescence" is reproduced from *Regions of Unlikeness: Explaining Contemporary Poetry* by permission of the University of Nebraska Press. Copyright © 1999 by the University of Nebraska Press.

Excerpts from *The End of Beauty* by Jorie Graham, Copyright © 1987 by Jorie Graham, are reprinted by permission of HarperCollins Publishers Inc.

Excerpts from *Region of Unlikeness* by Jorie Graham, Copyright © 1991 by Jorie Graham, are reprinted by permission of HarperCollins Publishers Inc.

Excerpts from *Materialism* by Jorie Graham, Copyright © 1993 by Jorie Graham, are reprinted by permission of HarperCollins Publishers Inc.

Excerpts from *The Errancy* by Jorie Graham, Copyright © 1997 by Jorie Graham, are reprinted by permission of HarperCollins Publishers Inc. and by Carcanet Press Limited.

Excerpts from *Swarm* by Jorie Graham, Copyright © 1999 by Jorie Graham, are reprinted by permission of HarperCollins Publishers Inc.

Excerpts from *Never* by Jorie Graham, Copyright © 2002 by Jorie Graham, are reprinted by permission of HarperCollins Publishers Inc.

Brian Henry's "Exquisite Disjunctions, Exquisite Arrangements: Jorie Graham's 'Strangeness of Strategy'" first appeared in the *Antioch Review* 56 (3). Copyright © 1998 by the Antioch Review, Inc. Reprinted by permission of the Editors.

Joanna Klink's "To Feel an Idea" first appeared in *The Kenyon Review*-New Series 24 (1) (2002). Reprinted by permission of the author.

James Longenbach's "Jorie Graham's Big Hunger," from *Modern Poetry after Modernism* by James Longenbach, Copyright © 1997 by James Longenbach, is used by permission of Oxford University Press, Inc.

Thomas J. Otten's "Jorie Graham's _____s" first appeared in *PMLA* 118 (2). Copyright © 2003 by the Modern Language Association of America. Reprinted by permission of the Modern Language Association of America.

Ann Shifrer's "Iconoclasm in the Poetry of Jorie Graham" first appeared in the *Colby Quarterly* 31 (2) (1995). Reprinted by permission of the publisher.

Helen Vendler's "Jorie Graham: The Moment of Excess" is reprinted by permission of the publisher from *The Breaking of Style: Hopkins, Heaney, Graham* by Helen Vendler, pp. 71–94, Cambridge, Mass.: Harvard University Press, Copyright © 1995 by the President and Fellows of Harvard College.

Helen Vendler's "Indigo, Cyanine, Beryl" first appeared in the *London Review of Books*, www.lrb.co.uk (January 23 2003). Reprinted by permission of the author and publisher.

Stephen Yenser's "Breaking and Making" is reprinted from *A Boundless Field: American Poetry at Large* by Stephen Yenser. Copyright © 2002 by Stephen Yenser. Reprinted by permission of the University of Michigan Press.

Jorie Graham

Introduction

THOMAS GARDNER

In two short essays published almost twenty years ago, Jorie Graham called attention to Wallace Stevens' notion of "The poem of the mind in the act of finding / What will suffice." "Those poems that move me are enactments of discovery, not retellings," she writes. "In those poems that change me the speaker is most often the protagonist, not the narrator. The narrator knows he will survive the poem. The protagonist never knows if he will even make it to the end; the poem itself becomes the act of survival, the act of flailing and probing, an open desire for grace or change. I think this is what Stevens meant. . . ."[1] Discoveries happen in the writing: "the poet using the . . . poem—the process of writing the poem—in order to find what will, for now, suffice."[2] What prompts those acts of mind has shifted over the course of Graham's career: the seemingly self-contained beauty of paintings; the explosive poise of myth; the largely-unexamined story of one's life; a silent lover; the disappearing world—all, as in Dickinson, just out of reach. As the linguistic approaches by which Graham opens and engages her sometimes stubbornly resistant materials have developed—that is, have been tested, exhausted, and reformulated—the dramas her poems enact have become increasingly more ambitious and detailed and pointed, prompting some reviewers to complain that her linguistic records aren't exactly poems anymore.[3] And yet, despite these changes, Graham's intentions have stayed remarkably consistent: to be awakened and changed, in the writing; to experience and to take responsibility for one's human presence in the world— flailing, touching, destroying; and to reproduce those experiences in the reader.

Graham's ambitions for poetry—what she calls the "courage—right there at the core of the act of composition— . . . not to let up on the belief in language"[4]—

has produced a body of work restless with its accomplishments, willing to entertain contradiction and complexity, and almost-theatrical in the questions it raises and the responses it ventures. Her visibility as a writer—nine well-received books in a little over two decades, fifteen years teaching at Iowa's Writers' Workshop, the current holder of Harvard's Boylston Chair of Rhetoric and Oratory, Pulitzer Prize, MacArthur Fellowship—is not only a recognition of undeniable poetic gifts, but also points to an increasing openness in American poetry as a whole to larger questions and experimental complexity. Her work demonstrates the value of refusing to align oneself with a too narrowly drawn set of pressures or predecessors or expectations. Such an openness, in Graham and others, has produced an American poetry deeply and unpredictably alive.

Helen Vendler's prominent reviews of four of Graham's early books, not included here, have drawn attention to the shifting styles with which Graham has traced the mind in action. In reviewing *Erosion* (1983), Vendler pointed to "the evenness of Graham's line and the gravity of her gaze" as she traces "those spiritual motions, impulses, currents, apprehensions, and emergings that intangibly make up our inner life." Examining *The End of Beauty* (1987), Vendler called attention to the "intrapsychic conflict between drift and shape" in the poems of that volume: the way "free and far ranging thought" is continually halted and broken off, the poet's lines "mimic[king] the fertile ruses of the mind—exploratory rush and decisive interruption, interrogatory speech and intermittent silence." Vendler used the image of "cloud chambers full of colliding protons" to describe Graham's "practice [in *Region of Unlikeness* (1991)] of connecting together moments widely separated in time and space and occurring on disparate mental levels." Working out initially unseen links between such moments, tracing "a zigzag of half-articulated suspicions, invocations, silences, hints, glimpses, stumblings, and contradictions," the poems in this volume refine once again the way they "picture . . . the mind making meaning." Focusing in her response to *Materialism* on rhythm (1993)—"the cascading or tumbling one of urgent presentation followed by a lapse into pause or exhaustion"—Vendler significantly shifted terms and began speaking about movements of consciousness: "The personal lyric represents the socially marked self; but the impersonal lyric represents what used to be called the soul, but might better, in Graham, be called consciousness," "the voice of metaphysical and moral consciousness. . . ."[5]

A number of the reviews and essays collected here extend and complicate this line of thought, describing—often by reenacting—the increasingly-foregrounded stylistic means by which Graham replicates movements of consciousness. In "Listening for a Divine Word," his examination of *The Errancy* (1997), Forrest

Gander attempts to describe "the radical and sensuous language [with which] Graham enacts a presence." He carefully details the way her "accretionary syntax, . . . allow[ing] for innumerable revisions" combines with the ability to keep multiple patterns of sound in motion, "looping one pattern of sound through another," to produce lines that "feather objective and subjective stances" in an ongoing process of "inscription, revision, and erasure." Brian Henry, in "Exquisite Disjunctions, Exquisite Arrangements: Jorie Graham's 'Strangeness of Strategy,'" follows a similar approach, noting a constant process of self-correction in "the various [inner] enactments" of her poems. This process is most visible, he claims, in her syntax—in which "grammatical disruptions . . . [work] against her own music and eloquence"—and her line. Henry calls attention to Graham's recent use of the "outrider" to "displace a word or phrase at the end of a line," seeing the "arrangement and rearrangement" made possible by such a device as a facet of her "disjunctive lyricism—a lyricism struggling against itself— . . . one of the primary dramas of her poems."

In "Jorie Graham's Big Hunger," James Longenbach also highlights the poet's ongoing quest "for new ways to dramatize the mind in motion," but cautions that one shouldn't be unthinkingly led by the conventional notion of the "breakthrough" volume to immediately associate growing stylistic complexity with formal and ideological open-endedness. In fact, he claims, Graham's second and fourth books (*Erosion* and *Region of Unlikeness*) share a manner of thinking which her third and fifth books (*The End of Beauty* and *Materialism*) consistently refuse. The first pair, he claims, thinks by means of analogy, juxtaposing or intertwining (in however fragmented a way) different stories. Only apparently "decentered and opened," these poems "do not so much enact the processes of consciousness as create, through juxtaposition or implied analogy, a static puzzle that the reader is obliged to solve." The second pair of books, by contrast, includes elements that "do not match up analogically, . . . but move steadily if inexplicably forward, linked by the arbitrary repetition of particular words." In describing Graham's most recent use of language to emphasize the body's role in acts of consciousness, Helen Vendler, in "Indigo, Cyanine, Beryl," reviewing *Never* (2002), also sounds a note of caution: "One can feel, reading the new work, a nostalgia for the shapeliness of the pure lyrics in *Erosion* and *The End of Beauty*. But no good poet can stand still. . . ." What Vendler finds in *Never* is something both familiar and new: an attempt to "reproduce, in what she believes to be an accurate way, the shimmer of body-mind as it attends to nature." Again, a shift in style makes possible this latest unfolding of consciousness: "Graham makes her single voice multiple by the proliferation of slashes, parentheses standing alone, brackets standing alone, and parentheses within brackets. . . . Writing of this sort represents an ambitious attempt to make language equal to our perceptive body, with its several senses always in mutual interplay with the phenomenal world."

In her remarks on Stevens, Graham links poems of enactment with "an open desire for grace or change," suggesting that the various activities performed in a poem—thinking, feeling, backtracking, leaping, stuttering, coming up short—have significant consequences, if one knows how to read them. Not knowing how to read them leaves one in the situation Wittgenstein assigned to his sister Hermine: "You remind me of somebody who is looking out through a closed window and cannot explain to himself the strange movements of a passer-by. He cannot tell what sort of storm is raging out there or that this person might only be managing with difficulty to stay on his feet."[6] What sort of storm? Joanna Klink, in "To Feel an Idea," suggests that we think of the "strange movements" of consciousness in a Graham poem as responses to, or attempts to inhabit, specific problems. Their actions become visible and readable within a problem's particular context. She writes: "Problems are not solved in poems, at least not in any philosophical sense; they are imagined. Poems allow you to feel, deep in their music, the impact and urgency and relevance of a problem. . . . To feel an idea means to inhabit the problem with the full force of your body and your mind, rather than just to think it. It creates a situation out of words which is concrete, visceral, real; one in which you are forced to consider deeply, to choose, to act, to be known by your actions." Shifts of style, then, or changes of initiating situations keep certain problems unsettled and urgent. Thinking, for example, about "the [problematic] border between the self and the world" that Vendler and others address, Graham points out: " I 'choose' occasions, therefore, with a mind to keeping the problem—with its moral, political, spiritual, and aesthetic implications—as alive to me as possible. Shifts in my 'style' are a large part of that process."[7] What a significant number of the essays collected here attempt to do, then, is begin the process of describing other storms or problems within which Graham's actions matter and might usefully be assessed.

One situation that Graham's poems consistently problematize and inhabit is the act of writing itself. In "Jorie Graham's Incandescence," I argue that, in constantly "turn[ing] her appalled eye on her own activity as she writes"—attempts and failures to know, remember, describe, liken, express—Graham is in fact trying to slow the act of knowing, suffer it and hold its suddenly live implications in her hands. In allowing herself to be drawn to the point where "language's drives to master and sort and go on have been [temporarily] checked," Graham is in fact able to explore whether "something [might be] gained in the space of error." By acknowledging and living within their limits, her poems ask a simple question: "What sort of response to the world . . . might be developed, in her own sentences, when the drive to master and narrate shatters. . . ?" In "The Place of Jorie Graham," written for this volume, James Longenbach focuses on Graham's two most recent books, *Swarm* (1999) and *Never*, examining their investigation of the lyric's uneasy rendering of place. For Longenbach, the two books, in two different manners, make visible the way lyrics "simultaneously conjure and disperse locations." The lyric "attempts to locate meaning in a landscape" while simultaneously admitting "that we know only the surface of things [even as] we crave depth." *Swarm*, in attempting to dissolve location so as to keep desire and distance alive, and *Never*, in attempting to capture "particular locations at particular times," come to much the same position: as place is dissolved, it rushes back in; as it is established, its meaning drains away. To foreground that, in the writing, is to "recognize that we inhabit the world intimately because we inhabit language"—a recognition which necessarily leads to using the lyric's fragile tools and expectations in a more tentative, self-revealing way.

A second problem within which Graham's poems unfold is that of the role of the body in experiencing the world. In "Countering Culture," Elisabeth Frost turns to Graham's emphasis on "the physical world—to matter and life in their troubling otherness and flux; and to our attitude toward that world, including our own bodies." If, in Graham, we "risk losing awareness of what is most basic to our existence—the body itself— . . . the culprit is rational thought, represented [in *Materialism*] by the philosophical tradition, here given a voice." Calling attention to the failures of a mechanical "pursuit of knowledge" and intercutting that drive with the notations of an observant eye, Graham, according to Frost, uses "philosophical language with a double charge, . . . the very diction of rational thought suddenly express[ing] intimacy, passion, longing." In "Jorie Graham: The Moment of Excess," her examination of Graham's various uses of the long line, Vendler notes that early on the line articulated a longing for "what Kristeva calls by the Platonic name of the *chora*—the presymbolic matrix of language, where rhythm and syllable and semiosis have not yet coalesced into sign and meaning." Later, as the poet's "struggle against the intellectual and formal dénouement of shapely closure" intensified, the line began tracking the gaze—finding in it another way of "representing the luxurious spread of experienced being, preanalytric and precontingent." And finally, in Graham's recent long noticings where "the poet's body becomes, kinesthetically, a form of the world's fluid body," Vendler suggests that we are drawn as readers to the "human body . . . replicating *itself* in its aesthetic body of words, rather than replicating the outside world in a direct mimesis."

Why this emphasis on the body? Playing off of the title of Graham's 1995 selected poems, Joanna Klink remarks: "To bring together what I experience of the world in my body, and the ideas by which I understand this experience, or to restore the body and senses to the mind, is the 'dream of the unified field,' the prayer behind every poem." To bring such notions as *self, history, choice, order, empire, owning, you,* or *I* down into the body allows one to "inhabit them in their complexity, to suspend them long enough that they might be received as freedom as well as a responsibility." While an idea grips the body, before the idea is "named, or its effect in the world is identified, determined, or explained," it remains in some senses up for grabs—an arena within which one can be tested and drawn toward a richer sense of knowledge and responsibility. As Willard Spiegelman suggests in "Jorie Graham Listening," another essay written for this volume, the body's ways of knowing also tend toward predictability and must themselves be challenged and resisted. Taking note of the "pronounced and increasing attention to sound" in *Never,* Spiegelman contrasts that with an "ineluctable preference of the eye to the ear," in "the activities of poetic 'thinking'" dramatized in her earlier poems. In those poems, notes Spiegelman, the poet consistently ignored the aural, or framed it with the visual, or turned it into something visual, as in his example of the sound of a bird becoming first "black talk" then sheer visual movement as it, "thrashing, wrinkling, dissipates." In her recent attempts to capture sound which "is temporal and more difficult to catch than light, harder to grasp than wind," Graham, for Spiegelman—closing her eyes in one poem then opening them to hear, for the first time, "the seven kinds of sound" of waves crashing—has discovered yet another way to engage the body and open a space for action.[8]

A third unsettled problem which Graham "inhabits" has to do with what she variously calls *the now, the present, the invisible,* or *the eternal.* In an important early essay, "Jorie Graham: Art and Erosion," Bonnie Costello argues that the poems in Graham's second book "aspire to the unity and completeness of an artifact rather than the residue of a process." Painting, Costello argues, "becomes her primary model for how we can pursue the invisible in the visible. . . . It forms an alternative space to the world of erosion, a form of 'rescue' from the flux, a means of centering vision and restoring unity beyond the grasp of reason and the word." Although she notes a number of qualifications to her claim—"Whether 'the invisible' is itself an effect of art rather than a separate reality is . . . a question . . . many poems in the volume invite"; the "poet fails by definition, as she yearns to approach the condition of presence evoked by the visual icon"—Costello insists that in this volume, unlike the work that follows, in which "the darting, temporally unstable images of cinema and television" dominate, the drive to construct an "eternal space set apart from the flux" remains central. Anne Shifrer, in "Iconoclasm in the Poetry of Jorie Graham," responds to Costello by arguing that we find in Graham a confrontation with "art forms as intricate, ceaselessly paradoxical and multivoiced layerings that shroud an ultimate metaphysical void." For Shifrer, the poems in *Erosion* discover in paintings depths which contradict the surface. Surfaces which seem to make the real accessible are reduced to "successive, mobile layers of image [that] may wrap the real, or they may be the real." What we are left with, once again, is the uncertain, self-critical movement of consciousness—the poem, as with the work of art it reads, "available as an experience rather than as an immutable, temporally transcendent object."

In his review of *Materialism*, "Postlyrically Yours," Calvin Bedient looks at Graham's attempt to filter "the real present from the nominal present" or to "think time and space into their proper strangeness, which is purer than we are." Graham invents something Bedient calls the "cogitative lyric"—contemplating phenomena "in the constant rhythm of moving forward and peeling back, applying a new phrase like a trowel or a scraper or both at once, getting *at* things, over and over, in their living actuality." Of course, since the "distance . . . between sight and *created* essence" is never eliminated, the poetry's "passion for the absolute" is always derailed, never satisfied. In his review of *Swarm*, Stephen Yenser examines a later version of this struggle. The volume's "broken sentences," he argues, are part of an "aggressive spiritual exercise," seeking to get "underneath" or "outside time." If the sentence is linked to time and the body, then Graham's "swarming" phrases—"on the move, unpredictable, part of a process, and always reforming [themselves]"—attempt a personal and stylistic "reformation" that has at its heart an impossible journey toward a Dickinson-like Master who exists "Somewhere—in Silence—." In a new essay written for this volume, "Toward a Jorie Graham Lexicon," Bedient returns to this notion of a derailed drive for the absolute and takes it a good bit further. Casting his essay as an alphabetized examination of crucial Graham terms—*beauty, the body, the glance*, and so on—Bedient performs an intricate enactment of this dilemma. Graham is still the "dramatist of the thinking of the invisible," driven to reach "the inherent sublimity of the present": the "purely here, purely now" or what one entry terms "*the invisible (underneath, something, something else, the x, the absolute).*" But the drive is always frustrated. To think the invisible means to leave *beauty* and *story* and *body* behind. Unlike Whitman and (surprisingly) unlike Stein, Graham writes from within "impasses of consciousness" in which "a transubjective real [is seen] as increasingly impossible to define." Why is such a poetry important? Because, Bedient claims, it assumes "both the historical and philosophical burden of the present." Graham "multiplies, scatters, and tilts lines of thought" in all directions, creating, through "cognition and perception . . . place-holdings where there is no place." Which is to say, she inhabits, and opens for the reader, the problem of the present, or the now

Along with the role of writing, the body, and the present—all "storms" consciousness engages and within which it unfolds—a final problem raised by these essays has to do with the immediate material conditions within which the poet finds herself. In "Jorie Graham's _____s," Thomas J. Otten argues that "lyric history might be [written as] an account of how consciousness makes its own image out of the materials and technologies that constitute a given cultural moment." As with the writing, the now, and the body, materials or material situations might also be problematized and productively dwelt within. Otten starts with a stylistic feature—Graham's blanks, as in the line "Like a _____ this look between us"—and argues that the device is "an emphatic mark of absence . . . absence and substance occupy[ing] the same point." The blank, like the lyric, "gives a degree of density and definition to the spaces between persons while remaining true to the facts of absence and distance that are so often the lyric's generating cause." But what the blank also points to and, Otten argues, critically "replicates," is "the nebulously material things characteristic of Graham's poems": "the virtual matter of late-century technology [that] alternately solidifies and dissolves"—dust in a projector beam, latex, formica, and so on. One problem her style engages, then, is how to make philosophically visible "the vagaries, the historical vicissitudes, of [the] material culture" she finds herself in.

Two final essays, both written for this volume, explore another problematic set of "material conditions" that consciousness makes visible and is made visible by. Cynthia Hogue traces Graham's interest in what Hogue calls "a different subjectivity"—one she describes as "in process, less *self*-centered and more aware of others," "a receptive channel." For Hogue, Graham's poetry "has as much to do with [this] ethical consciousness arrived at through embodied experience as with disembodied philosophical inquiry and aesthetics." What Graham embodies—or inhabits, with open eyes—is "the predictable plot of a particular gendered ideology imposed on women, and into which individual women disappear." Hogue examines a number of scenes in Graham in which a speaker, finding herself "inaugurate[d] . . . into the social contract" in a way that doesn't adequately reflect her, "stands before a mirror, shocked by some event out of childish security—that sense of being one with herself—into a sense of self-alienation and difference." In slowly inhabiting this problem, Graham discovers that this divided, "emerging subject, although less secure . . . , is also more tolerant of alterity"—a movement or change in consciousness made available to the writer by "complicating and refiguring [the problem] of feminine narcissism, self-reflection, and subjectivity."

Working along similar lines, Stephen Burt in "'Tell Them *No*': Jorie Graham's Poems of Adolescence" investigates an analogy he has observed between Graham's much-remarked-on desire to temporarily free herself from narrative closure and the struggles of adolescence. He looks in detail at *Region of Unlikeness*' "Fission," claiming that "the poem suggests not only an analogy but a homology (a shared source): what if the resistance to narrative time Graham so often depicts derives from a resistance to ways of 'being-seen,' to ways of becoming a woman?" That is, what if one of the problems generating her remarkable stylistic achievements is a return to the adolescent's impossibly complicated desire to both take on and refuse the "story of feminine development"? At the very least, as Burt and others here urge, this would suggest that "questions Graham's readers ordinarily view either within the domain of the lyric alone, or in the related domains of continental philosophy" might profitably be examined from a much wider variety of perspectives. As that happens, work devoted to tracing this poet's restless, self-critical achievement may well grow as many-sided and inventive as the poetry itself. This volume, in both consolidating and opening new approaches to Graham's work, offers itself as one step in that movement outward.

Notes

1. Jorie Graham, "Pleasure," in *Singular Voices*, ed. Stephen Berg (New York: Avon Books, 1985), 93.

2. Jorie Graham, "Some Notes on Silence," in *19 New American Poets of the Golden Gate*, ed. Philip Dow (New York: Harcourt Brace Jovanovich, 1984), 414.

3. See, for example, Adam Kirsch's review of *Swarm* in *The New Republic*, 13 March 2000, 35–42. He writes about a poem from *The Errancy*. "It is evident that one cannot read this poem as one usually reads a poem, with the confidence that the poet will tell us more or less what she is talking about." Or see Bonnie Costello's review of *Region of Unlikeness* in *The New Republic*, 27 January 1992, 36–39. She writes: "Restless with the answers she found before, her vision has become more ecstatic, more omnivorous, more abstract in each of her four books. It has also become looser and more notational, less concerned with shapeliness and eloquence."

4. Jorie Graham, "Poetic Statement: At the Border," in *American Women Poets of the 21st Century*, ed. Claudia Rankine and Juliana Spahr (Middletown, Conn.: Wesleyan University Press, 2002), 146.

5. Helen Vendler, "Jorie Graham," in *The Music of What Happens: Poems, Poets, Critics* (Cambridge, Mass.: Harvard University Press, 1988), 456–57; "Married to Hurry and Grim Song: Jorie Graham's *The End of Beauty*" and "Mapping the Air: Adrienne Rich and Jorie Graham," in *Soul Says: On Recent Poetry* (Cambridge, Mass.: Harvard University Press, 1995), 237, 233, 227, 231; "Ascent into Limbo," *The New Republic*, 11 July 1994, 27, 28.

6. Ray Monk, *Ludwig Wittgenstein: The Duty of Genius* (New York: The Free Press, 1990), 170.

7. Jorie Graham, " Poetic Statement," 147.

8. See as well an earlier essay by Spiegelman on Graham's eye: "Jorie Graham's 'New Way of Looking,'" *Salmagundi* 120 (Fall 1998): 244–75.

I

Jorie Graham

Art and Erosion

BONNIE COSTELLO

Jorie Graham emerged in the 1980s as a major poet, distinguished for her philosophical depth, her sensuous vision, the grandeur of her style and themes. In a decade of poetry stigmatized for its shrunken ambition, or sidetracked by politics and ideology, she celebrated the spiritual and metaphysical reach of art. In her first book, *Hybrids of Plants and of Ghosts* (1980), Graham limited her meditation primarily to tentative reflections based on natural objects. *Erosion* (1983) marked a striking maturity for this poet in finding a focus to the roving eye of *Hybrids*, and in understanding the iconic and even sacramental nature of her mind. Her language in this volume is marked by eloquence and sententious boldness, and she identifies her project more directly with that of monumental artists from the past. While ordered around a passion for mystery, the poems themselves aspire to the unity and completeness of an artifact rather than the residue of a process. Whatever twists of thought may arise in the poems end in a tied, integrated imagery, a tense unity.

Graham's emphasis on iconic representation and visual design in *Erosion* expresses at once her strong sense of the body and her resistance to the force of erosion. Painting rather than nature becomes her primary model for how we can pursue the invisible in the visible, how we can shape our limitations into a form that can surpass them. In relation to the word, the visual icon seems inexhaustible, infinitely deep, yet centered. Art is the implicit answer to Graham's query, "in what manner the body is united with the soule." It forms an alternative space to the world of erosion, a form of "rescue" from the flux, a means of centering vision and restoring unity beyond the grasp of reason and the word. In this celebration of beauty over knowledge, and art over history, *Erosion* is essentially a modernist text, whereas Graham's later work may be characterized as postmodern.

Erosion, loss, grief, the past, history, evolution, dispersion—these central facts of our world pervade the poetry. But they are almost always set against their opposite—the aesthetic transformation of the world as iconic design. The title poem, "Erosion" (56–57), asserts:

> I would not want, I think, a higher intelligence, one
> simultaneous, cut clean
> of sequence. No,
> it is our slowness I love, growing slower,
> tapping the paintbrush against the visible,
> tapping the mind.

The mind of the painter "tapping the paintbrush against the visible" and of the beholder may be sequenced, but the work of visual art is not. Indeed, its major distinction from literary art is its simultaneity, its spatial rather than sequential presentation. Graham sets her intelligence toward images detached from their surroundings, held in a private, contemplative space and made timeless through aesthetic transformation, even as she remains in a dimension of history. It is not surprising, then, that eight of the poems in *Erosion* describe established masterpieces of visual art. Ecphrasis is her chief rhetorical strategy. The word is approach and commentary; the icon holds out a promise of presence. Even as Graham questions the value of design or acknowledges the "tragic" aspect of the pursuit of the eternal, hers is an essentially optimistic view of art. "The beautiful," the centering of images into an order where mystery is held and glimpsed, is *Erosion*'s highest value.

In more recent work Graham has begun to decenter the image, thrusting it out of controlling aesthetic form and into personal and public history, unpacking and deconstructing its narrative and discursive implications. Film rather than painting has become her sister art. *Erosion* was a significant book for the eighties, however, because it boldly reasserted modernist values and ambitions which she has never entirely surrendered—the pursuit of the timeless, the impersonal, the beautiful over the brutality and flux of history, the desire of the mind for the eternal and the drive of art to pursue it. Now, however, vision occurs in moments wrested from chaos rather than preserved in sequestered icons.

Graham's strong pull toward an iconic center apart from the flux finds expression in both "Mist" and "Reading Plato." In each she conceives of a figure by which the transient world is arrested even as it is evoked. In "In What Manner the Body is United with the Soule," Graham pursues a single figure beneath the surface of the stream, which can be drawn out and elevated as art. The symbolist imagery of the poem presents the mutuality of body and spirit central to *Erosion*'s idea of art. Graham's iconic imagination often forms a permeable inside/outside opposition as well. In "Still Life with Window and Fish" the interrupted and reassembled images of the external world define an inner space, a new dynamic unity in still form. In other poems ("To a Friend Going Blind," "Kimono," "The Lady and the Unicorn and Other Tapestries," "At the Exhumed Body of Santa Chiara, Assisi") Graham imagines design in terms of fabric—the world securely woven into a tapestry or sewn into a garment. The complex metaphor of stitching suggests that art is a means of mending a world we experience as broken, uniting the horizontal and the vertical, the temporal and the eternal, in its movement. This tapestried nature also clothes a mystery, giving a sense of depth to the physical world, a vanishing point in the design. The numinous is not dispersed, then, but hidden and disclosed in art.

Several poems in *Erosion* deal directly with a masterpiece of visual art—by Piero della Francesca, Luca Signorelli, Masaccio, Gustav Klimt. In these poems Graham poses as beholder, in the world of erosion, reflecting on the work, its relation to her world, and the creative process of the artist. Graham's preoccupation with Christian subjects (the Resurrection, the expulsion from the garden of Eden, the birth of Christ), which will continue in later volumes, suggests the importance of her analogy between Christian paradoxes and the mysteries of art. In her treatment of modern works Graham continues to conceive of art as a process of drawing off and transforming the given to a fabric that will enclose something infinite as its secret center. But she no longer takes for granted the nature of the mystery and the purpose of its aesthetic covering.

In "Mist" (4–5) Graham describes the condition of consciousness ("this quick intelligence") we live in and act on. In our hungry rationality we are "blind" but "forever trying to finger the distinctions" between being and becoming, essence and existence. The mist represents the mind "making everything / part of itself," seeking "the whole idea" which eludes it. Our "geography" is better than our "history" as we try to map out a world in flux. But the mist also suggests, more traditionally, the condition of erosion in which we live and think.

The rational mind pursuing absolutes in a world of erosion ("the rose inside the rose that keeps on opening") fails, but the creative will provides an alternative:

>   and then
> this other still
> wherein it is a perfect rose
> *because* I snap it
> from the sky,
>
> because I want it,
>
> another, thicker, kind of sight.

In a world opening, being consumed, swimming, and waving goodbye, that is, the poet chooses an icon, not out of reason but out of desire. To counteract erosion she "snaps" a different mode of seeing, one thicker and thus more stable than the swimming, blind/deaf world of thought she has characterized throughout most of the poem. The rose is "perfect" not because it realizes a Platonic truth, but "*because*" her imagination draws it out from "the sky."

Similarly, in "Reading Plato" (6–7) Graham describes her friend making lures. This action is a "beautiful lie" because it is based on the representation of a "good idea" of forms "past death, past sight," suspended from the world of erosion. Graham is anti-Platonic, believing not in ideal, rational forms but in "the body // they were all once / a part of." But she admires these lures, initiating here a distinction she will make frequently, between the beautiful (the forms of art, which may surpass reason in their importance to us) and the true (which eludes the forms of reason). While constructed of fragments of nature we experience as broken, the lures have a unifying force. "A hook / under each pair / of wings," they reunite body and spirit as they are cast into the stream. Graham contrasts our dispersed, sensuous "knowledge of / the graceful // deer" to the fly made out of deer hair because it is "hollow / and floats" (the form of our dissecting, abstract knowing). But the iconic lure, cast into the stream, has led her to imagine back to the whole. We will see in other poems that the dismemberment of reality is redeemed by the construction of forms that permit a glimpse of numinous wholeness.

The relation of the icon to the stream is again the focus of the three-part poem "In What Manner the Body is United with the Soule" (12–15). This time what floats above the stream is not an artifact but an agency, a self, in the figure of a "miraculous / waterstrider" which can "measure ripples / for meaning." Graham's connection of this invisible "meaning" with art is explicit from the beginning. The first section of the poem considers, through the metaphor of the stream, the effect of music. The sounds, their "surface tension / which is pleasure" lead to the sounding of "meaning / —small, jeweled, deep-water— / flash." At the outset of the poem, then, the soul is understood in terms of the aspirations and effects of art. But music, the most abstract and temporal of the arts, must give way to iconic symbols for Graham. Indeed, in the next section that "flash" turns out to be "manuscripts / illuminated by monks" which are unearthed from "the mud / of the Arno." These verbal icons release their "gold" into the "lush browns" in which "all the difficulties / of the passage / of time" are caught and held. Thus they "illuminate" the mud as the mud preserves them through time. "The self" is the center of this reciprocity:

>   an act of
>   rescue
>   where the flesh has risen,
>   the spirit
>   loosened. . . .

In the final section of the poem Graham writes only of the natural world, but her symbolist images mirror and unite earlier images of art. The stream which has run through each section is here "smaller, / almost still," as if made ready for creation, a "delay" in the "hurry" of life and erosion that allows for artistic vision. The "jewels" of meaning in section 1 are now held as "tiny insect / life" which the waterstrider-self consumes. The "gold bee," an image perhaps of the inspiration or food of art, parallels the gleam on the ice over the mud that holds the manuscripts. The golden eggs of the waterstrider-self are the creative expression of this insight:

>   Of silence, mating striders make
>   gold eggs
>   which they will only lay
>   on feathers
>
>   dropped by passing birds
>   or on the underside
>   of a bird's tail
>   before it wakens and
>   flies off, blue and white and host
>   to a freedom
>
>   it knows nothing of.

The final movement here is clearly out of the stream, into the freedom of the disembodied spiritual, but the body is made, by the self, the vehicle of transcendence even as its direction may be elsewhere.

Each of the poems I have discussed deals with a condition of flux or erosion (figured as mist or stream), from which something iconic is constructed or fathomed, a "perfect rose," a "lure," an "elaborate gold frame," isolated parts that can evoke a whole. Along with this relation of icon and flux Graham frequently poses a relation of outside world and inside mind or art. Our minds want to draw the "outside" world into the "inside" structures of thought and representation. Graham presents this as a natural and positive impulse when driven by a regard for mystery, for the beautiful, rather than for rational meaning. The aesthetic, iconic "inside," while it is walled off from the world, evokes and transforms that world. This iconic space has its own indeterminate movement even as it resists temporality.

"Still Life with Window and Fish" (32–33) is a celebration of aesthetic space and a study of its attractions.[1] Fragments of the world "outside" the window (of her room, of her mind) are brought "inside," "dismembered" but also "remembered." They enter as shadows made when objects interrupt the passage of light—as what is seen in the window, held in the mind, or represented in ornamental designs. The "inside" forms a space where things are simplified and reassembled.

> The whole world outside
> wants to come into here,
> to angle into
> the simpler shapes of rooms, to be broken and rebroken
> against the sure co-ordinates
> of walls.

The "sure co-ordinates of walls," like the frames of art, designate a boundary in which images are sequestered from reality. But within the walls relations "blur" and "nothing starts or / ends," unlike the eroding world outside. Graham emphasizes that the space "inside" is partial and "broken," yet its delights are clear. The shadows, designs, and other images of the world outside are loosed from their physical boundaries:

> Here is a fish-spine on the sea of my bone china
> plate. Here is a fish-spine on the sea of my hand,
> flickering, all its freight
> fallen away.

The fish image returns here to suggest the transfiguration of the flux into an "indelible / surf," the surf-ace of art or imaginative transformation of reality. The self is drawn into this surf where the restless imagination can sustain itself against the tide of erosion:

> If I should die
> before you do,
> you can find me anywhere
> in this floral, featureless,
> indelible
> surf. We are too restless
> to inherit
> this earth.

This interior, formal space of "still life" provides a kind of rescue, then, from the world of erosion. Its very limitations and interruptions transfigure and save.

The same sense of an "inside" space which may "block the view" of the outside world but which, at the same time, may rescue us from erosion arises in "To a Friend Going Blind" (27). The complete integration of many associative links in this poem is testimony to art's power to unify. The poem begins with a description of walking:

> I had to walk this town's entire inner
> perimeter to find
> where the medieval walls break open
> in an eighteenth century
> arch.

Graham here recognizes both limitation and the artistic transformation of limitation which designs an inner space to be permeable to the outside, even to reveal it. The poet shifts abruptly to an apparently unrelated issue. "Bruna," a local seamstress, "is teaching me / to cut a pattern." Bruna is linked to the medieval town when her measuring tapes are described as "corn-blond and endless, / from her neck"—like Rapunzel's hair. Bruna is an artist, who, judging her "material" "for texture, grain, the built-in / limits," turns those limits into something useful and, incidentally, beautiful. As a kind of Rapunzel she can teach the poet, who can teach her imminently blind friend, to get imaginatively beyond the walls. We may remember that Rapunzel's lover was blinded by the witch until Rapunzel's tears fell upon his eyes and cured them. Bruna teaches how the outside world might come inside, transfigured, how limitation might provide access since the whole world itself seeks "interruption." Thus the poet's journey through the walled town is an imitation of the lesson from Bruna: "I wandered all along the street that hugs the walls, / a needle floating / on its cloth." Bruna teaches the usefulness of art: enclosed as we are within our tower, art can help us escape as Rapunzel's prince could not:

> When Bruna finishes her dress
> it is the shape of what has come
> to rescue her. She puts it on.

The controlling metaphor of "To a Friend," stitching, binds its two images (Bruna's sewing, walking the town's wall) into a kind of New Critical verbal icon. The metaphor informs nearly half the poems in *Erosion*. Stitching involves several varied but related desires for Graham: we desire to make of the world's raw material (and our own built-in limits) something that can "rescue" us from flux and that can give form to the numinous. We would bind together what is broken (the temporal and the eternal, life and death, the individual and the whole) and penetrate the gaps and cracks in our norms in order to create new wholes. Finally, we respond to the "beautiful," for the pleasure it gives and the mystery it shrouds. Stitching is an act of love, something that seeks to draw the objects of this world into a more permanent, shaped, beautiful "fabric" of art.

Graham expresses her measured faith in "stitching" in "The Lady and the Unicorn and Other Tapestries" (37). The ephemeral world is woven into the permanent fabric of the tapestry:

> If I have a faith it is something like this: this ordering
>   of images
> within an atmosphere that will receive them, hold them
>   in solution, unsolved.

That "unsolved" is importantly double—undissolved by erosion, yet perpetually mysterious (the tapestry is a "still moment"), unapproachable by the interpretive invasion of the word.

The title is curious since the poem never mentions the central subjects of the famous tapestry series. The Cluny tapestries depict the Lady and the Unicorn in various postures that symbolize the five senses. In certain of these and other unicorn tapestries quail are shown settled on or rising from a tree, but they are more decorative than functional in the pictures. Even in the famous hunt tapestry (at the Cloisters in New York), it is the unicorn, not the quail, which is pursued. But it is precisely the decorative impulse, the impulse to design rather than to symbolism, that interests the poet. Graham's strategy of peripheral vision in response to classic works of art allows her the freedom to invent new meanings for these overdetermined works and to explore the nature of art itself as an aesthetic rather than a symbolic activity. The opening lines of the poem (quoted above) might well apply, implicitly, to the effect of the tapestries as a whole, however, since the tapestries depict a mysterious "ordering of images" in which lady and unicorn stand as paradoxical companions (chastity and virility).

The quail provide the link between the artwork and the familiar natural world and allow the poet to imagine that world itself in terms of design: "the quail / over the snow // on our back field run free and clocklike, briefly safe." Art makes that moment of "safety" more enduring. Yet in the next breath she qualifies "the beautiful" as "our whitest lie," white because of its benevolence, a lie because its orders do not represent the realities of erosion. Art gives us a way of looking at the world, allows us to see the hunt itself as design—the quail's role that of "prey." The "ancient tree their eyes map out" is the tree of Eden (symbol of our erosion from the ideal) as well as the tree on which the quail are perched in the tapestries. In response to the Fall we slaughter the quail but also preserve them as decorative feast, as art:

> the quail are woven
> into tapestries, and, stuffed
> with cardamom and pine-nuts
>
> and a sprig of thyme.

The sprig of thyme is our memento of our fall, our temporality, marked within atemporal form. The tapestry artist holds these paradoxes "in solution, unsolved," unlike the hunter who would possess and destroy.

More often Graham's stitching metaphor connects with her imagery of clothing, with the idea of a numinous center within or behind the aesthetic pattern. Art is not only an ordering of images but a shroud of the infinite; its surface is arranged around a vanishing point. Graham returns repeatedly to the metaphor of the garment which wraps the eternal invisible. Whether "the invisible" is itself an effect of art rather than a separate reality is not a question Graham raises in *Erosion*, though many poems in the volume invite it.

"Kimono" (38–39) combines the ideas of art as design and as garment. The fluency and pictorial richness of fabric allow Graham to imagine the world of erosion in an aesthetic space. Stitched in visual delight with "valleys, clear skies, / thawing banks / narcissus and hollow reeds," the kimono's fabric represents our knowledge of the world. A boy depicted in this garden becomes our innocence, in which we mistake our knowledge for reality: "It means the world to him, this flat / archaic fabric / no weather worries." But formed into a garment, this limited knowledge becomes art and suggests something real and whole within it. The poet, wearing the kimono, identifies herself with a permanent spirit of the world that moves it:

> What he sees,
> in my garden, is the style
>   of the world
> as she brushes her hair
>   eternally beyond
>
> the casual crumbling forms
>   of boughs.

If the world is a kimono, erosion is the "style / of the world" where "reeds are suddenly / ravines" but not its essence. Something whole stands "eternally beyond" it as well, which we may glimpse through the "open door" of the shifting "green scrim." It is "late" in the evolution of our knowledge, the poet tells us often, for any transparency of truth. Yet even in this lateness, the human spirit, "a sacred store / of dares," glimpses the disrobing of nature, the disclosure of a unifying presence.

What makes this vision "late" and modernist rather than romantic is the self-conscious mediation of art. It is art, not nature, that allows us this glimpse into the whole. As a work of art, this fabric, this "beautiful lie," can wrap a "reality" which is an otherwise unknown "something"—its mystery. It is not our knowledge of the world but our knowledge transfigured as garment, our world transfigured as art, with its "abstract" branches, that allows, even intends, the glimpse suggested at the end of the poem into "something most whole," beyond erosion. Indeed, that "something" may only have identity through art.

The poet, through the metaphor of the kimono, gives herself a privileged position. She is caught in the "archaic fabric" like the boy but also takes the position of the object beheld, the spirit-woman inside the aesthetic surface. The switching pronouns, in which "I'm / wearing valleys" and "she brushes her hair" coincide in the subject, suggest a double stance of penetration and disclosure. Again the artist affirms the reality beyond art's "archaic fabric" only by positing that reality within art, as a place of unveiling.

In "Kimono" Graham apparently follows a traditional romantic paradigm of male consciousness as desire toward veiled female nature. She modernizes this paradigm by showing how art fosters it. And without subverting this paradigm she does complicate it by shifting her identity from object to beholder. In Graham the icon as clothed female figure represents a reciprocal aspect of art in which the beholder "going in" experiences a sense of mystery yielding itself, without a complete consummation. In "San Sepolcro" (2–3), about Piero della Francesca's image of the laboring virgin, the aesthetic mediation is explicit and the paradigm of vision as male desire is more clearly transfigured. But this basic reciprocity in the figure remains. This poem about a monumental work of art (conveyed in humble language) opens the volume *Erosion*, suggesting that the mediation of iconic representation controls many of the poems in their understanding of the relationship between the body and the spirit.

"San Sepolcro" again works with a contrast between the world outside and the more private, contemplative space of iconic representation. And again the representational space is associated with penetration and disrobing. But here art is not merely a matter of male desire extended by an inexhaustible, yielding female image. The sexuality implicit in "Kimono" (where the peeping Tom climbs the "gentle limbs" of a tree and observes nature as she "loosens her stays") is displaced by a metaphor of birthing. Graham is "one of the living," Mary a symbol of the mind's power to conceive eternity beneath the temporal, the "blue . . . mantle of weather"—thus partaking of both male and female mythology. Male and female stereotypes (penetrating mind and desired object) are transcended. The beholder-self of the poet is a transparent vessel ("snow having made me / a world of bone / seen through to"), but also active ("I can take you there"), enabled by this reciprocity. This structure is repeated in the presentation of Mary, whose figure paradoxically unites immaculate male mind ("How clean / the mind is, // holy grave. It is this girl") and female body waiting "to go into // labor." Mary's dress represents the threshold nature of the icon itself.

"San Sepolcro" begins with an invitation to move from the outside temporal world into, first, the interior world of the walled house, then to a picture whose colors evoke an idea of eternity. Thus again an apparent narrowing into limits allows for a sense of expansion. Graham opens like a tour guide but, in the manner of Elizabeth Bishop, goes on from the literal to the symbolic, and hence to the beautiful and the mysterious, from the profane ("Etruscan") place of San Sepolcro (with its assembly lines and open-air markets) to the elusive, undefined, "sacred" space of art, from the public to the private. The pivotal figure is the rooster, Christian symbol of betrayal and sacrifice, who stands between the world of "mist outside the walls," the unclear world of erosion, and the disclosure of the icon, "before the birth of god." Just here Graham defines the limits, the "tragedy" of art, which awakens in the beholder a desire for presence. The icon is not an incarnation; the "still moment" is "forever stillborn." "The living," approaching the icon, "go in" but never "arrive." Yet art's power to awaken our thoughts of the infinite insures its hold on us:

> but going in, each breath
>   is a button
>
> coming undone, something terribly
>   nimble-fingered
> finding all of the stops.

The model of veiled female as icon arises once more in "At the Exhumed Body of Santa Chiara, Assisi"(21). She is "pure even after a ton of dirt," in the world of erosion but not of it. Again the model of contemplation is one of desire forestalled. The poet's own worldly desire ("whether I leave him / or not") is delayed, as was the worldly desire of the earthly Chiara ("So and so you loved, / so and so you left"). These are left to the world of disappearances, replaced by a spiritual desire, a "deep[er] delay" in the contemplation of "nowhere" marked by the clothed, iconic figure.

Graham views the exhumed body of Santa Chiara, "queen of the chiaroscuro," almost as a work of art, a figure dark against a background of contemporary "blue." "Blue over your body in its afterlife / on its back in its black dress with gold trim." The phenomenon of Chiara's exhumed body is itself parallel to the phenomenon of art "as if the flesh were the eternal portion after all." This is not a Christian but a modern notion of the icon, recalling Wallace Stevens's secular reversal: "Beauty is momentary in the mind—The fitful tracing of a portal; / But in the flesh it is immortal."[2] Graham, too, approaches art as a means to approach the infinite rather than escape the body. The reciprocity of the icon rests in the paradox of the veil placed "in order / to be seen."

In *Erosion*, I have argued, Graham treats the icon as a form of rescue from the flux and as a veil which shrouds but also discloses the infinite. Her constant return to Christian images and subjects reveals an important analogy. But her secular treatment of these subjects also reveals a distinctly modernist cast to the analogy, one which erases ideas of transcendence to a spiritual other realm. Art itself becomes the redeemer, though the terms of redemption are not in arrival but in the "going in." Eternity is redefined so that it is bound to the earthly ("beneath motion, more flesh") even as it is released from flux.

Two of Graham's ecphrastic poems, "At Luca Signorelli's Resurrection of the Body" (74–77) and "Masaccio's Expulsion" (66–69), make this shift from Christian to modernist iconicity especially clear. Graham's return to the rhetorical strategy of ecphrasis emphasizes the aesthetic nature of the "nowhere" which absorbs her meditation.

The figures resurrected in Signorelli's painting are not raised by God but by art, drawn up "into the weightedness, the color, / into the eye / of the painter," and hurry toward "distance" and "perspective," the limitations of human time-space defined in terms of painting. The notion that these figures never wholly arrive, that "there is no entrance, only entering," itself derives from the experience of painting rather than from the painting's illusion and its Christian promise of resurrection. The still moment of figures caught in action and held into that action is never complete. There remains an inherent "gap," to use Graham's favorite word, between the painting and presence, between representation and desire.

Signorelli's frescoes, of which "The Resurrection" (the emphasis on "the body" is Graham's addition) is one of several at the cathedral in Orvieto, represent the pinnacle of his career. Graham has captured in this poem the central power of motion and bodily impact which is often celebrated in his work. She begins her poem by focusing the reader's attention immediately on the dramatic subject of the bottom half of Signorelli's fresco—bodies rising from openings in the earth, transformed from skeletons to fleshed figures:

> See how they hurry
>   to enter
> their bodies,
>   these spirits.
>   . . .
>   From above
> the green-winged angels
>   blare down
> trumpets and light. But
>   they don't care,
>
> they hurry to congregate,
>   they hurry
> into speech, until
>   it's a marketplace,
> it is humanity.

It is not quite true that the figures in Signorelli's fresco ignore the angels above them (who make up the top half of the fresco and are considerably larger and more prominent than the human figures). Many gaze in awe and ecstasy at these figures. But it is their resumption of human activity—dancing, bartering, debating—that interests the poet. "Hurry" is a key word for Graham, used six times in his poem and denoting our temporal nature (its paired term is "delay," involving the gap between our temporal natures and the eternal dimension we desire, the dimension opened by art). Art holds that hurry in its still moment.

By shifting from subjects to beholders Graham makes an important qualification to her idealization of art's beautiful lie, the same qualification she makes in "San Sepolcro," where the desire for arrival, for presence of the infinite (the birth of God), meets "tragedy." (The "at" in the title "At Luca Signorelli's Resurrection of the Body" emphasizes, as it does in "At the Exhumed Body of Santa Chiara," the threshold between history and art.) Unlike the Christian believer, Graham, as beholder of the icon, recognizes no "arrival," no complete presence. The ecphrastic poet fails by definition, as she yearns to approach the condition of presence evoked by the visual icon. For Graham this verbal/visual difference simply reveals the inherent limits of art to provide the arrival we yearn for. Thus "there is no entrance, / only entering," addressed to the figures in Signorelli's paintings as they "hurry" into representation, applies reciprocally (as it did in "San Sepolcro") to the condition of the beholder before the visual image.

Graham's next major shift in the poem is to the artist himself and his creative process. Whereas the figures in "The Resurrection" depicted the "hurry" of our temporal natures, the emphasis here is on patience and slowness. That patient penetration of the "wall / of the flesh" (like the opening garment in "San Sepolcro") is demonstrated in Signorelli's practice of studying anatomy through autopsy. This literal breaking into the body in search of "arrival," in search of its essential aspect, yields to a transformation from the fleshly to the iconic where it becomes inexhaustible, where "the flesh / opens endlessly, / its vanishing point so deep / and receding / / we have yet to find it." This absorption in the flesh as icon has a counterpart in a movement "from the symbolic" (where the flesh might simply serve to convey an unearthly message) "to the beautiful" (where the flesh is itself cast in an eternal dimension).

This idea of the "beautiful" defines the redemptive character of art, counterpoint to the "tragedy" of elusive presence. Graham may have drawn from Giorgio Vasari the apocryphal anecdote of Signorelli painting the body of his dead son. Vasari suggested that the son was the model for the pietà in "The

Deposition"; actually Antonio probably died of the plague, and it is unlikely that Signorelli used his body as a model.[3] But the legend suits Graham's vision of the redemptive power of art. Signorelli's act of drawing his dead son is implicitly parallel to the resurrection depicted in his famous fresco and described in the first part of the poem. But it is not the resurrection of the dead son so much as of the bereaved artist that we are left with, for Signorelli's mind enters the "open flesh" just as the spirits hurried into their bodies in his picture:

> It took him days
> > that deep
> caress, cutting,
> > unfastening,
>
> until his mind
> > could climb into
> the open flesh and
> > mend itself.

Like Bruna cutting and sewing in "To a Friend Going Blind," Signorelli forms, from the broken flesh, an icon, the shape which will rescue him if he puts it on. Visual art, more than poetry, involves this pursuit of the timeless through an immersion in the body.

"At Luca Signorelli's Resurrection of the Body" concerns a reciprocal need: the body's need for art to lift it out of the world of erosion, the mind's need for the body, for embodiment of its idea of the infinite. We see a similar compensatory and reciprocal principle at work in Graham's poem "Masaccio's Expulsion." The poem describes one in a continuous series of frescoes Masaccio painted in Florence, arranged so that the Expulsion clearly leads into the other images of biblical history, to which the poem alludes collectively. As in "Resurrection," Graham emphasizes the pictorial nature of the space as well as the illusion of reality. The poem begins with the grief of the figures and the common notion that the condition of representation is a fall, a loss of presence:

> Is this really the failure
> > of silence,
> or eternity, where these two
> > suffer entrance
> into the picture
> > plane[.]

The poem goes on to revise this negative judgment. Like Keats's "still unravished bride of quietness," art is not the failure of silence but the triumph of the visual. Graham goes on to find in the world of the paint, not just of the illusion, certain compensatory features. Having lost presence and immortality, these figures emanate their loss, and his "price" can "live forever" as art.

Graham begins with the figures of Adam and Eve refusing sight: "a man and woman / so hollowed / by grief they cover / their eyes / in order not to see." But the poet's position depends on looking, and her poem is, as it goes on, an appeal to redemptive features of sight. Art makes a "garden" of this fallen world, this "inexhaustible grammar" of history, "its dark and light" objects and shadows. This space of the "picture / plane" represents a narrowness in which the fullness of live being is reduced to "symbols, / / balancing shapes in / a composition," yet art provides a compensation for the loss of freedom it represents, a commemorative and aestheticizing power that rises up out of these limits. The pivot of this compensatory view is not in the central, symbolic subject matter of the frescoes but, as in "The Lady and the Unicorn," in a decorative detail:

> And perhaps
> it is a flaw
>
> on the wall of this church, or age,
>   or merely the restlessness
> of the brilliant
>   young painter,
> the large blue bird
>   seen flying too low
>
> just where the trees
>   clot.

This bird, "the gift of / the paint," appears on the fresco as a winglike blotch at the edge near Eve's thigh, incomplete as a bird shape but close enough for Graham to figure it as such. It becomes her image of the imagination, driven to seek form, to enter "a space too small / to fit in" but also hovering above that space.

That narrowing into embodiment has a reciprocal effect of expansion on the beholder. Graham's eye moves down from Adam and Eve to various figures "in the foreground" (more central in the alcove) who represent biblical history. But their pictorial power in "the gold air" of art raises them from their passage into the narrowness of history:

> There isn't a price
>   (that floats up
> through their miraculous
>   bodies
>
> and lingers above them
>   in the gold air)
> that won't live forever.

Art assures this immortality and causes the figures to "float up" from history and form. It provides the countermotion to the downward glance of Adam and Eve and the general lines of the fresco they occupy.

In the poems described above Graham affirms the triumph of the beautiful, the power of the aesthetic to raise the spirit above not only the flux of history but also the weight of symbolism, the mere interpretation of history. But as Graham turns her attention to art of the modern age and to the pressures of modern history, she begins to approach aesthetic value with more uncertainty. The weight of modern history carries a moral imperative that is hard to reconcile with aesthetic pleasure or notions of art's "beautiful lie" against time. While such issues revise Graham's thoughts about the role of the icon, however, they do not finally change her faith in its value or understanding of its structure.

The beholder in "Two Paintings by Gustav Klimt" (61–63) brings to the fin de siècle works a knowledge of subsequent history which she cannot help but impose on what she views (history is not, here, "hopelessly even"). She uses the juxtaposition of two paintings as if to corroborate her own archaic vision. Behind the idealized icon, a space of eternal beauty, lies a scream, the juxtaposition seems to say. Yet such an unveiling is by itself too simple; it is the relation between the veil and what lies behind it, the relation of desire, that interests Graham and determines the value of the aesthetic for her.

The first painting is a landscape, a "buchen-wald," or beech forest. Klimt painted a number of such landscapes, which expressed his spiritually and sexually symbolic vision in a network of prominent verticals and high horizontals. *Gustav Klimt* by Alessandra Comini is the probable source of many details in "Two Paintings by Gustav Klimt." Comini describes "Beech Forest I" as a "rhythmic grouping of elemental verticals and horizontals." The beholder's vision of the landscape stands between Klimt and twentieth-century history, so that his meaning-saturated environment takes on the meanings that postdate it, in which the term "buchen-wald" is forever blighted. Graham introduces the issues that have concerned her throughout the book—the aesthetic transformation of "flaws" into "the beautiful":

> Although what glitters
>   on the trees
> row after perfect row,
>   is merely
> the injustice
>   of the world,
>
> the chips on the bark of each
>   beech tree
> catching the light, the sum
>   of these delays
> is the beautiful, the human
>   beautiful,
>
> body of flaws.

The "injustice / of the world" is very broadly defined here as erosion itself because the word "buchen-wald" has not been introduced. Despite the opening disclaimer, the poem clearly presents the world depicted, the world of erosion—"leafrot," "mottled shadows," "broken skins"—caught in art, as evoking an elusive ideal of "something to lean on / that won't / give way." "The dead / in their sheer / open parenthesis" at this point simply stand as a contrast of the mortal world to the abidance of landscape and art. But these "dead" are the victims not only of our mortal but of our moral nature—the anonymous dead of the Holocaust, for whom the trees soon stand as symbols, not opposites. The continuities of landscape and art, and the aesthetic balance achieved in art, come into tension in the poem with the poet's knowledge of human brutality, the weight of the word "buchen-wald." For the post-Holocaust observer "late / in the twentieth / century," the yellow light is a "gaseous light." But against this view the poet holds out another, amoral view, inaccessible to her but embodied in the beautiful landscape, where

> To receive the light
>   and return it
>
> and stand in rows, anonymous,
>   is a sweet secret.

The air, like the male gaze, would penetrate this mysterious image of the trees, with "little hooks" that "poke," anticipating the pornographic image in the second painting. The "sweet secret" of the trees is, of course, their inhumanity, their innocence of history, the idea of the infinite they embody.

Graham's poem may in one sense describe a transformation in seeing from the nineteenth to the twentieth century, in which the idealization of the landscape is no longer possible and an unveiling of the oral horror beneath the masks of aestheticism is inevitable. But I think Graham's vision, and her view of art in particular, is too complex for this simple contrast. The beautiful holds its place, drawing us into mystery.

The tension between the moral and the aesthetic and the aestheticizing of the moral comes to a focus in the second half of the poem, in which Graham considers a very different painting by Klimt, an incomplete, pornographic rendering of the female body, clothed only in a transparent garment.[4] The woman's genitalia form a "mouth" "something like / a scream."[5] Her facial expression remains "bored, feigning a need / for sleep." For Klimt she is a figure of Freudian desire and repression, for Graham a figure perhaps of public indifference to the known horror of fascism.

Certainly the "scream" Graham identifies with this mouth establishes the parallelism between the two paintings through the idea of a violence beneath tranquil surfaces. The major interest of the poem, however, is not in the genital "mouth" (or the issues it raises about the male gaze in Western art), or in the bored face of the woman (with its political implications). Graham's central interest is, as always, the garment, which is not merely condemned as the cover-up for brutal obscenity. "The fabric // defines the surface, / the story, / so we are drawn to it."

Graham directly compares the "feathery garment" that Klimt had begun to paint over the figure to his rendering of landscape in the other painting, describing "its blues / and yellows glittering / like a stand / of beech trees." She remains ambiguous about how we are to evaluate this analogy or the placement of the garment itself. But the resemblance of this garment to other images of clothing in Graham suggests that she approves of it. Through the garment of art we glimpse what is otherwise unrepresentable.

But rather than pursue this metaphor (garment/story), Graham abruptly returns to the first painting by Klimt: "In // the finished painting / the argument / has something to do / with pleasure." In one sense the juxtaposition of the two paintings, weighted in favor of the unfinished one and the Holocaust allusion, turns pleasure into decadence or even cruel obscenity. Yet that "surface tension / which is pleasure" (in "In What Manner") "holds / the self // afloat" and draws us toward the unknown and unspeakable. Thus "pleasure" may become a vehicle of insight, beauty a route to unfathomable truth (whatever its moral register).

"Two Paintings by Gustav Klimt" is finally not an exposé but an assertion of the value of the veil. Still, "pleasure" stands as a highly vulnerable term by the end of the poem, as the "argument" of the second painting is inevitably grafted onto the first.

"Two Paintings by Gustav Klimt" repeats the erotic structure of the icon implicit in other poems I have discussed. Graham does not condemn, in fact she seems in sympathy with, this structure. The addition of the Holocaust imagery does not undermine this fundamental vision of art; it simply changes the character of the "secret" dimension of the icon and turns the promised wholeness behind the surface into an abyss. But this shift, and Graham's vagueness—which is not clearly ambivalence—about "pleasure" and elsewhere in *Erosion* about "the beautiful," may account for the dramatic change in her style and approach to the image in her next volume, *The End of Beauty* (1987).

For this ambitious poet each book is a critique of the one before. The very titles she has chosen map this out. Where *Erosion* imagines the construction of an integrated, centered eternal space set apart from the flux, even rescuing us from its absolute effects, *The End of Beauty* concerns itself with edges, boundaries, origins and ends, images unraveling into "minutes" and splitting into dialogue, the still moment dissolving into narrative. Graham has pursued this shift in recent work. Her focus is increasingly on the hurry of this world (this "region of unlikeness" no icon can transfigure) and the struggle to sustain a visionary stance within it rather than withdrawing into a contemplative one. The darting, temporally unstable images of cinema and television rather than the static images of painting have become her gauge. Digression rather than integration is the dominant aesthetic effect.

These and other qualities represent Graham's move from a spatial, modernist to a temporal, postmodern aesthetic, one that subscribes less to art as artifact than to art as process. One needn't make a value judgment to comprehend the necessity of this shift for the poet (one needn't, that is, see a plot in her development). But whatever place *Erosion* may take in the evolution of Graham's work, its value to us as achieved vision will remain.

Contemporary Literature

Notes

Quotations from Graham's poems are from *Erosion* (Princeton, N.J.: Princeton University Press, 1983).

1. The twentieth-century American painter Marsden Hartley made a painting with this title which may have inspired Graham. It is more likely, however, that the "still-life" to which Graham refers is her own mental transformation of an interior space.

2. Wallace Stevens, "Peter Quince at the Clavier," in *The Collected Poems of Wallace Stevens* (New York: Vintage, 1982), 91.

3. "Overwhelmed with grief as he was," Vasari wrote, "he had the body stripped, and with the greatest fortitude of soul, without tears or lamentation, he made a drawing of it, in order to have always before his eyes . . . what Nature had given him, and cruel Fate had snatched away." Quoted in Maud Cruttwell, *Luca Signorelli* (London: George Bell, 1899), 10.

4. See Alessandra Comini, *Gustav Klimt* (New York: Braziller, 1975). Comini's book opens with an account of thieves breaking into the artist's studio and discovering the unfinished painting known as "The Bride": "For here, even to the uninitiated, was an extraordinary revelation of what might be called a 'dirty old-master' technique. In opposition to the floating knot of figures covering the left side of the canvas, the splayed-out nude body of a young girl dominated the other half. Her face was averted in a profile turn to the right, and a mufflerlike wrap at the throat seemed to separate the head from its glimmering white torso, creating a startling effect of mutilation. The knees were bent and the legs spread apart to expose a carefully detailed pubic area upon which the artist had leisurely begun to paint an overlay 'dress' of suggestive and symbolic shapes" (5).

5. Karl Krauss, according to Comini, called Vienna in Klimt's time "an isolation cell in which one was allowed to scream" (13).

2

from Countering Culture

Review of Materialism

ELISABETH FROST

In this fifth collection, Jorie Graham is even more rigorously philosophical than in her previous books—most recently, *Region of Unlikeness* (Ecco, 1992) and *The End of Beauty* (Ecco, 1987). At stake here is the whole body of Western thought. The "materialism" of her title refers not to American middle-class values (although Marx does make an appearance in one poem), but to the physical world—to matter and life in their troubling otherness and flux, and to our attitude toward that world, including our own bodies. As in most Western philosophy, there is a marked distance in Graham's work between subjective experience and the objective world. Lines from the poem "Subjectivity," in which she explains her use of the third person to refer to herself, capture this divide: "I say *she* because my body is so still / in the folds of daylight." Physicality can even become a mere afterthought. An aside in a poem called "Invention of the Other" runs: "(*the body!* she thought, as if she had forgotten it)."

Apparently we risk losing awareness of what is most basic to our experience—the body itself—and the culprit is rational thought, represented by the philosophical tradition, here given a voice. Graham has included passages from (among others) Plato, Bacon, Dante, Wittgenstein, Whitman, Benjamin and—only slightly out of place in this procession—McGuffey (from his *New Fifth Reader* of 1857). It is a bold gesture, one typical of Graham's restless poetry, to include landmarks of Western thought and then, in effect, talk back to them—to challenge even as she exploits the familiar mind/body split.

Although most of the quotations are separate from the poems, Graham does carry on a dialogue with them and the "great works" they stand in for. Excerpting can be a form of rewriting, and her selections often undermine the writer's original intentions. I was surprised to learn that the great nature-lover, Audubon, detailed the killing of "specimens" that served as excellent subjects for his sketches. One anecdote found here involves a buffalo—an ironic reminder to the contemporary reader of our destruction of this country's native inhabitants: "The head was cut off, as well as one fore and one hind foot. The head is so full of symmetry, and so beautiful, that I shall have a drawing of it to-morrow." In Graham's excerpt, Audubon's fine aesthetic sense supplies no regret for the animal's killing and dismemberment. Ethics and aesthetics, she implies, can remain dangerously disjunct.

Graham reflects on the artist's complicity in a similar act of violence in "Subjectivity." The speaker discovers a monarch butterfly whose beauty captivates her: it is "butter yellow, fever yellow, / yellow of acid and flax, / lemon and chrome." Finding the creature inert, she assumes that it's dead, and is preparing to "make it flat" and insert it into a collection when a friend tells her that the butterfly is still alive. The object of her gaze reclaims the poem:

> the yellow thing, the specimen,
> rising up of a sudden out of its envelope of glances—
>
> a bit of fact in the light and then just light. (31)

The speaker manages to elude her own desire to possess, but the borders between preservation and destruction, artistic "appreciation" and imperialism, prove thin indeed.

This kind of moral dilemma leads Graham into territories she has explored in earlier work—the fields of myth and history. Juxtapositions of different narratives and historical periods within her poems suggest unexpected connections. "Annunciation with a Bullet in It," for example, joins scenes from a Holocaust survivor's diary with an account of her dog's death following a shooting. In "Concerning the Right to Life," descriptions of an abortion clinic during a protest alternate with descriptions of the speaker's concern for her fever-ridden daughter; the poem closes with excerpts from Christopher Columbus' diary, which remind us of colonization—also a trope for women's bodies.

For Graham, these connections are buried all too deeply in our culture. She presents a series of experiments by Sir Francis Bacon, the early scientist and preeminent humanist, that seems, in its very objectivity, to forecast our fatal disconnection from the material world and one another: "We took a glass egg, with a small hole at one end; we drew out the air by violent suction at this hole, and then closed the hole with the finger, immersed the egg in water, and then removed the finger." The pursuit of knowledge is mechanical and never-ending, as an ellipsis at the excerpt's conclusion (which occurs mid-sentence) indicates: "We took a leaden globe. . ." The "scientific method" involves a detachment of self from other that Graham also senses when she writes; in "In the Hotel," she tries to bridge the gap between herself and the reader, between what she writes and what we feel: "What do you / want, *you*, listening here with me now? Inside the / monologue, / what would you insert? What word?"

Virtually all the poems in *Materialism* are painful meditations on why such efforts fail. "Steering Wheel" describes a moment in which the speaker, backing a car out of a driveway, notices a "veil of leaves / suctioned up by a change of current." While the poem seems to meditate on the most external of facts—leaves swirling, a hat caught by the wind coursing down a street—the poem is finally about the fear of entrapment in one's own subjective experience. The final lines reflect on the meaning of the most basic rules of motion and gravity, "the law / composed of updraft, downdraft,"

> and angle of vision, dust, gravity, solitude,
> and the part of the law which is the world's waiting
> and the part of the law which is my waiting,
> and the part which is my impatience—now; *now?*—
>
> though there are, there really are
> things in the world, you must believe me. (5–6)

The closing plea reveals the speaker's uncertainty about objective reality, "things in the world" other than the self. Graham charges her lines with longing for the "real" world. But how can we break through "solitude" to reach "the world's waiting"? Her answer seems to be that the observing eye, the poetic self that is aware of both the material and the spiritual, must remain utterly self-conscious. Acute observation is the closest we come to genuine knowledge—closer than speculative philosophy has taken us.

As in "Steering Wheel," the most moving poems in the book use philosophical language with a double charge. In Graham's hands, the very diction of rational thought suddenly expresses intimacy, passion, longing. "The whole cannot exist without the parts," a speaker in one of the many sections of "The Break of Day" asserts. Then comes the voice of a different self, pleading for union, "Stay, stay." The "parts" are suddenly two people, full of need, and the philosophical dictum is transformed. The shift in tone bears witness to one of

Graham's greatest gifts—turning rhetoric against itself and allowing a simple moment or utterance to unfold in all its nuances. In *Materialism,* an ambitious collage of the language of "great works" and the language of poetry, Graham responds to rational philosophy with the poet's rigorous and practiced vision.

The Women's Review of Books

3

from Postlyrically Yours

Review of Materialism

CALVIN BEDIENT

As Jean-Luc Nancy says in *The Birth to Presence*, "a pure flow of time could not be 'ours.'" Jorie Graham's *Materialism* attempts over and over the birth to presence, to a time that is an uncanny sort of "property." Her poetry is the opposite of will-less blossoming; it strains for the gnat of a time and space that includes us, as God includes the saints. Graham's temperament is metaphysical; her single realm, material. Let her stress the visible as much as she likes, painting with words is not her project—all the descriptions in *Materialism* put together would not rival a single Marianne Moore stanza for optical sparkle. Graham's real object is to think time and space into their proper strangeness, which is purer than we are, even as her heart says, "Relent, stay, be the eternally manifested, not the eternally manifesting; I'm strained, *strained*, with being alone in your inhumanly self-emptying presences."

Bible-colored, poised to ring with alarums like *Moby-Dick*, Graham's poetry has the passion for the absolute that characterizes sublime art and, at the same time, the heart-poured dependence on surfaces that is the senses' mercy to the insatiably ravenous spirit. It is greatly divided, great with division—what it contains of the human world it may often thin almost to the bursting point, like a balloon wanting to line the whole universe, but only thus can the poet see through the small human order (all too thick a surround in most current poetry) to the seductions and evasions of the material grandeur of reality.

The third of the poems entitled "Notes on the Reality of the Self" is the oddest thing in *Materialism*, all of which reads like a peculiar new species of poetry. It roughly goes as follows: scene, bakeshop; character, "a man about to eat his morning's slice"; action, his eye-shut prayer of thanksgiving; problem, his momentary ontological blindness. Just when you think that this bakery is reality there come the lines:

> The knife, a felled birch left overnight
> for tomorrow's work on which the moonlight,
> in the eyes of no one, plays, gleaming, the knife
> sits awaiting the emptiness it will make appear
> where all along there had been emptiness
> implied.

"Round him / infinite spaces gnaw at his face." A loaf and infinite spaces: what is their connection? Merely, if not simply, this: from any given visible good ("The loaf is a crucial landmark"), the unfamiliar branches out like a path. *Take it*. "For days / he hunted for the tree. Found it." Then "Beauty . . . recognized!— / three redbirds in [the evergreens] and then two now, up and out, chasing the third, / bursting the air all round like water when the monster's / surfacing." For Graham, the visible world is a Moby-Dickish wonder-show of disappearances and bursting appearances, the bursting implying another disappearance. *Here* is already partly *there*, the knife a felled birch, for everything relates to everything else, if in a way that only the infinite genius of reality could map. So to "lift the knife" is to evoke "Corridor, stairway, front door—." And so the poem ends, passing outward.

To be so selflessly preoccupied with the widest implications of slices of space, with space's gnawings on the bread of faces, is extraordinary. In another age, Graham might have been a Christian theologian, gender allowing; or a pen-pierced candidate for sainthood. In ours, her miracle loaf is in a bakery, the cross is a felled birch played on by moonlight; her churchmen, redbirds; and resurrection the surfacing of a monster of endlessly unpredictable ways and limits (white whale, white birch, harpooned whale, felled birch, sliced white loaf . . . the price of being is to be cut into by absence).

The purity, if not the all but obsolete nobility, of Graham's project is bothered by too much lofty philosophical company—thirty-two or so pages of quotations from Plato, Sir Francis Bacon, Leonardo da Vinci, etc., some of which are beside *her* point (for instance, Wittgenstein on pictorial form, which she does not emulate). Compiling a Graham Reader (and she has the wit to quote from McGuffey's Reader) in order to educate her readers, she overdoes it in a way that suggests self-doubt. In reality, each of her brain cells is already full of heads bent over books in libraries, her nerve-endings are already the feelers of super-refined thought, her imagination is already an advancing phalanx of concepts hidden within concepts, so she can afford to snap her fingers at the inner prompting to show her knowledge, if she wishes.

A more serious impurity, because internal to some of her poems, is the hybridization of resistant historical matter—an earnest more of Graham's good heart and conscience than of continuing inquiry. Walter Benjamin's virtual prose poem on the angel of history ("he sees one single catastrophe that keeps piling wreckage on wreckage and hurls it in front of his feet," etc.) hangs like a silent, irrelevant gong in *Materialism*, whereas it reverberates terribly through every page of Carolyn Forché's *The Angel of History* (1980). Graham seems anxious to comprehend history in her book as an item, for the sake of comprehensiveness itself; but, in doing so, she reduces historical events to allegories of her own ontological anguish, leaving, as it were, real arms and legs hanging out. (Her absorption in human crises really belongs to a separate project, toward which she has been hankering and sidling since *Region of Unlikeness*, published in 1991.)

Pushing beyond even the intellectualized lyricism, the anti-nailing attenuations of *The End of Beauty* (1987), where Graham first reinvented the cogitative lyric, *Materialism* breaks into itchy-woolly ascetic contemplation of phenomena that seem (after an idea she cites from Jonathan Edwards) "newly created in each successive moment." (No history here.) At the same time, the poet forsakes the gender investigations of the earlier book (after all, she had done that) for a dissection of moments into their visual joints and organs. Here her passion is, in Emerson's words, "to form an acquaintance with things." If she lacks what Forché has in abundance, what George Eliot thought womanly, namely the ability to live in the experience of others, she has something perhaps equally rare, a soul innocence that echoes Captain Ahab's surprise, if not his dangerous sense of affront, when he says, in words the poet quotes, "Swim away from me, do you?" She may write nearer the heart of ontological trauma (the shock of there being a world at all, the further shock of its passing) than any poet since Rilke.

The writing in *Materialism* is not a school of conventional beauties: "ventriloquial breeze on which the / furry gypsy-moths from the immensities of x / now constellate" means to be, and is, a new kind of philosophical description, a sieve through which the hunger for surfaces (or is it for an *end* to surfaces?) continues to pour. The poetry is in the constant rhythm of moving forward and peeling back, applying a new phrase like a trowel or a scaper or both at once, getting *at* things, over and over, in their living actuality ("Nothing is virtual"). "Is there a new way of looking," the poet asks in the first poem, "Notes on the Reality of the Self"—"valences and little hooks . . . ?" Graham perhaps comes as close as anyone could to fashioning or feeling out little hooks, slippery or muffled hooks though they are.

The many strong poems in *Materialism* include the several "Notes on the Reality of the Self" (except for the dull one made up of quoted classic haiku—not to offend its many fans, but I find haiku slick compared to Graham's own rough planings of the real), "Subjectivity," "The Dream of the Unified Field," "The Visible World," "Existence and Presence," and "The Surface" (titles that half-read like entries in a philosophical index). The most magnificent is the perhaps overambitiously titled "Relativity: A Quartet"; here the poet hits upon a vehicle—and literally so, a train ride—that makes natural room for something of the variety of the human drama itself ("And I see on her arms the needle tracks," etc.), even as the poet as passenger remains attuned to her own going by, "as if matter itself were going / on and on to its own / destination" while laying "itself down frame by frame onto the wide . . . opening of our wet / retina . . . / all the astonishments . . . smearing onto us." The poem is somber with a sense of our violent human distance from "the fundamental uncreated essence," as with the sense that "there has never been anything / given to another, there has never been anything received from another." Hence the loneliness of Graham's quest to close at least the distance between sight and *created* essence, in a profound objection to the dangerousness of our species. Even though the longer poems splay away from a single object of contemplation or "unity" of time and place, what Graham here most trains her formidable powers of concentration on (if through a technique of almost alienatingly abstract description) is the fate—a sorrowful fate? a great fate?—of being an astonished "wet retina."

The Threepenny Review

4

Jorie Graham

The Moment of Excess

HELEN VENDLER

The breaking of style can occur on the largest scale, as when Hopkins invents a new rhythm distinguishing his later poetry from his earlier work; or it can occur, as in Heaney's writing, on the scale of a single poem, as the adjectival style called for by the poet's perplexity before the Grauballe Man is exchanged for the nominal style demanded by the trance of a memory-portent in "Deserted harbour stillness." Whereas a large-scale break in style like Hopkins' can scarcely be ignored by readers and critics, smaller breaks from poem to poem like Heaney's often go unnoticed, and the essential exposition through grammatical form of the thematics of the poem goes unremarked. When a poem is deprived, in critical discussion, of its material body—which is constituted by its rhythm, its grammar, its lineation, or other such features—it exists only as a mere cluster of ideas, and loses its physical, and therefore its aesthetic, distinctness.

I want to look, in Jorie Graham's work, at the unit of the individual line. Historically, the line has been the characteristic unit distinguishing poetry from prose; it is the most sensitive barometer of the breath-units in which poetry is voiced. The very shortest way of composing a line makes a single word (in Cummings and Berryman, even a single syllable or letter) constitute a line; the very longest manner of composition invents a line that spills over into turnovers, or, in a different move, suspends from its right margin an appended short line, what Hopkins called an "outride." When a poet ceases to write short lines and starts to write long lines, that change is a breaking of style almost more consequential, in its implications, than any other. Jorie Graham began as a writer of short poems in short lines, lines with a hesitant rhythm so seductive that one's heart, reproducing those poems, almost found a new way to beat. And then, with a burst of almost tidal energy, Graham began to publish long poems in long lines, poems that pressed toward an excess nearly uncontainable by the page. "Poetry," said Keats, "should surprise by a fine excess,"[1] and one form of that fine excess is the long line. "In excess, continual, there is cure for sorrow," Stevens observed in "A Weeping Burgher,"[2] and one of those cures for world-sorrow is the independent, provocative, and exhilarating excess of voicing represented by the long line. Graham's breaking of style, from short lines to long, invites us to consider these and other possible implications of her act.

But before I come to Graham's recourse to the long line, it may be useful to say a word about the general presence of the lengthened line in modern verse. There are two chief classical sources of the long line—the epic hexameter and the dithyrambic lyric: the first stands for heroic endeavor, the second for ecstatic utterance. When Hopkins compared "The Wreck of the Deutschland" to a Pindaric ode, he wanted to reclaim ecstatic and irregular form beyond what the eighteenth century had done; but it was chiefly in his sonnets, as we have seen, that he pushed the regular English line to its utmost length, for both effortful and ecstatic reasons. Toward the end of his life, he wrote of his "herds-long" lines:

> My cries heave, herds-long; huddle in a main, a chief-
> Woe, wórld-sorrow; on an áge-old ánvil wínce and síng—
> Then lull, then leave off.[3]

His several hexameter sonnets sometimes added outrides and even a coda; and finally, in the octameter lines of "Spelt from Sibyl's Leaves," Hopkins reached his breath-limit. As we have seen, Hopkins used the long line in several ways— as a container of heterogeneity, for instance, which could nonetheless rise to epic heroism: "Thís Jack, jóke, poor pótsherd, patch, | matchwood, immortal diamond / Is immortal diamond" (198). More interestingly, even, Hopkins used the long line to creep up on something by a chromatic series of words, each one melting ecstatically into the next by almost insensible half-steps: "Earnest, earthless, equal, attuneable, | vaulty, voluminous, . . . stupendous / Evening strains to be tíme's vást, | womb-of-all, home-of-all, hearse-of-all night" (190).

Like Hopkins, Whitman—who brought us the founding American free-verse line, deriving it from the Bible and Macpherson's *Ossian*—found the long line useful as a container for the heterogeneous; but he also used it to signify intellectual and speculative difficulties. It served Whitman, in its Hebraic coordinate form, for his ongoing repudiation of the old and embrace of the new: "I do not offer the old smooth prizes, but offer rough new prizes."[4] He also used it to signify spontaneity of speculation, and a ready turn to self-correction, as in the poem "Of the Terrible Doubt of Appearances," where a single line (l. 9) says of appearances:

> May-be [they are] seeming to me what they are (as doubtless they indeed but seem) as from my present point of view, and might prove (as of course they would) nought of what they appear, or nought anyhow, from entirely changed points of view. (120)

In spite of examples of length like those offered by Hopkins and Whitman, the English line tends stubbornly, when left to itself, to return to its more normative four- or five-beat length unless special heed is paid by the poet either toward shortening it—as Heaney deliberately did, for instance, in his volume *North* when he was seeking a more "Irish" music—or toward prolonging it, as Stevens did in a poem of Odyssean ongoingness called "Prologues to What Is Possible":

> He belonged to the far-foreign departure of his vessel and was part of it,
> Part of the speculum of fire on its prow, its symbol, whatever it was,
> Part of the glass-like sides on which it glided over the salt-stained water,
> As he traveled alone, like a man lured on by a syllable without any meaning.
>
> (*Collected Poems*, 516)

More could be said about the reasons why Whitman, Hopkins, and Stevens were pressed toward lengthening the English line—lengthening it against prescription, against historical habit, almost (one could say) against nature. But I want to move on to Graham, and ask why this pressure arises in her, so that her recent poems sprawl across the page in ways that startle and unsettle us, even while we are enthralled by their urgency, their effort, and their power.

The body Graham first chose for herself in verse was one that above all represented deliberation. That deliberation could be seen—to invoke an organic metaphor she uses in the recent poem "Opulence" (from *Materialism*)—as a stalk which arises slowly, puts forth a leaf, matches that leaf with another leaf on the opposite side of the stem, ascends a bit further, issues a branchlet, and then presses that branchlet to grow a twig. The narrow poems in Graham's first two books grew by antiphonal lines—the first line flush left, the second indented, the third flush left, the fourth indented, and so on. Step by step, accreting perceptions, the verse—to invoke a different metaphor—descended the page, creating a stairway (often of dimeter followed by monometer) for the reader. Here is a fragment of "Scirocco" from her second book, *Erosion* (1983):

Outside his window
    you can hear the scirocco
working
    the invisible.
Every dry leaf of ivy
    is fingered,

refingered. Who is
    the nervous spirit
of this world
    that must go over and over
what it already knows,
    what is it

so hot and dry
    that's looking through us,
by us,
    for its answer?[5]

We see in such lines, which owe much to Williams, the young poet's approach, increment by increment, to a mastery of the world. Most of the poems in *Erosion*, a book written in Graham's late twenties and early thirties, are composed in these stair-step short lines. They embody a process the poet at times calls erosion, at times dissection, in which something is crumbled, bit by bit, to dust; or something is opened, layer by layer, to view.

    The process of step-by-step investigation of the world is itself defended in the central question, "How far is true?" posed by Graham's harrowing poem "At Luca Signorelli's Resurrection of the Body." The son of the painter Signorelli has died, and the father, reaching beyond his grief, dissects the body:

        [H]e cut
            deeper,
    graduating slowly
        from the symbolic

to the beautiful. How far
    is true?
. . . .
    [W]ith beauty and care
        and technique

> and judgement, [he] cut into
> shadow, cut
> into bone and sinew and every
> pocket
>
> in which the cold light
> pooled.
> It took him days,
> that deep
> caress, cutting,
> unfastening,
>
> until his mind
> could climb into
> the open flesh and
> mend itself. (76–77)

This accomplished, steady, unflinching writing-in-short-lines (which deals out the lines, group by group, in regular six-line stanzas) represents, we could say, a faith in the power of the patience of mind; and in its deliberate respect for the resistance of matter, it intimates the "beauty and care / and technique / and judgement" that the mind must observe in the precise investigative use of its various scalpels. The question "How far is true?" is left open-ended, but that it is the poet's duty to take the symbolic through the beautiful into the true is not in doubt.

Toward the end of *Erosion*, Graham includes a disturbing poem called "Updraft," its title betraying a force which is the diametrical opposite of those sequential, incremental, and orderly processes—whether natural like erosion or intellectual like dissection—on which Graham's form had depended. The updraft, or convection current, of Graham's poem literally turns the atmosphere turbulently upside-down in tumultuous irregular lines:

> [A]ll the blossoms ripped suddenly by one gust, one
> updraft—mosaic
>
> of dust and silks
> by which we are all rising, turning, all
> free. (70)

The movement chronicled by "Updraft" is the dissolution of meaning into unmeaning. The poet, now distrusting the closure of form, implores a God-like figure to let Eve, the mother of creation, symbol of the world of formed shapes, slip back into the uncreated:

> so let her slip
> out of her heavy garment then, let her slip back
> into the rib, into Your dreams, Your
> loneliness, back, deep into the undress. . . . (71)

The undress exists "back / before Your needle leapt in Your fingers, meaning." The "undress," then, that the poet longs for is what Kristeva calls by the Platonic name of the *chora*—the presymbolic matrix of language, where rhythm and syllable and semiosis have not yet coalesced into sign and meaning. But since we cannot go backward to the *chora*, we must, in our resistance to closure, go forward, by entropy, into randomness and shapelessness.

The long line, therefore, is first generated by Graham as the formal equivalent of mortality, dissolution, and unmeaning. At this point in her writing, it is set against the persuasions of shapely organic form, and against the intellectual intelligibility that is the result of careful deliberative investigation. "The blood," says Graham in "Updraft," "smears itself against the mind," and this contest, as suffering body disfigures questing spirit, is continued in all of Graham's later books.

Erosion was followed by the volume uncompromisingly entitled *The End of Beauty* (1987), which marks Graham's definitive break with short-lined lyric. Though the old investigative antiphonies reappear once or twice ("Eschatological Prayer," "Noli Me Tangere"), the preeminent move in the book is a struggle against the intellectual and formal dénouement of shapely closure. Rather, there is now in the poet an assent—voiced in a long-lined poem called "Vertigo"—to uncertainty and unpredictability: this is the vertigo felt as one abandons old and predetermined ways in favor of the pull of the unknown beyond the precipice of the new:

> She leaned out. What is it pulls at one, she wondered,
> what? That it has no shape but point of view?
> That it cannot move to hold us?
> Oh it has vibrancy, she thought, this emptiness, this intake just
>   prior to
> the start of a story, the mind trying to fasten
> and fasten, the mind feeling it like a sickness this wanting
> to snag, catch hold, begin, the mind crawling out to the edge of the cliff
> and feeling the body as if for the first time—how it cannot
> follow, cannot love.[6]

The dizzying extension of the mind, as it crawls out to the edge of the cliff of the conceptual, presses Graham to her long lines and to their "outrides"—small piece-lines dropping down at the right margin of their precursor-line. Graham's combination of indefinitely stretching right-edge horizontality with occasional right-edge vertical drops refuses both the model of step-by-step upward mental advance and the model of investigative penetration inward from the beautiful into the true. Rather, Graham redefines the human aim of verse as an earthly, terrain-oriented lateral search (which can reach even the epic dimensions of the Columbian voyage) rather than a vertical Signorelli-like descent into depth or, as in "Updraft," ascent into prayer. Earthly desire itself is the thing allegorized by Graham's long horizontal line, desire always prolonging itself further and further over a gap it nonetheless does not wish to close. In this search by desire, mind will always outrun body. And the linear ongoingness necessitated by the continuation of desire means that the absence of shape, far from meaning dissolution and mortality, now stands for life itself.

In the poem "Pollock and Canvas," Graham, searching for a nontranscendent vertical which will be comparable to her earthly "desiring" horizontal, finds a metaphor for her line in the fluid drip of Pollock's paint between the body of the artist and his canvas spread on the ground. The line of paint, let down from the brush, is like a fishing line sinking without effort into the water: this cascading line is not epic, like the Odyssean one questingiy covering distances toward a horizon; rather, it is ecstatic, living in the possible:

> 17
> the line being fed out the line without shape before it lands without death
> 18
> saying a good life is possible, still hissing still unposited,
> 19
> before it lands, without shape, without generation, or form that bright fruit[.] (84–85)

At this moment, the long vertical line, "fed out," is pure middleness, the unposited, the possible, the "formless," the ethically indeterminate. It has not yet tethered itself to shape, to ending, to decision; it has not yet plucked the apple of the Fall.

To write a poetry of middleness, of suspension, is Graham's chief intellectual and emotional preoccupation in *The End of Beauty*. In that aim, she defers closure in many poems by a series of ever-approaching asymptotic gestures, each one of them numbered, and each advancing the plot by a micro-measure. Her model for this use of the long line seems to be the cinematic freeze-frame, by which an action sequence in film is divided, like the flight of Zeno's arrow, into minutely brief "shots," or elements. To place each of her elements into stop-time, Graham tries the experiment of numbering the freeze-frames sequentially, so that the unfamiliar appearance of a number punctuates on the page each quantum of perception delivered by a line or lines.

This experiment—affixing a number to each perception-packet—is tried in only six of the twenty-six poems in *The End of Beauty*, but these six are the dual self-portraits in which the volume finds its cohesion:

"Self-Portrait as the Gesture between Them"
"Self-Portrait as Both Parties"
"Self-Portrait as Apollo and Daphne"
"Self-Portrait as Hurry and Delay"
"Self-Portrait as Demeter and Persephone"
"Pollock and Canvas"

These poems have a collective importance beyond their mere number. Why, we must ask, does this forcibly stopped numbered version of the long line predominate in the self-portraits (of which "Pollock and Canvas," despite its title, is surely one)?

The self-portrait, as a visual genre, has always depended on some mirror-strategy by which the painter can depict an object normally inaccessible to vision: his or her own face. Not all self-portraits display the necessary mirror, but even those that do not do so prompt the viewer to some reflection on the difficulty of realization necessitated by such a portrait. Some self-portraits—Vermeer's of the artist in his studio, for instance—obliterate the face of the artist, as Vermeer substitutes the inscrutable rear view with black hat as an index of that necessary but suppressed subjectivity of the painter which plays a role in every painting, no matter how "objective." Parmigianino, as Ashbery has reminded us, paints himself reflected in a convex mirror so as to emphasize the distortion inevitable in any stratagem for self-representation.

Graham's facing up to the complex strategy of her own dual self-portraits is articulated most visibly in her numerically interrupted frames. They say: "Look at yourself in a frozen moment; write it down. Gaze again; write it down. And now glance a third time; and write it down." The alternations of consciousness as the pen succeeds the gaze are not concealed; rather, they are inscribed on the page, number by succeeding number. By "baring the device," as the Russian Formalists would say, Graham's self-portraits prevent an easy slide by the reader—or by the poet herself—into an introspection unconscious of problems of representation.

But what does the affixing of prefatory numbers have to do with Graham's break into the long line? The conventional view of the poetic line, as I have said, associates it with breath; and indeed, a good deal of theorizing about the material base of poetry links it to the inspiration and suspiration of the single breath as its measure. The physiological regulation of breathing makes natural breaths roughly isometric—in, out; in, out. And isometric breathing is the basis for regular lines, orderly and successive ones. But the gaze has no such isometric rhythm: a gaze can be prolonged at will, held for inspection, meditated on, and periodically interrupted. It is the gaze, rather than the breath, that seems to me Graham's fundamental measure in the numbered-line poems. By this choice of the gaze over the breath, Graham redefines utterance; and what utterance becomes is the tracking of the gaze, quantum-percept by quantum-percept, bundle by bundle. In Graham's recent poetry, a trust in the vagaries of the perceptual replaces the earlier poetry's trust both in the physiologically regulated order of breath and in a teleologically regulated order of truth. Since the apotheosis of the perceptual is necessarily an apotheosis of the moment, Graham is as interested in the (numbered) interruptive pause as in the significant perception; and her sequestering of the pause as a good in itself can be seen most clearly in "Pollock and Canvas," the most interesting test, in *The End of Beauty*, of her freeze-frame lines.

"Pollock and Canvas" is a poem in three Roman-numeraled parts, but only Part II affixes numbers to its lines. Part I is a conceptual summary (in the past tense) of Pollock's "drip" practice, linking him with the wounded King of *The Waste Land* and the Parsifal legends, a King suspended between life and death. The intermediate state of the King—alive but not life-giving, wounded but not dead—is summed up in Pollock's question as he bends over his canvas, refusing to let the brushtip touch it: *"tell me then what will render / the body alive?"* (*The End of Beauty*, 82). Pollock, though accomplished in the conferring of shape, resolves to keep his canvas safe from the death of final formal shape (*"his brush able to cut a figure / on the blank and refusing"*).

I pass over, for the moment, the numbered Part II, to look at the way the poem concludes. Pollock's Part I terror of the conclusiveness of final shape is answered in Part III of "Pollock and Canvas," which envisages a way *out* of formal shape. That formal shape (beauty, love, the figure), once it has been conferred on the canvas, permanently settles over a piece of life and determines it. The only way out of the conclusiveness of that formal shape is the admission into it of elements of chance; and Graham's figure for that possibility is God's rest after He made the world, a point at which the unintended, the serpent, can slip into Paradise:

> And then He rested, is that where the real
> making
> begins—the now—Then He rested letting in chance letting in
> any wind any shadow quick with minutes, and whimsy,
> through the light, letting the snake the turning
> in. (87)

Graham's conclusion is that the adventitious, the aleatory, the not-yet-true will eventually, without God's intending it, become part of the Creation:

> Then things not yet true
> which slip in
>
> are true,
> aren't they?

The things which slip in are part of the Keatsian "fine excess," and, since they are a "supplement" to what was intended, have their formal equivalent in whatever in the line seems arbitrary, unintended, added by chance, as though the line had had to expand to take such things in.

In "Pollock and Canvas," long lines exist, it is true, in both the Amfortas-suspension of Part I and the Jehovah-chance of Part III. But the quintessence of the species "long line" in the volume *The End of Beauty*—which I take to be the long line intermitted by the long numbered pause—is achieved in Part II of "Pollock and Canvas," where, though Pollock cannot entirely avoid the forward pull of temporality, he attempts to spatialize time as much as possible by inserting between each gaze a pause, representing ecstatic being:

> PART II
>
> 1
> Here is the lake, the open, he calls it his day; fishing.
> 2
> The lake, the middle movement, women's flesh, maya.
> 3
> And here is the hook before it has landed, before it's deep in the current[.] (82–83)

This pregnant section of the poem—enacting space, middleness, incarnation, illusion, suspension—speaks directly of what the double excess of the long line and the long pause mean to Graham—a way of representing the luxurious spread of experienced being, preanalytic and precontingent. This condition has Romantic affinities; but Graham does not want to be laid asleep in body to become a living soul. Rather, against Wordsworth, she almost wants to be laid asleep in mind to become a living body. Her *maya* contains no access to Wordsworthian transcendence; rather, she accepts its blessed stoppage in prolonged sensual illusion, that excess that is, in Stevens' terms, the cure of sorrow. The incarnation of this *maya* as it takes place "between the creator and the created" (83) is the Stevensian moment of credences of summer, of human existence without temporal entrance or exit, represented paradoxically by "of the graces the / 8 / most violent one, the one all gash, all description." This grace is the Muse of eternal process, who has replaced for Graham the meditated, investigative, and shaped Muse of product.

Graham's long line, representing being-in-process, continues, after The *End of Beauty*, into *Region of Unlikeness* (1991); but in the later, more autobiographical volume, the line drops its earlier partner, the open numbered space, which had represented being-in-pause. The gaze turns to single autobiographical self-portrait (which replaces mythological dual self-portrait), and the plot of narrative replaces bundled quanta of perception. Instead of dwelling on *Region of Unlikeness*, I want to turn to Graham's most recent book, *Materialism* (1993), because in it she combines the long line with its apparently ultimate narrative partner, the long sentence. Since the long horizontal line of extension in space toward the horizon is itself already formally effortful, it becomes even more epically taxing when it is joined to the long sentence (the conventional equivalent of temporal and conceptual complexity). To the long horizontal axis is added a long vertical axis. Graham had used long sentences to good effect as early as *Erosion*, but there they were strung down the page in very short lines. In The *End of Beauty*, the lines were longer, but the long sentences appearing there were usually interspersed with shorter ones, alleviating the effort of suspension. In *Materialism*, the combination of horizontal and vertical prolongation is carried out to the utmost degree, so that the poems literally construct visual plane areas ("tarpaulins," to use Ashbery's word from the poem of that name) in which words cover and spatialize being.

Total coverage is the ultimate effect toward which Graham has been tending with her long lines ever since they first appeared. This area-effect has affinities with other literary structures (the epic simile, the Miltonic verse-paragraph, the Whitmanian catalogue, the Moore encyclopedia-page), since all of these represent what Graham calls, in one of the titles of *Materialism*, "The Dream of the Unified Field." In that dream (in Graham's version), the whole world is

Jorie Graham: The Moment of Excess

extrapolated out from whatever center one chooses as origin. Stevens conceived of this effect, in "The Man with the Blue Guitar," as one in which the twang of the blue guitar would be "the reason in the storm," incorporating the whole of the storm while giving it a focal point and intelligibility:

> I know my lazy, leaden twang
> Is like the reason in a storm;
>
> And yet it brings the storm to bear.
> I twang it out and leave it there.
>
> (*Collected Poems*, 169)

Against Stevens' brisk storm, we can put Graham's enveloping storm in *Materialism*:

> The storm: I close my eyes and,
> standing in it, try to make it *mine*.
> . . . .
>   possession
> gripping down to form,
> wilderness brought deep into my clearing,
> out of the ooze of night,
> limbed, shouldered, necked, visaged, the white—
> now the clouds coming in (don't look up),
> now the Age behind the clouds, The Great Heights,
> all in there, reclining, eyes closed, huge,
> centuries and centuries long and wide,
> and underneath, barely attached but attached,
> like a runner, my body, my tiny piece of
> the century—minutes, houses going by—the Great
>   Heights—
> anchored by these footsteps, now and now,
> the footstepping—now and now—carrying its vast
> white sleeping geography—mapped—
> not a lease—*possession*.[7]

Graham compares this constant human desire for aesthetic possession of all space and time (the Great Heights, the long and wide centuries) to Columbus' desire to possess the New World; the hubristic dubiety of both enterprises is set against their spiritual ambition. Such undertakings are instinctive and unavoidable, Graham suggests, in creatures of mind and appetite. The human appetite desires metaphysical and intellectual, as much as material, gain. It is the limitlessness of the claims of intellect and of desire that Graham's recent ambitious poems are most inspired by, and most appalled by as well.

The appetitiveness of the mind, and the infinity of the world's stimuli, generate the excess of Graham's long horizontal lines, which generate, in their turn, her long vertical sentences. Any given poetic idea begins to produce, in Graham, a version of an aesthetic Big Bang with its vertiginous perceptual expansion and its receding conceptual distances. We can see this happening in the recent unpublished poem "The Turning." The poem is about dawn in an Italian hill town, and it begins with several brief successive noticings (not quoted here). Each noticing creates a brief sentence, and then stops. Nothing can take wing. The poet cannot yet feel her way into the heterogeneity, simultaneity, chromatic change, spontaneity, and self-correction present in all acts of extended noticing. Eventually, the reason for the fizzling-out of each perception is formulated: there is either a war between the world and its perceiver, preventing their interpenetration; or else there is an indifference between them, making them remain on parallel tracks without intersection:

> There is a war.
> Two parallels that will not meet have formed
> a wall.

In spite of successive tries, the desired tarpaulin, area, square, updraft, thrown cloth, has not yet been found. Not until inner feeling and outer perception begin to meld, and the poet's body becomes, kinesthetically, a form of the world's fluid body, can the world be re-created in language. The poet declares her creed: that the sun must come up in her before it can come up on her page; and it must come up on her page before it can come up for her reader:

> The sun revolves because of our revolving in
> the wall.

The wall is the poet's new perceptual blank sheet of paper. At the beginning of her observation of the dawn, nothing is inscribed on her mental "wall" except Stevens' command to himself at the end of "Notes toward a Supreme Fiction," where he addresses the Earth, saying that poetry requires *"that I / should name you"*:

> Fat girl, terrestrial, my summer, my night,
> How is it I find you in difference, see you there
> In a moving contour, a change not quite completed?
>
> . . . This unprovoked sensation requires
>
> That I should name you flatly, waste no words,
> Check your evasions, hold you to yourself
>
> . . . You
> Become the soft-footed phantom, the irrational
>
> Distortion.
>
> (*Collected Poems*, 406)

Faced with her recollection of Stevens' command, Graham, "phantom-eyed," must name the "soft-footed phantom," the earth as it presents itself on this Italian morning. But how is she to articulate the area, the cloth, the tarpaulin to be cast over this infinitely opening piece of reality without stiffening it into lifelessness?

It is within the moment of an unlooked-for chance event, when a single bird moves, that the poet finds she can rise unexpectedly with it into unimpeded voice, combining bird, soul, light, church-bells, swallow-flocks, and human beings into a single long—almost unending—sentence which constructs the second part of the poem (quoted here) from the words "Bright whites and citrines" to "I look down into the neighbor's garden":

> Bright whites and citrines
> gleaming forth,
> layerings, syllables of
> the most loud
> invisible
> that stick (no departure and no return) to their single
> constantly revised
> (I saw men yesterday, tuck-pointing, on their scaffold)
> lecture on what
> most matters: sun: now church bells breaking up
> in twos and threes
> the flock
> which works across in
> granular,

forked, suddenly cacophonic
         undulation
      (though at the level
of the inaudible) large differences of rustling, risings and lowerings,
                      swallowings of
                          silence where the wings
en masse lift off—and then the other (indecipherable) new
                    silence where
                    wings aren't
used and the flock floats in
unison—
      a flying-in-formation sound which
I can see across the wall (as if loud)—shrapnel of
            blacknesses
              against the brightnesses—
fistfuls thrown (as if splattered) then growing fantastically
                  in size (also now
                    rising swiftly) as
they come—a stem of silence which blossoms suddenly
as it vanishes from the wall—(turning, the whole
                    flock
turning) exfoliation of aural clottings where all wings open now
                        to break
and pump—vapor of accreting inaudibles—
innermost sound scratchy with clawed and necked
                  and winged
indecipherables (a herald)—whole flock now rising highest just before it
turns to write the longest version yet against the whole
length of the wall where the churchbells
have begun to cease and
one name is called out (but low, down near the Roman
                  gate) and one
car from down there sputters
up—(the light brightest now, it almost
                true morning)—
these walls these streets the light the shadow in them
the throat of the thing—birds reassembling over the roof
in syncopated undulations of cooing as they settle. . . .
I look down into the neighbor's garden.

In order to maintain itself, this long-lined and outridered long sentence depends on several grammatical techniques of prolongation—present participles, appositions, relative clauses both adjectival and adverbial, parenthetical insertions, a colon, additive conjunctions like "and," negations, comparisons ("as if"), co-temporalities ("also"), successivities ("then" and "just before"), repetitions ("now. . . now"), qualifications, and nominal simultaneities ("these walls these streets the light the shadow in them / the throat of the thing").

It is only of course after the fact that we can name these grammatical means accelerating the perceptual thrust of the sentence; during our actual stretched assimilation of this long cascade of words flung over a page we are, to put it imaginatively, participating in making the sun come up, the birds awaken, and the churchbells ring. Such an epic sentence—as the town turns from night to morning—is a human, and therefore effortful, *Fiat lux*. It cannot have the concision and effortlessness of the divine illumination of chaos, because it is made from a human sensing and concentrating body striving to comprehend a moment in one internalized physical and mental gestalt. And that human body is replicating *itself* in its aesthetic body of words, rather than replicating the outside world in a direct mimesis. The poet has to substitute, for the metaphysical divine will and the intellectual divine Logos, a frail human eye and an even frailer human will, which must concentrate fiercely to translate into internal kinesthetic sense-response "the most loud invisible" of the light and "the vapor of accreting inaudibles," the silent flocking of birds. The poet must translate these first into a consciousness of her own internal physical mimicry of the external stimuli, and then, in turn, she must translate that internal kinesthetic mimicry into the visible and audible signs of English, a language with its own internal constraints on expression. The order of linguistic signification, which succeeds the orders of perception and kinesthesia, is represented in the poem by the moment when "one name is called out." Every genuine poem, as Mallarmé insisted, aims at being "one name"—a single complex and indivisible unit of language proper to its moment and irreplaceable by any other. As the poet lifts the silent and the nonlinguistic and the nonpropositional from perceptual import to kinesthetic import into semiotic and rhythmic import, one form of suffering—seeing the day go by unregistered and unrecorded—is brought to an end.

The poet's subsidence into rest—after the epic but also ecstatic effort of turning dawn into words—is almost painfully brief: "I look down into the neighbor's garden." There are still things unheard, the poet reminds herself (the petal-fall); there are still things her transcription has been unable to incorporate (the pine tree unincluded in the long central sentence):

> What if I could hear the sound of petals falling
> >   off the head that
> >   holds them
> when it's time?
> What if I could hear where something is suddenly
> >   complete?
> The pinetree marionette-like against the wall—but still,
> >   unused.
> Whose turn is it now? Whose?

A new sentence begins to brew in the poet's compelled heart: she has "done" one bit of morning, the turn from dark to light, from nested birds to flying flocks, from silence to churchbells, from sleep to the crying of a single name—but "Whose turn is it now? Whose?"

The alternating rhythms of silence and naming become ever more anguishing in Graham's work, if only because each poem, at this point in her pursuit of the lyric, demands of her that she leave out nothing. This is a demand to which all serious artists eventually come—"O mother, what have I left out? O mother, what have I forgotten?" asks Ginsberg in "Kaddish"—and, implicitly, all readers test long lyrics by asking "What *should* have been included here by way of observation, reflection, qualification, and conclusion, and was, to the detriment of the poem, left out?" (Even shorter lyrics must, to succeed, convince us of their completeness; they do it by a sort of Dickinsonian implosion, in which an implied prehistory of ignited totalization is condensed into charred post-hoc indices of itself.)

At this moment in her writing, Graham chooses to show us her expanding universe by means of a slice of it in conic section. The cosmological excess that Graham has been insisting on recently can be read as a corrective to the current lyric of personal circumscription. It is especially a corrective (in its descent from Dickinson at her most metaphysical and Moore at her most expansive) to the lack of grandeur in much contemporary American poetry. Just as the personal is always in danger of becoming petty, so of course the grand is always in danger of the grandiose; and the Great Heights (as Graham has called them) can, unchecked, become parodies of themselves. Graham's capacity to descend from the Great Heights to an unremarkable single dawn in an anonymous town suggests that she understands the Whitmanian ecstatic sublimity of the ordinary as well as the Shelleyan heroic sublimity of aspiration. She has shown, in still other poems, that she possesses self-irony and historical irony, both of them useful balances to the vaulting mind and the universalizing voice that have impelled her approach to the edge of the precipice of perception by means of her triple excess—her long lines, her long pauses, and her long sentences.

From *The Breaking of Style: Hopkins, Heaney, Graham* (Harvard University Press)

Notes

1. John Keats, *Letters*, ed. Hyder Rollins, 2 vols. (Cambridge, Mass.: Harvard University Press, 1958), 2: 238.

2. Wallace Stevens, *Collected Poems* (New York: Knopf, 1955), 61.

3. Gerard Manley Hopkins, *Poetical Works*, ed. Norman H. Mackenzie (Oxford: Clarendon Press, 1990), 182.

4. Walt Whitman, *Leaves of Grass: A Comprehensive Reader's Edition*, ed. Harold W. Blodgett and Scully Bradley (New York: New York University Press, 1965), 155.

5. Jorie Graham, *Erosion* (Princeton, N.J.: Princeton University Press, 1983), 8–9.

6. Graham, *The End of Beauty* (New York: Ecco Press, 1987), 67.

7. Graham, *Materialism* (New York: Ecco Press, 1993), 85–86.

5

Iconoclasm in the Poetry of Jorie Graham

ANNE SHIFRER

Poems about paintings are abundant in the works of Jorie Graham, especially in her second volume, *Erosion*, which includes poems about Piero della Francesca's "The Madonna del Parto," Goya's "El Destino," Masaccio's "The Expulsion of Adam and Eve," and Luca Signorelli's "Resurrection of the Body," to mention but a few of her ecphrastic subjects. Indeed, Bonnie Costello, in one of the best essays written on Graham, suggests that ecphrasis is the "chief rhetorical strategy" of *Erosion*.[1]

Ecphrasis (a term now used to mean a verbal rendering and response to a visual representation, particularly a painting) is also a valuable entrée to Graham's ensuing volumes of poetry, *The End of Beauty* and *Region of Unlikeness*, and to her aesthetic philosophy generally. Some have argued that the appeal of ecphrasis for poetry resides in a painting's ability to "be" without meaning and to exist in apparent atemporal repose. Words, the medium of poetry, necessarily mean; words, when read, must occupy temporal sequence; thus, the argument runs, poetry envies its sister, painting, for the qualities poetry itself lacks. Graham, however, has a different, more complex relation to visual representation. Her exploration of connections between the medium of words and the media of visual representation abandons the traditional paradigm with its persistent and usually invidious comparisons. Graham examines both verbal and visual art forms as intricate, ceaselessly paradoxical and multivoiced layerings that shroud an ultimate metaphysical void. She also studies visual representation to amplify the resources of her craft.

Graham's poetic techniques have been deeply influenced by the practices of painters. In an interview with Thomas Gardner, she mentions Jackson Pollock in particular, saying that his work calls attention to the process of painting, to "the gap between the end of his gesture and the beginning of the painting." "I love," Graham exclaims, "to imagine that one-inch gap between the end of the brush and the beginning of the canvas on the floor."[2] It is this gap, "this nothing" in which the plenum of possibility is suspended, that is for Graham the most exhilarating moment of creation, a moment painting and poetry share. In *The End of Beauty*, Graham's third volume, blank spaces are placed within the poems to signify the gap between pen and paper and the openness of what might occur there. Part of the poem remains uncreated or left up to the reader's imaginative interaction with the poem.

Pollock has also influenced Graham in another way. His large murals cannot be seen, she claims, from any distance: Stand close, you can't see the whole canvas; stand back, you can't see the dripwork. Graham suggests that Pollock's work compels "us to stand at that difficult juncture of whole and partial visions. . ." (Gardner, 99). Vacillating back and forth, we begin to learn a type of seeing in which we sense the whole from within the limits of our individual perspective. Through viewing Pollock's paintings, we can develop, Graham thinks, a compensatory peripheral vision that negotiates between individual perspective and vision of the whole. This type of seeing is, Graham argues, essential to our survival as a species. Just as Pollock's murals require perspectival agility, so too do the poems in *The End of Beauty* and *Region of Unlikeness*. We, for instance, may find ourselves just getting comfortable within a perspective determined by the speaker's position, when we're tossed into an aerial view. Or we may be nesting within an introspective voice and then abruptly wakened to a perspective which includes us, as in the poem "Room Tone" when suddenly we're addressed: "Dear reader, is it enough for you that I am thinking of you / in this generic sort of way. . . ?" (*The End of Beauty*, 73). Or again, we may hear a "click" and a "click, click," a noise that suggests the poem's subject is being photographed or, more disconcertingly, that a picture is being taken of the reader reading.

This brief summary of how Pollock's painterly techniques have influenced Graham should suggest that the visual arts have been for her more than just a subject matter; they also have informed her sense of how poetry might be practiced.

Graham is also, however, drawn to the visual arts for what might be called perverse reasons. In an interview published in 1986, Graham was asked about the motives behind her ecphrastic poems, and she responded that paintings activate her rage, her rage to have things change:

> I don't *use* the paintings as much as spring off the scene in them which is strangely fixed and free from us and so makes especially evident our desire for transformation, our

tiny imperialisms of the imagination. Paintings are "finished" and stilled in ways few things in nature are, and therefore resistant in ways that make my rage to change more visible to me.[3]

Indeed, throughout *Erosion*, we see Graham subtly, and not so subtly, tinkering with masterpieces of Western visual art. In "San Sepolcro," she agitates and eroticizes the notably quiescent figure of Piero della Francesca's "The Madonna del Parto" (2–3). While Kenneth Clark describes this madonna as oriental in her tranquility, Graham has her unbuttoning her dress to enter into both labor and temporality.[4] The figure almost walks out of the fresco into the present space of the viewer. Similarly, in her description of Masaccio's "The Expulsion of Adam and Eve," Graham injects kinesis into the stasis of the painting. She addresses Adam and Eve directly, telling them to take their hands from their faces and step out of the confining frame of pictorial composition, "a space too small to fit in" (68). Again, Graham temporalizes the painting by insisting on taking its implied kinesis literally. (We are reminded that Adam and Eve did, after all, initiate Time.)

Although Graham's ecphrastic poems do acknowledge some of the surface of the paintings and some of their traditional significance, she changes them enough to call her at least "a strong reader," to use Harold Bloom's phrase for artistic appropriation, if not an iconoclast. What seems to provoke her iconoclasm is, in part, the traditions of meaning which help compose these artworks; but more, the very fact of their pictorial stasis, their apparent pretense to exemption from temporality. One might think that Graham is reinvoking that old and potentially invidious distinction between the verbal and the visual arts, i.e., that poetry is a temporal art and painting a spatial and static art. This is not, however, so. Both art forms can be understood as fixed and atemporal, and both can alternatively be understood as a field of transformative possibilities. Graham, of course, prefers the latter for reasons that I think are moral. What exasperates her about the visual arts is exactly what she finds and resists in the traditional conception and practices of poetry: the idea that art works of any medium should pretend to immunity from time and circumstance.

Since I read the ecphrastic poems of *Erosion* as a resistance to iconography and the idea that meaning can be stabilized, either within the work of art, or, if not there, within the culture and systems of signification that surround the artwork at the time of its creation, I was surprised when I read Bonnie Costello's essay on ecphrasis in *Erosion* because she describes it as a work that presents art as "an alternative space to the world of erosion, a form of 'rescue' from the flux . . ." (373–74), and she even suggests that Graham composes the visual arts "into a kind of New Critical verbal icon" (381) within her own temporal poetic creations. With this reasoning behind her, Costello calls *Erosion* a modernist work and Graham's later works postmodern. While Graham's later poems do increasingly insist on disrupting their own surfaces, I would argue that the seeds, if not the fruits, of postmodern ideas about art are very much present in *Erosion*.

To pursue this argument, I take Costello's ending point, her analysis of Graham's "Two Paintings by Gustav Klimt" as my point of departure. After an astute analysis of the poem, Costello concludes that Graham, while questioning the Klimt paintings, finally seems in sympathy with their treatment of surface because the pleasure it offers "draws us toward the unknown and unspeakable" (394). Although sharing much of Costello's understanding of this difficult poem, I disagree with her conclusion and instead feel that Graham verbally dissects the paintings and then ends her poem with an ironic comment on their surface innocence. Graham finally never trusts the surface calm of artworks, even though she at times may try to admire it.

"Two Paintings by Gustav Klimt" begins with a description of one of Klimt's paintings of a beech tree forest, in German a "buchen-wald." The shimmery trees and the forest floor dominate the foreground; a band of blue sky on the horizon establishes the depth of the wood. High in the trees, a few leaves shine brightly like gold foil. The well-known imprimatur of Klimt, the Egyptian glitter that decorates his women, would seem to be all but absent if it weren't for these small golden leaves.

The scene is seductively pleasant: Trees and ground seem to refract and reflect, becoming all one light on a fine ceramic glaze. But as Graham presents the painting to our view, she insinuates that the kaleidoscopic glitter of the beech trees is deceptively beautiful. The poem suggests that this exquisite, apparently innocent, landscape painting must be viewed in moral terms:

> Although what glitters
> >   on the trees
> row after perfect row,
> >   is merely
> the injustice
> >   of the world,
>
> the chips on the bark of each
> >   beech tree
> catching the light, the sum
> >   of these delays
> is the beautiful, the human
> >   beautiful,

>   body of flaws.
>   The dead
>   would give anything
>   I'm sure,
>   to step again onto
>   the leafrot,
>
>   into the avenue of mottled shadows
>   the speckled
>   broken skins. The dead
>   in their sheer
>   open parenthesis, what they
>   wouldn't give
>
>   for something to lean on
>   that won't
>   give way. I think I
>   would weep
>   for the moral nature
>   of this world,
>
>   for right and wrong like pools
>   of shadow
>   and light you can step in
>   and out of
>   crossing this yellow beech forest.
>   this *buchen-wald* (61–62)

The aggrieved dead, the victims of Buchenwald, seem to be waiting in these trees, longing to resume life. Their formlessness—the form the painter has failed to give them—is present, as one end of an open parenthesis, in the leafrot which metaphorically interfaces their skin.

In a characteristic move, Graham insists that seeing is impure; it is conditioned, in this case, by our knowledge of the holocaust even while Klimt's life and work preceded that event. Our light has changed: "[L]ate / in the twentieth / century, in hollow light, / in gaseous light" (62), when we gaze on a buchenwald, we can't help thinking of that other Buchenwald. To see the trees receive light and return it in apparently sheer and amoral beauty appears not to be possible. Light and dark become substantive and morally infused; the speaker of the poem walks through them. The lingering effluvia of the holocaust osmotically penetrate and infect the coppered blues and yellows of the painting.

The second half of the poem describes another painting by Klimt, "The Bride"; this painting seems subtly but firmly to corroborate Graham's reading of the "Buchenwald" and her eerie sense that a dismantled ethos lurks in the landscape painting. Shortly after Klimt died, an unfinished painting was found in his studio. One side is a tangled group of figures wrapped in the mosaic trappings for which Klimt is famous. On the other side is an uncompleted female figure, with legs splayed and a mangled composite head (that of a sleeping female face and what appears to be an aged male face or a death's head). One art critic, Alessandra Comini, reports that the painting was first seen by burglars, who broke into Klimt's studio on the day when Klimt had a stroke from which he later died. Comini describes what the burglars saw as follows:

> For here, even to the uninitiated, was an extraordinary revelation of what might be called a "dirty old-master" technique. In opposition to the floating knot of figures covering the left side of the canvas, the splayed-out nude body of [a] young girl dominated the other half. Her face was averted in a profile turn[ed] to the right, and a mufflerlike wrap at the throat seemed to separate the head from its glimmering white torso, creating a startling effect of mutilation. The knees were bent and the legs spread apart to expose a carefully detailed pubic area upon which the artist had leisurely begun to paint an overlay "dress" of suggestive and symbolic ornamental shapes. . . . The unfinished painting, by the mere fact that it was unfinished, contained the clue to the erotic premise of Klimt's great allegories involving female figures. The unknown ransackers of the studio had, sheerly by accident, caught the artist in the secret and revelatory act of flagrant voyeurism.[5]

Apparently Klimt had intended to cover the woman's body, including what Graham designates as "a scream between her legs," with his usual imbrications. Graham describes the painting as follows:

They say that when Klimt
    died suddenly
a painting, still
    incomplete,

was found in his studio,
    a woman's body
open at its point of
    entry,
rendered in graphic,
    pornographic,

detail—something like
   a scream
between her legs. Slowly,
   feathery,
he had begun to paint
   a delicate

garment (his trademark)
   over this mouth
of her body. The mouth
   of her face
is genteel, bored, feigning a need
   for sleep. The fabric

defines the surface,
   the story,
so we are drawn to it,
   its blues
and yellows glittering
   like a stand

of beech trees late
   one afternoon
in Germany, in fall.
   It is called
Buchenwald, it is
   1890. In

the finished painting
   the argument
has something to do
   with pleasure. (63)

Graham gives the painting two mouths, one of which was about to be silenced by "a delicate garment (his trademark)." Had Klimt finished the painting, we would not, presumably, know what lay behind it. The woman might have looked like other Klimt works—those beauties who appear to be drugged, embalmed or mummified, their delicate leers hovering between the erotic and a death grimace. A perverse tang—a love in death motif, which links the erotic with the enshrined death of women—is everywhere implicit in Klimt's work; but only in the unfinished painting is it possible to link his portraits of women so definitely with mutilation.

Graham's reading suggests that the decorative glitter with which Klimt covers his women (and his beech trees) conceals a deeper intention and reality, one we might never glean from the finished paintings themselves. With our knowledge of Klimt's painting process and our knowledge of history, we can no longer see his "Beech Trees" as a stand of beech trees. "In the finished painting the argument is pleasure," says the end of Graham's poem, a line which is chilling for its suppression of judgment, its suppression of the moral world for which we weep. It is a line forged, we might imagine, in an agonizing attempt to remain neutral; it is also a line which resonates, finally, with deepest irony.

Graham sees that the unfinished painting authorizes, even mandates, a reading of "Buchenwald" that refuses its surface beauty. The clue may begin in a transposition (*buchen-wald* becomes Buchenwald), which is then curiously ratified by the unfinished painting, with its unfinished burial which reveals the chasm dividing surface and depth. An ecphrasis that at first seems eccentric and even puritanical, which sees didactic polarities in a landscape painting, finally, by the end of the poem, seems highly relevant, perhaps indispensable to how we might understand Klimt's work as a whole. I, for one, now see his work differently.

My reading of Graham's reading of Klimt has, I think, illustrated that though Graham is deeply influenced by the visual arts, she is better seen as an iconoclast than as an icon maker. Indeed, when I presented this analysis at a conference, one art historian in the audience was deeply angry at Graham for distorting Klimt's intent. If Graham's attitude toward art were thoroughly modern in *Erosion*, I don't think her poems would win such anger. Traditional art historians are more likely to see Graham as an icon basher than icon maker. It is clear, I think, even in her second volume, *Erosion*, that Graham is troubled by the static, atemporal pretensions of art. She wants to make artworks move, change, and, most importantly, to submit to the preoccupations, perspectives, and needs of our present moment. For her, when art becomes an objet d'art, it becomes not-art. This is as true for poems as it is for paintings; she bears no particular hostility to the visual arts.

In fact, when she seeks to make her own art more aleatory and open-ended, Graham again turns to Jackson Pollock. His works, she suggests, are aclosural. They include chaos, and in her own poetry Graham strives to postpone closure, trying to find "forms of delay, digression, side-motions which are not entirely dependent for their effectiveness on the sense-of-the-ending, that stark desire" (Gardner, 84–85).

Graham's insistence on exposing the historical and experiential contexts of artworks both visual and verbal seems to arise from a fundamentally moral concern about the place of art and its role in history and our lives. Closural art, for

Graham, is linked to the imperial motive to contain and possess and to the eschatological sort of thinking that encourages us to think that we only have meaning through endings and completions. These proclivities in our lives and art are, for Graham, what is driving us towards apocalypse. As she says in her 1992 interview with Thomas Gardner:

> ... we have created a situation whereby we are only able to know ourselves by a conclusion which would render *meaningful* the storyline along the way.

Then, after reminding us of Jonathan Schell's *The Fate of the Earth*, Graham says that we live with a "secret sense 'well let's get it over with so that we might know what the story was, what it was *for*'" (Gardner, 84).

Interestingly, at this moment Graham looks to the visual arts for a clue about how to proceed with her own art: "I'm intrigued by medieval triptychs—in which the middle panel (the *present*) is larger than the side panels (past and future)—as a model" (Gardner, 84). Again, we sense her iconoclastic impulse at work, for we gather that in making the present frontal, Graham would revise the better part of Christian eschatology present in most medieval triptychs.

In addition to desiring art forms that would help change our thinking about the dependency of value on endings and completions, Graham also believes that art is only significant as it is experienced. All of the arts must be temporal in this sense. She asserts that art should always involve genuine risks, not just "risks fabricated for the purposes of getting a poem" (Gardner, 93). This risk is the risk of change: for the creator, for the person who experiences the art piece, and for the very artwork itself. In this, Graham's art might be allied to postmodern forms such as performance art and installations. Her own poems happen, she says, always in the present tense, *to her*, and she tries to make a present-tense, transformative experience available for readers.

Similarly, the rhetoric of her ecphrastic poems is always that of a present-tense temporality that makes the artwork available as an experience rather than as an immutable, temporally transcendent object. This approach to ecphrasis is an interesting twist because so often it has been suggested that poets turn to the visual arts because they admire, even envy, the nontemporal repose of paintings and sculpture. The allure of the visual arts for Graham is just the opposite: They activate her rage to subsume all art forms into the kinesis of personal change.

Poems, for Graham, should not be told by survivors. In reviewing Graham's third volume of poetry, *The End of Beauty*, for *The New Yorker*, Helen Vendler majestically sums up this impetus in Graham's poetry, tracing it back to an early essay written before the publication of *Erosion*:

In an essay called "Some Notes on Silence," explaining why she writes poems of inconclusive, ongoing presentness, Graham contrasts such poems with narratives, reminiscences, and prophecies—poetic forms that are strung on the temporal axis of past, present, and future. [P]oems in the past tense are told by a survivor of the experience recounted. Such poems are containers for understood experience rather than a precarious enacting of experience as it is being undergone. . . .

Rushing into temporality, Graham's new verse resembles Action painting in words.[6]

Graham's commitment to art forms which render the artist herself vulnerable becomes increasingly evident in *The End of Beauty* and *Region of Unlikeness*. Even the title of the latter comes to mean, as one reads the volume, the self which is never self-identical and the terra incognita wherein metaphorical unities come undone.

The opening poem, "Fission," suggests this fragmentation and also reveals a new dimension in Graham's employment of ecphrasis. Rather than using a painting as the "springing off scene," Graham describes a film, Stanley Kubrick's *Lolita*, based on Nabokov's novel of the same name. Both Helen Vendler and Bonnie Costello note a shift from the pictorial to the cinematic in Graham's work and see it as a symptom or sign of postmodernity in Graham's artistic practice. Vendler suggests that "the inevitable present tense of film," its rhythm of "this moment, then this moment," becomes the formal principle of Graham's poetry after *Erosion* (76); and Costello suggests that Graham's recent work decenters the image, "thrusting it out of controlling aesthetic form and into personal and public history. . . . Film rather than painting has become her sister art" (276).

While the comments of Vendler and Costello are both precise and evocative, their insights can be usefully enlarged by looking more closely at the poem "Fission." This poem is, I think, epic in its dimensions while also being intensely, almost obscenely, personal. What Graham begins in *Erosion* (that vivisection of masterworks which reveals the spurious insularity of aesthetic experience and pleasure) is carried further in "Fission." In this poem and in the later work generally, Graham applies her analytic, deconstructive gaze not only to the ecphrastic subject, but also to herself. While "Two Paintings by Gustav Klimt" focuses on the deceptive surface layering of Klimt's palimpsests, the focus of "Fission" is more inclusive and unstable. The poem begins with a description of *Lolita*: "the full-sized / screen / on which the greater-than-life-size girl appears" (3). Graham's description entangles both the film's subject and the film qua film. In virtual simultaneity, we are made aware of the film's encompassing contexts: the theater with its "real electric lights," the viewer of the film (the poem's speaker, a young girl, perhaps Graham herself, who sits in the audience with her father), and also the larger historical context.

It is, we learn, 1963, the year John F. Kennedy was shot and killed. The announcement of this event disrupts the kinetic flow of cinema and the aesthetic experience of the speaker. If historical awareness had an originary moment for Graham's generation, it would probably be John F. Kennedy's assassination. The sense of the tragic was inscribed in and by this event, as was, paradoxically, the personal. As is so often noted, everyone remembers what they were doing when they first heard news of this president's death.

It is this moment, the collision (or fission) of aesthetic experience with the public and the historical, that Graham explores in "Fission." A man runs into the theater, "asking for our attention," . . . "the man hoarse now as he waves his arms, / as he screams to the booth to cut it, cut the sound. . ." (4–5). I quote in this broken fashion because the film plays on as the man screams, and the poem's speaker describes her divided experience from more than one perspective. At times, she seems to be wholly inside the experience of viewing the film. At other times, perspective seems to embrace the larger context (and here one should remember Graham's admiration for Pollock's handling of perspective).

As the man continues to shout, various lights go up: first the electric lights of the theater, revealing "the magic forearm" (4) of the cinematic light coming from the projector. These additional lights turn the screen figures, Lolita with her heart-shaped sunglasses, her mother and Humbert Humbert, into leper-like figures. Next, "the theater's skylight is opened and noon slides in / . . . whiting the story out one layer further" (5). Lolita's flesh is turned into "a roiling up of grayness," "bits of moving zeros" (5). As the "real" lights of the theater deteriorate the image projected by the film light, and as the "more real" light of noon destroys the lights of the theater, and as all these lights wrap themselves about "the real," what ultimately gets revealed is the poem's speaker herself:

> Where the three lights merged:
>   where the image licked my small body from the front, the story playing
> all over my face my
>   forwardness,
> where the electric lights took up the back and sides,
>   the unwavering houselights,
> seasonless,
>
>   where the long thin arm of day came in from the top
> to touch my head,

> reaching down along my staring face—
> where they flared up around my body unable to
>
> merge into each other
>   over my likeness,
> slamming down one side of me, unquenchable—here static
>
>   there flaming—
> sifting grays into other grays—
>   mixing the split second into the long haul—
> flanking me—undressing something there where my
>   body is
> though not my body—
>   where they play on the field of my willingness,
>
> where they kiss and brood, filtering each other to no avail,
>   all over my solo
> appearance. . . . (6–7)

This solo appearance, a showing of the self to the self, is extremely painful. Graham compares the speaker's sense of exposure to being made suddenly naked. Light becomes a perversely erotic force, undressing her, fondling her body. The viewer, rather than the film, suddenly becomes the center of attention, or so, at least, she feels herself to be. Where Graham in "Two Paintings by Gustav Klimt" focuses on Klimt's exhibition of a painted woman's body, here she focuses on the exhibition of her own body.

The classic privacy of the cinema is violated, dramatically. The primary conditions of film as medium—the invisibility of the cinematic apparatus and the invisibility of spectators—are all at once exploded, revealing the voyeuristic privacy of the audience that Laura Mulvey discusses in her germinal essay, "Visual Pleasure and Narrative Cinema." It is not just that the speaker in Graham's poem becomes excruciatingly aware of her body; it is also that she becomes aware of her own desire, as it has been stirred by the film. "I wanted," she says, "someone to love" (6). And yet she resists being an object of desire; she thinks, "there is a way to not yet be wanted / . . . no telling what on earth we'll have to marry marry marry" (6). The speaker finds herself in what Mulvey would call the "traditional exhibitionist role" of woman; her eros, like that of the young Lolita's under Humbert Humbert's male gaze, is beginning to be fixed in her "to-be-looked-at-ness," to use again a phrase from Mulvey.[7]

The poem is full of exposures—the exposure of the cinematic apparatus, the exposure of the viewer, the exposure of the personal moment as a public moment. The public largeness of Kennedy's assassination redoubles the nakedness and embarrassment of personal desire. Desire, especially the desire of a young girl, seems minute and mortifying within the magnitudes of history. Cast within the trajectory of tragedy (if it is true that tragedy is only for males, as Camille Paglia claims), the girl could be made to feel even more small. Reading the poem as a note on "the girl" within the epic of American history, the girl sounds the smallest of sounds. The poem also suggests that desire, however small, is implicated in the violence of culture. To want to have ("no telling what we'll have to want next," the mind of "Fission" asserts) is, for Graham, to begin down the imperial road.

What will become history, the death of a famous male, destroys both the aesthetic experience of the girl and her ability to close herself within her own desire and identity. The girl becomes a bit like the nearly seven-year-old girl in Bishop's poem "In the Waiting Room," and perhaps even more like the girl in Alice Munro's short story "Wild Swans," whose sexuality is inappropriately kindled by an older man, a priest in fact, who fondles her on a train. One might expect Graham to proffer us an unqualified lament at the way in which innocence is stripped from the girl in "Fission." However, she does not. The fission or splitting apart of aesthetic experience that we witness in "Fission" is, for Graham, paradoxically, what the practice and experience of art should be. The iconoclasm of *Erosion* in which an art object is "read" to find depths which contradict the surface becomes an iconoclasm which is turned on the image of the poet: The poet herself becomes a succession of images that dissolves into other images. "Fission" is not the only poem in *Region of Unlikeness* that pursues this aesthetic; the whole first section contains poems in which historical violence intersects with the private life and effectively destroys privacy.

In moving her iconoclasm from the field of pictorial art to the mobilities of film, Graham becomes, I think, more readily able to suggest the processionality and kinesis of image and icon and also their immersion in history and time. By focusing on visual masterpieces of the past, *Erosion* seems to cast itself against the notion of image inherited from Modernism. Iconoclasm in *Region of Unlikeness* definitely moves within the postmodern maze of images, or what Baudrillard calls "simulacra."[8] The "precession of simulacra" that moves through "Fission" presumes no ultimate ground for mimesis; the image is never certainly an image of anything. The poem shows a speaker who moves through simulacra, including simulacra of herself. The image of Lolita is in one sense an image of the speaker herself, and as the film dissolves, dissolving Lolita's body, so also does the speaker's sense of her body dissolve. The lights with their "sifting grays into other grays" (7) turn her into an "almost leper" like Lolita.

For the Jorie Graham of *Region of Unlikeness*, who declared in her previous volume's title "the end of beauty," images are, if anything, a shroud to reality. I quote now the end of the poem "Fission":

> *choice* the thing that wrecks the sensuous here the glorious
> > here—
> that wrecks the beauty,
> > choice the move that rips the wrappings of light, the
> > > ever-tighter wrappings
>
> of the layers of the
> > real: what is, what also is, what might be that is,
> what could have been that is, what
> > might have been that is, what I say that is,
> what the words say that is,
> > what you imagine the words say that is—Don't move, don't
>
> wreck the shroud, don't move—(8)

"Choice," the only thing that gives the girl agency and being, must negotiate the most complex of regions and unlikenesses. Choice must sort through layer after layer, image after image. Successive, mobile layers of image may wrap the real, or they may be the real. Getting to the heart of the real, for Graham, means, I think, the pondering of a mass grave, not only the particular death of Kennedy but also the nothingness at the center of metaphysics, the nothingness of the female body. The shift from immobile to moving image in Graham's ecphrastic work and the iconoclasm which she exerts on the images of both media enable her to peer, reverentially I think, into the graves of both beauty and truth and to begin to construct a feminine subject who exists in agency rather than image.

Laura Mulvey ends "Visual Pleasure and Narrative Cinema" with this comment: "It is said that analysing pleasure, or beauty, destroys it. That is the intention of this article." Mulvey would destroy pleasure and beauty "in order to conceive a new language of desire" (8). Graham's iconoclasm is similar in its aim.

Notes

Quotations from Graham's poems are from *The End of Beauty* (New York: Ecco Press, 1987); *Erosion* (Princeton, N.J.: Princeton University Press, 1983); and *Region of Unlikeness* (New York: Ecco Press, 1991).

    1. Bonnie Costello, "Jorie Graham: Art and Erosion," *Contemporary Literature* 33, no. 2 (Summer 1992): 374.

    2. Thomas Gardner, "An Interview with Jorie Graham," *Denver Quarterly* 26, no.4 (1992): 80.

    3. Ann Snodgrass, "Interview: Jorie Graham," *Quarterly West* 23 (1986): 153.

    4. See Kenneth Clark, *Piero della Francesca*, 2nd ed. (Ithaca, N.Y.: Cornell University Press, 1981).

    5. Alessandra Comini, *Gustav Klimt* (New York: Braziller, 1975), 5–6.

    6. Helen Vendler, "Married to Hurry and Grim Song," *The New Yorker*, 27 July 1987, 75.

    7. Laura Mulvey, "Visual Pleasure and Narrative Cinema," *Screen* 16, no. 3 (Autumn 1975): 11.

    8. See Jean Baudrillard, *Simulations* (New York: Semiotext(e), 1983).

6

Listening for a Divine Word

Review of The Errancy

FORREST GANDER

Film director Mai Zetterling, given the opportunity to shoot one Olympic competition in the sixties, chose weight lifting. "I am not in-ter-ested in sports," she explained in a seductive Swedish accent; "I am in-ter-ested in ob-sessions." After the weighty quotations, the historical dialogues, the lapidary density of *Materialism*, Jorie Graham obsessively continues to create in her new book, *Errancy*, a kind of echo chamber of Western literary culture with Homeric and Greek mythological themes, with quotations and allusions to *The Waste Land,* and with references to the poems of Wallace Stevens, George Oppen, Rilke, Hart Crane, Coleridge, and Dickinson, among others. Her treatment of the Biblical story of Jacob wrestling with an angel becomes paradigmatic of man's encounter, fraught by miscommunication, with the other—both the human and divine other. Divine encounters, several poems suggest, may go unrecognized by those herds of us stuck in traffic, clutching lists of things to do. Though a few scintillating poems celebrate sexual love, the human encounters described in these new poems are often savage ones or ones in which thought has become tragically disconnected from emotion. Much of *Errancy* concerns the struggle to leaven fatigue and despair with feeling, to reawaken the full possibilities of being. In a radical and sensuous language, Graham enacts a presence complex and empathetic enough to wrestle some word of blessing from our millennium's dark last nights.

    The lines in *Errancy* are contractile, propulsive, often hyperextensive. They serpentine into quick arpeggios of near-rhyme, stretching across the page horizontally, curling into short appendixes tucked under the lines above them, flicking into dashes, coiling between parentheses. One sequence of sound patterns stressing vowel reverberations will be interwoven with secondary and tertiary sequences, creating complexly layered rhythmical movements. The first stanza of "The Scanning" is fairly representative.

> After the rain there was traffic behind us like a long kiss.
> The ramp harrowing its mathematics like a newcomer who likes
>   the rules—
> glint and whir of piloting minds, gripped steering wheels . . .
> Jacob waiting and the angel *didn't show.*
> Meanwhile the stations the scanner glides over, not selecting, hiss—
> islands the heat-seekers missed
> in the large sea of. . . . And after lunch
> the long-distance starts up pianissimo—telephone wires glinting where the
>   frontage road
> parallels the interstate for a little, narrow, while.
> Elsewhere, from the air, something *softens* the scape—
> which activity precedes, though doesn't necessarily require,
> the carpet-bombing that often follows—
> And the bands of our listening scan
> the bands of static,
> seeking a resting point, asymptotic, listening in the hiss
> for the hoarse snagged points where meaning seemingly
> accrues: three notes: three silences: intake
> of breath: turnstile?: a glint in fog?: what the listener
> will wait-into, hoping for a place to
> stop . . . Jacob waited and the angel didn't—

We hear first the echo of "k*iss*" in "*its*" and "mathemat*ics*." But even before those three notes are reinforced by "h*iss*," "m*iss*ed," "d*is*tance," and "pian*is*simo," Graham introduces a counterpoint, the growling consonance of "*g*lint," "*g*ripped" and "*g*lides" and the long *o*'s of "sh*ow*" and "*o*ver." Look how the word "show" recollects the second syllable of "harr*ow*ing" from the second line, and prepares our ears for the deep vowels in "pianissim*o*," "teleph*o*ne," "*o*ld," "r*oa*d," "narr*ow*," and "foll*ow*." But the music becomes increasingly intricate. Our ears must be attentive to keep pace with the changes in rhythm and pitch. The end-words "while" and "require" amplify the earlier chime of "wire." The first tonal key we heard—*iss*—returns toward the end of the stanza in "l*is*tening in the h*is*s" and "l*is*tener." Meanwhile, along with the long *a*'s of "int*a*ke," "w*ai*t," and "pl*a*ce," and the long *u*'s of "accr*ue*," "int*o*," and "t*o*," we hear the closely clustered detonations of new tonal patterns: "bands of our listening scan / the bands"; "Elsewhere, from the air"; "meaning seemingly." The words "hiss," "glint," "bands," "point(s)," and "three" are each repeated, along with a variant of the sentence fragment "Jacob waiting and the angel didn't show." The whole stanza, gaining momentum as it approaches the sequence of colons, undulates in the clause, "hoping for a place to stop" wherein the conceptual and rhythmical meanings converge. And stop.

There is a lot to say about this heady, improvisational music, even before we acknowledge the significance of the Biblical reference (at one level the poem is about miscommunication), the nod to Wallace Stevens ("for the listener who listens in the snow"), or the allusions—"heat-seekers," "carpet-bombing"—to an impersonal war (another example of the failure to communicate).

Graham's ingenious weave of tone-leading vowels, chords of rhyme, off and slant rhyme, creates a generative syncopative tension. Each subsequent occasion of hearing an unpredictable rhyme draws together matching sounds, compressing the interstitial words. Graham loops one pattern of sound through another, controlling the pacing with commas and dashes, and the rhythmic contractions and expansions muscle the poem along like a snake pulling itself forward around uneven anfractuosities in the landscape. The poems have a distinctly peristaltic momentum.

Such polyphonal sound patterns—the rifts in the riffs—give the poems in *Errancy* their propulsive energy. Profoundly, in their multilayered architecture they also function as analogues to Graham's phenomenology: the feathered objective and subjective stances, the coexistent perceptions of world and thought and poem. In the last section of "The Scanning," for instance, Graham can write simultaneously of a flock of geese taking flight, the dialectic between the numerous and the singular, and the poetic process itself:

> and the birds lift up—
> and from the undulant swagger-stabs of peck and wingflap,
> collisions and wobbly runs—out of the manyness—
> a molting of the singular,
> a frenzied search (unflapping, heavy) for cadence . . .

The poems are thrilling in their capacity to promote corollaries of meaning that reinforce and extend each other. So in the last lines of "The Scanning,"

> above us now, the sky lustrous with the skeleton of the dream of
>   reason—look up!—
> Jacob dreamer—the winged volumetrics chiseling out a skull
> for the dream—

the skeleton of the dream of reason is, of course, the vertebral line of flying geese (which image replaces the earlier one of war planes). So it is also the winged angel arriving to wrestle Jacob (as the poet wrestles with the poem) and to rename him (author of a nation, author of a poem). So it is also, literally, the vision of a skull chiseled out to make room for a new dream, a hopeful gesture—that active "look up!—" after the old dreams have imploded. These meanings are collaborative and inseparable.

How do her lines carry the weight of these simultaneous representations? Partly, it is because of Graham's accretionary syntax. Her sentences allow for innumerable revisions ("it held some light in it, / or, no, it twisted back, peeled back, some light") and elaborations in a style less common to English, perhaps, than to French or Italian, languages Graham heard as a child. When she writes, "beneath the glittering exterior-latex, beneath the storyline," she adds a signifying dimension with the second clause. Often, through metaphor, Graham collapses the distance between the revelation of a narrative and revelation of her own thinking about the narrative, as when—in a poem about Pascal's coat—she writes, "I have put on my doubting." Or she deftly pulls the thread of her own thought out of the narrative fabric, as when she writes in "Untitled Two," "Overheard sparrows snarl-up, and river, dive / making a dark clean thought, a bright renown. . . ." To make sense of these coextensive realms, the consciousness wedded to conscience, readers must recognize an increasing complexity of presence.

Everywhere in Graham's poetry, outside and inside, the activity of the world and discriminations of the mind interact in terms of inscription, revision, and erasure. In the title poem, suggesting that we, as a species, thought "we would comply, some day" to the notion of human perfectibility, Graham writes,

> we were *built* to fit and
> comply—
as handwriting fits to the form of its passion. . . .

Revelation, Graham insists, can come only through language. Later in the same poem, she writes, "she wants to be legible." "The Guardian Angel of Self-Knowledge" asks of those he observes, "How will they feel the erasures erase them?" In another poem, Graham describes "the grammar, so strict, of the two exact shoulders" of Pascal's coat, and the fabric's "grammatical weave." It is always language which describes and narrates the world. We see the weeping willow "dragging its alphabet of buds all along the gravelly walk" and "The sun . . . so poor here in its words." The carpenter is "ready to scribble" and the lightning is an "invisible inscription." Graham reminds us that there is no conception of the world, no place to be human, outside of language. Any new conception of being will require a new poetics, and this, Graham provides.

As key words migrate across the poems, much as they do in George Herbert's *The Temple*, rings of association pass through each other, investing themselves in new meanings. A much-repeated word like "swarm" (or "corridor," or "glance," or "spoor") and its variations ("aswarm," "swarming") will come to characterize the movement of a flock of birds, formations of people, debris before a storm, Pascal's decomposing coat, the whelm of thought, and the abstraction of "many-ness" in contradistinction to "singularity." Each key word is a field of signs. It doesn't stand still in its meaning, and there is no closure to our interpretation. The key words recur in various roles—as verbs, nouns, adjectives, adverbs—and in diverse metaphoric systems; often they do not refer even to the same concepts with which they were associated in their previous contexts. But these repeating words sustain a dramatic unity, and they tie the poems together as the work of one mind excavating, through language, the corridors that connect one thing with another.

We read "zero," for example, first in "The Errancy" as "zero / at the heart of the christened bonfire." In this case an expression for the spirit, it also reminds us of Emily Dickinson's "zero at the bone." It recurs later in the poem as part of a discrete image—"first fruit hanging ripe—oh bright red zero— / right there within reach." And "zero" continues to crop up, flowering on its own terms in new contexts, and then dehiscing across the collection into other poems and other connotations. In "The Guardian Angel of Private Life," the two words—"zero of"—huddle by themselves near the right margin. Syntactically, they are connected through the preposition to "the bright mock-stairwaying-up of the posthumous leaves." But visually they mingle with the words in the line directly below them: "zero of" "the heart." What develops through the repetitions is not a unity of meaning, but an endless impulse to propose meanings. "Zero" resurfaces in an image of liquid shade, the "swirling black zero we wait in / through which no god appears," and in an abstraction for a "hundred worn, black steering wheels, / gigantic sum of zeros that won't add." In "The Guardian Angel of Not Feeling," the speaker gasps: "oh look, the tiny heart / mouthing and mouthing its crisp inaudible black zeros out." The meaning of such key words, carrying into each of their occasions the history of their use in preceding contexts, becomes more than the sum of their meanings. In their multiple roles, Graham's key words are polysemous, binding the poems together in a matrix of interconnectedness.

And so the poems are sewn together like a garment, like Pascal's coat (imagined by Magritte in the painting reprinted on the book's cover) into which

Pascal's sister, at his deathbed, stitches his dream of reason, his "irrefutable proof of the existence of God," as we read in "Emergency" after the central poems "Le Manteau de Pascal" and "Manteau." The metaphor of Pascal's coat and the dream of reason might remind us, again, of Herbert whose poem "Divinity" is a meditation on the way that reason and definitions have "jagged" the "seamless coat" of Christ. But Graham's dream, on the deathbed of a millennium, is less apodictic, more tentative and gestural than either Pascal's or Herbert's.

Much of *Errancy* seems to be written at dawn (five poems include "Aubade" in their titles) after another rough night at the end of a century that has seen the failure of various utopian dreams. At such times, "Even the accuracy / is tired— the assimilation tired— / of entering the mind." The guardian angels specified in several poems speak sadly. They notice the list in our "exhausted hand" and importune us to "put it down." They see "The form of despair we call 'the world'" and bother to speak to us of "happiness." They tell us to "Behold . . . this" and we hear birdsong. But fatigue, habit, and disillusion as easily shatter countries as sink human spirits. When we look at the world through Graham's poems, we must recognize among ourselves the rapist, the child-beater, the drifter, the potential suicide, and the children crying for their murdered parents as well as the lover saying "I love you" and "saying the words again," the lover who in a beautiful act of stillness, says she will "take your breath into [her] hair." Graham's dream is to find a means to be true to it all. "How consent to that honor—," she asks at the end of "Little Requiem."

In the penultimate poem in the collection, "Recovered from the Storm," the speaker goes out among the broken limbs, torn-up bushes, and "drowned heads of things strewn wildly" about her yard at dusk in the wake of a storm, wondering "Am I supposed to put them back together—" It is too much confusion; no one could make it cohere. And yet she ends the poem with a gesture that in itself is all-important. Against chaos, against the terrifying force of barbarism, the gesture is all-important: "I pick up and drag one large limb from the path." Rather than offering a mystic expiation of the sins of the world, rather than facilely asserting that good will triumph, Graham proposes that in a "hostile universe" we can at best take one small step toward justice. In such humble acts—expressed in the "look up!" of "The Scanning," in the lovers of "Against Eloquence" kissing "as if trying to massacre difference," in the quivering, tender stillness of Eurydice bent over Orpheus, her mouth at his fingers "though not so much / as grazing them"—we may find not redemption, Graham suggests, but the inertia to prevail against the fatigue of a culture come to the end of its utopias.

Motivated by the dream to honor both singularity and manyness, Graham's most trenchant impetus is to connect thought and feeling into a sensually energized language of wakening presence. Within the poems, language itself is repaired, made capacious enough to transmit the divine, recharged with connectedness.

For two decades now, Graham's poems have been exercising the major muscles in the throat of our language. If you haven't been listening, I'm telling you there's a new music out there, and this book, *Errancy*, is its finest performance.

Boston Book Review

7

Jorie Graham's Big Hunger

JAMES LONGENBACH

Jorie Graham published her first book only sixteen years ago, but she has already produced a body of writing that feels like the accumulation of a lifetime. Like Yeats, who early in his career cautioned suspicious readers that "it is myself that I remake," Graham has been driven to turn against her own best discoveries, risking everything she has achieved. Each of her books is a new beginning; in *Materialism*, each poem feels like an interrogation of the one preceding it. Graham has been unwilling to settle for anything settled, and she sometimes discards achievements that other poets would be willing to nurture for a long time. A different kind of writer would winnow more scrupulously in private, sharing only the distilled residue of her dissatisfaction. But Graham's most self-conscious interrogations of poetry are driven by a kind of seriousness that impresses the most skeptical reader. The more she writes, the more necessary— the more truly elucidating—her public agon seems. Graham's achievement seems big because she is satisfied with so little.

Even individual poems seem poised between the contrary demands of the intimate and the cosmic. The linguistic texture of Graham's poems has always been distinguished by a tension between poetically precise and philosophically expansive kinds of diction; in *Materialism*, Graham transformed this tension into a structural principle. Her most recent poems tend to focus on an insignificant action—walking the dog, delivering her daughter's leotard, or picking up a dead butterfly. The poems themselves never seem little, however, for Graham creates (more than uncovers) the infinitely expanding web of psychic energies that makes each small moment possible. The result is a dramatization of what Husserl thought of as the "thickened" present: tracing the contours of a single action in the present, we feel the weighty convergence of the personal and cultural traces that cling to it. As Graham says in one of the five poems called "Notes on the Reality of the Self" in *Materialism*, she wants to "expand / each second, / bloating it up, cell-like, making it real." In the process, she forges a deeply sensuous poetry out of the slippage between language and sensation that so many American poets have worked to suppress—and she does so without capitulating to the opposite idealism, in which the claims of language supposedly override our desire to know the world intimately.

Graham's dramatization of consciousness can be so rapid and expansive that the insignificant action provoking the poem becomes difficult to find; but simple evidence for the action is always there. In "Recovered from the Storm" (collected in *The Errancy*, her most recent book), the action is simply and unexpectedly delineated in the poem's monosyllabic final line: "I pick up and drag one large limb from the path." The line is as unassuming as the action it describes, but because of the poem's breathless exfoliation of thought, the line is almost unbearably weighted with connotation.

> So this is the wingbeat of the underneathly, ticking—
> this iridescent brokenness, this wet stunted nothingness—
> busy with its hollows—browsing abstractly with its catastrophic wingtips
> the tops of our world, ripping pleatings of molecule,
> unjoining the slantings, the slippery wrinklings we don't even grasp
>   the icily free *made-nature* of yet?
> Why are we here in this silly moonlight?
> What is the mind meant to tender among splinters?
> What was it, exactly, was meant to be *shored?*
> Whose dolled-up sorceries *against confusion* now?
> The children are upstairs, we will keep them tucked in—
> as long as we can, as long as you'll let us.
> I hear your pitch. How containment is coughing,
> under the leafbits, against the asphalt.
> How the new piles of kindling are mossily giggling
>   their kerosene cadenza
> all long the block in the riddled updrafts.
> I pick up and drag one large limb from the path.

The achievement of this poem is that its final line—in itself so plain—is almost impossible to paraphrase. Negotiating the syntactical thicket that precedes it, we are made to feel the existential terror that Graham staves off by the necessary and yet poignantly inadequate act of dragging one (just one) fallen limb from the path. On the one hand, that terror feels threateningly domestic, the kind of fear that every parent of small children knows. On the other hand, the terror feels ominously metaphysical. In this poem of tiny consequence, Graham is audacious enough to refer openly to the two greatest modern poets of existential terror. She makes already well-known lines from Eliot ("These fragments I have shored against my ruins") and Frost ("a momentary stay against confusion") ring in our ears again. There is nothing cagey about these gestures toward the moderns. Graham wants us to feel the power of these lines, and she needs to let us know that the lines—however familiar they might be— are a necessary part of her poetic equipment. Her poems do not feel at all similar to those of Pinsky, Howard, or Clampitt, but, like them, Graham exemplifies what is best about contemporary American poetry; her distinctiveness is based on acts of inclusion, a hunger to align herself with a wide array of contemporaries and precursors.

For Graham, the problem with Eliot, Frost, or Stevens is not that their achievements are overpowering, but that their presence in contemporary poetry is not powerful enough. Having come of age at a time when Eliot had as much or as little to do with contemporary writing as Coleridge (Graham was born in 1950), she is young enough to feel that the moderns are separated from her by several generations of equally formidable writers. But these poets tended, says Graham, to narrow the scope of American poetry. However necessary and productive it was for them to endorse a "strictly secular sense of reality (domestic, confessional)," we need to return to the ambitious questions of spiritual and cultural redemption that preoccupied Eliot, Frost, and Stevens: "I think many poets writing today realize we need to recover a high level of ambition, a rage, if you will—the big hunger."[1]

I suspect that there is no postromantic poet who has not felt this hunger (the elegantly circumscribed world of Richard Wilbur is hardly unambitious), but Graham is right to suggest that a kind of expansiveness, a certain rhetoric of ambition, became difficult for poets after modernism. "We hear the *man* in *manifesto*," said James Merrill, thinking about the vast productions of Eliot, Pound, Stevens, and Williams: "these men began by writing small, controllable, we might say from our present vantage 'unisex' poems. As time went on, though, through their ambitious reading, their thinking, their critical pronouncements, a kind of vacuum charged with expectation, if not with dread, took shape around them, asking to be filled with grander stuff. As when the bronze is poured in the lost-wax process of casting, what had been human and impressionable in them was becoming its own monument." It was for this reason that Merrill was so deeply nourished by Elizabeth Bishop, a poet who (as Merrill put it in "Overdue Pilgrimage to Nova Scotia") refused "to tip the scale of being human / By adding unearned weight."[2] In contrast, Graham wants the "big hunger" to bring to American poetry a muscularity, not a flabbiness.

Merrill ultimately rejected the notion, implicit in his pun on *manifesto*, that "unearned weight" is accumulated only by men (though he was right to suggest that the conscious shirking of high ambition is often associated in American poetry with femininity). Similarly, Merrill's career makes us resist the notion that weight, earned or unearned, is necessarily accumulated more readily by the moderns than by their successors: *The Changing Light at Sandover* is one of the grandest poems produced by an American poet since Pound's *Cantos*. Merrill checked the portentousness of his poetic cosmology with a tone that varies from bemused to whimsical, and the moderns were similarly troubled by the specter of unearned weight, even when they indulged their appetites. Almost as soon as *The Waste Land* was published, Eliot began diminishing the poem as nothing but "rhythmical grumbling." Yeats was careful to publish "The Second Coming" beside "A Prayer for My Daughter," tempering his apocalyptic vision of "a rocking cradle" with a glimpse of his own child "half hid / Under this cradle-hood and coverlid." Lamenting the loss of the "big hunger," Graham does recognize that Merrill and Ashbery have kept modernist ambition alive: "the hugeness of their project seems so central," says Graham, "and the aesthetic differences that divide them ultimately so minor."[3] It consequently seems appropriate to say that a longing for the "big hunger" has coexisted with a fear of "unearned weight" in the poetry of both the moderns and their successors. As "Recovered from the Storm" suggests, Jorie Graham has embraced this tension and made from it a poetry all her own.

In her recent poems, Graham has perfected a style that is, in its own way, as grippingly idiosyncratic as Marianne Moore's. But her development has been swift; as I began by suggesting, Graham has not been shy about exposing her quest (a lesser word will not do) for new ways to dramatize the mind in motion. In retrospect, her career might be described in the way that Merrill characterized the careers of the moderns: her first two books, though different, contained small, controllable poems, while her third book, *The End of Beauty*, unveiled a far more challenging and ecstatic way of writing. This dramatic development was due mostly to a poet's passage from apprenticeship to an early mastery of her own language, a mastery that allows the poet to attempt more risky effects. But because Graham was precocious (the poems of her apprenticeship are highly crafted), it has been difficult not to read her passage from *Erosion* to *The End of Beauty* as an allegory for the play of larger forces. Bonnie Costello has ventured that *Erosion*, Graham's second book, "is essentially a modernist text, whereas Graham's later work may be characterized as postmodern."[4] Plausible as this statement is, our sense of what modernism was remains so fluid that Graham herself is able to read her own career in opposite terms. To her, the earlier work in *Erosion* is similar to the modest productions of poets who came of age in the wake of modernism, while *The End of Beauty* represents her first large-scale attempt to recover the "big hunger"—the formal audaciousness and cultural relevance she associates with modernism.

Graham has become, due in part to the heartfelt endorsements of Helen Vendler, the most prominent American poet born after the Second World War. It is consequently difficult to remember how controversial each of her books has seemed—how sharply she has turned against her own accomplishments and how unsympathetically those turnings have often been received. Costello, who admires *Erosion*, finds *The End of Beauty* and *Region of Unlikeness* problematic. Less thoughtful reviewers have said worse. But the controversy seems to me elucidating, because Graham so expertly resists the narratives we usually bring to postmodern poetry while, at the same time, she invites us to consider her poetry in relationship to those narratives. Like Ashbery, Graham does occasionally reinforce the logic of the "breakthrough," especially when she associates an idealized sense of aesthetic closure with an equally ahistorical notion of ideological oppression. But just as often she explodes this logic. If, as Costello has suggested, the recent work takes on the formal strategies currently associated with a garden-variety postmodernism ("darting images without explicit connections; a digressive, decentered approach to thought; the fragmentation of linear plots and arguments"), it is more important to remember, as Costello also points out, that Graham "has a fundamentally different orientation" from Ashbery and his cotillion: for them, poetry is not—as it is for Graham—"a matter of metaphysics, of sustaining the rigor of truth or opening words to ecstatic vision."[5] As "The Tree of Knowledge" suggests, Graham entertains "the old dream of an underneath," but she does so without complacency or idealism: she knows that "just appearance turning into further appearance" may as easily become an unexamined certainty as appearance giving way to the real thing.

Such contradictions—real or apparent—are the source of Graham's distinctive power. Especially since the publication of *Materialism*, it has become clear that Graham's poetry reaches in too many different directions to be accounted for by any linear narrative. Just as *Life Studies* looks like the crucial turning point only if we ignore the restless, searching quality of Lowell's entire career, *The End of Beauty* looks like a "breakthrough" only if we ignore the ways in which the book that followed it, *Region of Unlikeness*, now seems like a retreat to the presuppositions that underlie many of Graham's earlier poems. Until recently, this retreat was difficult to see: *Region of Unlikeness* appears to extend the stylistic extravagance of *The End of Beauty*, eschewing the controlled shapes of the earlier poems of *Erosion*. But style is not always linked unequivocally to vision, and one of the great strengths of Graham's poetry is that it weakens links that readers of postmodern poetry almost always take for granted. In other words, Jorie Graham is as frustrating and problematic a poet—I mean this as the highest compliment—as Eliot or Frost.

In "The Sense of an Ending," the long poem that concludes *Erosion* and foreshadows the concerns of her later work, Graham recalls her childhood acquaintance with "eyemachines" at a clinic: looking into the machine, each eye would see an "earthy thing, one to / each eye" and the mind would be "given the task: to bring them / together." These lines describe the way in which most of the poems from *Erosion* (and many from *Region of Unlikeness*) work: in contrast to recent poems like "Recovered from the Storm" these poems do not so much enact the processes of consciousness as create, through juxtaposition or implied analogy, a static puzzle that the reader is obliged to solve. In "At Luca Signorelli's Resurrection of the Body," for instance, Graham brings together Signorelli's fresco of "The Resurrection" in the cathedral of Orvieto with the story of Signorelli's dissection of his son's body. In the fresco, souls clamor to reenter human flesh that Signorelli has rendered perfectly; in the studio, Signorelli dissects cadavers in order to achieve that perfection. But the dissection of his own son suggests that something more than the demands of early modern empiricism was motivating the painter.

> It took him days,
>   that deep
> caress, cutting,
>   unfastening,
>
> until his mind
>   could climb into
> the open flesh and
>   mend itself.

Graham does not need to make any explicit gesture back to Signorelli's "Resurrection" for us to feel its relevance here. Looking at the fresco, she wonders if the souls are really "after" perfection as they hurry into human form; the people in the cathedral, muses Graham, could tell the souls that "there is no / entrance, / only entering." Similarly, the poem's hushed final lines suggest that the painter himself is "mended" not by seeking spiritual wholeness but by confronting the physical evidence of the most unbearable kind of human suffering.

"At Luca Signorelli's Resurrection of the Body" offers one of the most convincing examples of Graham's analogical method in *Erosion*; in other poems, this method produces poems that overdetermine their endings. "The Age of Reason" is divided into three discrete sections (as the Signorelli poem could have been): part one describes birds who settle on anthills, taking the insects— or sometimes cigarette butts or broken glass—into their bodies before they fly away; part two describes Werner Herzog's film of Georg Büchner's *Woyzeck*, in which the hero stabs his wife, throws the knife in the river, and "goes in" after it much as the knife "goes in" the body; part three attempts a synthesis, depending (as many of the *Erosion* poems do) on questions that instruct the reader: "How far is true / enough? / How far into the / earth / can vision go and / still be / love?" As in "At Luca Signorelli's Resurrection of the Body," Graham plays with different notions of "entering," groping for the place at which the mechanisms of violence and of love seem too similar to pull apart. If the poem is like the "eyemachine," however, it not only presents discrete narratives but conflates them, solving the poem's puzzle before we have a chance to feel its mystery. The poem may look more modest—more apprehensible, more controlled—than much of Graham's later work, but its shape is determined by a hunger for big solutions to big questions.

In offering this analysis, I am only repeating what Graham suggests about her own poems when, in "The Sense of an Ending," she describes a wolf pacing in a cage: "Too much clicks shut in that quick step / revolving on the one hind leg, bringing the other down just as / the swivel ends. . . . It's beautiful. You can hear / minutes stitching shut." Looking back to one of the most frequently invoked metaphors in *Erosion* (stitching), these lines also introduce the most prominent metaphor of *The End of Beauty* (clicking shut). Throughout both *The End of Beauty* and *Region of Unlikeness* (though in very different ways), Graham is appalled by the "click" of closure, having felt that she herself was seduced in *Erosion* by its beauty, its perfection. But in *Region of Unlikeness* she is once again seduced by closure even as she sustains her critique of it. The most ambitious poems from this volume ("Fission," "From the New World," "The Phase after History") do not read much like *Erosion* poems; instead of juxtaposing different stories, Graham fragments and intertwines them, making the poems seem (at first glance) decentered and open-ended. Yet these poems rely on the same kind of analogical thinking that distinguishes "The Age of Reason": however strenuously they lament the ethical or political repercussions of aesthetic closure, the poems themselves click shut.

In "From the New World" Graham braids together three different narratives: the recent trial of John Demanjuk, known as Ivan the Terrible at Treblinka; the story of a girl who emerged from the gas chamber asking for her mother, only to be raped and sent back in; and the story of Graham's own grandparents, who, after fifty years of marriage, were put into separate nursing homes. When Graham remembers visiting the grandmother who no longer recognized her, the stories begin to line up, making the poem's structure feel more spatial than linear: "I went into the bathroom, locked the door. / Stood in front of the mirrored wall— / not so much to see in, not looking up at all in fact, / but to be held in it as by a gas, / the thing which was me there in its chamber." Like the "eyemachine," the poem asks us to superimpose the narratives, equating the closed spaces of the bathroom and the gas chamber. And in both cases Graham wants to preserve the moment of possibility that the narrative forecloses; each girl is desperate to save her "thin / young body" from its all but certain end. But by drawing such a broad analogy between such bracingly different realms of human experience, the poem itself seems tightly closed: it focuses our attention so sharply on the similarities of the narratives that it seems oddly unconcerned with their differences. Graham goes so far as to say that "the coiling and uncoiling / billions" were there with her in the bathroom: "the about to be held down, bit clean, shaped, / and the others, too, the ones gone back out, the ending / wrapped round them."

Paraphrasing "What the End is For," Helen Vendler exposes the problem with these analogical poems: "The wish of the speculative mind to halt its drift and take visible shape leads not only to marriage but to atomic piles and B-52's."[6] One wants to know how, precisely, cognitive or aesthetic closure leads to mass destruction. For if what the poem says about narrative closure were true, then it would be easy—just by embracing different formal strategies—to end sexism and stave off nuclear disaster. Writing in defense of the Language poets, Jerome McGann once declared that "narrativity" is an "inherently conservative feature of discourse." But just because our experience of the world is discursive, shaped by narratives, it does not follow that we can change the world by disrupting specific versions of those narratives. Responding to McGann, Charles Altieri rightly pointed out that "there is no one social form—that hypothesis is pure Platonism, not Marxist materialism."[7] This logic may explain Graham's repeated condemnations of narrative closure: she is—at least in this regard—a kind of Platonist, a poet who sees the same issue of aesthetic form at the root of all social problems. As Graham herself has admitted with characteristic forthrightness,

"I'm so much at the outer limits of political action" that the poetry's social dimension is "probably a delusion I create for myself in order to get myself off the hook."[8]

Graham dismantles this delusion as often as she fosters it. In the early wake of modernism, when Robert Lowell called his first book *Land of Unlikeness* (translating the phrase *regio dissimilitudinis*), he wanted his strictly controlled poems to imply a corresponding spiritual vision—as the chaotic surfaces of Pound's and Eliot's poems did not seem to do. In contrast, the author of *Region of Unlikeness* is interesting because the formal and thematic aspects of her poems are often at odds with each other, undermining accepted notions of openness. Graham has offered the counterintuitive but convincing argument that Whitman is "a very *intellectual* sensibility writing desperately towards his body to recover it," while Stevens is "a poet so fully in the body, in his senses, and moving towards the conceptual and philosophical in order to complete himself." By this same logic, the egregiously fragmentary and digressive poet of *Region of Unlikeness* is preeminently a poet of closure. "We tend to define our poets by that aspect of sensibility they actually most lack and strive towards," continues Graham, and she herself strives most arduously to embrace poems that do not click shut.[9] That is why her poems—unlike the work of contemporaries who champion open-endedness with more consistently doctrinaire fervor—are so moving and unpredictable. In the closing lines of "Soul Says," the last poem in *Region of Unlikeness,* Graham seems desperate to discover a region of "likeness" in which all metaphors are literalized, all stories are the same story: one thing is *likened* to another thing but also *is* that thing.

> Now then, I said, I go to meet that which I liken to
> (even though the wave break and drown me in laughter)
> the wave breaking, the wave drowning me in laughter—

Beautiful as these lines are, they could not serve as the conclusion to *Materialism*. Little of what I've said so far is pertinent to Graham's recent poetry, and neither is it pertinent to most of *The End of Beauty*, the volume that appeared between *Erosion* and *Region of Unlikeness*. Graham once admitted that after publishing *Erosion* she completed and discarded almost an entire book of poems written in the manner of *Erosion*: among the poems included in *The End of Beauty*, "Imperialism" and "What the End is For" seem like the only remaining evidence of that effort; despite their jittery, disjointed surfaces, they too feel spatial in design (offering stories that we correlate). Other poems in *The End of Beauty* are written in a startlingly different manner—a more resolutely linear manner that, in retrospect, prepares us for the poems of *Materialism*. The title of one of them, "Self-Portrait as Hurry and Delay," may serve to describe them all: although the poems move inexorably and ecstatically forward, Graham slows down the movement, breaking the poem into discrete sections, often line by line. While she tends in the poems of *Materialism* to thicken a single moment of consciousness, Graham imagines in these poems the complexities that lurk between our moments as they pass. In the process, she offers a compelling critique not only of closure but of openness as well.

The End of Beauty contains five poems called "Self-Portrait." The first of them, "Self-Portrait as the Gesture Between Them," unfolds the story of the first human story: by plucking the forbidden fruit and handing it to Adam, Eve turns her back on the static truth of God, initiating a plot from an error.

> 27
> the feeling of being a digression not the link in the argument,
> a new direction, an offshoot, the limb going on elsewhere,
> 28
> and liking that error, a feeling of being capable *because* an error,
> 29
> of being wrong perhaps altogether wrong a piece from another set
> 30
> stripped of position stripped of true function
> 31
> and loving that error, loving that filial form, that break from perfection
> 32
> where the complex mechanism fails, where the stranger appears in the clearing,
> 33
> out of nowhere and uncalled for, out of nowhere to share the day.

These breathless final lines, hurrying forward even as Graham delays the end, suggest that human freedom lies in errancy and digression. And inasmuch as the lines seem to describe the poem's movement, Graham expresses her dissatisfaction with the "complex mechanism" of the analogical poems she wrote in *Erosion*. But elsewhere in *The End of Beauty* Graham reveals a deep suspicion of the freedom apparently embodied by this new kind of poem. What seems like the opening of all possibility in "Self-Portrait as the Gesture Between Them" immediately seems like the foreclosure of all possibility in "Self-Portrait as Apollo and Daphne." Pursuing Daphne, Apollo is all closure; he wants "to possess her, to nail the erasures," and all he can offer are the typical lines: *"will you forgive me?* or *say / that you'll love me for / ever and ever.*" Daphne, in contrast, is associated with the aleatory movement of a flock of birds: "the shrill cheeps and screeches of the awakening thousands, / hysterical, for miles, in all the directions." Daphne refuses to "give shape to his hurry by being / its destination," and since Graham is likewise attempting to undo the end (to forge a poetry that resembles the flock of birds more than the single-minded male), she seems to posit a realm of feminine experience that lies outside of narrative—a "given" world untouched by the "made." But Graham skewers this idealism in the final lines of the poem: the random bird calls "marry" in the air, suggesting that the plot of heterosexual desire cannot simply be evaded but must be more resolutely resisted from within.

Part of what makes the sequence of "Self-Portraits" in *The End of Beauty* so exciting is that they are sternly self-critical: each poem not only turns against the one before it but also turns on itself, collapsing the duality posited by its title. In "Self-Portrait as Hurry and Delay [Penelope at Her Loom]," Graham emphasizes more clearly that her own formal strategies of interruption and delay inevitably heighten our desire for closure. Although Odysseus threatens to wrap "himself plot plot and dénouement over the roiling openness," Penelope unweaves her tapestry, delaying the suitors, only to make them "want her more richly"; though Penelope's strategy is delay, her fingers dart over the weaving "like his hurry darts." However compromised, Penelope's power over the suitors is not dispelled. In Elizabeth Bishop's "Brazil, January 1, 1502," the Native American women are "retreating, always retreating" behind the landscape that exists only as a tapestry—an imposed system of European values—for the pursuing men; in "Self- Portrait as Hurry and Delay," Penelope has taken control of the tapestry itself, "beginning always beginning the ending as they go to sleep beneath her."

Even more tellingly critical of Graham's notion of openness is "Self- Portrait as Demeter and Persephone," the last of the five self-portraits. Once in hell, Persephone discovers a world with no shape, no beginning and, therefore, no end. She wonders how she will recognize anything in the future if she loses all sense of the past.

> She watched the smoke where it began what it left off
> What will I recognize it to have been she thought
> smoke smoke her fingers her eyes like static all over it
> Surely I can find it the point of departure she put her hand in
> The birds the beaks of the birds the song the heard song

> She reached in what is it begins at the end she thought
> Where is the skin of the minutes will it ever come off
> She reached in there was no underneath what was this coiling over her fingers
> She reached in she could go no further she was sealed off
> It pushed back against her it was hell she could finally lean
> It was the given and it was finally given

This and other passages in "Self-Portrait as Demeter and Persephone" offer some of Graham's most virtuosic writing. She eschews all punctuation, suggesting that the poem itself has reached a condition of openness beyond the conventions of grammar and syntax; however, the passage itself maintains that such a condition would be intolerable, even if it were possible. If we really could step outside of narrative, if we could live without any sense of an ending, attaining some sense of the given, of pure being, we would be in hell. And as Graham describes it, this static world of the given resembles the Eden we left behind in "Self- Portrait as the Gesture Between Them." Persephone emerges from hell as gratefully as Eve emerged from Eden, glad to "inhabit a shape," to "suffer completely this wind." Between these two poems, Graham has shown how little may be possible within the human world of narrative; but there is no doubt that this woefully constricted world is the only place in which meaningful resistance is possible at all.

In the penultimate poem of *The End of Beauty*, "Of Forced Sightes and Trusty Ferefulness," Graham casts her own lot with Persephone, giving herself over to the Shelleyan wind, to relentless forward motion: "through wind, through winter nights, we'll pass, / steering with crumbs, with words, / making of every hour / a thought." This positive argument (the finding of freedom within narrative) is far more complicated and interesting than Graham's negative argument (the unequivocal association of narrative closure with oppression). And one way to explain Graham's development would be to say that the spatial poems of *Region of Unlikeness* extend the negative argument while the linear poems of *Materialism* extend the positive argument. The final poem in *The End of Beauty* is "Imperialism," an analogical poem that, unlike the self-portraits, would not seem out of place in *Region*. But when Graham recently organized her selected poems, she placed "Of Forced Sightes" at the end of *The End of Beauty*, suggesting that it, rather than "Imperialism," prepares us for the more resolutely self-critical poems of *Materialism*. Another way to explain Graham's development would be to say that in *Region of Unlikeness* she recovered from modernism even more of the "big hunger" than she had in *Erosion*; in *Materialism*, she recovered from *The End of Beauty* an equally powerful distrust of "unearned weight."

Just as *The End of Beauty* contains five "Self-Portrait" poems, *Materialism* contains five poems called "Notes on the Reality of the Self." Graham does not return to the freeze-frame structure of the self-portraits, however; like "Recovered from the Storm" (the recent poem with which I began), these "Notes" focus on a deceptively simple action. "I let the dog loose in this stretch," says Graham midway through the first of the "Notes," the opening poem in *Materialism*: the line tells us the poem's entire plot, but our experience of the poem is dominated by Graham's rapidly unfolding drama of consciousness. She watches the river, "each handful of it closing over the next"; leaves are sucked into "the quick throes of another tentative / conclusion"; leaf-matter accrues "round a / pattern, a law"; and the river itself is "Spit forth, licked up, snapped where the force / exceeds the weight, clickings, pockets." *Clickings, pattern, conclusion, closing*: this is the vocabulary of oppression in *Region of Unlikeness*, but here Graham uses the same words to describe the unceasing river of consciousness. Flux is now imagined as a sequence of moments that, however conclusive in themselves, are immediately superseded: "each next right point, inter- / locking, correct, correct again, each rightness snapping loose." As if picking up where her sequence of self-portraits left off, Graham begins *Materialism* by discarding any sense of "roiling openness" that is not patterned, shaped, governed by law.

"What is inwardness?" asked Rainer Maria Rilke in one of his late poetic fragments: "What if not sky intensified, / flung through with birds and deep / with winds of homecoming?"[10] Graham's notion of selfhood throughout *Materialism* is similarly external; she dramatizes consciousness by focusing on the movement of the material world outside the self, ultimately suggesting that the self exists only inasmuch as it is composed of material phenomena. As Helen Vendler has pointed out, Graham can no longer compose self-portraits through mythological figures, as she did in *The End of Beauty*. Once the "instabilities of matter" are assumed by the self, it can no longer assert a "mastery over experience" through myth: the material self, Vendler continues, "is ultimately powerless over fate."[11] Not only has Graham given up the dream of openness, asserting that all experience is governed by patterns or laws; she also admits that the individual self has very little power to impose or disrupt those laws. In the second of the "Notes on the Reality of the Self," Graham makes this point by comparing the self to bushes that are affected in various ways by the evening light, the autumn wind, and the sounds of a marching band practicing in the field beyond the poet's yard. The band, "screeching, rolling, patterning, measuring," is a

  scintillant beast the bushes do not know exists
as the wind beats them, beats in them, beats round them,
them in a wind that does not really even now
          exist,
in which these knobby reddish limbs that do not sway
       by so much as an inch
its arctic course
      themselves now sway—

Real only inasmuch as it is motion, the self is composed of a world of whose existence it is unaware: the self is swayed but cannot assert itself in return. Yet the sheer verbal mastery of "Notes on the Reality of the Self" belies the notion of a self completely lacking in agency; other poems in *Materialism* will grant greater power to consciousness. And though the poems must be read in dialogue with each other, it is crucial that we see Graham diminishing so severely her sense of her own power, especially since the poems of *Region of Unlikeness* risked the impression of hubris by correlating personal and historical narratives.

  Because they also pull together wildly disparate materials, the most ambitious poems of *Materialism* ("Concerning the Right to Life," "The Dream of the Unified Field," "Manifest Destiny") may resemble the longer poems of *Region*. Their narratives do not match up analogically, however, but move steadily if inexplicably forward, linked by the arbitrary repetition of particular words. In "Concerning the Right to Life" the words *spot* and *red* reappear in otherwise unrelated sections of the poem; in "Manifest Destiny" the word *mark* accumulates a penumbra of different associations as it reappears in different contexts. "The Dream of the Unified Field" unfolds in an apparently more simple but ultimately more challenging way: although its six sections are similarly linked by the repetition of the words *white* (referring usually to snow) and *black* (referring to a leotard, starlings, a crow, and skin color), the poem unfolds with narrative ease, each section extending the story of the one before it: "On my way to bringing you the leotard / you forgot to include in your overnight bag, / the snow started coming down harder." This narrative action is not as tersely summarized as it is in "Recovered from the Storm" or the various "Notes on the Reality of the Self," but it is equally crucial to our experience of the poem. After delivering her daughter's leotard, Graham watches a flock of starlings fly through the snow and settle on a tree (which looks like a head that alternately "explodes" and "recollects"), and then hears a single crow within the swarm of smaller birds ("a voice inside a head, filling a head"). At this point, Graham herself is gripped by the overwhelming sense of emptiness: in contrast to the "head" she imagines in the tree, the pocket that held the leotard (her daughter's "dream") is empty, and so is her own skull.

> See, my pocket is empty now. I let my hand
> open and shut in there. I do it again. Two now, skull and
>   pocket
> with their terrified inhabitants.

Hinging on this moment of crisis, "The Dream of the Unified Field" tells the story of how Graham arrived at the understanding of selfhood she more calmly describes throughout the sequence of "Notes on the Reality of the Self." Feeling that there is nothing inside her, she returns to the window to watch her daughter dancing in the leotard. The scene evokes a memory of the ballet class she took from Madame Sakaroff, a Russian refugee. Changing into her own leotard, she overheard Madame speaking with an unnamed visitor: "*No one must believe in God again.*" Graham watched her teacher face herself in the mirror, approaching it until she touched her reflection, and Graham herself now approaches the window, watching her daughter dance, until she touches the glass. Speaking both to her daughter and to herself as a child, she asks, "what should I know / to save you that I do not know, hands on this windowpane?"

In response to the question, Graham undertakes the almost futile but necessary act of recomposing her self from the material world around her: "The storm: I close my eyes and, / standing in it, try to make it *mine*. An inside / thing." The poem breaks from its uncharacteristically placid narrative to one of Graham's most ecstatic flights of consciousness:

> wilderness brought deep into my clearing,
> out of the ooze of night,
> limbed, shouldered, necked, visaged, the white—
> now the clouds coming in (don't look up),
> now the Age behind the clouds, The Great Heights,
> all in there, reclining, eyes closed, huge,
> centuries and centuries long and wide,
> and underneath, barely attached but attached,
> like a runner, my body, my tiny piece of
> the century—minutes, houses going by—The Great
>   Heights—
> anchored by these footsteps, now and now,
> the footstepping—now and now—carrying its vast

> white sleeping geography—mapped—
> not a lease—*possession*—

In the smallest sense, Graham is describing the act of writing the poem we are now reading—the act of transforming a sequence of arbitrary observations and associations (snowstorm, leotard, starlings, crow, ballet class) into a logical narrative. In the largest sense, Graham is attempting to achieve the "dream of the unified field," the dream that all material phenomena might be described by a single paradigm. Graham's indomitable craving for closure reaches epic proportions in these lines: pulling The Great Heights into the vacant space of the self, her hunger has never been bigger.

But it is at exactly this moment that her fear of "unearned weight" also becomes stronger than ever before. The hubris implied by her metaphors (*colony, new world, wilderness, mapped, possession*) is exposed by a sudden and apparently unprecedented shift from the poem's narrative to lines adapted from the diary of Columbus's first voyage to the New World. Having begun with a domestic chore, ("On my way to bringing you the leotard"), "The Dream of the Unified Field" ends with one of the most primal narratives of Western culture.

> After the cross was set up,
> three sailors went into the bush (immediately erased
> from sight by the fast snow) to see what kinds of
> trees. They captured three very black Indian
> women—one who was young and pretty.
> The Admiral ordered her clothed and returned her to
>   her land
> courteously. There her people told
> that she had not wanted to leave the ship,
> but wished to stay on it. The snow was wild.
> Inside it, though, you could see
> this woman was wearing a little piece of
> gold on her nose, which was a sign there was
>   gold
> on that land—

This passage is linked thematically (though tenuously so) to the rest of the poem; it expresses Graham's fear of allowing her own life—her own emptiness, her own ambition—to overwhelm her daughter's. But in contrast to a poem like "From the New World," in which Graham nearly conflates personal and historical narratives, "The Dream of the Unified Field" compels us to feel the extraordinary distance the poem has traveled—to interrogate the means by which the poem achieves its leap between different registers of human experience. Because the narrative of "The Dream of the Unified Field" has so far been so apprehensible, we have not needed to pay much attention to Graham's repetitions of the words *black* and *white* in order to link the different sections of the poem. When the narrative falls away, that tissue of repetitions becomes crucial: the passage from Columbus's diary (*white* snow, *black* skin) is drawn into the poem, fulfilling Graham's dream of a "unified field" even as the passage implicitly criticizes the hubris of the dream.

Graham culls material from two entries from the diary, condensing and altering the language. Most dramatically, she adds the word *black* to describe the color of the Native American women; most implausibly, she adds the *white* snowstorm, a meteorological impossibility in the Caribbean.[12] I think Graham wants us to be startled by the utter implausibility of the snow. Although her poem ends in self-critique, a relinquishing of power, Graham cautions us through this blatantly illogical revision of Columbus's diary that she herself remains in control of the poem. If the hubris of the "dream of the unified field" needs to be checked, so does the idealism of the dream of relinquishing all control. As Graham herself has recognized, these complexities, these unresolved tensions, are the driving forces behind her poetry: she recently titled her selected volume—*The Dream of the Unified Field*—after what seems to me her most challenging and beautiful poem.

"What would we really know the meaning of?" asked Emerson: "The meal in the firkin; the milk in the pan; the ballad in the street; the news of the boat; the glance of the eye; the form and the gait of the body;—show me the ultimate reason of these matters; show me the sublime presence of the highest spiritual cause lurking, as always it does lurk, in these suburbs and extremities of nature."[13] Like Stevens before her, Graham makes poetry out of this question, struggling to find the most central knowledge in the most peripheral experience; like Stevens, she not only describes the struggle but makes us feel it in the movement of the poetry. In "The Dream of the Unified Field" the twin exigencies of the "big hunger" and "unearned weight" are made explicit by the poem's startling leap to Columbus, but their dialogue is implicit not only throughout the entire poem but throughout all of *Materialism*. In recent poems like "Recovered from the Storm" (which feels like a coda to "The Dream of the Unified Field"), Graham no longer needs to disempower herself so dramatically. Through the "vivid performance of the present"—delivering the leotard, picking up one fallen limb from the path—Graham discovers the highest spiritual causes in the suburbs.

When she said that American poets needed to recover the "big hunger" of the modernists, Graham did not specify which postmodern poets were responsible for domesticating modernist ambition. If only because so many poets have learned about the enabling virtues of modesty from Bishop, it would make sense if Graham had Bishop in mind; praising the early installments of *The Changing Light at Sandover*, Bishop cautioned (with ominous good humor) that the poem was "much too big" to write about on a "morning when I have to start cleaning house."[14] Graham herself has admitted that Bishop's music does not set her off as Stevens's or Berryman's does, and it's easy to imagine that Bishop would have found Graham's poetry far more unwieldy than Merrill's. But Graham has also emphasized that she feels a deep "temperamental affinity" with Bishop, an affinity that transcends stylistic decorum, and it's arguable that Graham, more than any other poet writing today, has realized Bishop's ideal notion of poetic movement: "not a thought, but a mind thinking" (the phrase Bishop borrowed from the critic Morris Croll). And while it's even easier to imagine that Bishop would have been bemused by the elaborate ambitions of the Language poets, Charles Bernstein has borrowed the same passage from Croll to underwrite his avant-garde project. As Bernstein describes it, his critique of "contemporary expository forms" involves the "attempt 'to portray not a thought, but a mind thinking.'"[15]

In part, this coincidence illustrates Robert Pinsky's belief that an enormous range of American poets are distinguished by a "fluidity of tone," an Emersonian blending of the cosmic and the domestic, the courtly and the vulgar, the ecstatic and the comic. The coincidence also suggests that style never tells the whole story of American poetry: poets who seem, because of their formal choices, to have little to do with one another may share the deepest goals or ambivalences. Remembering the early years of his career, when the academic and beat poets were standing off, John Hollander said that he "felt that there were guys on my team who weren't on my side, and there were guys on the other team who *were* on my side." Hollander is as formidable a stylist as Bernstein, a poet-critic who has invested a great deal of energy in the study of form; but he insists that "what makes a poet is not style alone, but something far deeper."[16] Although he continues to write in the elaborate forms he embraced as a young poet, Hollander insists that his poetry has changed radically—changed in ways that the "breakthrough" narrative, with its essentialized notions of poetic freedom, cannot describe.

If the narrative has been unaccommodating to poets like Hollander or Wilbur, whose styles have remained fairly consistent throughout their careers, it is even more deceptively unkind to poets like Ashbery or Graham, whose styles have changed dramatically. Graham's turn from the slender, controlled poems of *Erosion* to the apparently open-ended poems of *The End of Beauty* looks like one more occurrence of the "breakthrough" that several generations of twentieth-century poets have needed to embrace. But Graham's career is exemplary for different reasons. The poems of *Region of Unlikeness*, so different stylistically from those of *Erosion* and yet so similar in their thematizations of closure, confound the association of formal and ideological freedom. Like any poet writing at the peak of her powers, Graham is many different poets in one; within the parameters of her relatively brief career is a range of positions we all too easily condense into the false opposition of a poet like Wilbur and a poet like Ashbery. Consequently, a vision of American poetry that cannot encompass both Wilbur and Ashbery cannot encompass Jorie Graham alone. Neither can it do justice to Wilbur or to Ashbery. "There are no outsiders in these pages," says Graham in the introduction to her wide-ranging anthology of poetry in English, denying any poet the distinction of standing apart.[17] This is the kind of vision that will carry American poetry beyond postmodernism—whatever it will seem to have been—into the twenty-first century.

From *Modern Poetry after Modernism* (Oxford University Press, 1997)

Notes

Quotations from Graham's poems are from *Erosion* (Princeton, N.J.: Princeton University Press, 1983); *The End of Beauty* (New York: Ecco Press, 1987); *Region of Unlikeness* (New York.: Ecco Press, 1991); *Materialism* (Hopewell, N.J.: Ecco Press, 1993); *The Errancy* (Hopewell, N.J.: Ecco Press, 1997).

1. Thomas Gardner, "An Interview with Jorie Graham," *Denver Quarterly* 26, no. 4 (1992): 81.
2. James Merrill, *Recitative*, ed. J. D. McClatchy (San Francisco: North Point Press, 1986), 162, 161; *A Scattering of Salts* (New York: Alfred A. Knopf, 1995), 88. See also Allen Grossman and Mark Halliday's fascinating remarks on the rise and fall of modernist ambition in *The Sighted Singer* (Baltimore, Md.: Johns Hopkins University Press, 1992), 28–57.
3. Gardner, "Interview," 81.
4. Bonnie Costello, "Jorie Graham: Art and Erosion," *Contemporary Literature* 33, no. 2 (Summer 1992): 374.
5. Bonnie Costello, "The Big Hunger," *The New Republic*, 27 January 1992, 36.
6. Helen Vendler, *Soul Says: On Recent Poetry* (Cambridge, Mass.: Belknap Press of Harvard University Press, 1995), 237. See also Mark Jarman, "The Grammar of Glamour: The Poetry of Jorie Graham," *New England Review* 14, no. 4 (Fall 1992): 252–261.
7. Robert von Hallberg, ed., *Politics and Poetic Value* (Chicago: University of Chicago Press, 1987), 267, 305. See also Terry Eagleton, *The Illusions of Postmodernism* (Oxford: Blackwell, 1996): "It is not a question of denouncing closure as such, a universalist gesture if ever there was one, but of discriminating between its more enabling and more disabling varieties" (67).

8. Gardner, "Interview," 89.

9. Gardner, "Interview," 90.

10. Rainer Maria Rilke, *Uncollected Poems*, trans. Edward Snow (New York: North Point Press, 1996), 219.

11. Helen Vendler, *The Given and the Made: Strategies of Poetic Redefinition* (Cambridge, Mass.: Harvard University Press, 1995), 128–129.

12. See *The* Diario *of Christopher Columbus's First Voyage to America*, trans. Oliver Dunn and James E. Kelley, Jr. (Norman: University of Oklahoma Press, 1989), 203–207, 219–221 (entries for 6 and 12 December 1492). As Tzvetan Todorov suggests in *The Conquest of America*, trans. Richard Howard (New York: Harper & Row, 1984), 34–50, Columbus usually takes every opportunity to comment on the natives' skin color; however, in these entries he does not. The only time snow is mentioned (14 November 1492) is when Columbus notes that high mountains are *not* snow-covered. Graham also concludes "Concerning the Right to Life" with a passage derived from Columbus's *Diario* (23 October 1492), and she offers suggestive comments about the linguistic ramifications of the discovery of the New World in her introduction to *Earth Took of Earth: 100 Great Poems of the English Language* (New York: Ecco Press, 1996).

13. Ralph Waldo Emerson, *Complete Works*, 12 vols. (Boston: Houghton, Mifflin, 1903), I: 111.

14. Elizabeth Bishop, *One Art: Letters*, ed. Robert Giroux (New York: Farrar, Straus & Giroux, 1994), 597.

15. Charles Bernstein, *Content's Dream: Essays 1975–1985* (Los Angeles: Sun & Moon Press, 1986), 222. John Palattella points out this connection between Bishop and Bernstein in "After Such Knowledge, Knowledge Is What You Know," *Contemporary Literature* 35, no. 4 (Winter 1994): 791. See Graham's remarks on Bishop in Gardner, "Interview," 97–98.

16. Langdon Hammer, "Working Through Poems: An Interview with John Hollander," *Southwest Review* 80, no. 4 (Autumn 1995): 427–428.

17. Graham, *Earth Took of Earth*, xvii.

8

from Exquisite Disjunctions, Exquisite Arrangements

Jorie Graham's "Strangeness of Strategy"

BRIAN HENRY

> . . . the act of writing . . . grows dead and automatic if not constantly reinvigorated by strangeness of strategy.
>
> —*Letter from Jorie Graham to Charles Wright, quoted in* Quarter Notes

In a letter to his friend Robert Bridges, Gerard Manley Hopkins reluctantly admits, "I always knew in my heart Walt Whitman's mind to be more like my own than any other man's living." This confession stems primarily from Hopkins's recognition of some of his own prosodic strategies in Whitman's work. Although dissimilar in many respects, the bard from Brooklyn and the Jesuit indeed share rhythms and certain poetic attitudes; and the impacts of the pious Hopkins and of his iconoclastic doppelganger on contemporary poetry have been considerable. Because of Whitman's bold and boisterous example and Father Hopkins's equally bold yet devout one, it is somewhat surprising that few recent American poets have succeeded in fashioning a compelling poetic strategy out of the long line. Concentrated in the hands of a small number of poets, it seems more an aberration than an inheritance.

Perhaps the long line is just more difficult to write than the more manageable tetrameter or pentameter line. As it approaches the right margin, the poetic line flirts, often anxiously, with the boundaries of prose, requiring the poet to be even more attentive to language in order to avoid an attenuation of linguistic energy. Because, as Charles Wright has written, the "line must be strong all the way through and not finish in a dying fall" (*Halflife*, 3), the long line increases the poet's debt to language. Few poets can satisfy the burden of that debt.

[. . .]

Most recently, Jorie Graham has confronted this tradition by using and reinvigorating the long line in her poems. Although still in midcareer, she has established herself as one of the most thoughtfully unpredictable—as opposed to capriciously unpredictable—poets writing today. Like Wright, she has succeeded in introducing Dickinson's abrupt syntax and cadences into the sprawling Whitman line. Although Wright's lines might appear more fractured on the page than Graham's, her line-breaking actually is less orderly (Wright counts every syllable, preferring odd syllable counts, and uses regular stanzas) and is all the more severe because of her fluctuating line lengths and predominantly irregular stanzas as well as her refusal to inhabit a single line-breaking strategy from book to book or within a single book.

In her essay "Jorie Graham: The Moment of Excess," Helen Vendler celebrates and articulates the import of Graham's switch from the short line to the long line after her second collection, *Erosion* (1983). Vendler's reason for dividing Graham's work into two styles on the basis of line length rests upon her belief that the change from the short line to the long line is "almost more consequential, in its implications, than any other." While Vendler's enthusiasm for poets who are inclined to "break" earlier styles is warranted, her critical apparatus in this essay plays down the importance of other stylistic differences in Graham's work. The progression from the short line to the long line in Graham's poetry is certainly worth consideration, but it seems less significant than another stylistic divide in Graham's poems, noted but unexamined by Vendler: that between the left-justified poem of dramatically varying line lengths—from one to twenty-one syllables—and the poem with alternately indented lines. This split occurs primarily in *The End of Beauty* (1987), *Region of Unlikeness* (1991), and *Materialism* (1993). Although there are exceptions (no poetry can or should satisfy a single formula, however extensive the formula or devoted the formula-maker), the first type of poem tends to be shorter, more lyrically propulsive, more accessible, and less disjunctive than the second type of poem, which usually extends to several pages and, with its numerous unexpected dashes, parentheses, blanks, ellipses, and questions, actively resists the "kinetic flow" ("The Way Things Work") that characterizes her earliest poems. Graham's complex syntax initiates a series of grammatical disruptions that are instances of conflict for a poet visibly working against her own music and eloquence. This disjunctive lyricism—a lyricism struggling against itself—creates one of the primary dramas of her poems.

Because these poems contain so much flux—linguistic, psychological, emotional—they clearly are not offered as passive artifacts. Therefore, the memorability of a Graham poem presents readers with the familiar but unresolved issue of form and memory. Traditionalists and formalists would argue—and some have—that Graham's poems are not memorable because they do not rhyme or scan regularly, because they demonstrate a mind working rather than the polished product of a finished thought, and because they eschew or subvert plot and narrative. But if the reader works to engage them, Graham's poems are provocative and memorable. Their memorability resides not just in the various enactments—physical, philosophical, spiritual, visual—in them, but in the reader's experience of sifting through, struggling with, succumbing to—*experiencing*—the poems. Graham privileges enactment over mimesis, and Stevens' adage "To read a poem should be an experience, like experiencing an act" seems especially pertinent to her poems.

More recently, Graham has developed a third significant style: a hybrid of the other two, it is left-justified and violently disrupts its lyrical momentum as well as the poet's syntax and mental processes. To refer to this new style as a "hybrid" risks implying that it merely repackages Graham's two primary styles, when in fact most of the poems in this new style add a distinctive element: the Hopkins "hanger" or "outride" (also called "outrider"), which displaces a word or phrase at the end of a line and, rather than indent it (as C. K. Williams does) or drop it immediately below where it should be (as Wright does), positions it near the right margin as a mini-line. In Hopkins's preface to his poetry manuscript, published after his death, he explains the hanger and outrider as "licenses" he allows in his theory of sprung rhythm, defining them as "one, two, or three slack syllables added to a foot . . . so called because they seem to hang below the line or ride forward or backward from it in another dimension than the line itself." Graham's outriders, however, are rarely slack; they not only hang at the right margin, but ride the crest of the white space before them, actively occupying the page and forcing the reader to read down the page as well as across it. Although not innovative in itself, the outrider in Graham's recent poems has contributed to a major new style. No other poet has written this way before.

This style appears as early as *The End of Beauty* ("Vertigo," "The Veil"), but does not emerge with any frequency until *Materialism* ("The Dream of the Unified Field," both poems titled "In the Hotel," several of the "Notes on the Reality of the Self," individual sections of "The Break of Day," "Opulence," "Young Maples in Wind," and her *ars poetica* "The Surface"). By incorporating intense musicality, familiarity (most readers have encountered a left-justified poem before), syntactical disjunction, unpredictable lineation (from a monosyllabic word to twenty-eight syllables), and spatial disturbance, her new style is both recognizable and unsettling. And it requires readers to revamp their approach to poetry. Graham employs this style in nearly all of the poems in her most recent collection, *The Errancy* (of the thirty-eight poems in the book, only "Manteau" and twelve lines of "Flood" use the alternately indented lines that characterize many of Graham's earlier poems, and fewer than half a dozen poems avoid the outrider), and the style establishes the vigor of most of the poems.

But Graham emboldens this new style even further in *The Errancy* by introducing the double outrider in five poems ("Flood," "How the Body Fits on the Cross," "Emergency," "The Scanning," "The Turning"), yet again pursuing and attaining the "strangeness of strategy" that for her revitalizes "the *act* of writing":

> over the short wet grass—bunchy—the river behind presenting
>   lapidary
>   faithfulness—*plink*—
>
> ("The Scanning")

Of course, style and stylistic shifts, however dazzling, do not make a poet worth reading. For Graham, such style-shedding and -creating has more than aesthetic purposes: "the taking on, only apparently arbitrary, of stylistic devices—the inhabiting of them until they become the garment of one's spirit life, the method by which one touches the world, the means by which one can be touched oneself, and changed. . . . The changes I made in my 'technique' are changes that occurred in my life: I became the person I couldn't have otherwise been by these small devices, habits" (*Quarter Notes*, 44). Graham's ability to make her "small devices" and "habits" more than superficial changes in technique affirms the coexistence of stylistic development and inner change in the poems.

Similarly, if Graham had nothing to say in her poems, her poetry, despite its stylistic bravura, would be unremarkable, for style devoid of subject matter is "the spider's web without the spider—it glitters and catches but doesn't kill" (Wright, *Halflife*, 21). But Graham's poetry constantly pursues large subject matter: the interactions among personal, historical, and metaphysical forces or, in her own words, "my whole past (family, inheritance, the problematics of memory—historical and personal—the *history*, the wars Europe endured, etc.)" (*Quarter Notes*, 45). This insistence upon her "whole" past accounts for the ambition of her project as well as its immensity. Her epigraph to *The Errancy*— "Since in a net I seek to hold the wind" (from Wyatt's well-known sonnet "Whoso list to hunt: I know where is an hind")—succinctly and confidently declares the primary aim of the poems that follow.

In her previous book, *Materialism*, Graham seems more content to watch and describe the wind than catch it, whereas in *The Errancy* she seems more grounded and purposeful. The first and last outriders in *Materialism* and *The*

Errancy inform Graham's main preoccupations in each volume. In *Materialism*, "presence" and "permanences" point to the philosophical and metaphysical atmosphere of the book, which includes many passages from thinkers such as Plato, Sir Francis Bacon, Audubon, Wittgenstein, and Walter Benjamin. In *The Errancy*, "debris" and "unused"—on the lowest rung of the physical hierarchy—illuminate the primary shift in focus between the books: Graham has descended somewhat from the heights of philosophical discourse to the grittier plains of human experience. Although she never has shunned or avoided human experience in her poems, *The Errancy* is devoid of the philosophical passages that populate *Materialism*, and many of the poems in *The Errancy* rely heavily on sensory experiences. Because "The eye only discovers the visible slowly" ("Le Manteau de Pascal"), these poems do not reside wholly in the visible "*world of things*" ("The Guardian Angel of the Private Life"); but they inhabit recognizable terrain as they explore the poet's personal map of that world, operating mostly "between the pleats of matter and the pleats of the soul" ("The Guardian Angel of the Swarm"). Throughout the collection, certain words call attention to Graham's vacillation between the tactile and the intangible, neither of which excludes sensual perception. She gravitates toward a vocabulary of vision ("gaze," "stare," "squint," "look," and especially "glance," variations of which appear at least two dozen times), transformation ("arrange," "rearrange," "changed," "changing"), ascension ("rising," "upwards," "lifting," "updraft," "upthrust"), luminosity ("gossamer," "filament," "radiant," and especially "gleaming" and "glinting"), turbulence ("roiling," "foaming," "swirling," "floating," "swarming," "teeming"), boundaries ("edges," "hinge," "folds," "gate," "doorway," "window," "pane"), incipience ("unfolding," "awaken," "blossoming"), and stasis ("settling," "restored"). These words contribute to the moods, movement, and textures of the poems in the book, and their recurrence from poem to poem establishes various threads—lexical, emotional, imagistic—among the poems.

As the five poems titled "Notes on the Reality of the Self" and the five "Self-Portrait" poems contribute to the cohesiveness of *Materialism* and *The End of Beauty*, respectively, the six "Guardian Angel" poems and the seven "Aubades" outwardly distinguish *The Errancy* as an autonomous book rather than as a collection of disparate poems. This cohesiveness is further enhanced by the various companion poems in the book—"The Strangers" and "Studies in Secrecy," "The Scanning" and "So Sure of Nowhere Buying Times to Come," "Untitled One" and "Untitled Two," "Oblivion Aubade" and "Sea-Blue Aubade," "Red Umbrella Aubade" and "The Hurrying-Home Aubade," and "Le Manteau de Pascal," "Manteau," and "The Guardian Angel of the Swarm"—and by the crepuscular poems—"The Scanning," "The Errancy," "Little Requiem," "The Strangers,"

"Of the Ever-Changing Agitation in the Air," and "Recovered from the Storm"—which pivot against the aubades.

Although many of the poems in *The Errancy* begin by focusing on a quotidian detail or action—sitting in the car during a traffic jam, arranging flowers, watching a crow on a powerline, going outside after a storm, walking along a river—their persistent veerings into territories brimming with complexities make Graham's poetry anything but ordinary. Her ability to locate the metaphysical within the mundane depends upon her manner of perception and how things fare in "the open sea of [her] / watching" ("Willows in Spring Wind: A Showing"). Always aware that "It can never be satisfied, the mind, never" (Stevens, "The Well Dressed Man with a Beard"), Graham's mind in these poems is both terrible (sublime) and inviting (beautiful):

> The monster of the mind moves easily among its marls,
> . . .
> moves gently over the playing field,
> dragon of changes and adjustments,
> mightiness of redefining and refinement.
>
> ("In the Pasture")

In her poems—as in the poetry of poets like Stevens and Ashbery—objects are secondary to her perception(s) of them. This relationship between the interior world of the poet and the exterior physical world repeatedly manifests itself in her poems, most strikingly in "Thinking," which is a revision of Stevens' "Thirteen Ways of Looking at a Blackbird." Here the blackbird is a crow, continually altered by the poet's gaze ("It was a version of a crow, untitled as such, tightly feathered / in the chafing air"; "All round him air / dilated, as if my steady glance on him, cindering at the glance-core where / it held him tightest, swelled and sucked"; "If I squint, he glints"; "his hive of black balance"; "Every now and then a passing car underneath causing a quick rearrangement") until the bird's gaze acquires its own transformative power: "[the crow] eyeing all round, disqualifying, disqualifying / all the bits within radius that hold no clue / to whatever is sought. . . ." When the crow finally moves from the powerline, Graham's description and rhythms recall these lines from Hopkins's "The Windhover":

> how he rung upon the rein of a wimpling wing
> In his ecstasy! then, off, off forth on swing,
> As a skate's heel sweeps smooth on a bow-bend: the hurl and gliding
> Rebuffed the big wind.

Few poets would even try to emulate such splendor, but Graham's baroque lines hold up well in comparison:

> then wing-thrash where he falls at first against the powerline,
> then updraft seized, gravity winnowed, the falling raggedly
> reversed, depth suddenly pursued, its invisibility ridged—bless him—
> until he is off, hinge by hinge, built of tiny wingtucks, filaments
> of flapped-back wind

Here, and elsewhere in the book, Graham composes a muscular music based largely on iambs and spondees, constructing a brilliant verbal mosaic that accretes as it courses (consider the subtle and lissome thread that connects "gravity," "raggedly," "ridged," "hinge by hinge," and "wingtucks," or "falling," "suddenly," "invisibility," "bless him," "built," "filament," and "flapped-back").

Graham's treatment of the crow in "Thinking" illuminates the primary role of the poet in *The Errancy:* arranger and rearranger. This "blessed rage for order" can seem quite commonplace:

> Am I supposed to put them back together—
> these limbs, their leaves, the tiny suctioned twig-end joints—?
> these branches shoved deep into my silky glance—?
> these maples' outtakes streaked over the lawn—their thorns, their blithe
> footnotes. . . ? And the trellis cracked from the weight of the freefall?
> And the boxelder standing like an overburdened juggler—
>
> ("Recovered from the Storm")

The effectiveness of this ekphrasis, applied to storm debris instead of to the customary work of art, is heightened by Graham's strategy of seeming to exhaust her catalogue in each line. "[T]hese limbs, their leaves, the tiny suctioned twig-end joints" would sufficiently convey an image of the aftermath of a storm, but Graham continues to raise the ante in a list that culminates with a startling and precise simile. This sort of imagistic arrangement, and subsequent rearrangement, emerges as one of Graham's most compelling descriptive strategies.

But Graham's question in "The Errancy"—"What was it was going to be abolished, what / restored?"—recognizes the destructive possibility of this process of arrangement and rearrangement: as soon as something is gained, something else is lost. Graham, therefore, is often self-corrective in her arrangements, refocusing her lens ("The angel was on the telephone. / No, Jacob was on the telephone"), questioning her own perceptions ("I tried to house it—no, I tried to gorge it"), or rewriting her own words ("one ribbony with bits of valor, / or is it stringy now with *blips of laughter?*"). The dynamic between abolishment and restoration establishes the tension of many of these poems, and it announces itself in the beginning of the first poem in the book, "The Guardian Angel of the Little Utopia":

> Shall I move the flowers again?
> Shall I put them further to the left
>   into the light?
> Will that fix it, will that arrange the
> thing?

By assigning "thing" its own line, Graham brings increased attention to her preoccupation with arrangement, highlighting the poetic activity as well as the physical one she performs in the poem. Moving the flowers during a party while the guests sit downstairs "stuffing the void with eloquence" becomes a social act—it facilitates a "setting for their fears / and loves"—as well as a part of "all these tiny purposes, these parables, this marketplace / of tightening truths." Although Graham distrusts loquacity, with its "tiny carnage / of opinions" and "whips of syntax in the air," in herself and others (an idea that appears prominently in "Against Eloquence," a forty-five-line poem with thirty-seven dashes and seven questions), she knows that lyric poets, "wanting only that the singing continue, / if only for a small while longer" ("How the Body Fits on the Cross") must sing, no matter how temporary the song. The social transaction—her "little utopia"—implied by moving the flowers leads Graham to a line from Henry Vaughan's "Distraction"—toward language—before she relies on the gaze rather than on language in the final gesture of the poem:

> Oh knit me that am crumpled dust,
> the heap is all dispersed. Knit me that *am.* Say *therefore.* Say
> *philosophy* and mean by that the pane.
> Let us look out again. The yellow sky.
> With black leaves rearranging it. . . .

By ending "The Guardian Angel of the Little Utopia" with the gaze, and by directing that gaze out the window, Graham engages in a discourse between interior and exterior space that appears throughout *The Errancy*, most prominently in her aubades:

> Get up, get up. You are to walk and talk again, and breathe, and move.
> And breathe.
> Any manner of *want*, any world will do—any tint of mind—
> lift up the shade.
>
> ("Spelled from the Shadows Aubade")

This sort of self-admonition frequently galvanizes Graham into action, turning her from the interior space she inhabits to the unknown exterior space beyond the window, with the eye itself becoming a threshold: "my eye, my flapping / doorway-in. . . . Or, no, not flapping, not even mildly tethered to a blessed / randomness, no, just stuck ajar. . . ." ("Miscellaneous Weights and Measures").

For Graham, the dialectic between interior and exterior, with the window as one threshold and the eye as another, is especially meaningful at daybreak, between the "winglike silences of just-before-dawn" ("Red Umbrella Aubade") and "the dawn like something rusty starting its engines up again" ("The Hurrying-Home Aubade"). However, Graham's aubades are never conventional morning songs. "The End of Progress Aubade" and "The Hurrying-Home Aubade" continue, from *The End of Beauty*, her examinations of the Orpheus and Eurydice myth. Poised on the verge of daylight, these poems seem appropriate channels to a tale poised on the edge of the underworld. In the similarly innovative "Easter Morning Aubade," the backdrop for the tension between interior and exterior is physical and psychological rather than architectural: "She tried to clench the first dawnlight *inside her skull*. / Tried to feel it slather in there and make a form." Instead of holding the exterior world at bay, or entering it only through the gaze, this "she" attempts to literally internalize it:

> Felt the meadows the light held inside its flowing coat,
> sewn into there, silkiest lining—the seams, the property-lines perfect—
> and pulled them in, and laid them down along the floor of it.
> There was a green hill with a thin white road, she laid that in.
> There was a speckling, as where cypress have been struck, in rows,
> to indicate approach, and then a temporary house—she drove those in
> and laid them flat in there.

Because Graham later introduces the sleeping soldiers who awaken "to the blazing *not-there*" in Piero della Francesca's *Resurrection*, the primary action of the poem seems to occur outside the picture frame and therefore outside the viewer's (and artist's) gaze. The violence of such landscape-leveling becomes its own reminder about the possible menace outside the window.

When considered beside the aubades, the crepuscular poems seem even more aware of that menace. The actions of these poems, occurring at the end of day, seem at best wearisome and at worst terrifying. The "dread fatigue" that arrives with dusk resonates with one of Graham's notes at the back of the book, from Linda Gregerson's *The Reformation of the Subject:* "'discourse' derives from *discurrere* ('to run back and forth') as 'error' or errancy derives from *errare* (to wander). . . . Knightly errancy, then, begins with a gaze. . . ." Because of her reliance on the gaze, Graham follows the motions of discourse and errancy in these poems. Such to-and-froing after the initial gaze, and the ineluctable rearrangements that follow it, can be spiritually and physically exhausting, as in "The Errancy," which is an elegy for the "struck match of some utopia we no longer remember the terms of":

> here, we stand in our hysteria with our hands in our pockets,
> quiet, at the end of day, looking out, theories stationary,
> . . . .
> Utopia: remember the sensation of *direction* we loved,
> how it tunneled forwardly for us,
> and us so feudal in its wake—

Because the aubades and crepuscular poems seem at odds with each other in the possibilities they present, it is significant that the last poem in the book, "Of the Ever-Changing Agitation in the Air," is set at dusk. The poem presents a simple scene: a man dancing, "his hands to his heart," as "[t]he doorways of the little city / blurred." The despair that appears in the other crepuscular poems is absent in this oddly light-hearted and giddy poem, and even the violent undertone of its ending seems subdued in its domesticism:

> *liberty* spreading in the evening air,
> into which the lilacs open, the skirts uplift,
> liberty and the blood-eye careening gently over the giant earth,
> and the cat in the doorway who does not mistake the world,
> eyeing where the birds must eventually land—

These lines, cut short by a dash, close a book that begins with a question ("Shall I move the flowers again?"). By beginning and ending in indeterminacy, and by refusing to succumb to the kind of prolonged lyricism that leads to the now-conventional Rilkean epiphany of many poems, *The Errancy* effectively demonstrates Graham's awareness of the problematics of closure, of eloquence, and of arrangement and rearrangement. This stance, neither original nor particularly rare, becomes both when established by a poet committed to serious arrangements and rearrangements of language, perception, and inner life. If the "hysteria" initiated by the absence of "the sensation of *direction*" in *The Errancy* threatens to drag the poet into a deadening stasis, her hunger for such rearrangements allows her to avoid languor.

With her linguistic resourcefulness, metaphysical obsessions that yoke the philosophical to the personal, and keen eye and capacity for description, Graham already has fashioned a powerful body of work. Since *The End of Beauty*, her poetry has been working toward exquisite disjunctions and exquisite arrangements that question and adjust perception, defy closure, resist eloquence, disrupt syntax, revitalize lineation, and unabashedly examine the role of the poet in (shaping) the world. With *The Errancy*, she has further enriched her penchant for stylistic innovation while pursuing important subject matter and demonstrating intellectual and emotional energy. Consistently ambitious and accomplished, Graham undercuts her own ambition and accomplishments by shedding styles, scrutinizing and remaking older ones, and creating new ones. The ability to do so intelligently and meaningfully places her achievement alongside such poets as Ashbery and Wright. And her determination to forge new styles with flair and daring testifies to the heights attainable through such stylistic vitality.

The Antioch Review

9

from Jorie Graham's Incandescence

THOMAS GARDNER

Jorie Graham, in her work, has been consistently drawn to confrontations with what she describes as an "other": "God, nature, a beloved, an Idea, Abstract form, Language itself as a field, Chance, Death, Consciousness, what exists in the silence. Something not invented by the writer. Something the writer risks being defeated—or silenced—by."[1] In such confrontations, dramatized in poems where the acts of remembering or describing or likening take center stage, the poet's desire to know and hold and possess is both fanned into full life and brought up short. What is attractive about that process? Why write, as Graham does, "I need to feel the places where the language fails, as much as one can?"[2] Describing a poetry reading where the pace and movement of another writer's language resisted her desire to make immediate sense of things, Graham sketches an answer to that question:

> Listening to the poem, I could feel my irritable reaching after fact, my desire for resolution, graspable meaning, ownership. I *wanted* to narrow it. . . . It resisted. It compelled me to let go. The frontal, grasping motion frustrated, my intuition was forced awake, I felt myself having to "listen" with other parts of my sensibility, felt my mind being forced back down into the soil of my senses. And I saw that it was the resistance of the poem—its occlusion, or difficulty—that was healing me, forcing me to privilege my heart, my intuition—parts of my sensibility infrequently called upon in my everyday experience in the marketplace of things and ideas. I found myself feeling, as the poem ended, that some crucial muscle that might have otherwise atrophied from lack of use had been exercised.[3]

The other's resistance, then, both exposes and frustrates the desire to know. In the place of knowing, the other "force[s] awake" another part of the poet's sensibility—one in which responsiveness is freed from the drive to master. Graham calls that "crucial muscle" the heart or intuition, suggesting that the listener finds herself more responsive because more fully engaged. Such many-sided responsiveness I take to be the primary goal of Graham's poetry.

The work of the philosopher Stanley Cavell, focused on many of these same issues, helps explain why Graham might think to discover an awakened language within a painful encounter with limits. Cavell's work focuses on the problem of skepticism. Raising "the question whether I know with certainty of the existence of the external world and of myself and others in it,"[4] skepticism, for Cavell, voices "philosophy's discovery of the limitation of human knowledge . . . in its radical form."[5] Claiming that the skeptic's refusal to settle for anything less than perfect knowledge of the world is in fact a "refusal to acknowledge his participation in finite human existence,"[6] Cavell goes on to explore other responses to this truth which skepticism raises but turns away from in disgust. The "truth of skepticism," he writes, "is that the human creature's basis in the world as a whole, its relation to the world as such, is not that of knowing, anyway not what we think of as knowing."[7] In Wittgenstein and Thoreau, Cavell finds that non-certain relation to the world enacted. Both writers, understanding that "our capacity for disappointment [by words] is essential to the way we possess language,"[8] continually enact skepticism's disappointed demand for certainty in order to access what it turns away from: "our shared home of language"[9]; "this haphazard, unsponsored state."[10] As with Graham desiring and failing to grasp the poem she heard read, being awakened to a new sort of listening apparent once such knowing had been put aside, Thoreau and Wittgenstein, in this view, are attempting fully to "inhabit our investment in words, in the world."[11]

For Cavell, "Thoreau is doing with our ordinary assertions what Wittgenstein does with our more patently philosophical assertions—bringing them back to a context in which they are alive."[12] Graham's work, I would suggest, is involved in just this process. As the "other" her poems encounter shifts throughout her career from works of art and our mythological heritage to personal experience and the puzzles of matter, each resistant surface brings her back, as she writes, into an acknowledge of limits and permits her to explore what comes to life there. We find in her work what Cavell calls "endless specific succumbings to the conditions of skepticism and endless specific recoveries from it, endless as a circle, as a serpent swallowing itself."[13] What I would like to do here is examine four of Graham's early books, four turns of that circle, tracing the progressively more ambitious ways she suffers and is forced awake by what she calls "the erosion / of the right word, what it shuts."[14]

The poems in the first book I will examine, *Erosion* (1983), work out a response to limits by studying a series of exemplary objects (often paintings) or situations. Often initially resistant, these models draw from her an interwoven set of responses which chart much of her work in the books which follow. At the same time, a number of poems in *Erosion* go beyond simply working out this theory and attempt to enact it, coming alive in the gap generated by resistance. After working through her response to exemplary objects, I'll turn briefly to these more active poems in *Erosion*, then trace the continuation of such work in recent books.

Erosion's opening poem, "San Sepolcro" (*E*, 2–3), establishes most of the tensions that charge her poems. It begins with the lyric's classic move—a cold crisp morning in the Italian mountains ("milk on the air, / ice on the oily / lemon-skins") convinces the writer that the dream of grasping meaning, of taking a reader or listener through to one's core, is possible:

> In this blue light
>   I can take you there,
> snow having made me
>   a world of bone
> seen through to.

The speaker plays that drive out, further unfolding it by associating the blue light off the snow with a painting of Mary "unbuttoning / her blue dress, / her mantle of weather, / to go into / labor." "Come, we can go in," she remarks, eyes on the painting's calm invitation to enter and know and see, beckoning to her reader who is, she imagines, waiting to be "take[n] . . . there":

>   This is
> what the living do: go in.
>   It's a long way.
> And the dress keeps opening
>   from eternity
>
> to privacy, quickening.
>   Inside, at the heart,
> is tragedy, the present moment
>   forever stillborn,
> but going in, each breath
>   is a button

>   coming undone, something terribly
>   nimble-fingered
>   finding all of the stops.

What happens in these lines is that as the drive to "go in" is played out it gradually thickens and slows to a halt, something one sees over and over in the work of Elizabeth Bishop. "It's a long way," Graham writes. What had looked like a doorway to "eternity"—the word in several senses becoming flesh—never opens all the way, leading only to a sense of separation and inevitable "privacy." The poet's lyric drive to capture "the present moment" and the painting's wonder at "the birth of god" are equally "stillborn," become equally tragic. And yet, that confrontation with limits is also described as a "quickening," for something deeply human comes to life in this space where she feels both a sense of tragedy and the delicious, "nimble-fingered" (terrible, but so dexterous) drive to know and open and enter. The rest of *Erosion*, essentially, looks for ways to account for and describe the sense of "quickening" occurring in the space between these two realizations.[15]

A number of poems in *Erosion* think about this quickening space by concentrating on the nimble-fingered way we seek to know; they imagine both the powerful drive to enter and the sudden suck of its collapse. That is one way, they propose, to describe the terrible unease of the human condition. "Kimono" (*E*, 38–39) plays out the drive to know by means of its mixed tone. The speaker is in her backyard, wearing a kimono—its pattern showing "valleys, clear skies, / thawing banks / narcissus and hollow reeds / break through"—and brushing her hair. She knows that a small boy is hidden in the evergreens on the side of her yard, watching. Though she realizes that "the casual crumbling forms / of boughs" on her kimono are simply lies, representations, and that it is very "late" in our history "for the green scrim to be / [thought of as] such an open / door," she is also taken by the boy's drive to see in or see through. Bending, thinking about the gaps of her clothing opening and shifting, she muses about what the boy embodies—that "soothing" thought that we can cross such "enchanted gap[s], this tiny / eternal / delay which is our knowing"—and plays Mary for him: "something / most whole / loosens her stays / pretending she's alone." It's a complicated gesture, for as she teases and withholds, she both enacts what Robert Hass would call the impossibility of that "old story" and stares in bemusement at our shared desire for it to be so. "At Luca Signorelli's Resurrection of the Body" (*E*, 74–77) is a darker playing out of this impulse. It mourns this sense of limit rather than teasingly going along with the game one more time. What Graham probes is Signorelli's vision of the dead "hurry[ing] / to enter /

their [resurrected] bodies" at the end of time. "[P]ulling themselves up / through the soil / into the weightedness, the color, / into the eye / of the painter," they seem obsessed with what the poet calls their "entrance," through the body, into "names, / . . . happiness." Why hurry? she asks. Is it better? Can a home for the spirit ever be fully located in the fixed and weighted body? These questions probe the painting but are deflected again and again, by the spirits' haste. Soberly, she acknowledges that though we know "there is no / entrance, / only entering," though we know "the wall / of the flesh / opens endlessly," though Signorelli himself, studying the dead body of his son, "with beauty and care / and technique / and judgement, cut into / shadow, cut / into bone and sinew" and never arrived—though we know all of this, we still try, over and over. At best, she concludes, describing, in a sense, the rhythms of her own voice in this volume, one might emulate the painter's patient suffering of ambition and tragedy and attempt, along with the spirits, to know and enter, but in a manner "stern and brazen / and slow."[16]

Both "Kimono" and "Signorelli" explore knowing's limits by playing out the desire to arrive—slowly, giddily, achingly. If it could only be so, these poems seem to lament. A more complex set of poems not only plays out that impulse but tries to picture what is gained in acknowledging its limits. I'll look at one—an early poem, "Scirroco" (*E*, 8–11), which sets up the issue. Visiting the rooms in Rome where Keats died, that sense of limit confirmed by a glimpse of Keats's papers behind glass, "some yellowing, / some xeroxed or / mimeographed," the poet finds visible there two allegories for "the nervous spirit / of this world" which drives us to look and seek to know. One is the hot wind by which the ivy outside "is fingered, / refingered / . . . [this spirit] that must go over and over / what it already knows." The other is the grapes on the terrace whose "stark hellenic / forms" will "soften / till weak enough / to enter / our world." If the wind fingering what it knows is a version of nimble-fingered attempts to know and undress and "unfasten" (*E*, 77), the softening grapes are the stark forms which collapse when resisted.[17] Woven together, Graham proposes—trying and failing to know, holding yourself there—these two approaches might bring us to some sort of "quickening":

    Therefore this
  is what I
must ask you
   to imagine: wind;
the moment
  when the wind

>   drops; and grapes,
>   which are nothing,
>   which break
>   in your hands.

The poems in *Erosion* which point the way forward are those in which Graham begins the difficult task of modulating the certainty of her own uses of language: forcing the poems to contend with what would threaten their ways of moving; letting them drive toward failure in order to discover what might awaken in that blinded collapse. I will look at two. "The Age of Reason" (*E*, 16–20) begins with a description of a bird "anting":

>   which means,
>   in my orchard
>   he has opened his wings
>   over a furious
>
>   anthill and will take up
>   into the delicate
>   ridges of quince-yellow
>   feathers
>   a number of tiny, angry
>   creatures
>
>   that will inhabit him

That extraordinary activity—mastering the world's otherness in a manner both painful and exhilarating—seems a temptation we are simply incapable of refusing: "Who wouldn't want / to take / into the self / something that burns / or cuts, or wanders / lost / over the body?" The bird, like Signorelli's spirits at the resurrection of the dead, acts out a version of a human drive. He functions as a sort of emblem. In the second section, Graham stands aside from that drive, thinking about the extremity of that gesture by paralleling it with an equally troubling human act—the end of Werner Herzog's *Woyzek* in which, "after the hero whom / we love / who is mad has / murdered / the world, the young / woman / who is his wife, / and loved her," the central figure throws his murder weapon into a river. He is Othello as Stanley Cavell describes him, murdering the world he loves in order to possess it completely. Carefully echoing her language about the bird (and touching on similar ways of describing knowledge's movement "into" things scattered throughout the book), Graham tosses away in disgust that bold desire to "take on / almost anything." She allows the drive to crumble and acknowledge its own blindness:

> In the moonlight he throws
>   his knife
>
> into the wide river
>   flowing beside them
> but doesn't think it has
>   reached deep
> enough, so goes in
>   after it
>
> himself. White as a knife,
>   he goes in after it
> completely.

But then something important happens. As if suddenly realizing that such attempts at mastery are not confined to madmen and lovers, Graham turns her appalled eye on her own activity as she writes.[18] To use another Cavell term, she "measures" herself against what she has just realized.[19] She suffers herself our "built-in limits" (*E*, 27) as knowers and lovers. Calmly, steel in her voice, she looks at the writing scene she is in the middle of. Because the world we would love "resist[s]" us, she remarks quietly, "we have / characters and the knife / of a plot / to wade through this / current." Like Elizabeth Bishop with the colonizers in "Brazil, January 1, 1502," she finds herself linked to the lover using the knife.[20] We too—as the patient attention of this poem unwittingly demonstrates—are driven and never satisfied, giving up only when the world we would absorb has been lost in being narrowed into name, scent, and symbol:

>   For what we want
>   to take
> inside of us, whole orchard,
>   color,
> name, scent, symbol, raw
>   pale
>
> blossoms, wet black
>   arms there is
> no deep enough.

Though perhaps the echo of Pound slightly softens the collapse here—the suggestion being that all of poetry shares in this criticism—this seems to me the most important move *Erosion* makes. Here, I would suggest, the volume "quickens."

It does as well at "Patience" (*E*, 42–45). Graham begins by celebrating memory, one of the ways we finger and refinger the world:

> There is a room now
>   buried
> in late morning
>   sunlight
> that will not
>   change
>
> in which a woman
>   & a small
> girl who is not
>   me
> although I am
>   her patience
>
> are ironing

Through that fixed, unchanging memory, the poet has found a way to describe "her patience," a trait she still defines herself by. There seems to be an "open door" back to this emblematic moment; it is held open by means of "a perfect shaft / of light / the rudder for / the scene." However, as if remarking silently to herself on the "lateness" of such an enchanted view of knowing oneself, Graham begins to overplay memory's desire to sort and order: "We iron to find / the parts / in each thing, making / a tidy body / that folds away / into itself." Cavell would call this "succumbing" to the urge to know for sure. Graham calls it "feed[ing]" memory's form of knowing, doing to herself what she had done to the boy in "Kimono" or had watched, horrified, the spirits attempt in the Signorelli poem:

>   Tell me
> where that room is now,
>   that stubborn
> fragrant bloom? The fragile stem
>   from here

> to there is tragedy, I know,
> 	the path we
> feed it by until it cracks
> 	open at last

Overplaying the fragile claims of memory makes visible what it normally hides—that it is a tragic declaration about distance and not a guarantee of connection. The power of this piece is that the overplaying and collapse happen in the writing, in the act of remembering. What is suddenly visible, in that collapse, is a much larger world than the one the poet had been carrying around:

> & it's all right Maria is
> 	so tired
>
> even the sweetness of
> 	wisteria
> hurts, all right she has
> 	just lost
> her son, a policeman, &
> 	is crying
>
> as she irons

This had originally been a broken, rudderless experience. What the poet finds, eyes equally on that painful scene and on the writing scene, is how quickly, years ago, she had turned from that initial disorientation and narrowed it to something safe and domestic. How quickly, she acknowledges, she turned the "living vine" into "twistings of . . . wicker," turned pain and the feeling of being lost, "as if themselves [held] beneath / the blue / and eye-shaped iron," into "the style, / the innocence." As memory dissolves, then, as one suffers the collapse of its confident fingering, the world not mastered quickens and flares.

If *Erosion* is concerned mainly with identifying and investigating emblems of Graham's developing poetics, *The End of Beauty* (1987) follows the lead of such poems as "Patience" or "Two Paintings by Gustav Klimt" or "The Age of Reason" and tries to actively inhabit the process of feeling the wind strain and die, the discovery the follows knowing's collapse.[21] Where *Erosion* often turns to paintings to measure its writing activity against, *The End of Beauty* turns to our culture's grand stories—resistant and needing to be struggled against, but part of us all. In entering such stories, the poems enter dramatizations of finitude. The book is built around five central poems which unfold biblical or mythological situations that put into play the same drive to know and its rich collapse which we saw framed and reframed in *Erosion*. Graham labels these poems "Self-Portraits" in order to spell out the way their explorations offer, in Cavell's terms, "allegories or measures" of her own "investment in words, in the world."[22] As she feels her way into them, she attempts to see herself, and suffer herself, there. Each self-portrait tries to describe the charged gap between knower and the world, and each asks what can be made of that space. Surrounding each self-portrait with a cluster of poems displaying the tension or process the portrait establishes, Graham develops, in *The End of Beauty*, a rich, cross-pollinating investigation.

The book begins with Eve handing Adam the forbidden fruit from the tree of the knowledge of good and evil: "Self-Portrait as the Gesture Between Them" (*EB*, 3–8). Graham worries the gesture much as she had those of Signorelli's dead or that of the bird anting. What does the gesture show about the tensions in knowing or plotting or shaping? she asks. Breaking the poem into numbered sections, breaking it phrase by phrase at moments of concentration and intensity, she slows the gesture down.[23] She establishes an interval outside the straightforward piling up of sentences in order to inhabit its implications. Eve's gesture, she writes, was a "rip in the fabric where the action begins, the opening of the narrow / passage." It was a narrowing down of many possibilities into a single choice, which was then followed by another, somehow related, and so on—the "action." Graham calls that: "The passage along the arc of denouement once the plot has begun, like a limb, / the buds in it cinched and numbered, / outside the true story really, outside of improvisation." But, she continues, acknowledging the deep need the gesture responds to, of course they chose such a narrowing—one always does: "But what else could they have done, these two, sick of beginning, / revolving in place like a thing seen, / dumb, blind, rooted in the eye that's watching." Radically slowing the poem, the poet's eye slashes back and forth across that first movement into knowing, trying to see and feel the drive as it originates. Eve must have wanted "freedom," she speculates: the ability to think of Adam in "secret," "turn[ing] him slowly in the shallows," a desire which would have grown (like a fruit) into something more complicated and needy and incomplete. If so, if Adam in her mind became something "owned but not seizable, resembling, resembling," then that "gesture between them," responding to form's (or resemblance's) nagging lack, would naturally have followed. Can you complete me, she must have asked, driven by the first stirrings of the desire to know, and in asking that must have handed over her freedom for the unending series of questions and answers, shapes followed by other shapes, minutes by minutes, that make up our world:

           until it must be told, be
                              14
taken from her, this freedom,
                              15
so that she had to turn and touch him to give it away
                              16
to have him pick it from her as the answer takes the question
                              17
that he should read in her the rigid inscription
                              18
in a scintillant fold the fabric of daylight bending
                              19
where the form is complete where the thing must be torn off
                              20
momentarily angelic, the instant writhing into a shape

But in the same instant that form is completed and she is read, Eve loses all. Her story becomes Adam's story: "the scales the other way now in his hand, / the gift that changes the balance." The drive to know comes up short, the movement out of "improvisation" into "narrowing" leaving Eve with "the feeling of being a digression not the link in the argument, / a new direction, an offshoot, the limb going on elsewhere, / . . . a piece from another set." And yet, the poet goes on, looking at that broken-off gesture one more time, perhaps there's something attractive about that "error, . . . that break from perfection," for what it makes possible is an intimacy that acknowledges the simultaneous presence of estrangement—here, in time—"where the complex mechanism [of knowing] fails, where the stranger appears in the clearing, / . . . out of nowhere to share the day." So, this gesture which initiates and stands for our finite condition is a charged one: it is a bid for freedom and its rich loss, a narrowing that opens on something else, wind and grapes in the same exchange. To put it simply, Graham's first self-portrait discovers a generative estrangement possible in knowing's collapse, something gained in the space of error.[24]

"Self-Portrait as Both Parties" (*EB*, 14–16) charts the poet's position in a second way, by means of the Orpheus and Eurydice story. If the gesture between Adam and Eve shows both loss and the possibilities of estrangement in the movement from improvisation to plot and structure, what does the loss of Eurydice as Orpheus turns back to gaze at her show? Think of the silt of a river being touched by "the open hands of the sunlight," the poem suggests. Call the sunlight Orpheus and the "slow bottom of the river" Eurydice. The drive to possess immediately makes itself felt: "How would he bring her back again? She drifts up / in a small hourglass-shaped cloud of silt where the sunlight touches, / up to where the current could take her." But she is soon lost. Like Eve's movement into "resemblances," Orpheus's need to know has the loss of the object of his attention built into it:

> And though he would hold her up, this light all open hands,
> seeking her edges, seeking to make her palpable again,
> curling around her to find crevices by which to carry her up,
> flaws by which to be himself arrested and made,
> made whole, made sharp and limbed, a shape,
> she cannot, the drowning is too kind,
> the becoming of everything which each pore opens to again,
> the possible which each momentary outline blurs into again,
> too kind, too endlessly kind,
> the silks of the bottom rubbing their vague hands
> over her forehead

Description inevitably breaks down; Eurydice won't be "made sharp and limbed." The "possible," the bottom where outlines blur and distinctions drown, is "too kind," its gravitational field overwhelming.

Turning to this story a second time in the poem that immediately follows, "Orpheus and Eurydice" (*EB*, 17–19), Graham begins to explore its hold on her, as she writes. She enacts the Orpheus-in-her drawn by the garden's hissing snake to turn around and glance and lose the world she loves:

> Up ahead, I know, he felt it stirring in himself already, the glance,
> the darting thing in the pile of rocks,
>
> already in him, there, shiny in the rubble, hissing Did you want to remain completely unharmed?—
>
> the point-of view darting in him, shiny head in the ash-heap,
>
> hissing Once upon a time, and then Turn now darling give me that look,
>
> the perfect shot, give me that place where I'm erased. . . .
>
> . . .
>
> And yes she could feel it in him already, up ahead, that wanting-to-turn-and-cast-the outline-over-her
>
> by his glance,
>
> sealing the edges down

Perhaps Orpheus turned because he was driven by a force that would only quiet when it played the game of knowing all the way out to its collapse: "Because you see he could not be married to it anymore, this field with minutes in it / called woman, its presence in him the thing called / future—could not be married to it anymore, expanse tugging his mind out into it, / tugging the wanting-to-finish out." And perhaps Eurydice understood the attraction of being grasped at and lost, of finding herself unspoken for again: "now she's looking back into it, into the poison the beginning, / giving herself to it, looking back into the eyes, / . . . looking into that which sets the _____ in motion and seeing in there / a doorway open nothing on either side." If so, and if both responses tug at the poet as she writes, then perhaps the Orpheus and Eurydice in her attempts to outline and seal down precisely *because* what follows is a generative silencing of that drive: "When we turn to them—limbs, fields, expanses of dust called meadow and avenue— / will they be freed then to slip back in?" I would suggest, then, that although allowing naming to exhaust itself in a world-unhanding blankness (Orpheus and Eurydice) is different from entering into resemblance's estranged intimacy (Adam and Eve), they are responses to a single problem. They are ways of unfolding knowing's collapse.

The third speculative poem in this sequence, "Self-Portrait as Apollo and Daphne" (*EB*, 30–34), tries to get at what might be gained by acknowledging the limits of knowing in yet another way. Eve's gesture leads to "finite . . . options," Orpheus's to a "put[ting] to rest" (*EB*, 17) of the "glance." This poem opens up something else. Graham begins by describing what she calls the first "phase" of their story—the "chase scene" as the god pursues the nymph: "The truth is this had been going on for a long time during which they both wanted it to last." One can read that sometimes delicious, sometimes oppressive contest everywhere: in words pursuing things, in the wind attempting to handle the world, even in the sun glinting off "bits of broken glass / . . . for just a fraction of an instant / (thousands of bits) at just one angle, quick, the evidence, the landfill, / then gone again, everything green, green." To put it simultaneously in linguistic and sexual terms:

2
How he wanted, though, to possess her, to nail the erasures,
3
like a long heat on her all day once the daysounds set in, like a long analysis
4
The way she kept slipping away was this: can you really

> see me, can you really know I'm really who . . .
> His touchings a rhyme she kept interrupting (no one
> believes in that version anymore she whispered, no one
> can hear it anymore, *tomorrow, tomorrow,*
> like the different names of those girls
> all one girl). . . .

Eventually, of course, Daphne, out of desperation, halts this phase and is turned into a laurel tree: "She stopped she turned, / she would not be the end towards which he was ceaselessly tending, / she would not give shape to his hurry by being its destination." Her change leaves open "the distance between them, the small gap he would close," but it is no longer a probing, teasing, tearing battleground. She becomes neither the morning's glinting glass nor its screeching birds but rather:

> the air the birds call in,
> the air their calls going unanswered marry in,
> the calls the different species make, cross-currents, frettings,
> and the one air holding the screeching separateness—
> each wanting to change, to be heard, to have been changed—
> and the air all round them neither full not empty,
> but holding them, holding them, untouched, untransformed.

Apollo wants to possess, and Daphne knows the terror of becoming his ending: together, dramatizing a tension within the poet as she writes, they suggest a response to our condition in which one holds the world without touching it, handles it without reaching out to transform it. Robert Hass has called this the haiku's "clear, deep act of acceptance and relinquishment";[25] Elizabeth Bishop describes it, in lines Graham must be remembering here, as "thousands of light song-sparrow songs floating upward / freely, dispassionately, through the mist, and meshing / in brown-wet, fine, torn fish-nets."[26] It's an attractive possibility—a non-possessive openness.

The fourth portrait, "Self-Portrait as Hurry and Delay" (*EB*, 48–52), is subtitled "Penelope at Her Loom" and uses her weaving / unweaving ruse to propose yet another way of inhabiting knowing's limits. What Penelope must be doing, the poet gradually realizes as she struggles with the story, is creating, in the gap between "the here and the there, in which he wanders searching," a place where desire, in all of its positive and negative implications, is kept alive. (That's a slightly different formation from creating a space where desire leaves the world untouched or where it appreciates its own slide into a collapsed state.)

Here, holding "for an instant in her hands both at once, / the story and its undoing / . . . the threads running forwards yet backwards over her stilled fingers," Penelope allows desire (or choice) to make itself visible and felt without being forced to drive towards an "ending." On her loom, we see "The opening trembling, the nothing, the nothing with use in it trembling—." The shroud is "nothing" because it has come undone, but it trembles in that stalled space because it is still charged by human drives and uses: to be home, to know for sure, to hold tight, and so on. Think of Odysseus at sea; those desires tremble on the loom:

> like the light over the water seeking the place on the water
> where out of air and point of view and roiling wavetips a shapeliness,
>   a possession of happiness
> forms,
>
> a body of choices among the waves, a strictness among them, an edge
>   to the light,
>
> something that is not something else

By keeping herself from the suitors, Penelope keeps the possibility of such a "possession of happiness" free for Odysseus: "It is his wanting in the threads she has to keep alive for him, / scissoring and spinning and pulling the long minutes free, it is / the shapely and mournful delay she keeps alive for him." But, perhaps more to the point, she keeps desire itself—costly, beautiful, wanting to wrap itself "plot plot and dénouement over the roiling openness"—alive and visible, keeps it as something to be attended to. That too must be something writing does.

The final and most powerful piece in this series is "Self-Portrait as Demeter and Persephone"(*EB*, 59–63). It begins the book's conclusion and holds many of its strongest poems in its gravitational field. To inhabit knowing's limit as both Demeter and Persephone means "suffer[ing] [it] completely"—living over and over the cycles of having and losing, of being in a story and being released from it. Every year, Persephone goes "out into the open field through the waiting the waving grasses / way out to the edge of that drastic field of distinctions." Every year she finds herself bride of the underworld:

> She took off the waiting she stood before him without nouns
> He held her where are the images he said we will destroy them
>   you are in hell now there is no beginning
>
> the outline is a creature that will blur you will forget him
>
>   as for motive that shapeliness let us splinter it let us scatter it

And yet, set apart from nouns, images, outline, or shape, every year Persephone finds herself returning to all of that: "Look she said I have to go back now if you don't mind waiting." Demeter, of course, has her own cycle. She lives in "the knowable / clucking I've been looking for you all day," gradually devastating the world as the inevitability of that loss dawns: "the made grieving . . . like a mother or winter / the great gap grieving all form and shadow." What would it mean to imagine our relation to the world through both figures? Think of it as Persephone returning to the world devastated by Demeter's love and grief and wanting: "The first thing she saw when she surfaced was the wind / wrapping like a body round the stiff stripped trees / that would bend more deeply into that love if they could." Then combine the stories. Under the influence of Persephone's generative return, think of those same trees, exploded into leafiness while Demeter's winter grief still howls its terrible, blanked desire:

> that would bend more deeply into it inventing (if they could)
>
>   15
>
> another body, exploded, all leafiness, unimaginable
>
>   16
>
> by which to be forgiven by which to suffer completely this wind

An explosion which is also a leafing out, a bending into what simultaneously responds and destroys—inventing such a tormented form as this to inhabit knowing's contested space is what the poems which conclude *The End of Beauty* attempt.

Let mention just one. In "Imperialism" (*EB*, 94–99) the poet acknowledges Cavell's "truth of skepticism" by means of the image of a shadow moving across a dusty road, touching a bank, a hole, and so on. The shadow works like the mind:

>   the shape constantly laying herself down over the sparkling dust
> she cannot own—
>   What can they touch of one another, and what is it for
>
> this marriage, this life of Look, here's a body, now here's
>   a body, now here,
> here. . . .

She enters and feels out that space by remembering an argument from the night before. The way her partner's face seemed to flutter in the kerosene lamp—

"something like clear light then / soiled light / (roiling)"—was like the unsettled shadow across the road, as was their inability to converse cleanly and "keep the thing clear—the narrative of / bentwood chair and hinge and trim." In that space, she remembers, a story came alive and then sputtered out: "And there was a story I wanted / to tell you then but couldn't / (just where she came on into us and we pushed back with / better rephrasings)."

A broken-off story in an open space, canceled eventually by "better rephrasings." What value is that? As she works back to it now, she begins to answer. The story she had thought of had been about being taken by her mother, when quite young, to the Ganges where she had seen bodies burned on pyres and the ashes shaken into the river. "Later she had me walk on in. / Strange water. Thick. I can recall it even now." That is, she walked into a skeptical space where bodies and shapes dissolved. Not unexpectedly, she woke up that night screaming, suffering again that loss of bodies and shapes. The broken-off story, she realizes now, was an image of what form looks like in such a swirling dissolve, an image of form momentarily opening the powerfully alien world around us, and then collapsing:

 —But what I remembered last night to tell you

is a white umbrella a man in the river near me was washing
 and how the dark brown ash-thick riverwater rode
in the delicate tines as he raised it rinsing.
 How he opened it and shut it. Opened and shut it.
First near the surface then underwater—

And perhaps that is what form does in the space it suffers and can't hold—opens and shuts, the world riding, visible but untouched, through it. Or not entirely untouched, for the world, too, opens and shuts, as the poem's last lines make clear, "narrow[ing] down to [a mother's] love" then flaring out to a terrible vertiginous openness: "no face at all dear god, all arms—."

In *Region of Unlikeness* (1991), Graham rephrases this investigation as an attempt to inhabit and suffer what she calls "the sentence in its hole, its cavity / of listening" (*RU*, 114). She asks again what sort of response to the world—this book calls its "listening"—might be developed, in her own sentences, when the drive to master and narrate shatters over its limits: "(Where the hurry is stopped) (and held) (but not extinguished) (no)" (*RU*, 125). The book's "Foreword" recalls the use of large cultural equivalents in *The End of Beauty* and suggests that we might measure our entrance into the poet's struggle—"How do you feel?" (*RU*, 101), she keeps asking—against Augustine's trembling awareness of the "region of unlikeness" he inhabits far from the "whole," Heidegger's "drawing toward what withdraws," Isaiah's inability to find a proper equivalent for God, or John's "wilderness" of waiting in *Revelation*. Yet the book itself turns from those larger equivalents and looks instead at the resistant details of the poet's own memories. The book is more like "Patience" than it is like "Orpheus and Eurydice," though its drama takes place in an area shared by both: story's stalled spaces which the poet, as she writes, attempts to inhabit and "paint . . . alive" (*RU*, 44).

"Fission" (*RU*, 3–8) sets up many of these concerns. Its title, reluctantly acknowledging the breaking apart that knowing has put into human hands, points to a moment of unraveling shared by many; the speaker remembers being in a movie theater and hearing the news of Kennedy's shooting. As Graham prods the memory, the various ways we shape the world and move toward an end become charged and fragile and at issue. As the poem begins, the movie's soundtrack is suddenly shut off, the houselights come on, a skylight opens, and a man races down the aisle trying "to somehow get / our attention." The movie continues, however, and the man's unwitting call to attend to the space or gap where the "magic" story we've rested in seems to fray and dissolve echoes throughout the book:

> I watch the light from our real place
> suck the arm of screen-building light into itself
>   until the gesture of the magic forearm frays,
> and the story up there grays, pales—them almost lepers now,
>   saints, such
> white on their flesh in
>   patches—her thighs like receipts slapped down on a
>   slim silver tray,
> her eyes as she lowers the heart-shaped shades,
>   as the glance glides over what used to be the open,
> the free

The movie is Stanley Kubrick's *Lolita*. This is the moment when the sunbathing girl, roused from a shapeless slumber by her mother's call and the flaring desire of Humbert Humbert, comes to consciousness. Her face—what a later poem calls "the forward-pointing of it" (*RU*, 119)—dominates the screen as her world is narrowed and yanked into a plot. What one is called to attend to is the region of unlikeness made visible when Lolita's face and her Orpheus-like "glance" over what previously had been "open" are reduced to:

> a roiling up of graynesses,
> vague stutterings of
> light with motion in them, bits of moving zeros
>
> in the infinite virtuality of light,
> some *likeness* in it but not particulate,
> a grave of possible shapes called *likeness*—see it?—something
> scrawling up there . . .

Her expression—the possibility of expression, let's say—isn't eliminated; rather, likeness's hold over the world is suspended and the possibility of a new sort of "scrawling" emerges. The speaker is pulled into this uneasy space as well—"the story playing / all over my face my / forwardness"—and describes it now as a kind of halt or pause: "there / the immobilism sets in, / the being-in-place more alive than the being, / my father sobbing beside me." What the poet realizes, and will take the rest of the book to explore, is that she is in a place where action has been discredited and whited-out and is yet demanded. To speak or to choose or to struggle with the way words take over memories is to risk fission's unwrapping of the real; to not do so is to rest in a skepticism that leaves the world dead and untouchable. That is what comes alive on the face as the light frays:

> *choice* the thing that wrecks the sensuous here the glorious
>   here—
> that wrecks the beauty,
> choice the move that rips the wrappings of light, the
>   ever-tighter wrappings
> of the layers of the
> real: what is, what also is, what might be that is,
> what could have been that is, what
> might have been that is, what I say that is,
> what the words say that is,
> what you imagine the words say that is—Don't move, don't
>
> wreck the shroud—don't move—

The poems which follow frame the question of how to speak in this roiled-up space ever more uneasily. "From the New World" (*RU*, 12–16), for example, works through an event related during the trial of the Cleveland steelworker accused of being the Nazi executioner Ivan the Terrible—the story "about the girl who didn't die / in the gas chamber, who came back out asking / for her mother." Although she is shaken by the brutality of Ivan ordering a man "on his way in to rape her" and thus start the stalled story back up again ("the narrowing, the tightening"), the poet finds her own progress halted before the girl's frail, agonized voice in that "unmoored" space, asking for her world back. What to make of that? Acknowledging her own complicity in story's drive toward an ending—"God knows I too want the poem to continue, / want the silky swerve into shapeliness / and then the click shut"—she lets it drop and holds herself before that whispered "*please*." Graham makes a number of almost desperate attempts to find equivalents for the girl's pleading. Was it like realizing, as a child, that her grandmother had so lost her faculties that she had erased her granddaughter? Or like, some years later, the grandmother herself, now in a nursing home, her "eyes unfastening, nervous," focused on nowhere? The point of these comparisons isn't their fit, as the strain of trying to imagine the whirling-walled bathroom the child had fled to as a "chamber" in which she is "held in . . . as by a gas" suggests.[27] Rather, what is important is the way the resistance of these stories has forced her to an almost immobile space, "a grave of possible shapes called *likeness*" (5). How does one speak there, if likeness doesn't hold? How does one make sentences?: "At the point where she comes back out something begins, yes / something new, something completely / new, but what—there underneath the screaming—what?" It's an almost unmanageable question, charged and desperate and alive:[28]

> *like what*, I whisper,
> *like* which is the last new world, *like, like*, which is the thin
> young body (before it's made to go back in) whispering *please*.

As "Manifest Destiny" puts it, most of the poems in *Region of Unlikeness* can be described as suffering or "pay[ing]" language's price in spaces where such "zero[s]" open (*RU*, 28). The title poem (*RU*, 37–40), for example, uses the speaker's memory of waking, as a thirteen year old, in a man's room, to establish its moment of charged suspension:

> You wake up and you don't know who it is there breathing
>   beside you (the world is a different place from what it
> seems)
>   and then you do.
> The window is open, it is raining, then it has just
>   ceased. What is the purpose of poetry, friend?

Trying to get at the resistant memory, like the struggle with myth or paintings in her previous books, slows the poet's language and makes it visible. Why is she writing? For what purpose? She attempts an answer by watching herself as she writes, tracking both her desire to not engage the memory—"He turns in his sleep. / You want to get out of here. / The stalls going up in the street below now for market. / Don't wake up. Keep this in black and white"—and her fear that she thereby risks running "right through it no resistance / . . . right through it, it not burning, not falling, no / piercing sound." As she fills in color and context, sketching an ending, she declares herself ready to pay in order to keep the human responsibility of remembering alive, in order to hold herself in its unmastered zero:

> If I am responsible, it is for what? the field at the
> end? the woman weeping in the row of colors? the exact
> shades of color? the actions of the night before?
> Is there a way to move through which makes it hard
> enough—thorny re-
> membered? Push. Push through with this girl

The tug of these questions seems to awaken her language, for at the end of the poem she is pulled, in Wyoming "Twenty years later" walking among hatching butterflies, back to that live interval:

> and below the women leaning, calling the price out, handling
> each fruit, shaking the dirt off. Oh wake up, wake
> up, something moving through the air now, something in the ground
>   that
> waits.

"Waiting" is one of *Region*'s repeated terms for what one does in that charged, temporarily immobile place where language's drives to master and sort and go on have been checked. In the space of waiting, we pay or suffer our finitude; we examine and take responsibility for our lives in language. "Picnic" (*RU*, 41–45), for example, gets at the term by struggling with the memory of her father's betrayal, "near the very end of childhood": "Then someone's laugh, although they are lying, / and X who will sleep with father / later this afternoon." It's clear, as the poem begins, that although the poet would like to "Pay attention" to this break in her childhood, the memory has become so "inaudible" over the years that it has been dismissed as a probable lie, like all the others: "The light shone down taking the shape of each lie, / lifting each outline up, making it wear a name. / . . . (so does it matter that this be true?)." That's the stalled spot that this poem inhabits—memory, and in fact all shaping and naming, having been skeptically eroded away. Why write? Why enter that impossible place? "And why should I tell this to you, / and why should *telling* matter still, the bringing to life of / listening, the party going on down there, grasses, / voices?" Such a world seems dead or shrouded—as Graham puts it, it is "sated, exhausted."

What she does, however, is wait and stare at the memory, staying with it until she finds a place that's thorny and difficult—where that distance from what she was then to what she is now can't be bridged by the outlines one so easily draws. Waiting draws that out:

> one of me here and one of me there and in between
> this thing, watery,
>   like a neck rising and craning out
> (wanting so to be seen) (as if there were some other place dear god)—.

She follows that "watery" uneasiness to another, perhaps below-the-surface memory of "father with X": "When I caught up with them they were down by the pond." Then, remembering her desperation to calm things—"I looked into the water where it was stillest"—, she touches its still-live terror and disorientation:

> Have you ever looked into standing water and seen it going
> very fast,
>   seen the breaks in the image where the suction shows,
>   where the underneath is pointed and its tip shows through,
>   maybe something broken, maybe something spoked in there

And there is more to be found in the waiting, for she remembers now, as she writes, what must have been her mother's acknowledgment of the break and her refusal to cover it over with an outline or lie. Later that day, her mother "came up into the bathroom" and, the two of them staring into a mirror, took her daughter's face in her hands and applied make-up. What was that—the way "She shadowed the cheek, held the lips open, fixed the / edge red," and then as the light started to go, the way "The silver was gone. The edges on things. The face still glowed— / bright in the wetness, there"? That, she now realizes, was her mother's way of insisting that one could stay aware in "the opening which is *waiting*"—that one could take responsibility in that dissolving, sucking wetness by acknowledging the fragility of the lines we work with and within:

>   We painted that alive,
> mother with her hands
>   fixing the outline clear—eyeholes, mouthhole—
> forcing the expression on.
>   Until it was the only thing in the end of the day that seemed
>
> believable,
>   and the issue of candor coming awake, there,
> one face behind the other peering in,
>   and the issue of
> freedom. . . .

In many ways, these poems try to do just this: they seek to peer into an ungrounded charged space where the price of expression, of choice, is real and alive. Writing becomes a place where being candid and where facing the trials of "freedom" are still possible.

The book concludes with two rival poems on the implications of waiting or immobilism, as if to suggest that the issue of what is gained in the gap is a still-unsettled one. "Who Watches From the Dark Porch" (*RU*, 97–108) is a powerful attempt to pull the reader into the gap, in this case the skeptical sense that this very poem, "is a lie . . . / . . . Thing / so beautifully embalmed in its syllables." That is a sense we all share, experienced every time we stare at a scene and find "the possibilities (blink) begin to exfoliate" or find a "right version and more right versions, / each one stripping the next layer off her" and the world disappearing under a bewildering series of "veil[s]" that continue to gather even as we discard one and then another. Graham calls that a hole, or a region where likeness won't hold, where suction takes the image. The poet invites the reader into that uneasiness and calls it, in this poem, a struggle between "Matter" and "Interpretation." She sets up a situation: you're on a porch on a summer evening ("sit, here is a soft wood seat / in the screened-in porch") and you hear a sound from next door: "A child's sound. Maybe laughter—no—maybe a scream." The poem "quickens." What if, from the porch, you can't interpret, can't tell? How would you respond to the possibilities unknitted and live in your hand?

> Now I will make it impossible to tell the difference.
> Now I will make it make no difference.
> Now I will make there be no difference.
> Now I will make it. Just make it. Make it.
>
> How do you feel?

What the reader discovers, along with the poet, is a real temptation to use one's awareness of the finitude of outlines or interpretations as an excuse to hide and not meet the world: "If I am responsible, it can't be for everything. / May I / Close my eyes for a minute?" She enacts that temptation by imagining turning on the TV to drown out the sound—which is to say, skeptically turning on our awareness of the fragility and disposability of our interpretive takes on the world:

> Maybe if I turn the TV on?
>   Let's graze the channels? Let's find the
> storyline composed wholly of changing
>   tracks, click, shall I finish this man's phrase with this
>
> man's face, click, is this the truest news—how true—what are
>   the figures
>   . . .
>   —see how even you can't hear it
> anymore, the little shriek, below
>   this hum
>   . . .
>   —flecks of
> information,
>   fabric through which no face will push

There is no face showing through this shroud of self-canceling data because there is no willingness to listen or pay—an awareness of limitation yielding permission to not move forward: "no messy / going / anywhere, / rocking, / erasing each forwards, / . . . here in the place where it's all true so why move." This is a clearly disturbing possibility—that a skeptical response to limits, to its familiar stalled space opening up, might as easily be a retreat as a "waiting" for strangeness to "slice" over you. Think of that as a voice which dissolves the world, which "said *still*, said / don't wait, just sit, sit—Said / no later, no matter." In saying it doesn't matter, in turning from the struggle with it, there is suddenly no matter. "There," she writes, in horror about that feeling, "you got it now. You got it."

Finally, "The Phase After History" (*RU*, 111–121) attempts something different in the same space. Its version of the collapse of straightforward history or confident interpretation is the experience of having a junco loose in the house, its panic turning the house into a "diagram that makes no / sense . . . [a]

wilderness / of materialized / meaning." The house she suddenly inhabits—in which nothing is settled, wrong-turns everywhere—is like "a head with nothing inside" or even "Like this piece of paper" she's working on. How to inhabit this stalled space? One bird escapes on its own; the poet tries to edge the other one free, but can't complete the story: "I start with the attic, moving down. / Once I find it in the guest- / bedroom but can't / catch it in time, / talking to it all along, / hissing: stay there, don't / move—absolutely no / story—." Eventually, she is reduced to "waiting" and "listening," creating what she hopes might be described as "a large uncut fabric floating above the soil— / a place of *attention*." Sitting there, listening for the bird to thwack a resistant surface or bright pane of glass, the poet thinks of a friend in a Psych Hospital who had "tried to cut off" his face—that is, our "forward-pointing," our confidence in expression. He thought of it, apparently, as "an exterior / destroyed by mismanagement. / Nonetheless it stayed on." Sickened by his desperation but challenged by that stark memory of his "face on that mustn't come off," Graham speculates that perhaps being "returned to the faceless / attention, / the waiting and waiting for the telling sound" is a step forward rather than a retreat. Perhaps listening for the other—for the world's strangeness—, an experience heightened by the collapse of the face, poem, or the house's order, is a step in getting a new sort of face back:

> The head empty, yes,
>
> > but on it the face, the idea of principal witness,
> >
> > > . . .
> >
> > How I would get it back
> sitting here on the second-floor landing,
> > one flight above me one flight below,
> listening for the one notch
> > on the listening which isn't me
>
> listening—

It is the strength of this uneasy book that as it circles back to the opening poems and their questions of what to make of "immobilism, the being-in-place more alive / than the being" (8) or of the sense that likeness has been dissolved— "At the point where she comes back out [and] something begins, yes, / something new, something completely / new, but what?" (16)—it is the strength of this book that as it circles back, the answer is still out of reach.[29] Or the answer is the attentive wait itself: "something new come in but / what? listening" (120). Graham calls this, finally, "emptiness housed," her "eyes closed to hear / further."

Graham's next book, *Materialism* (1993), engages the limits of knowing by means of an intricate meditation on making sense of the world through description. Once again, one notes the increasingly personal way each new book enters this issue, moving from stilled paintings to still-active myths, and now from the writer's own stories to the play of her eyes. *Materialism* begins with an account of a river's "dance of non-discovery"—its constantly erased surface patterns "nailing each point and then each next right point, inter- / locking, correct, correct again, [yet] each rightness snapping loose"—and asks whether an equivalent acknowledgment of the limits of description might produce in us "a new way of looking" (*M*, 3–4). We can think of this as a possible response to *Region*'s "something completely / new, but what?" Poem after poem dramatizes the way the eye, "clawing for foothold," performs its "long licking across the surface of / matter" (*M*, 99, 132). Typically, the poems begin in the morning, as the "glance—surveyor of edges—descends / . . . gnawing the overgrowth, / crisscrossing the open for broken spots" (*M*, 8), or on waking in the dark, desperate to "mark . . . the pleating blacknesses of hotel air" (*M*, 58). Consistently, there is the sense, as one morning poem puts it, "that we are *in a drama*" (*M*, 127). The various desires and terrors and implications brought to consciousness by tracking the eye's swing are slowed and studied, and the "Monologue of going and going" is halted so that the reader might join the poet in understanding what is actually at stake as we stammer and stroke the world into sense.

Materialism quite deliberately sets its meditations in the midst of Michael Oakeshott's larger "conversation in which human beings forever seek to understand themselves." As we have seen in previous books, an echoing network of shared terms and images links Graham's own attempts to make and unmake meaning with those of such figures as Wittgenstein ("[pictorial form] is laid against reality like a measure"—*M*, 93), or Jonathan Edwards ("the continuance of the very being of the world and all its parts . . . depends entirely on an *arbitrary constitution*—*M*, 110–11), or Brecht ("the theatre must alienate what it shows"—*M*, 64). Where previous books used such established voices to set up clearly staged struggles—think of Klimt, or Augustine, or Ovid—*Materialism* seems an example of that "air" in "Self-Portrait as Apollo and Daphne" in which "the calls the different species make, cross-currents, frettings" are all alive at once. That is a different sort of "measuring" of one's own voice. Sometimes quoted, often subtly adapted, these other voices form a chorus—challenging and extending and undercutting the writer's own struggles. The most powerful of these engaged-with voices is Elizabeth Bishop's—never named directly, but in her careful descriptive progress and unnerving skids into its limits so present that the entire book reads as a sort of fierce and heightened adaptation of her work. Graham's comments on Bishop in an interview, in fact, can be taken to summarize the "new way of looking" *Materialism* charges itself with developing: "You have to undertake an act which you know is essentially futile, in the direct sense: the words are not going to seize the thing. But what leaks in between the attempts at seizure *is* the thing, and you have to be willing to suffer the limits of description in order to get it."[30] What is discovered "in between," in the space opened up by an object's resistance, is perhaps most simply described in one of the book's epigraphs, adapted from "Crossing Brooklyn Ferry." "Expand, being," Graham has Whitman write, in response to objects that remain stubbornly other and independent of our eyes' embrace, "keep your places objects. / . . . We use you, and do not cast you aside—we plant you permanently within us; / We fathom you not—we love you." Essentially, what this book asks is whether Whitman's dream can be realized—whether suffering the limits of description and admitting that we neither fathom nor own objects might lead to that expanded sense of "being" Whitman calls "love."[31]

An early poem in the book, "Subjectivity" (*M*, 25–31), powerfully illustrates how Graham enters this conversation, taking the "uttering tongues" of the epigraphs as "hints" (as Whitman puts it elsewhere) and voicing their music her own way. "Subjectivity" begins with the poet attempting to describe a motionless monarch butterfly she'd found and brought inside to study. As is typical of her work in this volume, the intensity of her gaze generates a series of striking metaphors for the butterfly's markings which then take on a life of their own as possible assessments or measurements of that gaze. The markings become: "Black bars expanding / over an atomic-yellow ground"; an "incandescent" yellow pushing "out (slow) through the hard web"; the "yellow of cries forced through that mind's design"; "a structure of tenses and persons for the gusting / heaven-yellow / minutes"; a "bright new world the eyes would seize upon— / pronged optic animal the incandescent *thing* / must rise up to and spread into." This seems to me extraordinary writing. The world under her attention blazes into "incandescence"—a incandescence generated by the opposition between the hungry-for-empire bars, designs, and syntactical orders which we can call, for short, the poet's eye and the as-yet unclaimed world the eye lights upon. The scale continually flickers and shifts—the optic nerve, the sentence, and the colonist all claim, essentially, the same territory—as Graham describes, without yet being able to explain, the allegory she's been presented with: the "gaze's stringy grid" and the world "almost burn[ing] its way / clear through / to be."

How is it that the distance between the mind's web and the world's atomic separateness yields neither domination nor emptiness but incandescence? This is the response to skepticism we've seen the poet moving toward in each book. How does that open space quicken, or come alive, or re-gain a face? There is "something new, something completely / new, but what?" (*RU*, 16). Graham, as always, tries to answer by, quite literally, feeling her way into the issues. She is intent, as Cavell puts it about Thoreau, on understanding, through "endless computations of words" that "Words come to us from a distance." She knows that "Meaning them is accepting that fact of their condition."³² In this volume, Graham enters the "condition" of her language by holding it up against the world around her. Noticing a ray of sunlight moving across the floor, Graham waits and lets it approach her, all "twang and a licking monosyllable." She invites the beam to become an allegory and a measure of her own descriptive desires. She feels herself, as the poem slows to a crawl, turned into a thing examined and then lifted up suddenly to consciousness—brought from "her" to "me" by the light's licking glance:

> making her rise up into me,
> forcing me to close my eyes,
> the whole of the rest feeling broken off,
>
> it all being my face, my being inside the beam of sun,
>
> and the sensation of how it falls unevenly,
>
> how the wholeness I felt in the shadow is lifted,
> broken, this tip *lit*, this other *dark*—and stratified,
> analysed, chosen-round, formed—

What she senses, from inside the process, is the wholeness description has broken-off and blinded, chosen and lit; she feels most acutely the I (the eye) staking its inadequate claim. This is Apollo and Daphne discovered within one's own eyes, Lolita's roiled-up face made one's own. That awareness produces an uneasy charge as she returns to the butterfly, acutely aware of her gaze "licking for crevices, imperfections," trying "to make it flat— / as if it were still too plural" and sensing "the *underneath* the mind wants to eliminate" in its drive to "smear, coat, / wrap, diagram." That sense, that there's an underneath untouched by the "almost icy beams I can feel my open eyes release," begins to drive the poem and then, so quickly the reader almost drops the book in surprise, suddenly blazes into visibility as a neighbor happens by, explains that the butterfly had only been stilled by the morning's cold, and, freeing it from her eyes, returns it to the sun. It blazes against her markings and is gone:

>   the yellow thing, the specimen
> rising up of a sudden out of its envelope of glances—
>
> a bit of fact in the light and then just light.

What these poems seek to do, playing off of another version of incandescence discovered in "Young Maples in the Wind," is carry writer and reader into such an uneasy confrontation with limits that the human condition is brought to life: "—can we, together, / make a listening here, like a wick sunk deep in this mid-temperate / morning-light, can we make its tip—your reading my words—burn" (*M*, 137). Let me touch on several examples in which she quiets the drive to know, admits it comes to nothing, and attempts such a listening. "Concerning the Right to Life" (*M*, 14–20) begins with a series of striking descriptions of a rose—it is a "rough muscle, / drenched veil . . . / . . . the possible / sprung from / possibility / into whipped red / choice. /. . . around it—shuddering—the invisible / ripens"—and then asks what happens when one stands before that flashing "accretion of discardings" and allows it to "judge" one's own attempts at form. Once again, Graham "tr[ies] to feel" her way into the implications of form and choice performed by the rose's ordering of the invisible. She dramatizes what is at stake in its "thrashing forking red" by listening to opposed voices at an anti-abortion protest and then walking through the crowd and into the clinic being targeted. Sitting inside, acknowledging her own tendencies to keep her language "immaculate" and to think of a writer's "freedom of choice" as something like "illustrious sleep," the poem's speaker begins to listen to the voices outside and, drawn into that contested space, finds her words taking on "materiality." Juxtaposing those rival voices—"some / voices screaming *right to life*, some others screaming / *choice choice*"—and then complicating each term—through such rights "held *self- / evident*" we've ruthlessly "*take[n] possession / of the earth*"; perhaps there are realms where "*there is no choice*"—Graham allows those tensions to "roil" or complicate the "immaculate" terms she wants to use in her own speech. Nothing is settled, other than the sense that now, when words are chosen, despite the sheer fragility of language, perhaps something will have been "displaced," an "underneath" will have been encountered, some tragically alert choice will have been chanced, there between language and the world. The poem makes its own formal choices contested ground, a place to listen and flare and expand into alertness.

"Relativity: A Quartet" (*M*, 34–43) works a variation on this pattern. Another interruption occurs; a train loses power and stops, and as the view outside her window is put on hold, the poet finds herself in another stalled linguistic space, the "Monologue of going and going interrupted." Once again, language's confident single voice is, like Penelope's web, unwoven into a number of voices as the stalled train becomes a stage set. Two voices, the views out both sides of the train, come alive in this space and the poet is forced to engage them. Across the aisle is a stoned couple, asleep. Through their window, before their "uncomprehending" eyes, the sea lies apart and "unseized." No longer "lay[ing] itself down frame by frame into the wide / resistenceless opening of our wet / retina," the sea is simply "mere, / still, being." The world lies immaculate, untouched, but as before this is a position that isn't held for long. Through the other window the poet sees "a scribble of leaves." She feels herself drawn to "look close," "see through," and "enter" into that second world—so much so that she discovers rising within herself the language of *Job* and *Isaiah* and the *Psalms* as her instinctive turn away from "gaping eyelessness" toward form re-enacts God's initial struggle with his "adversary: the [unshaped] waters":

> Green leaves: cloth to shroud the Deep:
> ride above the deep:
> > ride in your chariot of shapeliness:
> clean: shut: not this and not this:
> > destroy with one seed the monster's skull:
> thrust with one stem a sword into its heart—
>
> And the waters fled *backwards*—
> And the endlessness fearfully surrendered—

That great primordial need to shape, surprised into voice, then gets bracingly undercut as a second meditation on form begins, initiated by the girl across the aisle who refuses to be covered up. Perhaps form is not a cloth over the deep but a "cover up," in all the current uses of that phrase: "We have been monitoring developments," and so forth. And perhaps the language of stem and seed, sword and surrender has produced not a livable world but the laughing madman suddenly snapping into focus the sleepy corridor of a train much like this one:

> looking for what he's missed,
> laughing, gun at the end of his arm, over his
> > head, swinging back,
> tentacular, spitting seed, him the stalk of
> > the day, scattering seed, planting it deep—

What this entire meditation does, I think, is leave the act of seeing and making sense suspended in a very uneasy territory. There is no longer the option of simply clothing the deep nor of falling back into a stupor; there is a choice to be made here, a risk to be engaged with when we enter into language. What the poem does, I take it, is force the reader to crouch down with the writer—"on our knees"—as she opens up a sort of theater within which she insists that we speak. And as she describes the deep tensions loose on that stage, as she lets the limits of speech spark towards incandescence—*"my portion of time / my portion, full"*—she once again turns towards the reader and asks:

(can you stand it?)
   (get down and hide)
(live fast, cloth over a sea, breathe, breathe)

What Graham's poems ask in many different forms and voices, is whether language might remain the medium in which we live our lives. They ask whether we can both acknowledge our distance from words and use that distance to think with. To refer to *Materialism* one more time, they ask whether words, like a bullet "blazing" in a museum case recording the tooth marks of a soldier's silent scream during an amputation, might display "the toothed light" of thought making visible what it never dreams of owning:

How can the scream rise up out of its grave of matter?
How can the light drop down out of its grave of thought?

How can they cross over and the difference between them swell with
   existence?   (*M*, 100)

"Expand being," Whitman writes. Expand *in the writing*, Graham replies, where the "yellow of cries [is] forced through that mind's design" (*M*, 26), where "the difference between them swell[s] with / existence."

From *Regions of Unlikeness: Explaining Contemporary Poetry* (University of Nebraska Press, 1999)

Notes

   1. Jorie Graham, introduction to *The Best American Poetry 1990*, ed. Graham and David Lehman (New York: Macmillan, 1990), xxvii.
   2. Jorie Graham, "Some Notes on Silence," in *19 New American Poets of the Golden Gate*, ed. Philip Dow (New York: Harcourt Brace Jovanovich, 1984), 409.

3. Jorie Graham, *The Best American Poetry 1990*, xvi.

4. Stanley Cavell, *Disowning Knowledge in Six Plays of Shakespeare* (Cambridge: Cambridge University Press, 1987), 3.

5. Stanley Cavell, *In Quest of the Ordinary: Lines of Skepticism and Romanticism* (Chicago: University of Chicago Press, 1988), 5.

6. Stanley Cavell, *Themes Out of School* (San Francisco: North Point Press, 1984), 60.

7. Stanley Cavell, *The Claim of Reason: Wittgenstein, Skepticism, Morality, and Tragedy* (New York: Oxford University Press, 1979), 241.

8. Stanley Cavell, *In Quest of the Ordinary*, 5.

9. Cavell, *Quest*, 186.

10. Stanley Cavell, *The Claim of Reason*, 439.

11. Stanley Cavell, *Conditions Handsome and Unhandsome: The Constitution of Emersonian Perfectionism* (Chicago: University of Chicago Press, 1990), 61.

12. Stanley Cavell, *The Senses of Walden: An Expanded Edition* (Chicago: University of Chicago Press, 1992), 92.

13. Stanley Cavell, *Disowning Knowledge*, 30.

14. Jorie Graham, *Erosion* (Princeton, N.J.: Princeton University Press, 1983), 56 (hereafter cited as *E*). Other Graham books cited here are *The End of Beauty* (New York: Ecco Press, 1987) (*EB*); *Region of Unlikeness* (New York: Ecco Press, 1991) (cited as *RU*); and *Materialism* (Hopewell, N.J.: Ecco Press, 1993) (cited as *M*).

15. Bonnie Costello, in "Jorie Graham: Art and Erosion," *Contemporary Literature* 33, no 2 (Summer 1992), 373–395, offers a careful look at *Erosion*. Her claim that the book asserts "modernist values and ambitions"(374)—that is, that its "poems . . . aspire to the unity and completeness of an artifact"(373)—is quite different from mine. Where my eye goes toward the poems' "quickening" at the tension between the drive to go in and the tragic knowledge of the distance which will subvert that drive, Costello tends to return to the power of art. For example, concerning the end of this poem, she writes: "'The living' approaching the icon, 'go in' but never 'arrive.' Yet art's power to awaken our thoughts of the infinite assures its hold on us" (385). As I suggest in my introduction to the special issue in which this essay appears, Costello's piece also makes clear that *Erosion* can't sustain such a "desire for presence" and points the way toward Graham's three most recent books. Costello also offers valuable and differently focused readings of poems that I discuss here, including "Kimono," "San Sepolcro," and "At Luca Signorelli's Resurrection of the Body."

16. Helen Vendler, "Jorie Graham: The Moment of Excess," in *The Breaking of Style: Hopkins, Heaney, Graham* (Cambridge, Mass.: Harvard University Press, 1995), links the short lines of this poem to the mind's "precise investigative use of its various scalpels" (77). In an extended reading of this poem in "Jorie Graham: The Nameless and the Material," from *The Given and the Made: Strategies of Poetic Redefinition* (Cambridge, Mass.: Harvard University Press, 1995), Vendler writes movingly of the uneasiness of this poem and the way the poet "persistently questions the premise of the painting." See 99–104.

17. Writing about *Region of Unlikeness*, but responding to all of Graham's work, Helen Vendler describes this contrast as "the tension between existence and death. These are its ultimate terms; but the tension is also expressed as that between other polarities, such as continuity and closure, indeterminacy and outline, being and temporality, or experience and

art. . . . The Graham muse sings two siren songs: one says, 'Hurry: *name* it'; the other says, 'Delay: *be* it'" (223–224). See "Mapping the Air," in *Soul Says: On Recent Poetry* (Cambridge, Mass.: Harvard University Press, 1995), 212–234.

18. I would contrast this view to that of James Longenbach in *Modern Poetry after Modernism* (New York: Oxford University Press, 1997). Concentrating on the analogical method of this and similar poems but not taking into account Graham's unsettling turn toward her own work, Longenbach claims that this last section of "The Age of Reason" "solve[s] the poem's puzzle before we have a chance to feel its mystery" (164).

19. Stanley Cavell, *The Senses of Walden*, 61.

20. See my discussion in the introduction to *Regions of Unlikeness: Explaining Contemporary Poetry* (Lincoln: University of Nebraska Press, 1999), 14–16.

21. See my discussion of "Two Paintings by Gustav Klimt" in *Regions of Unlikeness*, 22–25.

22. James Longenbach writes of these "Self-Portraits" that "they are sternly self-critical: each poem not only turns against the one before it but also turns on itself, collapsing the duality posited by its title" (*Modern Poetry*, 168). Helen Vendler, in "Jorie Graham: The Nameless and the Material," writes that the poems suggest "that there is always a 'gesture between' two points of opposition; that there is a way to be 'both parties' at the same time; and that one may find a way to create an alternating current, so to speak, between the weaving of life into the temporary closure of a shaped text, and the unweaving of that text into a less closed form" (106–107).

23. Helen Vendler describes this as "anatomiz[ing] the moment of suspension in being by isolating each of its successive seconds in its own numbered freeze-frame." See "Mapping the Air," 225–226.

24. In a strong reading of this poem, Charles Altieri remarks that Eve locates here "an alternative power": "writing can be a mode of insisting on a strangeness that transforms being estranged into a constant process of spinning out and realizing one's constantly shifting investments" (48, 51). See "Jorie Graham and Ann Lauterbach: Towards a Contemporary Poetry of Eloquence," *Cream City Review* 12 (Summer 1998), 45–72. Calvin Bedient does some interesting work with the notion of Eve "be[ing] free through digression" in this poem in "Kristeva and Poetry as Shattered Signification," *Critical Inquiry* 16, no. 4 (Summer 1990): 807–829.

25. Robert Hass, *Twentieth Century Pleasures: Prose on Poetry* (New York: Ecco Press, 1984), 305.

26. Elizabeth Bishop, "Cape Breton," in *The Complete Poems 1927–1979* (New York: Farrar, Straus & Giroux, 1983), 68.

27. For an opposed reading of the issue, see James Longenbach, who argues that "by drawing such a broad analogy between such bracingly different realms of human experience the poem itself ["From the New World"] seems tightly closed" (*Modern Poetry*, 165).

28. Helen Vendler notes that this poem drives toward the question "What is Being *like*?" See "Mapping the Air" in *Soul Says*, 228–231.

29. Helen Vendler reads this poem more darkly than I do, concluding after a thorough explication (249–253) that the poet is suspended in an "indeterminacy of . . . possibilities." See "Fin-de-Siècle Poetry: Jorie Graham" in *Soul Says*.

30. Thomas Gardner, *Regions of Unlikeness*, 230.

31. On suffering the limits of description, see Helen Vendler, who remarks that in this book Graham "attempt[s] to describe the material world with only minimal resort to the usual conceptual and philosophical resources of lyric (once so dear to her), and to make that description a vehicle for her personal struggle into comprehension and expression. . . ." ("Jorie Graham: The Nameless and the Material," 129).

32. Stanley Cavell, *The Senses of Walden: An Expanded Edition,* 64.

10

from Breaking and Making

Review of Swarm

STEPHEN YENSER

Jorie Graham's *Swarm* is abuzz with beginnings and rife with endings. To complicate matters, more than most volumes it asks to be read all at once. In this regard it is akin to other determinedly experimental, metaphysically ambitious, spiritually aware, eclectically informed, obsessively revised, and self-consciously subversive projects. If T. S. Eliot's *Four Quartets* were to collide with *The Waste Land*, the debris pattern might look like this. Among recent books, Frank Bidart's *Desire* and Michael Palmer's *Sun* share qualities with *Swarm*—qualities that appear earlier in David Jones's *Anathemata*, which Graham credits in her mercifully selective endnotes, and the work that made these others possible, Ezra Pound's *Cantos*. An aggregate of perceptions, reflections, monologues in the voices of mythical characters, and glosses on other works in a variety of free verse forms, *Swarm* seems to want to have no edges, no boundaries, no unchanging shape. When we read in the book's penultimate utterance (like most others here, it is not a complete sentence) of "the atom / saturated with situation," we have to remember "the atom still at the bottom of nature" in the first poem and all of the references to atoms between. "More atoms, more days, the noise of the sparrows, of the universals" is one of Graham's vividly disconcerting attempts to summarize at once the world—from its simplest component (at root *atom* means "not cut" or in Graham's formulation "already as little as can be") to its comprehensive and axiomatic principles—and this collection.

This book's universe (everything "turned into one") is a congregation of mixogamous bits each "saturated with situation" or thoroughly imbued with its context—though the concept of "context" might have to be altered: "Bless, blame, transvaluate— / Change context— / Unexpect context," she counsels us in "Eve"—so that as in a swarm of bees the distinction between unicity and multiplicity seems irrelevant. "To swarm," the jacket copy reminds us, "is to leave an originating organism—a hive, a home country, a stable sense of one's body, a stable hierarchy of values—in an attempt, by coming apart, to found a new form that will hold." If that rather overbearing definition leaves the species *Hymenoptera* in its rapidly broadening wake—the wake of the *Arbella* and its flotilla might come to mind instead—it nonetheless suggests the behavior of these poems. As in her earlier *Region of Unlikeness*, St. Augustine supplies the epigraph to this volume ("To say I love you is to say I want you to be"), and it might be that in conceptualizing its "swarm" we should think also of his description of God as a circle whose center is everywhere and whose circumference nowhere. Graham's "Prayer," an unusually straightforward poem indebted to Friedrich Hölderlin, ends with these lines: "I called you once and thought you once. / You travel to me on your allotted paths, // a light embrace, miraculously omnipresent."

In any case God is relevant. The first poem in *Swarm* presents itself as a fragment "from The Reformation Journal," and its title's religious overtones are soon reinforced. The poem begins with a bold statement as to how to read this book. As in *The End of Beauty*, where she numbered them, Graham separates her lines, in this case with extra leading and sometimes an asterisk:

> The wisdom I have heretofore trusted was cowardice, the leaper.
>
> *
>
> I am not lying. There is no lying in me,
>
> *
>
> I surrender myself like the sinking ship,
>
> *
>
> a burning wreck from which the depths will get theirs when the heights have gotten theirs
>
> *
>
> My throat is an open grave. I hide my face.
>
> *
>
> I have reduced all to lower case.
>
> I have crossed out passages.
>
> I have severely trimmed and cleared.
>
> *
>
> Locations are omitted.

Uncertain readings are inserted silently.

Abbreviations silently expanded.

*

A "he" referring to God may be capitalized
or not.

A rejection of her mode hitherto—which had been increasingly disjunctive but which she now wryly views as retrograde and cowardly and identifies with "the leaper," a figure that would be appropriate in George Puttenham's nomenclatorial inventions in *The Art of English Poesie* (where we find other terms we could adapt to our advantage here, including *the trespasser, the straggler,* and *the disabler*)—this passage outlines the new aesthetics, the reformation of the poet.

The new aesthetics springs from the Augustinian motivation to confront candidly whatever the case may be. Although we might find it hard to trust a statement such as "There is no lying in me," Graham certainly intends no irony—nor is she, I think, disingenuous. Regardless of whether she can possibly vouch for her own honesty, her claim implies an ambition and sets a standard. The aim is that of the aggressive spiritual exercise. Graham has not yet quite eliminated all humor from her poems, but the grim irony of the fourth line quoted earlier is about as funny as she gets (she asks near the book's end, "what do I do with my laughter"), and for the most part she is engaged in a struggle so strenuous that it makes one think of Jacob, teeth gritted, as it were, muscles bunched, bearing down as though in childbirth. And let the reader beware: to approach this book in good faith you must commit yourself to some version of the same agon. There are no extended luscious passages here, no spacious pastoral interludes in which you can loaf and invite your soul, no discursive retreats, no plots grassy or otherwise to fall back on. Indeed, there are precious few uninterrupted sentences. Some time ago Graham seems to have taken literally Pound's advice to "Leave blanks for what you do not know," and here her implicit ignorance joins with a certain *askesis* to produce as *hard* a text as I have encountered recently. One has to get at it in a new way—a way roughly analogous to that in which one first got at John Berryman's *Homage to Mistress Bradstreet* or Emily Dickinson's more elliptical poems in their manuscript forms. Some poets need to devise a language within the language.

The Dickinson poem Graham alludes to and says in an endnote "animates the book throughout" is number 640 in Thomas Johnson's edition of *The Complete Poems*. As Graham informs us, the title of her "For One Must Want / To

Shut the Other's Gaze" misquotes the fourth stanza of Dickinson's poem, one of her fiercest proclamations of love in separation. In the original, "One must wait / To shut the Other's Gaze down," but that verb is evidently not avid enough for Graham. The situation of the Dickinson poem, however, is to Graham's purpose. Beginning "I cannot live with You— / I would be Life— / And Life is over there," it addresses a lover who eclipses the deity: "Your Face / Would put out Jesus'," Dickinson blasphemes, and

> You saturated Sight—
> And I had no more Eyes
> For sordid excellence
> As Paradise.

Because of the ruinous potential of the love,

> We must meet apart—
> You there—I—here—
> With just the Door ajar
> That Oceans are—and Prayer—
> And that White Sustenance—
> Despair.

Graham's poem, whose imagery harks back to that of the shipwreck in the opening lines of the book, is a dark night of the soul in which she reflects on her predecessor's plight and her own:

> What are you thinking?
> Here on the bottom?
> What do you squint clear for yourself
> up there through the surface?
>
> Explain   door ajar.
> . . . .
> Here: tangle and seaweed
> . . . .
> Explain   saturated.
> Explain   and I had no more eyes.

Whether Dickinson's problematic poem is ultimately religious or not, Graham's must be, in the sense that it reiterates the search for the God mentioned at the outset. God also appears, I take it, in another guise with Dickinsonian connotations: "A wise man wants? // A master," Graham admits in "Underneath (9)," and then later in "Underneath (Always)":

> But, master, I've gone a far way down your path,
> emptying sounds from my throat like stones from my pockets,
> emptying them onto your lips, into your
> ear warm from sunlight.
> Not in time. My suit denied.

Not in time: Graham uses the phrase three more times in the ten lines following. The echo of Eliot's phrase in "Burnt Norton" has here two senses: the quester is too late, as it were, yet it is precisely only "not in time" (outside time, that is) that she can be successful. Near the end of her book, speaking as Eurydice, the poet still asks, "Where is my master? with whom share death?"

Graham casts her search in psalmic terms in "Probity," in one of the simplest passages in the volume:

> I have shown up sweet lord
>
> have put my hand out
>
> have looked for a long while
>
> have run a hand along
>
> looked for a symbol at the door
>
> a long while
>
> devices   prejudices
>
> have felt for the wounds
>
> have tired eyes

But they also might not be served who stand and wait. In Graham's relationship, too, there is still that "Door ajar / That Oceans are—and Prayer" between the two principals. Like Thomas the doubter she has "felt for the wounds," but unlike him she has been neither satisfied nor shamed. To be sure, the "sweet lord" she seeks does not always resemble Jesus. She also identifies deity with "atoms" (the "saturated" motif is just one link between the meditation on Dickinson and the book's opening and closing poems) and "universals." But whatever deity is, it has to do with *telos*, which has to do with death. In "Underneath (8)" the devastating possibility is put like this:

As in they shall seek death
     *
and shall not find   it
     *
What if there is   no end?
     *
What if there is no
     *
       punishment.
     *
As in   *it is written.*

God has to do, as that last phrase hints, with narrative. The speaker's search is a journeying across a "Desert / Dune," as one poem is called, a pursuit as by ghost riders over a wasteland ("invisible crowd, dust-risen faces . . . then cooling sand, then crack of voices riding by, // some laughter ticked-out over sand, // deeper and deeper into the open") of "the seriously wounded narrator" (not the poet, nota bene), who would be the author of "the true story" ("Underneath [9]"). The Fisher-King also puts in appearances as Odysseus, Agamemnon, Oedipus, Lear, and others, while Graham's "invisible crowd" recalls the "crowd [that] flowed over London Bridge," and perhaps also, in a book called *Swarm*, "those hooded hordes swarming / Over endless plains." But Graham's story is more fragmented than Eliot's.

 It is at the point precisely of story, of narrative, that writing and teleology intersect. To write consistently in full sentences and in lines without lacunae or to provide a "true story" would be for the poet to collude in the creation of the fable of purpose and unity. To break the sentence is to admit that the *sentence* is: to be broken. ("What if there is no // * // punishment?" What if Thomas cannot be shamed?) The pun on *sentence* is featured, along with related others, in "Fuse," in which the speaker is the Watchman in the beginning of Aeschylus' *Agamemnon* who waits, alone and seemingly interminably, for the lighting of the last in a chain of beacons that relay the news that Troy has fallen. "It is a sentence the long watch I keep," because until the watch is ended, it is a kind of punishment. The fragmented sentence is the sentence levied upon the Watchman. Later he tells us that, waiting for the "syntax" of signal fires to complete itself, he is "Always drowsy. Never spelled." ("Thy name is all, if I could spell," George Herbert exclaimed. What if the beacon is never lit?) "Dear sentence so filled with deferral": the apostrophe is the Watchman's and the poet's. The grammatical sentence beginning thus is itself never completed but after forty lines frays out in several directions and in this respect seems to refigure the book. Of course to the extent that the sentence is a life sentence, its conclusion can only be in death. Maybe death bestows meaning, in short—but it might also be that there is no end, no purpose. Perhaps "Chance replaces punishment," as the last poem hypothesizes. In other words, "Explain   accident," as Graham has it elsewhere.

One of the crucial accidents in *Swarm* repeats an event recorded in *Region of Unlikeness* in a poem called "The Phase after History." The first indication of it in this volume is in the second poem, "Try On":

Wings thickly lifting off the hidden
nest.

The sound of a hand-sized stone hitting dry ground
from a certain height.

Other inchoate references appear now and again, and then more than fifty pages later, in "Underneath (1)," they all come into focus:

Painful to look up.
No. Painful to look out.

Heard the bird hit the pane hard.
Didn't see it. Heard nothing
drop.

To look out and past the shimmering screen to the miles of
grasses.

Now when we look back through such small foreshadowings as "Wrecks left at the bottom, yes. // Space   birdless" to that first mention, and to its anticipation in "I surrender myself like the sinking ship, // * // a burning wreck," the poem coheres around the image of the bird—probably a sparrow, because sparrows appear elsewhere in *Swarm*, so that Hamlet's meditation on accident and providence is drawn into the orbit of the image, which image also helps to account for another rich phrase, repeated three times, in the opening poem: glassy ripeness. Whatever else these words signify, they could refer to the instant of the bird's death in the collision with the windowpane. *Glassy* might glance at Paul's promise in 1 Corinthians 13 to the effect that we shall one day, instead of apprehending God as through a glass darkly, see him face to face, and *ripeness* might well call up Edgar's pronouncement in *Lear* ("Men must endure / Their going hence, even as their coming hither: / Ripeness is all"), and in any event we will reflect on Graham's insistent if always undermined conjunction of death and revelation. As she has it in her concluding poem, in almost her last words,

> The woman of clay;
>
> I wanted to be broken, make no mistake.
>
> I wanted to enter light—and everywhere its mad colors.
>
> To be told best not to touch.
>
> To touch.
>
> For the farewell of it.

The speaker is in part Mary Magdalene wanting to touch the risen Christ ("Noli me tangere," he warns her), but she has read the later *Cantos*. In "Canto XCII," for instance, Pound beseeches "Lux in diafana, / Creatrix," that his daughter be able to "walk in peace in her basilica, / The light there almost solid"—and we find an "Invisible basilica your willingness its floor" in Graham's "Daphne," where she also writes "Let light come into taste light," as well as "light touching everything / grace and slenderness of its touching" in juxtaposition with "to make the basilica of divine hazard" in her "Underneath (Uplands)." If, earlier in this same poem, which is "Underneath (Calypso)," we might suspect another more eccentric allusion to EP, especially since, according to his *donnée* he is the Odysseus to whom Calypso speaks—

> Why should the exile   return home?
>
> Era?   Period?

—we might be forgiven on the basis of the dense intertextuality of the book, which is in the end not a collection of poems or a sequence, really, but indeed a swarm.

Images comparable in structural importance to that of the bird abound in the book. In a longer essay one could follow among others the changes rung on the "door ajar," veils, empire, mirrors, and conjunctions of ear and mouth. That is the nature of *Swarm* as one warms to it: it's busy as bees, coherent but uncontainable, on the move, unpredictable, part of a process, and always reforming itself. The wineglass shattered underfoot in the Jewish wedding ceremony portends wholeness. For her part, Graham is deeply antinomian, perhaps philosophically anarchist, but never chaotic. She is grammatically and punctuationally promiscuous in the service of fidelity to a kaleidoscopic vision of things as she thinks they are, things that again remind us of Hopkins, things

> variegated   dappled   spangled   intricately wrought
>
> complicated   abstruse   subtle   devious
>
> scintillating with change and ambiguity

Graham's final lines (which might allude to Michelangelo's painting of Adam's initial human movement as well as to Eve's transgression and Mary Magdalene's impulse) are as follows:

> To be told best not to touch.
> To touch.
>
> For the farewell of it.
>
> And the further replication.
>
> And the atom
>
> saturated with situation.
>
> And the statue put there to persuade me.

Statue derives, of course, from a root meaning "to stand, to be placed, to be erected," while *persuade* comes from words having to do with sweetness, pleasure, enticement. Graham's book concludes—pauses, rather, on a threshold—with an emblem sonorously, sensuously saturated with inception.

From *A Boundless Field: American Poetry at Large* (University of Michigan Press, 2002)

II

To Feel an Idea

Review of Swarm

JOANNA KLINK

> And out of what one sees and hears and out
> Of what one feels, who could have thought to make
> So many selves, so many sensuous worlds,
> As if the air, the mid-day air, was swarming
> With the metaphysical changes that occur,
> Merely in living as and where we live.
>
> —*Wallace Stevens,* "Esthétique du Mal"

In one of Jorie Graham's earliest poems, "The Geese," from *Hybrids of Plants and of Ghosts*, she writes about "a feeling the body gives the mind / of having missed something" (38). I know this feeling when I read her poems; you may have experienced it. Readers of Graham's work are often moved by her poems even while finding that the language is difficult—hard to process because it is abstract, but easy to feel in its urgency, its music, its expansiveness and baroque diction. There is a reason you might experience, in her poems, this feeling of the mind frantically outrunning the body, or the body reaching out across a great, ocean-like distance, through confusion and grim pain, with all its senses brightened, to meet the mind. The effort in each of Graham's books has been to bring the body and the mind in right relation to each other, to bring them so close that a surface seems to form between them—an edge, an iridescence, a "fine inner lining," as she calls it in "Le Manteau de Pascal," "a grace" (*Errancy*, 64).

Of course, all poets want to connect thinking and feeling. At the other extreme from poets like Williams, for whom the interembeddedness of experience and idea is given, Graham, in her own wholly distinctive way, confronts these domains as mutually resistant and, sometimes, as radically separate. She seeks, in the company of other High Moderns such as Eliot and Stevens, to construct a relationship between them. By the term "idea," in this context, I mean forces perceived to be outside the self that would shape and organize experience, forces general enough to include your experience and mine at once. Although Graham often encounters experience and idea as explosively incompatible, nevertheless she believes them to be equally real. To bring together what I experience of the world in my body, and the ideas by which I understand this experience, or to restore the body and the senses to the mind, is the "dream of the unified field," the prayer behind every poem. As she writes in a poem from *Swarm*, the effort is to "[hold] the mind in   like a wish   so deep" (7). Graham's project, then, daunting and dynamic enough to span seven books of poetry, involves two motions of spirit: on the one hand, coaxing ideas—in their pre-entanglement with things—out of the visible world, that they might be apprehended and recognized; on the other hand, translating ideas into physical realities, bringing them down into the body so that they are particular, concrete, visceral, known. In both motions, Graham struggles to make the collective life something deeply felt, deeply lived.

You can sense an idea "entering" the world in Graham's poems whenever a form starts to settle over the words, forcing the onrush of language into fixed syntactical arrangements or strict numbered sequences; when phrases are interrupted or broken off; when blanks and dashes are inserted; when story, plot, and closure start to bear down on a lingering incident; when strings of questions appear. This difficulty you feel in the language is the resistance the body feels to an organizing idea. Because finally the speakers in these poems *want* to feel, want to let forces beyond the self—of reason, say, or history—open up, to inhabit them in their complexity, to suspend them long enough that they might be received as a freedom as well as a responsibility. This accounts for the persistent emphasis in Graham's poems on delay. As an idea is drawn toward enactment (not its enactment, in the sense of its illustration or example, but *an* enactment—an embodiment in a person's life), the poem tries to hold open its exigencies as long as possible. Graham throws her voice into an ever-widening present, allowing each moment to open up, keeping the sensation alive as long as she can. She does this differently in each book, but generally speaking she tends to resist story-line and linear, cause-and-effect thinking; to string out clauses literally to their splitting point with parentheses, descriptive asides and revisions within the line; to weave together personal anecdotes, myth, metanarrative, and self-conscious commentary (as she does in "The Phase after History" and "Le Manteau de Pascal") so that the music doesn't have to end.

What shuts this process down is, in the rhetorical sense, "definition." When an idea is named, or its effect in the world identified, determined, or explained, its grip on the body is lost. In Graham's poetry, there is an important, uncomfortable difference between inhabiting an idea and possessing it. (This is the principle concern of her book *Materialism*.) If it can be located intellectually (in my life, equality involves such and such), there is no need to feel it, precisely because there is nothing left to discover. Most poems are in search of some truth or understanding; they are not pictures of a confident mind presenting an already fully understood and trusted attitude. As "Underneath 8" expresses this,

> Make the sore   not heal   into meaning.
>
> Make the shallow waters   not take seaward   the mind.
>
> Let them wash it back continually onto the shore.
>
> Let them slap it back down onto the edges of the world.
>
> Onto the rocks. Into light unturned by wave. Still sands.
>
> Deposit back on the stillest shore all the messages tossed.
>
> Do not take   back in   the soundtrack.
>
> Let the cities stay where they were shouted out.
>
> Let the horizon   lower its heavy   lid.
>
> Agree   to be   seen.
>
> Deposit   silt
>
> Dream of   existence.
>
> Refuse   rescue.
>
> Overhear   love.
>
> *
>
> Where definition   first comes upon us   empire. (68–69)

The hope in this passage is that the horizon of meaning "agree to be seen," be discovered and concretely lived; that it might lower its heavy lid but not extinguish us entirely. While Graham wants to feel ideas at work in our lives, she does not want to be fully determined by them. As the "Le Manteau de Pascal" suggests, it is not that we are completed but that we are "filled with the *sensation* of being suddenly completed" (*Errancy*, 69). It is the presence of organizing ideas that compels such intense feeling in the first place.

"Empire" derives from the Latin *imperium*, to command absolute power, as an emperor might command sole authority over an imperial dominion. And of course the word also refers to the territories or peoples dominated, as in "the Roman Empire," and both meanings—the force of command and the region under command—are relevant in Graham's collection *Swarm*. For Graham, "empire" is among other things a metaphor for conceptual universality: the poems in this book try to stave off the dominion of ideas, which can crush personal freedoms, while harnessing some of their inclusive power—that power which makes us citizens. As the last phrase of the long poem "Probity" expresses this,

> we used to say it was a campaign
>
> to the edge of   empire.
>
> it is (101)

Graham's poems explore that region before self-definition slides into determinism; it is a campaign to the edge. But we need the empire—the general life, those forces that define us—in order to be able to say "it is," in order to know where the self starts and stops, where its delicate edges are. In the idiom of *Swarm*, which tries to get underneath the foundations of Western civilization and culture, if the city of Rome is never built up completely, it cannot be broken down. This lingering on the verge of definition is meant to keep that enforced separateness of generality from smothering the self. As Wallace Stevens (one of Graham's instructors in this problem) writes in "The Auroras of Autumn," an idea

> . . . is like a thing of ether that exists
> Almost as predicate. But it exists,
> It exists, it is visible, it is, it is.[1]

To make an idea visible—just visible enough that it feels real—is the task of Graham's poetry.

In two recent reviews of *Swarm*, Richard Eder and Adam Kirsch have suggested that Graham's new poems free themselves of the phenomenal realm altogether, that they withdraw from the sensuous world into such heights of abstraction that they sacrifice comprehension. Calling the poems in *Swarm* "private," both critics nevertheless call attention to one of the central experiences of reading her work: the mysterious, often violent, intermingling of ideas and sense-perceptions. For his part, Eder does not offer an interpretation of the larger project of *Swarm* and admits that "even as the brain struggles," the poems are physically bracing.[2] A good deal of his review is devoted to drawing attention to those very passages where Graham's sense-detail is most powerful. Kirsch, although acknowledging that "the way it feels to think is . . . one of the major subjects" of Graham's poetry, strains to interpret discrete poems in *Swarm* and determines that "there is no phenomenal presence" whatsoever in the poems, no "immediately comprehensible story. Indeed, the phenomenal experience of her poetry is a theoretical experience."[3] Of course, Kirsch uses these terms in unconventional ways. He lends "theoretical" a distinctly pejorative cast, so that it is not only synonymous with exegesis and the "assignment of themes" but involves opacity, over-conceptualization, statements about the limits of communicability, and deliberate obscurity. Likewise, he uses "phenomenal" in a thoroughly positive sense to encompass the poem's sound, its "literal meaning" (35), its plot, and anything else about the poem that he feels should declare itself outright. If we overlook for the moment some basic problems associated with using "theoretical" and "obscure" interchangeably, and with conflating many levels of meaning into one (*The Waste Land* is in trouble if, in order to have phenomenal presence, a poem's plot must be immediately apparent), we can see that Kirsch registers an active tension between two extremes of Graham's sensibility. The fact that Kirsch is left to conclude Graham's poetry is "about" the frustration of our perception indicates, at the very least, that he registers the resistance of thought to perception in her work. Indeed, both Kirsch and Eder acknowledge—look right into the face of—the acute sensory reach toward abstraction in *Swarm*, but they misread the orientation of these poems, which involves casting out from, and then drawing thought down into, the body. Insofar as Graham's poems fight to feel beyond the confines of a single self into a realm of collective experience, they risk, like those of the High Moderns, being "difficult," but it is exactly such an orientation that keeps Graham's poetry from being private or obscure. The complex energies in her language are an expression of the extent to which her voice is pitched outward, seeking ways to make the boundaries of a self more fluid and expansive.

Sense-details are at the core of most descriptive and figurative language. They arise when any kind of information—feelings, things, concepts—is filtered through the five senses. Sense-details summon a physical state in the reader, which is to say that you feel something suddenly and precisely. For Graham, to sense an idea means to touch it, hear it, taste it—it is transparent blue, it echoes, it's damp and sour and raw. Of course, sense-details not only place you back into your body and make you feel alive, they also ground your belief in a poem; they help convince you that an abstraction is as real as marble or flesh or crying birds. In Graham's prior books, and especially in *The Errancy*, close observation draws ideas out of the visible world. This is one of the techniques she takes from poets like Keats, Hopkins, and Bishop. She addresses things themselves—clouds, willow trees, floodwaters—and out of her engagement with these materials, out of watching and sensing, ideas arise. The presumption is that the ideas are there, just below the outermost surface of things, and that the task is to look hard and pay attention, for it is where things resist your desires—where they insist on their own nature apart from your subjective designs—that ideas take shape. In this kind of encounter, because ideas emerge from the bright outline of the world, the reader encounters them already couched in sense-detail. The concluding stanza of the poem "Try On" is a case in point:

> Wings thickly lifting off the hidden
> nest.
>
> The sound of a hand-sized stone hitting dry ground
> from a certain height.
>   *
> Holding the mind in   like a wish   so deep (7)

The heavy wings rise up against gravity in the first phrase, and you hear a low, rustling sound. The second phrase presents the opposite motion: a single stone after free-fall, dropping quickly, and the brief thud it makes on contact. Before you understand that the bird and the stone are at the mercy of laws of nature, you feel-hear tensions between gravity and flight at work in the concentrated effort to hold inward the mind. In effect, by the time this event has been classified (together these motions comprise what it feels like, to hold the mind inside), the reader has already recognized it *physically* as a conflict. This same process takes place over the course of entire poems. At the beginning of "Le Manteau de Pascal," for instance, there is a tactile description of Pascal's overcoat. The coat is "coarse," "elastic," a "wool gabardine mix" that bears a "grammatical weave" (65). Each button is "a peapod getting tucked back in," there is "harm with its planeloads folded up in the sleeves," and night-air inside the rips in the coat, and birds. The poem fits more and more of the world into the coat, so that when you arrive at the last section, when the idea of doubt is finally named—"I have put on my doubting, my wager, it is cold"—what you *hear* is: "I have put on my body, my wager, it is cold," because everything that was put into the coat now comprises a body. You believe, because you feel it, that Pascal's doubt involves his whole body, and that the body of the world is at risk.

Graham's other strategy for allowing ideas to acquire sense is to start with speculation and gradually bring it inside, to feel it issue into material. This strategy was explored most thoroughly in *The End of Beauty*, where different forms of closure and plot were slowly "admitted" (often to a breaking point) into human scenes patterned on myth. That book re-poses a central question from *Erosion*: "How far is true enough? How far into the earth can vision go and still be love?" ("The Age of Reason" 19)—or, how far into the body can vision go and still be felt? The end of beauty borders on the beginning of understanding, of ideas entering into the world to organize our lives, to help love along, to make it urgent. The poems from *Swarm* proceed with this same kind of investigation, where ideas like "history" and "universal law" seem to exist apart from the world and are drawn inside—often forced into—the speakers' lives, to the point where any stable sense of self starts to disperse. Because *Swarm* is formally very different from Graham's previous work, it is useful to consider how this process works in the new poems.

Swarm is a book of love poems. Love involves the whole cosmos; it involves feeling *and* knowing the beloved. Every action undertaken in this book, every description and realization, has some bearing on love—that elusive process which refuses any separation between body and mind. The main idiom of this book is to be underneath (there are fifteen poems that have "Underneath" as part of their title). The speakers in *Swarm* find themselves caught under their lovers' bodies, under the law, under judgment, under God. They seek some way to come to terms with these different forms of compelled obedience, to get, in effect, under Empire, below whatever sense of self has been colonized above ground, into the foundations of ancient Rome and Carthage, into the distilled remains of the Forum, the buried past. The foundations of the kingdom are in the body. The speakers want to inhabit the ground, the dirt, the cold soil from graves, so that depth becomes a metaphor for inwardness—slipping into tombs, digging deeper, feeling your way into ash and dark earth. Here the process of discovery is undertaken because there is always something more real, more authentic, farther underneath. The idea of history becomes dynamic when you take it inside your body, when you feel its materials—prints in the dirt, silt, burnt things—when you understand that these are the materials into which all bodies recede. As Graham writes in the poem "2/18/97," "Underneath, always, the soil that brightens and darkens" (13). Underneath, ultimately, are "the wondrous things," the treasures as yet "unperceived" (5)—selves hidden or buried, ourselves at our most private, individual, real. "O my beloved," says the speaker in "Underneath 9," "I speak of the absolute jewels" (11). The hope of these poems is that even our most private selves are connected—in the invisible buried city, in time, in the black earth itself, as pieces of clay and dust—and that, instead of being defined by sprawling claims of an Empire upon persons, "we be founded on infinite smallness" (5).

The tension in these poems between the idea of history and the person in history expresses itself formally. On the page, the poems seem suspended. Phrases proceed sometimes without logic, without punctuation, sometimes even without situation. In *Swarm*, ideas made inward splinter and unsettle the self, which has to rearrange itself into a different order to keep speaking, to survive not having a "first person." The title of the book calls attention to this activity. Like a swarm of insects or honeybees hovering together in the air, densely in motion, the self reassembles its parts—grains, bits of filament, syllables—in order to remain whole but still fluid. The swarm is a mediating, angelic cluster, a colony in which one can retain one's identity and yet participate. The urge to dismantle the first person and recoalesce into a more expansive self is something various "experimental" poets of the last century have explored, and certainly the poems from *Swarm* are indebted to the fractured, reaching prosodies of poets as different as David Jones and Michael Palmer. Graham recalls Jones's thematic preoccupations as well (especially as these are worked out in *The Anathemata* and *The Sleeping Lord*), staging her poems in the period of Rome's rise and fall. She is thinking about the foundations of Western culture, its productive and destructive collisions with the private self, about the ways such conflicts can create voice and a sense of identity.

As Helen Vendler has observed, many of Graham's poems manifest a kind of vertigo-effect, a "rapid zooming, in alternately short and long lines, between getting close and gaining distance."[4] In these poems, instead of accelerating a moment in history as she does in *The End of Beauty*, revealing all the things that can happen in a freeze-framed second, Graham slows it down, magnifies the instant, and as a result the lines are much shorter. There is a kind of condensation of attention that occurs in each poem, and moving from image to image is an archeological activity: you exhume the ruins of an object or a situation until it starts to take on sharp feature and relevance. The short line is an indication that the world appears in shards and must be built up, line by line—that the self has not yet been organized into a first person who can speak in full sentences. And yet a self *does* speak. A number of the poems begin with fractured, insistent demands, like "Needed explanation," "Explain   given to / explain   born of," "Pick   a card." A line, in other words, is built out of very little and has to carry a great deal of voice. Likewise, in the minimalism of this style, the speaker cannot avail herself of many words. Because there is a scarcity of names, there is pressure on each word to convey more meaning, to call up more history, to reach out more precisely to what's there. (This is in profound contrast to *The Errancy*, which is propelled by a radiant flood of diction. There the "I" can fill and empty itself of language as it needs, because language is abundant.) The stage directions that surface periodically in *Swarm* evidence this physical struggle for words. Frequently the speaker motions toward what would make her most whole, as in "Middle Distance":

> The "frontier labyrinth" (gestures)
>
> All the people in history (gestures further)
>
> The heart in my throat (spotlight on wilderness) (37)

Or the speaker is left, stagestruck, helplessly enacting desires without being able to articulate them in formal sentences ("For One Must Want / To Shut the Other's Gaze"):

> (Offstage: pointing-at)
> (Offstage: stones placing themselves on eyes) (55)

Having to build a self out of fragments, having to begin again in language, is the central problem of *Swarm*. The atom "[lays] its question at the bottom of nature" (4), and here the questions are always: what is the least one can say, in order to be understood; what is the least one can sense, in order to feel alive; what are the fewest materials a self needs, in order to hold together; what can you give up, in love, and still remain who you are; what is most minimally given, certain, true.

At those places when the speaker is most shattered, when the universal terms don't fit the private life, the poems tend to point it out, and one word that comes up repeatedly is "enjambment." "This is love," the poem will say, "this enjambment." At first glance it may seem peculiar that when the speaker is most stuck, most compromised by forces outside herself, it's called love. But these are the places where the speaker is the closest—the least separate from—other selves. The word *enjambment* comes from the French *enjamber*, meaning to step across, to straddle, to encroach upon. Many of Graham's new poems are built out of enjambed lines. Although the lines are broken up horizontally with gaps and caesurae, the phrases are threaded through—vertically—with spirit. Something, you feel, is not going to let them fall apart. This is love, this wanting to hold and be held up by something outside oneself.

The price of enjambment—love—is confusion; your sensibility disturbed;

your first person suspended. As the borders between lovers are undone (Daphne and Apollo, Clytemnestra and Agamemnon, Calypso and Ulysses), and as Rome's northern borders collapse, the speakers in these poems are faced with bewildering pain. The formal paring-down that happens in the line and in the diction is a figure of suffering. It is present as well in the images of desiccation and dust that run through the book: the recurrence of high noon, of choking, of straining to see above ground in excess sunlight, of razing forest, clearing or felling trees, of not being able to visualize an end. But this state of airlessness and middleness can be suffered—is willingly suffered—because there is the promise of life further underneath, the promise of regathering and re-feeling a more spacious sense of self. As different speakers acknowledge at various points in the book: "having lived it / leaves it possible" (4). When the speaker in "*from* The Reformation Journal" says, "Oh my beloved   I'm asking" (5), she does so in the hope that the beloved can be reached, that the ground will hold them both up, that the idea or the spirit will (as the Sibyl says) "come down through the sentences / to breathe" (25). In its most vulnerable form, this is the hope that human beings have that life will help them.

The "ground" here is the dirt, the foundation, the idea that exceeds my life and your life and supports us both. It is also, as I've been suggesting, the ground of language. In what is perhaps the most beautiful poem in this book, "Underneath (13)," Graham writes:

in our work we call this emotion

how a poem enters into the world

there is nothing wrong with the instrument

as here I would raise my voice but

the human being and the world cannot be equated (102–3)

Not only is it impossible that the world bend according to our wishes, it is not finally desirable. You and I, world and self, cannot be equated and *must* not be equated. But there is a middle ground where persons give up some sense of themselves for the sake of what we have in common—ideas and ideals—and where ideas shape themselves, become less general and less damaging, in the presence of another laughing, breathing person. A middleness, a lovely space opens up which allows ideas—including things "not yet true"—to slip into the real and become true ("Pollock and Canvas" [*End of Beauty* 87]). The mutual undoing between idea and person happens in this penultimate poem of *Swarm*, in the always breaking and regathering ground of language, and in the lyric refrain of "push past," "have faith," "undo":

> touch where it does not lead to war
>
> show me   exact spot
>
> climb the stairs
>
> lie on the bed
>
> have faith
>
> nerves wearing only moonlight lie down
>
> lie still patrol yr cage
>
> be a phenomenon
>
> at the bottom below the word
>
> intention, lick past it
>
> rip   years
>
> find the burning matter
>
> love allows it (I think)
>
> push past the freedom (smoke)
>
> push past   intelligence (smoke)
>
> whelm   sprawl
>
> (favorite city)   (god's tiny voices)
>
> hand over mouth
>
> let light arrive
>
> let the past strike us and go
>
> drift   undo
>
> if it please the dawn
>
> lean down
>
> say   hurt   undo ("Underneath 13" 103–5)

Like the poems that precede it, this poem does not acknowledge a difference between sex and love. Here the body of the beloved and the body of meaning—what that body means to the lover—have the same meaning. This blurring between person and idea is what enables the speaker, at last, to say "We exist":

there is in my mouth a ladder

climb down

presence of world

impassable   gap

pass

I am beside myself

you are inside me   as history

We exist   Meet me (105)

Problems are not solved in poems, at least not in any philosophical sense; they are imagined. Poems allow you to feel, deep in their music, the impact and urgency and relevance of a problem. In Graham's poetry, one overarching problem is how to make shared experience intensely inward, intensely felt. In an essay about silence that she wrote a long time ago, Graham says that what interests her most is how to "wrench a uniqueness, an identity, from the all-consuming whole" and, the other side of this problem, how to be "united with the unknown, to break out of this separateness" we feel.[5] Her poems imagine ways of bringing universals—the world of idea and spirit—into experience, of "press[ing] spirit into service" (as she says in the Hölderlin prayer), of seeing mind restored to body and sense. The difficulty in Graham's poems comes from the pressure of one world (the world we have in common) laid down upon another (the world of the self). In *Swarm*, Graham imagines to its utmost possibility how this "hallowed" world of ideas might find its way down into the sensuous realm, how a person might loosen the constraints of being a self without giving it up completely:

(you should see how the appointed

take their lethal

medicine, here in Carthage

love, in

Rome) (to make themselves marble) (although some blur

even as they drink) (far from the

patria) sweet thing of mine

I hold in with my

boundaries my having watched for so long

the ruined temple wondering

how does the hallowed come down to

the swag of clay and night as a broken

arch. The bluebird cries. ("Probity" 95–96)

How far is true enough? How far into the earth can vision go and still be love? Says the poem: there is no deep enough. To feel an idea means to inhabit the problem with the full force of your body and your mind, rather than just to think it. It creates a situation out of words that is concrete, visceral, real; one in which you are forced to consider deeply, to choose, to act, to be known by your action. The way you work for meaning when you read Graham's poems is part of this process, and so are those moments when you feel that something has been arrived-at, broken-through-to, or revealed. As Wallace Stevens writes in his essay "The Noble Rider and the Sound of Words," the poem allows us to feel the beauty within the conflict, to feel "the imagination pressing back against the pressure of reality. It seems . . . to have something to do with our self-preservation; and that . . . is why the expression of it, the sound of its words, helps us to live our lives."[6]

From *The Kenyon Review*

Notes

Quotations from Jorie Graham's poetry are from *The End of Beauty* (New York: Ecco Press, 1987); *Erosion* (Princeton, N.J.: Princeton University Press, 1983); *The Errancy* (Hopewell, N.J.: Ecco Press, 1997); *Hybrids of Plants and of Ghosts* (Princeton, N.J.: Princeton University Press, 1980); *Materialism* (Hopewell, N.J.: Ecco Press, 1993); *Region of Unlikeness* (New York: Ecco Press, 1991).

1. Wallace Stevens, *The Collected Poems* (New York: Alfred A. Knopf, 1991), 418.
2. Richard Eder, "A State of Withdrawal," *New York Times Book Review*, 2 January 2000, 9.

3. Adam Kirsch, "The End of Beauty," *The New Republic*, 13 March 2000, 42, 41.

4. Helen Vendler, "Fin-de-Siècle Poetry: Jorie Graham," in *Soul Says* (Cambridge, Mass.: Harvard University Press, 1995), 246.

5. Jorie Graham, "Some Notes on Silence," in *19 New American Poets of the Golden Gate*, ed. Philip Dow (New York: Harcourt Brace Jovanovich, 1984), 413.

6. Wallace Stevens, *The Necessary Angel: Essays on Reality and the Imagination* (New York: Random House, 1951), 36.

12

Indigo, Cyanine, Beryl

Review of Never

HELEN VENDLER

This new volume of poems by my Harvard colleague Jorie Graham, in its U.S. edition, bears on its jacket a detail from Vermeer's *The Astronomer*, showing the hand of the astronomer as it touches, almost affectionately, the zodiacal globe it is about to spin. Although the star-gazer cannot make physical contact with his remote field of vision, the caressing way his finger lies on the surface of the globe suggests his intense intimacy with the sky. The window that sheds light on the globe, enabling the astronomer to see it, presents the light of earth meeting the light of mind. We might take the astronomer as a figure for the poet, reaching forever towards a contour of sense-experience deeply known in the body, but unavailable in language except through the mind's mediation. Even the most intellectual poets begin as children enthralled by the senses through which the world is made known to them. The subsequent obsessive adult drive towards representation, entangling sense and mind in a Gordian knot, poses the problem underlying poetic composition: how to make a third thing, a linguistic one, in which the senses represent mind, and mind re-creates the senses. Every achieved poem is built on the paradox by which an object (the poem) reproduces, on the virtual plane of language, sense and mind moving inextricably together, as they do in every act of consciousness.

How to follow the flickers of consciousness without reducing it to "pure mentality" (that Platonic fiction) is one aim of the poetry of Jorie Graham; another (as Vermeer's all-comprehending globe suggests) is to accept consciousness as a universal without prior limitation by identity or location; a third is to caress the universe as one examines it. Graham named her marvelous selected poems (1974–94) *The Dream of the Unified Field*: perhaps *Never* could be thought of as the dream of a potentially unified (if now disunited) globe. The volume evolves in tandem with human evolution, beginning with the sea from which we came (contemplated by the poet alone at the shoreline) and ending with the altars we have deserted, as she finds herself in a church on Holy Saturday, herself the witness and recorder of "the taken-down God." In *Never* there are four poems with the word "prayer" in their title (representing that upward gaze so frequent in Graham's work); there are two called "Evolution" and several mentioning the sea or shore ("Gulls," "Dusk Shore Prayer," "Ebbtide," "Estuary," "Surf," and "High Tide"). An endnote to the first "Evolution" reveals the state of mind in which *Never* was written:

> During the 1850s, while Darwin was concluding *On the Origin of Species*, the rate of extinction [for species] is believed to have been one every five years. Today, the rate of extinction is estimated at one every nine minutes. Throughout the writing of this book, I was haunted by the sensation of that nine-minute span . . . My sense of that time frame [and its inevitable increase, even as we "speak"] inhabits, as well as structures, the book. It is written up against the sensation of what is now called "ecocide." I was also influenced by, among other texts, the "World Scientists' Warning to Humanity," sponsored by the Union of Concerned Scientists (1993).

To feel an extinction (a *never*) taking place every nine minutes, six species vanishing beyond recall every hour, more than a hundred per day, is to undergo a vertiginous sense of disappearance and irremediability. The world within which we have evolved is not ours for long, not as we have known it. In any case, the result of the fear of species extinction is to make Graham's lines even more intricate in their observation of the flux and reflux of the natural world. It is only very slowly that she makes her way from the seashore to the divine and human forms with which the book will close—the taken-down God, a homeless woman. The book's coda portrays evolution as what has impelled us into language, as nature thereby wills the representation of her contours into being. Literature is not a dream, distinct from the real from which it arises; nor is it a fever, a hysterical or diseased condition; rather, it is the painstaking transmutation and elaboration in language of what the expectant mind attentively receives. (My paraphrase does not represent the wave-like pushing of the tides of reality onto the shore of representation fitfully and thrustingly taking place in Graham's closing lines.)

In order to create on the page the mind in action, pushing and pausing, cresting and deepening, Graham has been driven, over her writing life, to many strategies. Before I return to *Never*, and its almost desperate moves towards amplitude of poetic response, I want to mention briefly earlier attempts by Graham to understand the relation of mind and world. In a recent interview (1996), she summed up the tension in her work between "encounter" and "resistance" as it changes over time:

> In each of the books, I essentially had an encounter with something I would consider "other," something that resists the will of the speaker. In . . . *Erosion*, the encounter was primarily with paintings—and what intrigued me about visual representations was their apparently eternal nature, the ways in which the events could not be altered and yet were always *taking place* . . . In . . . *The End of Beauty*, the place of paintings in that dynamic was taken by myth . . . In the book after that, *Region of Unlikeness*, I tried to use the kind of fact we think of as autobiographical as the texture against which I was testing my sense of what *knowing*, or *thinking*, or *feeling* is . . . It was an imaginative vertigo that was very useful for me, at that time. Obviously if I believed that facts were truly *real* I would just write out the narrative! Rather, because I believe that the thing that can be invented by the *presence* of the facts—what swirls around them, the cloud-chamber if you will, is real—much more so, perhaps, than the who-did-what-to-whom—I used it in that book.
>
> The book entitled *Materialism* in fact tries to use physical place as the resistant material.

These remarks concern the thematic or imaginative material for the books under discussion; I want to add a description of their corresponding stylistic ventures. The antiphonal symmetries of *Erosion* (1983) showed the mind in dialectical motion; in and out, back and forth. We find there a naked early phrasing of the longings that continue to animate *Never*: a desire that our sense-questings should "mend" and "change" us. To this, Graham adds that the world also desires, as we receive its conflicting aspects, that we should "mend" or "calm" its incoherences in our reciprocating consciousness:

>   Oh how we want
> to be taken
>   and changed,
> want to be mended
>   by what we enter.
>
> Is it thus
>   with the world?
> Does it wish us
>   to mend it,
> light and dark,
>   green

and flesh? Will it
   be free then?
I think the world
   is a desperate
element. It would have us
   calm it,

receive it.

("Scirocco")

The dialectical back-and-forth of *Erosion* proving too Procrustean a form for the myriad and flexible motions of the mind, Graham next resorted, in *The End of Beauty* (1987), to a filmic style, freezing the mind's action, frame by numbered frame. The paradigm for this step-by-step process is Penelope unweaving as she weaves, keeping alive in her mind Ulysses' desire for her by prolongation of her own desire for him:

<blockquote>

16
Yet what would she have if he were to arrive?
Sitting enthroned what would either have?
It is his wanting in the threads she has to keep alive for him,
scissoring and spinning and pulling the long minutes free, it is
17
the shapely and mournful delay she keeps alive for him the breathing
18
as the long body of the beach grows emptier awaiting him
19
gathering the holocaust in close to its heart growing more beautiful
20
under the meaning under the soft hands of its undoing

("Self-Portrait as Hurry and Delay")
</blockquote>

This self-scrutinizing frame-by-frame style was abandoned when continuous narrative memory was required for the autobiographical poems of *Region of Unlikeness* (1991). Memory oscillates (I quote from the poem "Picnic") between a past moment ("It was one day very near the end of childhood") and the same past moment revived as a living moment ("After lunch we took a walk"). Spliced into these two ways of "doing" memory is the "real" present-tense moment of writing, which compulsively swerves back into the past-which-is-nonetheless-present:

> Should I tell you who they are, there on the torn
> page—should we count them (nine)—and then the girl who
> was me
> at the edge of the blanket,
> two walking off towards what sounds like a stream now?
> Pay attention. Years pass. They are still there.

By the time of *Materialism* (1993), Graham has taken on the challenge of representing the self not only through its dialectics, or its reflexive consciousness, or its memory, but through its simulacra of the world. It was an astonishing leap of confidence. The poet says, implicitly: "If I describe how the world looks to me, you will know who I am." Sometimes altogether suppressing the "I," the poems (especially the several inscribed under the single title "Notes on the Reality of the Self") try to make the world think itself through the poet, so that she can, with her interpreting mind, supplement the current of a swollen river, "Expression pouring forth, all content no meaning." The multiple aspects of any observed scene compel her into a perspectival poetry: "I see it from here and then / I see it from here." No perspective can say "there": each one says "here." Doing justice to all aspects of the "unified field" (which can be seen only aspectually, degree by degree) requires longer poems, or sequences, with mini-sequences inside the main ones. The difficulty of adopting the aspectual principle can be seen in a (relatively short) passage that attempts to grasp the inscape of a crow. I quote only the opening of the passage, in which we are shown first a close-focus painterly examination of the crow's colors, then colors mutating in motion, then a summary view of the bird as a whole form:

> Closeup, he's blue—streaked iris blue, india-ink blue—and
> black—an oily, fiery set of blacks—none of them
> *true*—as where hate and order touch—something that cannot
> become known. Stages of black but without
> graduation. So there is no direction.
> All of this happened, yes. Then disappeared
> into the body of the crow, chorus of meanings,
> layers of blacks, then just the crow, plain, big,
> lifting his claws to walk thrustingly
> forward and back—indigo, cyanine, beryl, grape, steel . . .
>
> ("The Dream of the Unified Field")

This description keeps veering away from the eye into mental categories that attempt to dominate the eye, to bring meaningfulness to seeing. "What do I mean by *true*?" I mean "something that can become known." What do I mean by "something that cannot become known"? "An irreconcilable contradiction—as where hate and order touch." "I cannot fix a single blue or a single black as a name for this iridescent surface which, even as I define it as a mixture of blues and a mixture of blacks, mutates, as the bird walks, into a kaleidoscopic swirl of indigo, cyanine, beryl, grape, steel. . . ." "If I can't order the color into something known and *true*, can I perhaps order it under a scale, a graded spectrum, going from A to Z, in a direction running from darker to lighter, perhaps?" "No: there is no graduation or direction. No *truth* there." And in fact, as the poet then discovers, all these close-up aspects of color—irreconcilable, undirected—vanish in a longer view: they "disappear into the body of the crow" only to reappear in the glistening of his pacing walk. (The subsequent lines of this section extend to an X-ray anatomical view, a far-focus glimpse of the crow in flight, and the attempt to fix the form in memory, followed by an evaluation of the truth or falsity of representation.)

In *Materialism*, Graham proposes that since all resemblances are drawn from the natural world, everything we are and everything we think must be implicitly reproducible in phenomenal terms. She quotes in her preface Whitman's hymn to "appearances" from an early version of "Crossing Brooklyn Ferry":

> We *realize* the soul only by you, you faithful solids and fluids;
> Through you color, form, location, sublimity, ideality;
> Through you every proof, comparison, and all the suggestions and determinations of ourselves.
>
> You have waited, you always wait, you dumb, beautiful ministers!
> We receive you with free sense at last, and are insatiate henceforward . . .
> We fathom you not—we love you.

Whitman's faith in the evolutionary congruence of mind and object guaranteed, for him, the sufficiency of sense phenomena, those "dumb, beautiful ministers," as emblems of sublimity and ideality and proof. The modern poet is more likely to see universe and mind as incongruent, the one resisting any fixed interpretation by the other. *The End of Beauty*, with its mythological and marital dual self-portraits (as Adam and Eve, as Orpheus and Eurydice), had preserved the individuated subjectivity of the speaking voice. Once phenomena speak through the voice, however, the self is as fractured as the aspectual world. Forward direction is lost as the mind, in fission, hovers like diamond-dust over the scattered phenomena, and will not or cannot go forward to a formed conclusion, a shape.

This predicament yields the frantic exhaustion of "The Errancy," the title-poem of Graham's 1997 collection, which combines unstoppability and disappointment. As the poem evolves, it dissipates the forces it gains, then briefly forces its dissipation to cohere, and then watches its achieved coherence disperse into inefficacy. One of its summary passages remembers a lost utopia:

> Utopia: remember the sense of *direction* we loved,
> how it tunneled forwardly for us,
> and us so feudal in its wake—
> speckling of diamond-dust as I think of it now,
> that being carried forward by the notion of human
> perfectibility—like a pasture imposed
> on the rising vibrancy of endless diamond-dust . . .
> And how we would comply, some day. How we were *built* to fit and
>   comply—
> as handwriting fits to the form of its passion,
> no, to the form of its passionate bearer's fingerprintable i.d.,
> or, no, to the handkerchief she brings now to her haunted face

What style can we find which will leave behind our "feudal" selves that paid homage to providence, progress, and perfectibility, and enable us to find authentically modern selves that admit their tears—their contingency and fractionation and dispersal? The long forward drive of "The Errancy" belies its own professed disbelief in forward drives, while the disappointments of arrival ("aren't we tired? aren't we / going to close the elaborate folder") are contradicted by the last words of the poem, which reiterate the inescapable cycle of fulfillment and disintegration and dream: "oh perpetual bloom, dread fatigue, and drowsiness like leavening I / feel—"

In each of her books, Graham has rethought—by means of style—her relation to the world, a world which has included, besides natural phenomena, persons (grandparents, parents, companions, a daughter), sketches of her personal past, and historical events such as the Shoah, the assassination of John F. Kennedy, the perpetual alert of B-52s in the American prairie, or the Kyoto Accords. Still, her most shocking alteration of former habits occurred in *Swarm* (2000), in which her sentences disintegrated utterly. Her chief thematic preoccupation in *Swarm* is reflected in the many poems (16 of them) bearing the word "Underneath" in their title. Images of burial, of Eurydice in Hades, of falling into an excavated grave, of a flower being forced back down into its stalk, are matched by language that is (as the title of one poem has it) "spezzato," broken into small bits. "Tu ti spezzasti," "You broke yourself into pieces," says Ungaretti. A former way of life is being renounced in a string of "nevers" that forecast *Never* itself:

> All the rest I swear given back whole
> Never again empowered.
> Never again a thing that can come shaped
> out of a mouth—the world
> put in (have I already let it go) the world
> taken back out . . .
> Leave me the thing that cannot be thought—I will not
>   think it.
> ("2/18/97")

Swarm is a book more intelligible to those acquainted with Graham's work than to newcomers, since many of its broken lines gesture back to earlier integrations: Rome, the resurrected Christ, Eurydice. "Underneath (3)," for instance, interrogates the repudiated past and the diction associated with that past. Social phenomena (marriage, daughterhood) have become unreal; disjointed phrases repeat themselves in the brain; material things atomize themselves; birds make not song but noise; concepts, too, make noise unintelligibly filling the mind; as for the body, it weeps. We can see Graham's repudiation of her former sites of meaning in "Underneath (3)," which holds up to scrutiny the repudiated part and its conventional diction.

> explain   given to
> explain   born of
>
> explain preoccupied
>
> asks to be followed
> remains to be seen
>
> explain preoccupied
>
> mind all summer long filling with
> more atoms more day
> noise of the sparrows
> of the   universals
> have you counted the steps
>
> have you counted your steps

is crying now

(is crying now)

(is crying now)

"Underneath (13)" declares that "the human being and the world cannot be equated." The minimalism that is the stylistic consequence of incongruence and solitude and dissolution of past faiths dominates *Swarm*, in which the decomposition of the sentence is almost complete.

At the most crucial point in *Swarm*, the speaker sees "what appears to be / a pile of wretched flesh in a corner mildly brown." It turns out that this decaying body represents "the first person," and in "the desire now to lose all personal will" the speaker casts it off:

Look, I can rip it off (the pile in the
                            corner)

(once it beheld wondrous things)

. . .

  I'm writing this in the cold

keeping the parts from finding the whole again

page after page, unstitched, speaking for sand

Look I push the book off my desk

into the flood

("*from* The Reformation Journal [2]")

Having destroyed the sentence which (with its forward integration) represented her former first-person self, and having, like Prospero, drowned her book, what is the flayed poet of *Swarm* to do?

She will bring into being the new volume, *Never*, its title recognizing not only the extinction of the past but also further extinctions present and to come. She resolves to speak as an "impersonal" self whose "I" enunciates natural process, refusing the temptations of subjectivity ("O stubborn appetite: *I*, then *I*, / loping through the poem"). This resolve leads to a series of minutely articulated opening poems, in which the poet, standing at the Whitmanian and Stevensian shore where land and water, sea life and human life meet, contemplates the world in its purely physical motions, the ebb and flow of tides, the formation and dispersal of waves, predatory gulls and their food, the neighboring woods and their birds. The stylistic aim becomes the registering of sense perceptions not seriatim (as in the earlier phase-by-phase noticing of the colors of the crow) but simultaneously. Graham wants to bring into the lyric a polyvocality like that of those "impossible" opera recordings in which a single soprano sings (by overdubbing) both parts of a soprano duet. Graham makes her single voice multiple by the proliferation of slashes, parentheses standing alone, brackets standing alone, and parentheses within brackets. (A different graphic way of rendering this effect might be an "orchestral" one, in which phrases would appear on an upper and lower stave enclosing a medial vocal line, representing the way in which the thoughts of a single mind counterpoint each other.) Graham's brackets seem to enclose alternative phrases that the poet does not want to choose between: "No peace [of mind] [of heart], among the other / frequencies." The parentheses sometimes seem to indicate gestures or glances, as when wet sand is said to be "glassy (this side), packed smooth (that)," but more often are used to hold in mutual suspension a number of simultaneous phenomena, each one netted by a parenthesis. "Ebbtide," for instance, shows us a tidepool in which sandgrains advance in ranks to the conjunction of two rocks, where algae signal the entry-point from which the sandgrains will drop down into the pool and become silt. My sentence "describes" this fact, but Graham's lines want to create it in all its observed particularity and simultaneity. Hence her five sequential parentheses as we arrive at the algae:

>   algae
> signaling the entry point—(swarming but
>   swaying in
> unison, without advancing) (waiting for
>   some arrival)
> (the channel of them quickening)(the large espousal)(light
> beginning now to *touch* what had been only
>   underwater story)—
> until the gleaming flow of particles is finally
>   set down, is
>   stilled.

If Wallace Stevens had been writing this, he would have evened up the material inside each parenthesis into a pentameter, and would have written the phrases in apposition:

> Algae signaling the entry point . . .
> In unison, without advancing,
> Waiting for some arrival,
> The channel of them quickening,
> The large espousal,
> Light beginning now to *touch* what had been only underwater story.

Such a line-by-line formulation inevitably registers the events as a linear narrative harmoniously advancing. But Graham—with her parentheses for perceptions, her brackets for mental events, her dashes, her virgules, her Ammonsesque colons, and her spiky and suspenseful line-breaks—insists on the drama of simultaneity, as the mind absorbs many perceptions at once (the swarm of algae, their motions, their appearance of waiting for the arrival of the sandgrains, their quickening as the wave pushes in the sand, the meeting of sand and algae, the sandgrains and algae picking up a glister from the light).

Writing of this sort represents an ambitious attempt to make language equal to our perceptive body, with its several senses always in mutual interplay with the phenomenal world. It regularly ensconces perception not only within metaphor (that large espousal of inner and outer) but also within a glancing use of the pathetic fallacy (the algae "waiting for some arrival"). Graham asks patience of her readers as she invites them into the cloud-chamber of her attention, where numerous particles collide and part. Matter and antimatter (so to speak) cancel each other out, quanta of energy arise and vanish, electrons are gained and lost, atoms combine into molecules and disintegrate. She really wants us to "see" the motions of the world, if only because they bring us, by analogy, as close as we can come to the motions of consciousness. She is willing to indulge in extreme mannerism in order to reproduce, in what she believes to be an accurate way, the shimmer of body-mind as it attends to nature. And from the motions of nature she wants to build a new and reliable consciousness, one that will be as moving and integral as outworn religious and philosophical systems.

The daring and drama of *Never* increase as the book flows on from nature to culture. The poems are, in their length and unstoppable language, virtually unquotable in a short review. But to illustrate the drama of the writing, let me cite one passage from "Kyoto," in which Graham asks us to imagine one of those surpassingly beautiful formal *allées* of Europe, in which a long plot of grass is paralleled on each side by marble statues in *contrapposto* representing divinities (Diana with her bow and arrow) or mythological beings (Perseus with the head of the Gorgon). Such statues are encyclopedic embodied forms of European culture, with centuries of meaning in the stories behind them, centuries of classical sculpture behind their Renaissance shapes, centuries of conceptual and ethical thought in their allegorical extensions:

> Remember:
>   the statues you were looking at [in the
> old world] row after row in the beautiful garden,
> veined-marble after spring rain (so-called), weight placed on the one
> leg or the other, as if in gravity, although also actually
>   in gravity,
> arm on a hip, arm holding a
> book, a sword, a severed head—a bow, stone quills—some grapes
> proffered, long gazing out, long avenues of principles, adorned, with self,
>   with
> representation, naked for the most part, trees just-in-leaf all down
>   the lanes,
> and everywhere *principle*, hidden but manifest, what we have made
>   link up in the
> spine of time [the body of human making]—[.]

Having established her *allée*, and without breaking her long sentence, Graham swings her gaze from the Old World to the New and back again, asking us to engage in a thought-experiment concerning a possible future:

> I ask you now [with unexpected ease]
> [with rapid extension of mind, leaping] to come back from
>   here
> to the statues lining the avenue [mind/gaze now darting down it with
> a strange foraging hope] [as if feeding very quickly and furiously],
> ask you to see them blow up: to dust: all "at once": or "one at a time":
> down the wide avenue: lining both sides

The enormous human achievement of art, of shape-embodied thought, a nourishment after which the soul hungers, can (as we know) vanish by swift destruction (or slow attrition). What will we put in place of the integrations we have lost? And who will record those sublime integrations of the past before they disappear altogether?

As the scribe of the past becoming the present, "taking it down" as an amanuensis, Graham records in "The Taken-Down God" (on Holy Saturday) the way in which the carved body of Jesus has been taken down (in another sense) from the cross (to be restored only at the Mass for Easter). After a harrowing description of the steel-thorn-crowned crucified body on the church floor and of the faithful kissing its feet, the poet (brought up in Italy among the dramas of ritual) asks herself: "What are you carrying. You must / jettison it now." The poem comes to its thematic center in the baldest of sentences about the devastating loss of culture and the urgent yearning for a new structure of being. No parentheses here, no brackets, no virgules, no colons, only naked need:

> We write. We would like to live somewhere. We wish to
>   take down
> what will continue in all events to rise. We wish to not be erased from the
> picture. We wish to picture the erasure. The human earth and its appearance.
> The human and its disappearance. What do you think I've been about all this
>   long time,
> half-crazed, pen-in-hand, looking up, looking back down, taking it down,
> taking it *all* down. Look it is a burning really. See, the smoke
> rises from the altar.

This riveting seven-page poem is all drama, in which the reader is urged into active and strenuous co-operation (at the end restoring the Christ to the cross for the churchgoers, but also leaving the church: the last words are "you go out this door").

The pendant to "The Taken-Down God" is the second closing poem, "High Tide," a frightening meditation on the attempt at an ethical response to anonymous human misery. We begin in medias res as the poet sees a deranged homeless woman on the street:

> She held a sign that said Emergency [nothing else].
> Handwritten in pencil on the corrugated strip of boxtop.

Emergency ("[all caps]") is, so to speak, the woman's name: it is the identifying word she has chosen.

>   She: a woman of sixty: long gray and
> matted hair, many grays, also some blue in it: no light received or
>   fed back by
> her skin: and talking all day to the forever-descending in-
>   visible[.]

As the poet passes, the woman, "rags upon rags wrapping her," notices her. "I feel scribbled-in. Something inattentive has barely / written me in." Every day the poet sees the woman, and the woman sees the poet: "So I come close to her. / It takes form and time. Who would have expected it / would end this way. The journey out." When the "high tide" of the poem's title journeys out, it deposits debris on the shore, and the homeless woman is a piece of that debris. Graham makes the link in a flashback to tangled shore matter, which resembles the woman's entangled "rags upon rags." (The poem owes something to Whitman's great self-elegy "As I Ebb'd with the Ocean of Life.")

At dawn one day, the poet (coming back from the emergency room, prescription in hand) sees the woman sleeping on the brick sidewalk, the flap of her sleeping-bag exposing her cheek to the cold. Bending down to fold the flap "back over the freezing face, wind rattling wildly in my / paper sack, my face blown flat with cold" the poet grazes the woman's cheek—and finds

>   it's not
> a cheek, it's paste—or gum and some admixture—
> pull the hair back and it's not hair, it's wool and phloxed-up
> random yarns, old woolen caps stuffed in a stocking
> face, with gum laid on—or is it latex paint—onto
> the cheek, making a chin: it is a puppet: it is a place
>   *
> holding a place

The mind plunges down into what the empty simulacrum represents: the attempt to hold a sidewalk-place lest another take it, "this strict / eight feet of sidewalk in America," an America fixed in its fantasy-Utopias, "dreaming always of here from an // elsewhere, from a nowhere." The human debris left behind fuses with the shore debris, and the empty wrappings of the homeless with the empty sepulchre of Christ. The flurrying thoughts that close the poem are those of a balked mind, weighing questions of indifference and responsibility, the civic "created equal" and the unpayable debt it may impose, now and here:

> crashing, the wave deposits its gift: difference: indifference:
>
> and the long sepulchre: identity: open: *meanwhile* in the arms of
> *elsewhere:* someone has pushed the rock aside: I see
>
> the loan: I see its terms (maybe): I see the payable and
> the unpayable: the open-ended credit: created: equal: look.

It may be that with these closing poems—contemplating the taken-down God and the dearth of civic care—Graham has stretched the lyric to its utmost social extension. After each new book by Graham, I wonder what she will do next. Her courage in remaking her style over the years is exemplary (Yeats: "It is myself that I remake"). She has not shrunk from her large self-set tasks: to make language fit the mind's motions, to accept the burden of uncertain modernity, to describe phenomena passionately and exactly, to claim what she can (in the absence of a common culture) for feeling, for knowing, for thinking. The three languages of her upbringing (Italian, French, English), the countries in which she has lived (Italy, France, the United States), her mixed background (Jewish from her mother and Irish-American from her father) and her mixed fields of academic study (literature and film-making) account in part for her comprehensive, ever-evolving and inclusive view of the physical world and of human identity. She has learned from both classic and modern masters from Dante to Bishop, and her linguistic resource, especially in description, is astonishing. In the long sequences, she risks everything, and perhaps cannot always keep the several parts from flying apart—but the wildness of the risk is itself exhilarating to encounter. One can feel, reading the new work, a nostalgia for the shapeliness of the pure lyrics in *Erosion* and *The End of Beauty*. But no good poet can stand still, and to read under Graham's powerful impetus is to have one's consciousness, like molten glass, pulled into unforeseen—and sometimes almost unbearable—shapes.

From *London Review of Books*

13

Jorie Graham's _____s

THOMAS J. OTTEN

In her third book, *The End of Beauty* (1987), Jorie Graham begins to include in some of her poems blanks, word-length line segments denoting language's absence, like the kind meant to be filled in on a questionnaire or a grammar school quiz. These instances of italicized absence seem quite distinct from the extra-wide spaces between words Graham began using in the same book, spaces that draw out a caesura and therefore have a primarily temporal character. The blanks, on the other hand, are always part of a sentence's grammatical structure; hence, they almost always have a clear logical function even as they almost never have a clear solution or answer. In spite of the insistence in a poem in *Region of Unlikeness* (1991) that "you know this / already don't you fill in the blanks," only rarely do the poems with blanks present cues sufficiently explicit that a word seems to enter the gap and hover within the space of its own erasure (14). More often, the blank stays blank, and the apparent problem of filling in the right word gives way to the deeper problem of knowing how to read language's exclusion. Thus, the blank generates a strange ontology because while it is an emphatic mark of absence, Graham's usage endows it with substance: it usually serves as a noun, is usually used as a direct object or an object of a preposition, and is often a place or thing. Nothingness acquires a feeling of solidity as Graham's syntax endows this sign with what this sign excludes. What is so baffling, so conceptually difficult, about lines like "Mud, ash, _____,_____" and "corridors, windows, a meadow, the _____" and "Like a _____ this look between us" is that absence and substance occupy the same point and thus call on the reader to entertain simultaneously ideas that should logically exclude each other (*EB*, 25, 64, 65).

Understood in this light, the blank begins to emerge both as a stark graphic representation—an utterly simple picture—of lyric and as a reflection of late-twentieth-century material culture, a way of writing the surfaces and textures of contemporary everyday life. Considered from one angle, the blank reduces to their purest expression the alienating distance and opacity that give the lyric I its definitive and painful privacy. At the same time, the blank also replicates the nebulously material things characteristic of Graham's poems, things that hover on the furthest edge of a firm ontology, like the dust in the beam of a movie projector in "Fission" or the thin sheath of spandex stretched across a body in "The Dream of the Unified Field" or the floating colors, detached from any object, in an abstract expressionist painting that figure in "For Mark Rothko." Like those entities, the blank has a wavering materiality, one that renders the distance between persons as both a gap and a substance, a medium, something almost tangible. The blank and the things (or "things") associated with it become a concrete model for lyric, a way of giving a tenuous materiality to the tensions of the genre. "Materialism" is, in fact, one of Graham's key terms (it is the title of one of her books), just as one of her key images is the hole, whether a rip in fabric or a hole in the ground. While that term and that image may seem to pull in different directions, here they are virtually synonymous, for what Graham means by "materialism" is more akin to an ontological problem than it is to an assertion of the sufficiency or even just the primacy of the physical world. Like the ephemeral materials of late-century technology, like the gap between persons or between poet and reader, like the blanks themselves, holes are a hard case for the philosophical problem of what there is, almost a materialization of the ontological question. In this essay, then, I will argue for the inseparability of generic and material history as I seek to show how lyric's definition is subject to its changing physical analogues. Graham's blank offers the chance to see how the lyric genre intersects with the vagaries, the historical vicissitudes, of material culture.[1]

That there is something specifically lyrical about Graham's blank is signaled by the way it creates a visual pun on one of the definitive moments for lyric in the tradition of English poetry, Milton's meditation on his blindness in book 3 of *Paradise Lost*, a moment where the epic poet looks inward with the kind of intense loneliness that would become a dominant mood for the short poem of subjectivity.[2] In this passage, spiritual insight compensates for the poet's darkened physical sense of vision, a dialectic captured in small by the word *blanc*, which names darkness as whiteness and occlusion as revelation:

> But cloud instead, and ever-during dark
> Surrounds me, from the cheerful ways of men
> Cut off, and for the Book of knowledge fair
> Presented with a Universal blanc
> Of Nature's works to me expung'd and ras'd,
> And wisdom at one entrance quite shut out.
> So much the rather thou Celestial Light
> Shine inward, and the mind through all her powers
> Irradiate, there plant eyes, all mist from thence
> Purge and disperse, that I may see and tell
> Of things invisible to mortal sight. (3.45–55)

In "Untitled," a poem in *Region of Unlikeness* (17–18), Graham compresses the poetics of the Miltonic passage into a terse "And of what we spoke of in the dead of _____ once long ago." This is one of the few places where you can with reasonable certainty fill in one of Graham's blanks, since earlier lines in the poem and the impulse to complete a stock expression both work to fill this white space with "night." With its latent semantic meaning poised against its physical appearance, this blank materializes and performs the ambiguity of Milton's *blanc*, first because its white transparency yields a moment of readerly occlusion and then because when in a split second the moment of *éclaircissement* comes, that clarity consists of darkness. Graham's blank substantiates the dialectic between physical blindness and spiritual insight that in *Paradise Lost* is epitomized by the shifting, contradictory meanings of *blanc*, a word that in seventeenth-century usage can mean white or gray and that by means of its etymology shades into *black* (*blank* and *black* both derive from the Indo-European base *bhleg-*, "to burn, to gleam" [Bloom 78]). This Miltonic heritage makes clear that Graham's blank encapsulates and intertwines issues of separation and substance: it means being "[c]ut off," enjambed from "the cheerful ways of men" into a wavering space of cloud and clarity, of "things invisible," a space filled with ungraspable matter, whether mist or light. The "Universal blanc"—the space of poetry, as "-versal" underscores—materializes the sense of lack, endows absence itself with substance.[3]

The image in Graham's poetry that lends a paradoxical solidity to this absence filled in with itself, the image that endows this absence with something like a structure, is the hole, an entity Graham variously characterizes as a void, a palpable substance, and an aperture: an "empty" (the word is used as a noun) and a "gaping hole" (*EB*, 20; *Ey*, 11). In "To the Reader" (*EB*, 23–25), one of her first poems to include blanks, Graham articulates her theory of reading and her *ars poetica* around the image of a hole in the ground. In this poem, a girl "who is me" digs up a square yard of earth in the middle of a meadow, marking its edges with lines drawn with a spade, measuring its strata of leaf, loam, and clay with a ruler, and pulling apart its details—seedpods, moss, "riffraff the wind blew in"—with a tweezers (*EB*, 23–24). Recording her measurements in a notebook and preserving samples in plastic bags, she is working on a project "for Science Fair," an assignment that requires her to excavate this small plot and "to catalogue and press onto the page *all she could find in it* / and name" (23). The poem depicts this scientific project as the beginning of Graham's poetic one: this plot of ground is where "this begins," where writing originates. Even without that direct statement, it is clear that this poem is about poetic composition: perhaps the most sustained metaphor in English and American poetry is the figuring of poetry as cultivation, the lines of verse as rows of crops, the metaphors and rhetorical flourishes as flowers arranged in a garden.

"To the Reader" falls squarely within that tradition even while radically revising it. Instead of handing readers a flower, the poem hands them a _____, an analysis of the contents of a hole, an analysis that hovers above vacant space: "her hole in the loam like a saying in the midst of the field of patience, / fattening the air above it with detail, / an embellishment on the April air" (*EB*, 24). The hole serves as a material model for lyric because it gives a degree of density and definition to the spaces between persons while remaining true to the facts of absence and distance that are so often the lyric poem's generating cause. The work of lyric is that of "fattening . . . air"; it transforms the gap between the writer and the reader this poem overtly addresses into a substantial medium. Hence, it follows that late in the poem, when the speaker asks, "Where do we continue living now, in what terrain?" the answer is "Mud, ash, _____, _____" (25). The poem lists as parallel items the ungraspable, amorphous, protean substances of mud and ash with the redoubled and substantiated marks for absence that complete the line; the implication is that such nebulous matter is the ground of contemporary culture, that it epitomizes our experience in the world of spaces and things.

A second way of understanding this question and its answers is that the poem's continued life is somehow a matter of nebulous substances, holes, and blanks. This is the idea, the theory of reading, the poem explores in the extraordinarily complex image at its end. The poem depicts itself as a

> hole on the back of [a] man running
>
> through which what's coming towards him is coming into him, growing larger,

> a hole in his chest through which the trees in the distance are seen
> growing larger shoving out sky shoving out storyline
>
> until it's close it's all you can see this moment this hole in his back
>
> in which now a girl with a weed and a notebook appears.
>
> (*EB*, 25)

The hole in the ground with which the poem has identified itself becomes a cognitive space that is in turn fleshed out by the hole in the running man's back. The hole, the poem, becomes a perceptual tool that can take in the surrounding landscape and people it with the figure of the girl with weed and notebook. The poem ends, then, by offering us a model for how it does its work, a model in which Graham thinks through the matter of intersubjectivity by appealing to the strange materiality of holes. In the Magritte-like scenario with which the poem closes (a scenario that not only resonates with René Magritte's reversals of the represented and the real but also partakes of some of the painter's clinically surreal gruesomeness), the reader's experience is depicted as one of seeing through a nearly vertiginous series of holes, a series that connects the perceptions of the man, the girl, and the reader's own self.[4] But even if this very partial explanation holds, a formidable conceptual opacity remains here at the end of the poem, where the hole image is most highly elaborated; a sense of cognitive blockage sets in just where the poem offers an image that promises a clear aperture, windows between various selves. The poem's holes seem simultaneously transparent and opaque, void and material.

As "To the Reader" suggests, contemporary poetry "begins" with the hole, the blank. In other words, it begins with what T. J. Clark has described as modernity's "blankness," its "great emptying and sanitizing of the imagination" as "agreed-on" traditions lose their force and contingency fills their place. In modernity, Clark writes, "meaning is in short supply" (7). Clark's argument helps to suggest why it is that blankness and absence, the language of negation, come to be the modernist dialect. For Graham's emphatic use of empty space comes with a nearly century-old tradition trailing behind it. Reading the twentieth-century portion of *Earth Took of Earth*, Graham's anthology of her "indispensable poems" (xvii), one encounters the "nothingness" of the illusive transformations of Ezra Pound's Canto 2 (129), the "isolate flecks" with which William Carlos Williams closes "To Elsie" (126), the mythical "old stories" set adrift in the white space of the page in Robert Duncan's "A Poem Beginning with a Line by Pindar" (212), the definition of a poem as "erasures" in Donald Justice's "Poem," and the gap of immolation (an incineration of tradition) that appears at the end of Adrienne Rich's "The Burning of Paper instead of Children": "*burn the texts* said Artaud" (271). "Nothing" is one of modernism's key terms, a crucial word for Robert Frost—who counterpoises it with the indefinite "something," as Richard Poirier notes (317)—and for Wallace Stevens, whose "Snow Man" becomes "nothing himself" as he "beholds / Nothing that is not there and the nothing that is." Graham subjects this tradition of absence to a materialist reinterpretation; modernism's metaphor of nothingness receives in the holes of "To the Reader" as much concreteness as it can hold. Here it will be helpful to bring to bear two philosophical perspectives on holes and things. The first will be from recent analytic philosophy; the second will be Marx's historical materialism.

In an essay entitled "Holes," the philosophers David Lewis and Stephanie Lewis take up the question of whether a hole is a purely linguistic, immaterial entity or a real, material object, albeit one that is hard to describe. On the one hand, the word *hole* could be a description of a particular kind of shape, a word that designates an attribute, which ordinary speech misleadingly turns into a substantive: a piece of cheese can have holes in it, but that does not mean there is such a *thing* as a hole (3). On the other hand, perhaps holes are indeed material objects, not because they are filled with air or ether (although this possibility does briefly arise) but because they are defined by their material edges; what we call a hole would more accurately be labeled a "hole-lining" (5). As A. R. Ammons (another great ontologist of contemporary American poetry) puts it in his recent long poem *Glare*, "[E]ven nothing has a / rim around it, which makes it a / something" (117–18). The weaknesses of this solution, as the Lewises point out, are that defining the hole lining would then be perfectly arbitrary ("How much cheese do you include as part of one of these holes?") and that a hole would be then defined as solid substance, the opposite of what we intuitively think a hole is (6). As "Holes" unfolds and its competing intuitions and hypotheses accumulate, the hole emerges as a totally equivocal entity, a focal point for the endlessly contradictory relations that nonetheless govern the ways in which we take in and express the spatial and material world: a hole is an absence with a material edge to it, emptiness with a grain of substance, demonstrably a fiction—even a wholly linguistic entity—yet a fiction that points to a decidedly concrete thing that is also nothing.

Some of this uncertainty about what a thing (or nothing) is pertains as well in another philosophy of thingness—Marx's theory of the commodity, from which Graham quotes in the long poem "The Break of Day," originally entitled "Materialism" when it was first composed (*M*, 112–27). In the passage quoted, from *Capital*, Marx writes, "A commodity appears at first sight an extremely obvious, trivial thing. But its analysis brings out that it is a very strange thing, abounding in metaphysical subtleties and theological niceties" (Marx, 163). Once it enters the market, Marx writes in the same passage, an object is no longer an "ordinary, sensuous thing" but instead "changes into a thing which transcends sensuousness" as it forms the basis for a relation between persons, a relation it also negates, occludes, blanks out. Objects are everything to Marx: the pages of *Capital* are virtually overstocked with coats and gold and pins and flax and glass bottles and coal and bread. At the same time, objects are nothing in *Capital*, things whose physical substance dwindles away in importance when it is compared to the social significance that is nowhere discoverable within them.

These are the contexts in which we should understand the formulations in Graham that endow nothingness with a tenuously positive identity, that often specify an absence with the definite article: "the nothing-on-the-page," "the nothing with use in it," "a part of the place but cut out from the place," "The mind with the white hole in it," the "thick . . . empty" (*EB*, 47, 49, 85; *RU*, 53, 20). As we have seen in "To the Reader," Graham identifies her aesthetic with the problematic nature of holes and characterizes the work of poetry as that of solidifying a gap, "fattening the air . . . with detail." In "The Guardian Angel of the Swarm" (*Ey*, 81–84), a poem published ten years later, Graham thinks through more explicitly the ways in which she has predicated her writing on the materiality of absence. This poem quotes and reworks passages from Gilles Deleuze's book on Leibniz and the baroque. Graham turns to Leibniz because on Deleuze's reading he can be understood as materializing the spaces between persons and materializing them into a kind of perceptual matter. The distance between us as we sit beside each other or the distance between you and this page becomes the stuff, the substantiated space, of perception: as the next-to-last lines of the poem observe, "[T]he facade is riddled with holes, although there is no void / (a hole being only the site of a more rarified matter)," a formulation taken almost verbatim from Deleuze (*Ey*, 84; cf. Deleuze, 28). In Leibniz, there is nothing outside or apart from the monad, the basic and impenetrable unit of substance; hence, matter may have "different styles," but there is no such thing as an empty hole (*Ey*, 81). In *Toy Medium*, a recent study of materialism and lyric, Daniel Tiffany points out the persistence of Leibnizian thought in lyric poetry, especially lyric's penchant for things that hover on the border of materiality, like ether, rainbows, snow, and atoms (212).[5] Here I would like to go a step further and explain why this tradition is present and what it does in the specific instance of Graham's poetry. Leibniz answers here because his philosophy offers a universalist doctrine that does not deny holes and fissures, that can wrest a kind of concord and coherence from the riddled world without falsifying the world into an unruptured whole. The theory of the monad may be the closest thing in the history of philosophy to a grand unified theory of gaps, an ontology of a continuous material surface—"the dream of the unified field," Graham calls it in the title of her volume of selected poems—that is composed of units totally separate, fractured into disunity. Further, Leibniz's account of matter turns out to be oddly consonant with the particulate and virtual nature of contemporary materials like halogen, latex, plastic, and acrylic, substances named in *The Errancy* (58, 34, 13, 59). The Enlightenment philosophy becomes a tool that brings to light—heightens the visibility of—our own physical world.

Like her visual quotation from Milton and like her penchant for angels—the debate over whose physical substance spurred a huge cottage industry in Milton's time—Graham's conception of the hole reaches back to seventeenth-century materialism, the origins of modern materialism, but the intuitions and topoi of that tradition are brought to bear on a range of materials deeply characteristic of our own time, materials that define and shape the "terrain . . . [w]here . . . we continue living now," as "To the Reader" puts it. I will develop this point by detailing a list of substances, snapshots or swatches of Graham's material world. Alternatively, the following might be considered a catalog of Graham's technemes, the term by which Philippe Hamon designates the basic units of substance, the objects and resources that concretize ambiguity at a given moment in technological and literary history (192). My four examples are the beam of a movie projector, a latex shade, the property of color, and a Formica countertop. Taken together, they will lead to a closing indication of what is at stake for criticism of lyric poetry in the history of such surfaces.

In a poem called "Fission" (*RU*, 3–8), the speaker recalls the November afternoon in 1963 when as a young girl she sat in a movie theater watching Stanley Kubrick's *Lolita*. The image on the screen is of Humbert's first view of Lolita herself and then her reciprocal glance back at him through her famous sunglasses, her "heart-shaped shades" (4). The beam that creates these images is described as a "corridor of light / filled with dust," a "tunnel / of image-making dots licking the white sheet awake"; with this phrasing, the poem substantiates the pathways of sexual desire, finding in the dust motes and dots of light an ambivalent materiality that reflects both the emotionally real and so phenomenologically substantial presence and the vicissitudinous nature of the erotic pathways that connect persons (3, 4). As it "lick[s] the white sheet awake," the projector's beam reflects onto the speaker's face and finds its echoing reflection in her psyche as well; the film's story of the growth of a very young woman's sexual self-awareness repeats itself as the illuminated image on the screen "lick[s]" the "small body" of the speaker and she finds herself "want[ing] someone to love" (6). These reflections and quasimaterialized links dissolve—undergo fission, as the poem's title has it—when a screaming man runs to the front of the theater and delivers the news that President Kennedy has been shot. As the man struggles for the crowd's attention, the image on the screen begins "whiting . . . out" in successive stages: first it "grays" and "pales" as the houselights come on, and then it becomes "a smoldering of whites" as the theater's skylight is opened (4–5). Like the electron that splits the atom, the assassin's bullet breaks the bonds that hold the material—and so, for Graham, the affective—world together; dematerialized in the white light of fission, the image on the screen becomes "vague stutterings of light," "bits of moving zeros" in an "infinite virtuality," "not particulate." Early in the poem, persons had been held together by vision, the medium of love (Lolita's heart-shaped glasses), which had seemed so palpable that it resembled the physical contact between bodies (the beam "laps" and "lick[s]" the screen). Now the space in which vision operates has become an empty gap, one that provokes desperate attempts to bridge it: the man who announces the shooting waves his hat and weirdly slams "one hand flat / over the open / to somehow get / our attention," the speaker's father cries, a woman in the row behind begins to pray (5). Like the blanks, which in the reader's experience switch back and forth between substance and emptiness, the virtual matter of late-century technology alternately solidifies and dissolves, a fluctuation that comes to reflect the vicissitudes of the interpersonal.

In a poem near the beginning of *The Errancy* called "Spelled from the Shadows Aubade" (34–35), the speaker awakes with her eyes focused on a "latex shade," blank but with its "borders . . . gleam[ing]" from the rising sun. The room is still "grainy" and full of shadows, but the shade's edges are defined, "harshed-up" by the dawn until, at the end of the poem, the shade emerges as a "frame of light." The shade thus takes on the "dilation" and the "special luminosity" that Geoffrey Hartman identifies as the properties of mediating phenomena in modern poetry; it is like the fog and smoke in Wordsworth, nebulously material stuff that blurs the edges of the external world so that things outside the perceiving mind come to seem like intellectual substance (166). In the instance of Graham's latex shade, mediation is thickened into matter as the shade particulates, granulates, and atomizes into "lightflecks"—"bright bits of busyness"—the space between the lyric I and the outside world. Latex is an emulsion—rubber or plastic globules suspended in water. Considered as such, the medium of vision is a solid fluid, equivocal matter nearly though not entirely opaque; it lets through flitting shadows that could be flags or birds or clouds and leaves. Latex is also sticky and elastic and so epitomizes a recurrent impulse in Graham to convert the act of vision into adhesive matter that stretches between subject and object, to imagine the "iridescent sticky stare" as composed of "molecules of watching" that glue together perceiver and perceived (*RU*, 102; *M*, 132). Latex is also one of those highly adaptable and malleable multiuse products that reappear endlessly in the domestic environment, metamorphosing into glue, shades, paint, and synthetic rubber; as *The Errancy* unfolds, it remarks on this replication, noting first the latex shade, then, in another aubade, "the glittering exterior-latex" of a neighbor's house, and then the "sheen" of the interior latex a child's eyes "luster on" (34, 36, 92). Hence, latex substantiates a link between inner and outer, between a "tint of mind" and the objects the mind takes in (34). In such moments, the theory of vision Graham's poems articulate chooses tangibility and substance over transparency, even if—as in the case of the shade or the blanks—opacity is the price for that materialism.

In a poem called "The Lovers" (*EB*, 64–65), Graham imagines the interlocking gaze of a couple as "the glance, between them," "the glance afloat." The glance, the means of connection, is also described as a "howling and biting gap"; it is "[l]ike a _____ this look between us." The problem the poem tries to work out is how to give definition to this distance, this gaze—how to imagine it as something more than "dear nothingness," how to make visible the space across which persons connect emotionally. The poem likens the risky feeling of "a small terrified happiness" to "an idea of color / like an idea of color sinking to stain an instance, a *thing*"; hence, the poem imagines the _____ as a transient emotion and then gives that moment in time a wavering ontological status that is both nebulous, like an idea, and permanent, like a stain. The conceptual ambiguity and the physical properties associated with color here point toward a particular kind of painting; they evoke unprimed canvases saturated by poured or sprayed pigments, the color-field paintings of Mark Rothko and Morris Louis and their contemporaries. In an early poem entitled "For Mark Rothko" (*HPG*, 36–37), Graham similarly construes Rothko's aesthetic as one that depends on giving diaphanous color continuity over time and hence making something visible:

> Shall I say it is the constancy of persian red
> that permits me to see
> this persian-red bird
> come to sit now
> on the brick barbecue
> within my windowframe. Red

Like one of Rothko's nearly monochromatic paintings, the image this stanza frames offers closely related shades—the brick red, the persian red, the "Red" the stanza break strands from syntax—that waver between definition and dissolve, between keeping color continuously visible and blanking out vision by saturating it with an expanse of reds. Color becomes substantial—perhaps even "a *thing*," as "The Lovers" indicates—but substance is itself at issue.

In another poem about abstract expressionism, "Pollock and Canvas" (*EB*, 81–89), Graham writes that Jackson Pollock's aesthetic seeks "to paint nothing," a precisely equivocal phrase that itself grammatically hovers between the equally relevant alternatives of representing nothing and coating it with paint (88). As the "and" of her title suggests, Graham's poem about Pollock happens in the space between the brush and the canvas, "the blank," which Pollock "hover[ed]" above (82); color becomes an action that takes place in the gap, "mid-air," a whatness that will not stay put (84). In a 1967 essay on Jules Olitski's color-field spray paintings, Michael Fried defines the ontological question at work in Graham's concept of color, the historical shift in painting's representation of the material world that manifests itself in "The Lovers" and the poems about Rothko and Pollock. Characterizing the diaphanous, misty hazes of Olitski's canvases, in which color seems to exist as a thing in its own right, Fried argues that such paintings ask, "Why should a color be *of* an object at all, why can't color escape objects altogether?" (145). As "the idea of color" in "The Lovers" suggests, relationships between persons in Graham hover within this ontological schism in which color thickens the blank and bestows a "constancy" (*HPG*, 36) upon vision even as color loses its implications of solidity, its need to belong to an object. The equivocal materialism Graham discovers in new techniques and technologies like spray paint drives a wedge between objects and their properties. Hence, in a poem called "Room Tone" (*EB*, 73–76), two lovers who come "as close as one can" to another are "like the gloss of the thing and the thing," as the identification of things with their qualities fractures into proximity and the ontological questions of light and color stand in for the question of what a relationship is and whether it is real (74).

By now it should be clear that connection and separateness are what is at issue in the blank and in the substances that give that blank their substance. These forms of equivocal matter equivocate at the point where it is an askable question whether the spaces between us connect or divide, whether the transitory is present or absent, whether the amorphous is solid or dissolved. That this kind of material ambiguity is also a matter of ethics is developed most powerfully in "From the New World" (*RU*, 12–16), a poem centered on narratives of the Holocaust and thus placed in a context in which the burden to preserve memory—to keep something present, as an object does—is in tension with the conviction that materialism and image making and even just poetry are out of place, suspect because they reduce the distinctive atrocity of the death camps to the status of one stylized aesthetic object among many. The materialized blanks, the stuff of late-century culture, become a way of giving shape and solidity to an ethical dilemma, even a way of giving substance to the question of whether aesthetic objectification is a morally salutary response to annihilation.

In "From the New World," the speaker visits her grandmother in a nursing home at a time when the old woman's ability to remember persons and events is slipping away. The poem unfolds within the historical horizon of a trial in Israel of a concentration camp guard, identified in the 1980s by former camp prisoners. Hence, the visit to the grandmother occurs in a framework of testimony, evidence, and verification; on its microcosmic and macrocosmic levels, the poem works at the point where identity and experience are in danger of being lost, disavowed, or annihilated. This sense of erasure extends to the poem's speaker and to the poem's connection to other moments in Graham's work. It extends to the speaker because while she is explicitly identified as the poet, this identification happens in a negation and only there: the one time the poet's name appears is when the grandmother fails to recognize her, telling her, *"[N]o, you are not Jorie—but thank you for / saying you are. No. I'm sure. I know her you / see"* (*RU*, 13). This sense of relation as aporia extends to the poem's connection to other poems because while Graham's closest readers could be expected to associate—literally or thematically—this rest home with the one that names the poem "At the Long Island Jewish Geriatric Home" in *Erosion* (24–26), a book published eight years earlier, that relation is never firmly established. Jewish identity becomes a matter for indirection, for pronominal vagueness, as the speaker says that the experience in "From the New World" is "the one time I knew something about us / though I couldn't say what" (*RU*, 12).

The poem takes on the problems of how to imagine—to make into an image, to materialize—this sense of erasure, of absented reference, and how to forge some credible link between these experiences of annihilation (the death camps and the grandmother's loss of memory) without falsifying either one. In the now voluminous commentary on the Holocaust and art, these problems emerge as one of how to keep the Holocaust present without simultaneously redeeming its horror into something palatably humanized; as Adorno famously and radically termed it, the problem is whether it is not in fact "barbaric" to "continue to write poetry after Auschwitz" (87). More specifically, if the Holocaust is to be kept present, it must be translated into contemporary terms, a translation in which its indescribable horror must—so this anxiety goes—be compromised. As Ulrich Baer puts it in an essay on present-day photographs of the extermination camps, "How do we remember the *shoah* without forgetting that this event undermined the human capacity for memory and questioned the notion of survival in ways we are still struggling to comprehend?" (43).

In its opening and again at its close, Graham's poem makes this anxiety explicit by questioning the sufficiency of its own language. In its opening, the poem first invokes the gas chambers and the trial in Israel and then asks:

> Can you help me in this?
> Are you there in your stillness? Is it a real place?
>   God knows I too want the poem to continue,
>
> want the silky swerve into shapeliness
>   and then the click shut
> and then the issue of sincerity. . . .
>
> (*RU*, 12)

Faced with the incomprehensibility of the events it has summoned, the poem verges on blanking out its link to the reader, prematurely ending in silence, and then casts under suspicion the desires in this context for aesthetic pleasure ("the silky swerve into shapeliness") and for closure ("the click shut"). Like Adorno, who in his essay on the politics of literature after Auschwitz suspected both the "aesthetic stylistic principle" and the process of what he disparagingly called "working through the past" (88), Graham here questions the rightness and fitness of qualities that make poems poems. At its close, "From the New World" imagines a prisoner surviving the gas chamber, and then the poem stutters in a faltering repetition, "*Like* what, I wonder . . . *like what*, I whisper . . . *like, like*. . . ." (16). The substitutions of figurative language—the logic of *like* and *as*—are left dangling in incompletion because as tropes of comparison they are precisely unsuited for representing the incomparable. As Philippe Lacoue-Labarthe argues in his commentary on Paul Celan, one can only articulate the post-*shoah* abyss by stuttering, by "drawing a blank" (18, 19).[6]

Between these opening and closing performances of the ethical dilemma the Holocaust poses for the poetic image, the poem seeks to materialize that dilemma, seeks out an image that can reflect annihilation without falsifying it into something monumental and enduring. In the poem's narrative, this effort takes the form of the speaker's search for some refuge where she can compose herself after the shock of her grandmother's failure to recognize her, a non-recognition that resonates with the simultaneous trial of Ivan and the history of the death camps he guarded. When the speaker locks herself in the adjoining bathroom, these two moments of effacement come together in a profoundly uncomfortable association of death camp and nursing home as places where memory is erased, as places where Jews come to die. The speaker imagines that the bathroom is a gas chamber; there is gas on the floor ("something there on the floor now dissolving") and the room is filled with the visionary presence of the Holocaust's victims ("they were all in there . . . the about-to-be seized, / the about to be held down . . . hands up to their faces" [13]). For just a moment, the poem takes in the bathroom's accessories, first "the mirrored wall" and then "The sink. The gold-speck formica. The water / uncoiling" (14–15).

These details may seem of little significance, especially given the cataclysmic nature of other references in the poem. And yet "formica" all by itself captures and crystallizes most of the poem's work and the poem's ethical problem, both because it contains the word *form* and so suggests the process of giving form to the shapeless and absent, and because it carries with it the sense of metaphoric substitution (*Formica* derives from the material's origins as a substitute for mica in electrical insulation). In response to its own anxieties over the morality of the image, the poem materializes the process of dissolving as it wrests a moment of perception from substances that ultimately efface the perceiving subject. The clinical surfaces the poem details are ones that erase individual characteristics: they are institutional surfaces that will not stain and so can easily be purged of the traces of former occupants as new ones take their places. In other poems, Graham associates this kind of laminate material with mimesis: an "imitation-woodgrain tabletop" in *Materialism* (12), a "face that seems to shine / in the linoleum" in *The Errancy* (38). Here in "From the New World," that association is even more pronounced as the bathroom's mirrored wall, Formica countertop, and flowing water make the room a space of endless reflection. Hence, in this poem the space of erasure is also a space of mimesis and of particulate materialism. The poem switches back and forth between abyssal intimations of the final solution and an exaggeratedly close-up view of the material world; similarly, the poem represents a range of materials with careful specificity (noting the "goldspeck" details, for example), but those materials turn out to be not clearly defined images but instead specks, grains, dust motes, water draining away, fields on the point of visual dissolve. Like the blanks, like "the face that seems to shine / in the linoleum," Graham's imagery casts a human presence on matter that concretizes dissolution. Adorno's worries that artistic representations of the Holocaust would compromise its distinctiveness by rendering it one object among many and would endow it with a satisfying or at least alleviating sense of narrative closure are answered here by a metaphysics that keeps the question of matter hovering, that finds in the products of late-century technology a substantiated resistance to closure.

In "From the New World," the Holocaust emerges as a kind of ultimate circumference for the tenuousness of relationships, for the substantial emptiness between persons. In Graham, interpersonal relations in the late twentieth century are shadowed by Nazi genocide and by nuclear annihilation, as in "Fission."[7] These shadows become what Graham calls the "event horizon" for the interpersonal, a frame that bounds the understanding of some occurrence or routine action, shaping the constructions it is given and intensifying its import. More specifically, material processes and intimate personal relations—the daily life that continues in the face of atrocity—are tinged with and recoded by their widest historical and global context (the poem "Event Horizon" concerns the act of washing a stain from a red dress while the events at Tiananmen Square are unfolding [*Materialism*, 50–54]). The quotidian and the cataclysmic continually blend because in Graham's historical materialism the act of washing a dress is not some reassuring constant but is instead an image that reflects a changing horizon, one frequently filled with atrocity. The mimetic substances that figure relationship in Graham's poetry—water, mirrors, laminated surfaces, beams of light—reflect gaps and shadows. The blank, the space of connection, reflects the abyss that surrounds it.

What emerges in this way of understanding the blanks and the other characteristic substances of Graham's poetry is a culture in which the interpersonal takes on so much psychic weight that it comes to seem like a substantial thing; at the same time, the interpersonal is largely undefined by any larger frame and so is terrifyingly open and amorphous. Hence, in "The Lovers," "this look between us" is "[l]ike a _____" as relationships are both nullified and endowed with heightened or even exaggerated import. Here it will be revealing to notice some loose analogues between Graham's metaphors and those of social theorists who have worked to sum up late-modern experience. In *Sources of the Self: The Making of the Modern Identity*, Charles Taylor writes of a "bleached" sense of self, a self that is "ungrounded," defined only in terms of its own Cartesian awareness of itself, shorn of constitutive relations and set adrift in moral space (49, 175, 25). The modern self is "punctual," reduced to a single point in a vacuum, and so for Taylor the "map of our moral world" is full of "gaps" and "erasures," canceled relations to all that lies beyond the unimaginably small circumference of each component dot (49, 11). In *Modernity and Self-Identity*, Anthony Giddens distinguishes intimate relations in our time from those in tradition-bound eras by noting that relations today are "not anchored in external conditions of social or economic life"; such intimate bonds are "free-floating," experimental, "open," insecure, and "risky" (89, 91). Because they lack the definition provided by externally established protocols, such relationships have a "core" of "reflexive questioning" (91). Similarly, because sexuality is liberated from its reproductive telos, it becomes "plastic" and malleable (*Transformation*, 178). In *The Postmodern Condition*, Jean-François Lyotard argues that the social order can no longer be considered the unified totality claimed by the modern sociology of functionalism or be divided into the two antagonistic classes described by modern Marxism; rather, society is composed of selves woven into "a fabric of relations that is now more complex and mobile than ever before" (15). The postmodern social bond for Lyotard is a matter of the "'atomization' of the social into flexible networks of language games," utterances that follow elastic protocols and that make each self a linguistic "nodal point," utterances no longer contained by a master narrative (17, 15).

Thus, when social theorists conceptualize contemporary identity and the relations it is both stripped of and constituted by, these theorists' images take on qualities of the protean substance, the substance drained of color, and the abyss or gap that is construed both as a field open to new possibilities and as a terrifyingly empty space. The language of social theory becomes lyrical when it attempts to render the object of its inquiry as a physical object, when it needs to thicken and substantiate the space between persons while also acknowledging that space as a gap. The language of the interpersonal becomes an idiom of the materialized indefinite, an idiom in which social relations and material history shape each other. This sense of the materialized indefinite is why, I think, a moment in Walt Whitman echoes so powerfully in Graham, the moment where the poet asks, "What is it then between us?" in "Crossing Brooklyn Ferry" (310).[8] In Graham's implicit rereading of the line, Whitman's sentence becomes not a rhetorical question that collapses the temporal distance between speaker and addressee but instead something like a positive statement: between us lies what, the substantiated indefinite of contemporary materials, "[l]ike a _____." The mobility of pronouns' referential anchorages becomes the grammatical analogue of the slippages that constitute our contemporary sense of the material and the interpersonal.

I have been describing in this essay a material idiom of mediation, a repertoire of images and substances that shape and reflect back to us our understanding of social bonds, of affective ties, of what is between us. As the term *idiom* implies, these substances come to seem a kind of language, come to shade an understanding of what language is and how it does its work in the gap between persons. Hence all the materials this essay has examined allegorize the properties of writing: the projector's screen and the latex shade resemble blank pages, while "latex" carries an echo of "latent text"; paint is a medium of representation; Formica is in various senses a mimetic substance, and the particulate nature of its specks, like the dust in the projector's beam, imitates letters scattered across a page, "dots" that "connect" (*RU*, 106). In social theory, too, matter becomes "graffiti on air," as Graham calls it (*M*, 67): in Giddens, the "core" of the contemporary interpersonal relationship is a process of "reflexive questioning"; in Lyotard, the social realm "atomiz[es]" into "language games," as he puts it in *The Postmodern Condition*, or consists of "abyss[es]" and "gaps" between the language of moral prescription and the community that would be formed by such usages, as he puts it in *The Differend* (123, 144), a book Graham quotes in *Materialism* (72–73).[9] Hovering on the edge of what we think of as substantial, the language of contemporary lyric returns the pressures of modern intimacy to us as an ontological question; such poems represent their own language as graffiti—spray paint—in the moment before it settles on a surface, in the moment that it makes visible an emptiness, a hole.

This essay has attempted a materially specific reading of lyric imagery; it has tried to follow Graham's poems as they hone in on flecks of dust or glinting specks in Formica, the small spaces in the material world where intimacy is objectified and tested. I am arguing for a kind of attention to the materials and surfaces—the history—that lyric criticism has become tremendously proficient at abstracting away as it defines lyric in terms of recurrent, seemingly transhistorical rhetorical patterns: lyric is defined as a chiastic reduplication of means and ends (by Timothy Bahti), as the figure of apostrophe (by Jonathan Culler), as a moment in which language's allegorical and representational functions confront each other (by Paul de Man). In Sharon Cameron's work, timelessness itself becomes the defining characteristic of the lyric genre; what happens in lyric is "arrested, framed, and taken out of the flux of history" as incident is "sever[ed] . . . from context" (71).

Such analyses are triumphs of genre criticism, extraordinarily successful at generating reading methods widely portable across a range of disparate moments in literary history (Bahti's examples range from Shakespeare to Hölderlin to Celan, Cameron's from medieval lyric to Stevens). But these victories come at the price of a minute history, the history of subjectivity's changing material shapes and textures. If my reading of Graham's blank is accurate, then lyric history might be an account of how consciousness makes its own image out of the materials and technologies that constitute a given cultural moment, an account of how evolving materials yield an evolving idiom of identity and the interpersonal. In this argument, lyric emerges as the most intimate material history that literature records, the genre in which the gap—even just the physical distance—between a speaker and a world of objects is at its narrowest, the genre most dependent for its intelligibility on material things as they fill in and bestow a sense of location on the blank antecedent of the first-person pronoun. What material history can contribute to the study of lyric, then, is to show how subjectivity changes as isolation, connection, and desire are thought through the substantial and ephemeral things that surround the self. As the example of Graham's blanks suggests, lyric is a most sensitive register of how changing technology shades acts of self-definition.[10]

From *PMLA*

Notes

1. The blanks have received only the most passing of critical commentary, and the impression that emerges from this commentary is that they are an eccentricity that will not bear too much inspection. In a review of *The End of Beauty* published in the *New Yorker*, Vendler suggests that these gaps are the marks the poet makes "when she comes to a concept not yet conceivable" ("Married" 74), and then Vendler drops the matter entirely in her more recent, longer essays on Graham ("Nameless" and "Moment"). Gardner briefly suggests that the blanks appear when "naming . . . exhaust[s] itself" (181). Bedient treats the blanks as part of Graham's "elaborate system of deferrals of closure" (827); Costello makes the same point but far less sympathetically: "Graham's blanks represent a poetic failure—honest, perhaps, but hardly satisfying" (37–38). Longenbach, in an essay on the problematics of closure in Graham, never mentions the blanks, even though they seem highly pertinent to his theme. My own argument assumes that a dramatic change in the way lines of poetry are structured signals the presence of other, larger changes—in the way a genre is conceived, in the social relations that genre conceptualizes, in the imagery that finds its way into a poem—and that the blank is not so much a failure of language (as other critics have suggested it is) as a mark for changing material and social realities that cannot be adequately named in any other way.

2. On the various genres—including lyric—contained in Milton's epic, see Lewalski.

3. For further evidence that Graham thinks in Miltonic terms of this ambiguous materiality as the space of the interpersonal, see "Self-Portrait as the Gesture between Them (Adam and Eve)," the first poem in *The End of Beauty* (3–8). As its title implies, this poem recasts personal identity as interpersonal relations, which are in turn defined as operating in an amorphous, highly fraught zone of physical gesture (the poem's title refers to Eve's handing of the fruit to Adam).

4. For Graham's association of Magritte and holes, see the poems in *The Errancy* based on Magritte's *Le manteau de Pascal* (1954), a painting that depicts a huge and slightly ghostly topcoat full of holes that the stars of the night sky peep through.

5. Tiffany's explanation of the equivocal nature of matter is one of the aspects Graham singles out in her blurb for his book: "*Toy Medium* moves the question of Art's encounter with Science to an utterly original point of conflagration: where matter is mostly not matter" (qtd. in Tiffany, first unnumbered p.).

6. For further discussion of the breakdown of poetic logic and aesthetic mastery in Holocaust poetry, see the analysis of Celan's later work in Felman (25–40). In her commentary

in *Stupidity* on Wordsworth's "The Idiot Boy," Ronell builds on Lacoue-Labarthe's work by arguing that poetry identifies itself with the stupid, the nearly inarticulate: when it encounters an experience of "extreme unreadability," poetry is most itself, stripped down to its rhythms, to the tones of nondenotative language, like the stuttering of "From the New World" or the unintelligible "burrs" of Wordsworth's boy (272). In such moments, language fails but poetry succeeds. The argument is important for explaining how the semiologically void can convey a meaning that cognitively intelligible uses of language would falsify.

7. "What the End Is For" explicitly uses images of military technology to figure the dissolution of an interpersonal relationship (*EB*, 26–29); "History" and "Annunciation with a Bullet in It" attest to the presentness of the Holocaust (*Ey*, 64–65; *M*, 66–77).

8. The poem is quoted twice in *Materialism*, once as an epigraph to the volume and again as one of the extended quotations that appear between Graham's own poems (x–xi, 108).

9. The material quoted from Lyotard concerns the notorious controversies surrounding the verification of the reality of the Holocaust (*Differend*, 3–4, 8); Graham's poem places these controversies in an imagistic and thematic framework concerned with the materiality of language, the "one universal, stubborn black / out of which—*in* which?—the dark words *seem*" (*M*, 75). In this instance, the poem's images for writing—and hence for connections between persons and the sharing of histories between them—are almost literally shadowed by the Holocaust, while the unsureness of connections between persons is conveyed by the kind of amorphous materialism I have been seeking in this essay to identify.

10. For examples of the kind of work I am advocating here, see Fumerton on jewels, miniature portraits, and Renaissance sonnets; Scarry on paper and glass in Donne's lyrics; and Noland on machines and French poetic modernism. Like the present essay, these pieces of criticism proceed from the assumption that the lyric I "remains inarticulate until processed through a filter," as Noland puts it (202), and hence from the assumption that lyric's history must be a materialist history of the I's changing filters and mirrors.

Works Cited

Adorno, Theodor W. "Commitment." In vol. 2 of *Notes to Literature*, edited by Rolf Tiedemann, translated by Shierry Weber Nicholsen, 76–94. New York: Columbia University Press, 1992.

Ammons, A. R. *Glare*. New York: Norton, 1997.

Baer, Ulrich. "To Give Memory a Place: Holocaust Photography and the Landscape Tradition." *Representations* 69 (Winter 2000): 38–62.

Bahti, Timothy. *Ends of the Lyric: Direction and Consequence in Western Poetry*. Baltimore, Md.: Johns Hopkins University Press, 1996.

Bedient, Calvin. "Kristeva and Poetry as Shattered Signification." *Critical Inquiry* 16, no. 4 (Summer 1990): 807–29.

Bloom, Harold. *The Breaking of the Vessels*. Chicago: University of Chicago Press, 1982.

Cameron, Sharon. *Lyric Time: Dickinson and the Limits of Genre*. Baltimore, Md.: Johns Hopkins University Press, 1979.

Clark, T. J. *Farewell to an Idea: Episodes from a History of Modernism*. New Haven: Yale University Press, 1999.

Costello, Bonnie. "The Big Hunger." *New Republic*, 27 January 1992: 36–39.
Culler, Jonathan. "Apostrophe." In *The Pursuit of Signs: Semiotics, Literature, Deconstruction*, 135–54. Ithaca, N.Y.: Cornell University Press, 1981.
Deleuze, Gilles. *The Fold: Leibniz and the Baroque*. Trans. Tom Conley. Minneapolis: University of Minnesota Press, 1993.
de Man, Paul. "Lyric and Modernity." In *Blindness and Insight: Essays in the Rhetoric of Contemporary Criticism*, 166–86. 2nd ed. Minneapolis: University of Minnesota Press, 1983.
Duncan, Robert. "A Poem Beginning with a Line by Pindar." Graham, *Earth*, 204–12.
Felman, Shoshana. "Education and Crisis: or, The Vicissitudes of Teaching." In *Testimony: Crises of Witnessing in Literature, Psychoanalysis, and History*, by Felman and Dori Laub, 1–56. New York: Routledge, 1992.
Fried, Michael. "Jules Olitski." 1967. *Art and Objecthood: Essays and Reviews*, 132–47. Chicago: University of Chicago Press, 1998.
Fumerton, Patricia. *Cultural Aesthetics: Renaissance Literature and the Practice of Social Ornament*. Chicago: University of Chicago Press, 1991.
Gardner, Thomas. "Jorie Graham's Incandescence." In *Regions of Unlikeness: Explaining Contemporary Poetry*, 168–213. Lincoln: University of Nebraska Press, 1999.
Giddens, Anthony. *Modernity and Self-Identity: Self and Society in the Late Modern Age*. Stanford, Calif.: Stanford University Press, 1991.
———. *The Transformation of Intimacy: Sexuality, Love, and Eroticism in Modern Societies*. Stanford, Calif.: Stanford University Press, 1992.
Graham. Jorie. *The Dream of the Unified Field: Selected Poems 1974–1994*. Hopewell, N.J.: Ecco, 1995.
———, ed. *Earth Took of Earth: 100 Great Poems of the English Language*. Hopewell, N.J.: Ecco, 1996.
———. *The End of Beauty*. New York: Ecco, 1987.
———. *Erosion*. Princeton, N.J.: Princeton University Press, 1983.
———. *The Errancy*. Hopewell, N.J.: Ecco, 1997.
———. *Hybrids of Plants and of Ghosts*. Princeton, N.J.: Princeton University Press, 1980.
———. *Materialism*. Hopewell, N.J.: Ecco, 1995.
———. *Region of Unlikeness*. New York: Ecco, 1991.
Hamon, Philippe. *Expositions: Literature and Architecture in Nineteenth-Century France*. Trans. Katia Sainson-Frank and Lisa Maguire. Berkeley: University of California Press, 1992.
Hartman, Geoffrey H. *The Unmediated Vision: An Interpretation of Wordsworth, Hopkins, Rilke, and Valéry*. New Haven: Yale University Press, 1954.
Justice, Donald. "Poem." Graham, *Earth*, 238–39.
Lacoue-Labarthe, Philippe. *Poetry as Experience*. Trans. Andrea Tarnowski. Stanford, Calif.: Stanford University Press, 1999.
Lewalski, Barbara. "The Genres of *Paradise Lost:* Literary Genre as a Means of Accommodation." *Milton Studies* 17 (1983): 75–103.
Lewis, David, and Stephanie Lewis. "Holes." In vol. 1 of *Philosophical Papers*, by David Lewis, 3–9. New York: Oxford University Press, 1983.
Longenbach, James. "Jorie Graham's Big Hunger." In *Modern Poetry after Modernism*, 158–76. New York: Oxford University Press, 1997.

Lyotard, Jean-François. *The Differend: Phrases in Dispute.* Trans. Georges Van Den Abbeele. Minneapolis: University of Minnesota Press, 1988.

———. *The Postmodern Condition: A Report on Knowledge.* Trans. Geoff Bennington and Brian Massumi. Minneapolis: University of Minnesota Pres, 1984.

Marx, Karl. *Capital: A Critique of Political Economy.* Vol. 1. Trans. Ben Fowkes. New York: Vintage, 1977.

Milton, John. *Paradise Lost.* In *Complete Poems and Major Prose,* 173–469. Ed. Merritt Y. Hughes. Indianapolis: Bobbs, 1957.

Noland, Carrie. *Poetry at Stake: Lyric Aesthetics and the Challenge of Technology.* Princeton, N.J.: Princeton University Press, 1999.

Poirier, Richard. *Robert Frost: The Work of Knowing.* 1977. New ed. Stanford, Calif.: Stanford University Press, 1990.

Pound, Ezra. Canto 2. Graham, *Earth,* 127–31.

Rich, Adrienne. "The Burning of Paper instead of Children." Graham, *Earth,* 268–71.

Ronell, Avital. *Stupidity.* Urbana: University of Illinois Press, 2002.

Scarry, Elaine. "Donne: 'But Yet the Body Is His Booke.'" In *Literature and the Body: Essays on Populations and Persons,* 70–105. Ed. Scarry. Baltimore, Md.: Johns Hopkins University Press, 1988.

Stevens, Wallace. "The Snow Man." In *The Collected Poems of Wallace Stevens,* 9–10. New York: Vintage, 1954.

Taylor, Charles. *Sources of the Self: The Making of the Modern Identity.* Cambridge, Mass.: Harvard University Press, 1989.

Tiffany, Daniel. *Toy Medium: Materialism and Modern Lyric.* Berkeley: University of California Press, 2000.

Vendler, Helen. "Jorie Graham: The Moment of Excess." In *The Breaking of Style: Hopkins, Heaney, Graham,* 71–95. Cambridge, Mass.: Harvard University Press, 1995.

———. "Jorie Graham: The Nameless and the Material." In *The Given and the Made: Strategies of Poetic Redefinition,* 91–130. Cambridge, Mass.: Harvard University Press, 1995.

———. "Married to Hurry and Grim Song." *New Yorker.* 27 July 1987: 74–77.

Whitman, Walt. "Crossing Brooklyn Ferry." In *Complete Poetry and Collected Prose,* 308–12. Ed. Justin Kaplan. New York: Lib. of Amer., 1982.

Williams, William Carlos. "To Elsie." Graham, *Earth,* 124–26.

14

The Place of Jorie Graham

JAMES LONGENBACH

"I have crossed out passages," Jorie Graham tells us in the opening poem of *Swarm*, "I have severely trimmed and cleared."[1] Following the syntactical swoops and figurative flights of *The Errancy*, the poems of *Swarm* feel chastened, as if Graham needed to deny herself the satisfaction of her most hard-won pleasures. Most stringent is the fact, as she puts it, that "Locations are omitted" from the poems (*S*, 3). How do we read a book of lyric poetry that threatens to be spoken by no one from no place? I say *threatens* because the poems would be easier to read if they were clearly and unequivocally spoken by no one from no place. The poems are challenging because they simultaneously conjure and disperse locations.

Which is what all lyric poems do, not just those that advertise their acts of omission. Listen to Graham's "Untitled Two," from *The Errancy*.

> and then one girl, like a stairway appearing in the exhausted light,
> remembers the *reason* with a fast sharp gasp,
> and laughter rises, bending, from the chalice of five memories,
> as they move past us towards the railing of the lot,
> one stepping over, quick, one leaping high, giggling—red hair above her
>   as she
> drops—two whispering, one hands in pockets looking down
> as she, most carefully, leans into the quick step
> over the silver rail—oh bright forgetting place—then
> skips to catch up with the rest,
> and the rail gleams, and the rail overflows with corrugated light. (*Ey*, 27)

These lines describe the movement of several teen-aged girls through a congested parking lot. The cars "gather round, gloat, tangle, clot," and their drivers are a "gigantic sum of zeros that won't add" (*Ey*, 25, 26). In contrast to this unassimilated hoard of nameless people, the girls seem liberated: they move freely, speaking to one another. But if "Untitled Two" dramatizes the idea of a shared inner life, that idea remains elusive. We see the girls laughing and whispering; we feel the metaphysical weight of Graham's metaphors for these actions ("like a stairway appearing in the exhausted light"), and we experience the rush of movement embodied in her effortlessly convoluted syntax. But we never know what the "reason" motivating these clearly rendered actions might be.

At the center of *The Errancy* lies "Le Manteau de Pascal," a meditation on the coat in which Pascal was buried—the coat in which Pascal's sister sewed the philosopher's never-revealed proof of the existence of god. At the center of the poem is a line that will be repeated four times: "You do understand, don't you, by looking?" (*Ey*, 65). With each repetition the question seems less rhetorical, more urgent. It registers not only an awareness of how little we have understood but also the conviction that all we can do is look again: whatever we know about the spirit within the body, the meaning within the poem, we know as surface, an exterior. "Dreams are nothing other than a particular *form* of thinking," said Freud, emphasizing that the surface is all an interpreter knows: "It is the *dreamwork* which creates that form, and it alone is the essence of dreaming."[2] Throughout *The Errancy* Graham weaves a vividly sensuous surface—a coat—enticing us with the possibility of a reason without necessarily positing it. "It has a fine inner lining," says Graham, "but it is / as an exterior that you see it" (*Ey*, 64).

To say that a poem wears its essence like a coat might seem like a justification of a concertedly abstruse manner of writing, but in fact the same thing may be said of the pointedly lucid poems of Elizabeth Bishop.

> A small bus comes along, in up-and-down rushes,
> packed with people, even to its step.
> (On weekdays with groceries, spare automobile parts, and pump parts,
> but today only two preachers extra, one carrying his frock coat on a hanger.)
> It passes the closed roadside stand, the closed schoolhouse,
> where today no flag is flying
> from the rough-adzed pole topped with a white china doorknob.
> It stops, and a man carrying a baby gets off,
> climbs over a stile, and goes down through a small steep meadow,
> which establishes its poverty in a snowfall of daisies,
> to his invisible house beside the water.

> The birds keep on singing, a calf bawls, the bus starts.
> The thin mist follows
> the white mutations of its dream;
> an ancient chill is rippling the dark brooks.[3]

In the thirty-nine lines that precede these final stanzas of "Cape Breton," no human presence enters the landscape. Although it is Sunday, the churches are empty; bulldozers stand idle. But rather than offer a respite from this quizzical sense of emptiness, the emergence of people in the landscape exacerbates it. The priest isn't wearing his vestments—why? The glimpse of a man carrying a baby seems to promise a depth of human feeling, yet he disappears to an "invisible house"—a house which the lay of the land won't allow us to see but which, more than that, feels literally invisible. Singing birds and bawling calves seem only more or less as animated as the moving bus: everything in the landscape is shrouded equally in a mist that seems to be the most motivated presence in the landscape even as its empties the landscape of interiority.

Despite its clarity, "Cape Breton" is a poem of terrified desperation: it records a sequence of failed attempts to locate human meaning in a landscape that sloughs us off. Like "Le Manteau de Pascal," it acknowledges that we know only the surface of things but at the same time admits that we crave depth. "Whatever the landscape had of meaning appears to have been abandoned," says Bishop, who immediately posits an "interior" she cannot see: an interior "where deep lakes are reputed to be, / and disused trails and mountains of rock / and miles of burnt forests."[4] Nothing Bishop goes on to describe here (lakes, trails, mountains, burnt forests, sparrows, mist, fish-nets) exists. The passage is a catalogue of what she presumes the surface of the landscape is holding back in its "interior"—figments of an imagination that needs desperately to affirm its own interiority by positing an essence in the world outside. If Bishop seems initially like a poet who feels certain that we understand simply by looking, the ultimate effect of her poem depends on the absence of what we crave.

Poems often take place in identifiable locations, many of them literal, some of them historical verifiable. "Untitled Two" takes place in a parking lot, "Cape Breton" at Cape Breton. But if the named location of Bishop's poem seems clear enough, the locations of Graham's poems feel increasingly less relevant. Does this trajectory represent the attenuation of a remediable problem or a recognition that the problem is not a problem at all but an inevitable aspect of lyric poetry, something that may be suppressed or exploited? Listen to a poem from *Swarm*.

> What are you thinking?
> Here on the bottom?
> What do you squint clear for yourself
> up there through the surface?
>
> Explain   door ajar.
> Explain   hopeth all.
> Explain   surface   future   subject-of.
>
> Pierce.
>
> Be swift.
>
> (Let's wade again.)
>
> (Offstage: pointing-at)
> (Offstage: stones placing themselves on eyes)
>
> Here: tangle and seaweed
>
> current   diagram   how deep?   I have
>
> forgotten.
>
> Don't leave me. I won't. (*S*, 55)

These opening lines of "For One Must Want / To Shut the Other's Gaze" are located, as they themselves insist, *here*: on the bottom of the ocean, beneath the surface, among tangle and seaweed. But imagining that location doesn't help us to read the poem; like most of the poems of *Swarm*, it feels challengingly disembodied, all cry and no occasion—as if we were challenged to imagine the interior space below the surface without any knowledge of the surface. More helpful is the fact that the poem's title is a misquotation from Emily Dickinson's "I cannot live with You," a poem about the intensity of being merged with the beloved. "Explain   door ajar," says Graham. "So we must meet apart— / You there—I—here— / With just the Door ajar / That Oceans are," says Dickinson, emphasizing that a state of perfect unity destroys the distance on which the passion of love depends.[5] The *here* of Graham's poem is more richly understood as this metaphorical ocean rather than a literal one; it is a place of almost unbearable union that paradoxically preserves distinctions, a place where the merging of selves creates not understanding but a craving for explanation. And in its final lines, the poem honors that craving even as it refuses to satisfy it: while insisting that "the real plot was invisible" it also asks us to "name the place." As if to stress that we've come to this poem not for knowledge but for the experience of what it feels like to know something, "For One Must Want / To Shut the Other's Gaze" concludes with the question with which it began: "What are you thinking?" (*S*, 56).

Following this question is the title poem of *Swarm*. Its subtitle answers the injunction to name the place ("Todi, 1996"), and its first five lines offer a narrative perspicuity that is generally resisted throughout the volume.

> I wanted you to listen to the bells,
> holding the phone out the one small window
> to where I thought
> the ringing was—
>
> Vespers scavenging the evening air,
> headset fisted against the huge dissolving
>
> where I stare at the tiny holes in the receiver's transatlantic opening
> to see evening-light and then churchbells
>
> send their regrets, slithering in—
> in there a white flame charged with duplication—.
> I had you try to listen, bending down into the mouthpiece to whisper, hard,
>
> *can you hear them* (two petals fall and then the   is wholly
> changed) (yes) (and then another yes like a vertebrate enchaining)
> yes yes yes yes
>
> We were somebody. (*S*, 57)

In these lines, "the long ocean between us" (*S*, 58) is no metaphor but the Atlantic ocean; the speaker in Italy telephones the auditor in the United States, beckoning him to listen to the church bells. And if "For One Must Want / To Shut the Other's Gaze" is about unity that depends on the preservation of distinctions between two people, "The Swarm" is about the desperately misguided attempt to overcome that separation, wearing away the edges on which the passion of intimacy depends. For while the poem does begin in a manner that seems to capitulate to the injunction to "name the place," the poem quickly reveals the complexity of even the simplest act of naming. We cannot rest comfortably with our knowledge of the literal because language is inevitably threatening to transform the literal into the metaphorical. For what are the bells "scavenging" the evening air? Why does the speaker "stare at" the receiver rather than listening to it? Is the speaker really asking the auditor to hear "two petals fall" or are the petals an emblem of the difficulty of hearing the bells across the ocean? In any case, this increasingly desperate attempt to name the place and surmount the distance collapses in the simple declaration that "we were somebody." And the implication is that the relationship between the speaker and the auditor is itself a figure for the relationship between the poem and its reader: to name the location flatly, to leave nothing unexplained, is to render the poem undesirable and the reader unacquainted with desire. As "Underneath (1)," the poem following "The Swarm," puts it, "you were too / close for me to make / out in- // dividual words" (*S*, 61).

"Underneath (1)" comments on "The Swarm" in the same way that "The Swarm" comments on "For One Must Want / To Shut the Other's Gaze," complicating further our sense of what it means to "name a place." Reimagining the transatlantic telephone conversation, this poem concerns the transmission of information from auditor to speaker rather than speaker to auditor. And as in "The Swarm," purely auditory information is quickly translated into visual information. "All I / heard," says the speaker, "was the wind rushing into my / opening the ear like a field" (*S*, 61), and the field becomes a place.

> Near noon all the tall grasses for an instant stiff at
> attention,
>
> then a sturdy nervousness from left to right—
> deep bending of the light—
> light carried across on the backs, in on the tips—
> the screengrid forced so deep into the eye it's in
> disappearance—or the mind—as
>
> you   will
> have   it
> No   where
> No   two
>
> silvers alike although all bendings or bowings
> identical
> except for the fact of
> difference. (*S*, 60)

If these lines are evidence of the mind's inexorable craving for location and explanation, they also suggest that locations, whether literal or figurative, are constantly changing; even if our desire for the certainty of location is satisfied we cannot be sure that the location specified for one moment of experience will be relevant to the next moment. This place, this field, remains consistent with itself only inasmuch as it exists in a continuous state of becoming. It is composed of individual elements that are threateningly similar to one another but never identical; what joins them is the insurmountable fact of their "difference" from one another, a difference that reminds us of our inevitable difference from this place. If we know the place intimately, we do so not in spite of our distance from it but because of the distance.

The increasingly radical enjambment of the lines of these poems forces us to experience that distance, and the formal drama of the whole of *Swarm* involves a movement from poems in which syntax (however fragmentary) is equivalent with line to poems in which syntax overrides line not only to create particular patterns of intonation but to disrupt any clear sense that there is a natural or inevitable relationship between the syntax and the lineation. At the end of "Underneath (1)" the constantly shifting "fact of / difference" that distinguishes our experience of the field also distinguishes our experience of the poem, which divides into two columns which may be read separately or continuously.

yr voice not such	the sun entering
yr saying	the hotel window
so filled with	from the street
yr exhalation	and cries on it
it drowns itself	strangely the right color for
drowns in the *mine* of	cries
itself—all desire	crossing the history
yielding to secrecy	of inwardness vs insideness
spume of syllables	the seepage of
we were hungry	this was our century (*S*, 62)

Here, the failure of two voices to honor their distance in a transatlantic telephone conversation is mended in the lineation of the poem, which does not allow us to locate the voice of the poem in any one particular place. Dickinson's "Door ajar / That Oceans are" is preserved by the lineation, which tempts us with the particular unity of semantic units that still remain stubbornly distinct. To demand a more complete unity is to be denied the expectation that something (we don't know what) could be left for us to experience.

That expectation is crucial to our experience of any poem because it is an inevitable part of our experience of figurative language, no matter if the poem takes the form of "For One Must Want to Shut / The Other's Gaze" or "Cape Breton." In Graham's poem language feels less determinedly referential than in Bishop's, but her poem is not written in a different language; we are not at liberty to decide when words will have meanings. We may be more or less aware of the intricate relationship of words to things, however, and in this sense "For One Must Want / To Shut the Other's Gaze" foregrounds the complexity of any poem's relationship to its place. All poems are troubled about their own locations because their language is troubled by its referentiality; they recognize that the effort to include a clear sense of a location in the poem may become indistinguishable from the effort to omit it.

Listen to Wordsworth:

> The day is come when I again repose
> Here, under this dark sycamore, and view
> These plots of cottage-ground, these orchard-tufts,
> Which, at this season, with their unripe fruits,
> Among the woods and copses lose themselves,
> Nor, with their green and simple hue, disturb
> The wild green landscape. Once again I see
> These hedge-rows, hardly hedge-rows, little lines
> Of sportive wood run wild, these pastoral farms,
> Green to the very door; and wreaths of smoke
> Sent up, in silence, from among the trees,
> With some uncertain notice, as might seem,
> Of vagrant dwellers in the houseless woods,
> Or of some hermit's cave, where by his fire
> The hermit sits alone.[6]

These lines are located, as they themselves insist, *here*: under a dark sycamore. When Wordsworth revisited the place in 1798, Tintern Abbey was a refuge for homeless beggars and the wretchedly poor; the landscape around it was scarred by the early excesses of the industrial revolution. Only a little of that historical evidence appears in Wordsworth's poem ("wreaths of smoke" sent up "as might seem / Of vagrant dwellers in the houseless woods, / Or of some hermit's cave"), but that evidence, combined with the fact that the poem's title skirts the anniversary of Bastille Day ("Lines written a few miles above Tintern Abbey, on revisiting the Banks of the Wye during a Tour, July 13, 1798"), persuades the literary critic Marjorie Levinson to conclude that "what we witness in this poem is a conversion of public to private property, history to poetry": the place is left out of the poem. Jerome McGann speaks similarly of the poem's "displacement" of social conditions, then of "erasures and displacements," and finally of "annihilation": the poem annihilates its history.[7]

This argument equates displacement with omission; however, Freud is adamant in *The Interpretation of Dreams* that displacement is the opposite of omission: it is the means by which repression is subverted, allowing forbidden thoughts to be admitted into a dream. To suggest that by omitting a clear delineation of place the poem converts history to poetry is to presume omission to be repression—a problematic rather than an inevitable aspect of a text. It is to suggest that because language has a complex relationship to what it represents, there must be something better than the language of poetry—a more reliable way to insure that the location of a poem is contained in the poem. To wonder about a poem's conversion of history to poetry is consequently to reiterate the poem's resistance to itself. And to think of "For One Must Want / To Shut the Other's Gaze" as a categorically more difficult kind of poem than "Tintern Abbey" or "Cape Breton" is to ignore that resistance.

Throughout her career, Graham has resisted her own best discoveries relentlessly. She is no more willing to idealize her formal choices than to idealize beauty, and her most daring turn occurred when she followed *Swarm* with *Never*, a book whose poems refuse the glamour of aesthetic extremity. For rather than seeming to extend the formal experimentation of *Swarm*, these poems return to identifiable locations and more normative lineation. "How can I believe in that," asked Keats when he first saw the Lake District he had come to know from Wordsworth's poems. He was not referring to the sublime grandeur of the landscape: "The magnitude of mountains and waterfalls are well imagined before one sees them. What astonishes me more than any thing is the tone, the coloring, the slate, the stone, the moss, the rock-weed."[8] Keats's question is the epigraph to *Never*, and the poems represent a massively patient attempt simply to record the tone of things as they appear in particular locations at particular times. "Over a dock railing, I watch the minnows," begins the first poem in the book. "I am beneath the tree," begins the second (*N*, 3, 4). Readers who found *Swarm* excessively difficult found *Never* more immediately apprehensible, but what matters about these two books is not their difference from each other; what matters is the way in which their difference forces us to inhabit the question of their similarity. One book cannot help but to conjure locations as it disperses them; the other cannot help but to disperse the locations it conjures.

"Begin with the world," says Graham in the final line of "Afterwards," "let it be small enough" (*N*, 5). But having made the decision to record the object world as faithfully as possible, locating the object in space and time, how does one evade the temporality of the act of recording? Even if language were fully capable of locking the object in a particular moment in time, would one want it to do so? "How shall we say this happened," asked the Objectivist poet George Oppen, whose work is driven by the beautiful realization that it is not easy to begin with the object world.[9] Graham begins "Afterwards" by recording her observation of two starlings emerging from a hawthorn, their bodies literalizing the presence of their song.

> When two
> appear in flight, straight to the child-sized pond of
> melted snow,
> and thrash, dunk, rise, shake, rethrashing, reconfiguring through
> reshufflings and resettlings the whole body of integrated
> featherwork,
> they shatter open the blue-and-tree-tip filled-up gaze of
> the lawn's two pools,
> breaking and ruffling all the crisp true sky we had seen living
> down in that tasseled
> earth. How shall we say this *happened*? (*N*, 4–5)

Repeating Oppen's question at the end of this passage, Graham makes us feel it rising from the effort of observation. She emphasizes the ambiguity of the word "happened" but the word "this" is equally difficult to calibrate. Is "this" the flight of the starlings, their shattering of the pool of melted snow? If so, why does this "child-sized pond" become "two pools" after the starlings have entered it? Is "this" the fracturing of the pool itself? And is this fracturing an event that actually happens or a metaphor for what appears to have happened, the "breaking" of the "true sky" reflected in the water? Throughout *Never* Graham is poised "head-down and over some one / thing" (*N*, 26), but her devotion to her place becomes more vexed to the degree that it becomes more passionate.

Like Oppen, Graham thrives on vexation; it is the source of her pleasure, the record of her being in the world. In the opening lines of "Gulls," she doesn't really describe herself as focused relentlessly on "one / thing"; the phrase refers to seagulls standing in shallow waves. But inasmuch as Graham is focusing her attention on starlings or seagulls or waves, she wants us to feel that words inevitably distract us from what they also point towards. This effect is not due to a lack of precision in language; it is the result of precision: the more pressure Graham places on a word's denotative power, the more manifold its proliferating associations become. In addition, since the starling or the seagull or the wave is constantly in motion, the precisely denotative word is always lagging behind or lurching ahead of the object. To say that these lines from "Gulls" are about a "wave" is to deny the poem the pleasure of asking more questions.

> So then it's sun in surf-breaking water: incircling, smearing: mind not
> knowing if it's still "wave," breaking on
> itself, small glider, or if it's "amidst" (red turning feathery)
> or rather "over" (the laciness of foambreak) or just *what*—(among
> the line of also smearingly reddening terns floating out now
> on the feathery backedge of foambroken
> looking)—*it is*. (*N*, 27–28)

What it is: Graham does not relent from her devotion to place—"the charmed circle of yes of / what happened" (*N*, 100)—but each wave passes, becomes some other thing, no sooner glimpsed than gone. Like the imagined field in "Underneath (1)," the wave is a thing constantly in process, its solidity contingent on the fact that it is always becoming different from itself. What's more, the rendered wave becomes a figure for the poet's language, which also exists in a constant state of flux, its drive to predication constantly diverted by apposition and subordination. In the final movement of "Gulls," which began with seagulls that act like a poet, head bent down over one thing, the poet's language is likened to a seagull, swift over the sand.

> my clutch of
> words
> swaying and stemming from my
> saying, no
> echo. No stopping on the temporarily exposed and drying rock
> out there
> to rub or rest where nothing else
> grows.
> And truly swift over the sands.
> As if most afraid of being re-
> peated.
> Preferring to be dissolved to
> designation,

> backglancing stirrings,
> wedged-in between unsaying and
> > forgetting—
> what an enterprise—spoken out by
> > me as if
> to *still* some last place, place becoming even as I speak
> > unspeakable—(*N*, 28–29)

There is no crisis of representation here, no sense that by inhabiting language we make the mistake of converting history to poetry. To recognize that place becomes unspeakable as it is spoken is to recognize that we inhabit the world intimately because we inhabit language; the complicated relationship of words and things is not in itself noteworthy. So if locations are studiously omitted from the poems of *Swarm*, how should they be said to have been included in *Never*? Approaching the question from opposite sides, each book offers "the meditation / place demands" (*N*, 38).

In "a creative and spontaneous being," said D. W. Winnicott, one finds "a capacity for the use of symbols," by which he means figurative language in general. Children spend most of their time in a psychic space that is neither completely internal nor completely external—the "potential space" of play.[10] Dismantling Freud's stern opposition between reality and pleasure principles, Winnicott maintained that adults may too readily capitulate either to a world of inanimate objects on the one hand or to a world of uncontested fantasy on the other: the healthy adult continues to live in increasingly complex and tenuous versions of potential space. Hovering between the literal and the figurative, the language of poetry creates that space. All language has this capacity. But because we don't necessarily expect a poem to be useful in obvious or immediate ways, the language of poetry is liberated to create that space aggressively. Call it the valley of the River Wye, call it Cape Breton, call it the beach at Jorie's house: it is the place where we live.

Notes

1. Jorie Graham, *Swarm* (New York: Ecco Press, 2000), 3 (hereafter cited as *S*). Other Graham books cited here are *The Errancy* (Hopewell, N.J.: Ecco Press, 1997) (cited as *Ey*); and *Never* (New York: Ecco Press, 2002) (cited as *N*).

2. Sigmund Freud, *The Interpretation of Dreams*, vols. IV and V of the *Standard Edition of the Complete Psychological Works*, ed. and trans. James Strachey (London: Hogarth, 1970), 5: 507.

3. Elizabeth Bishop, "Cape Breton," in *The Complete Poems* (New York: Farrar, Straus & Giroux, 1983), 68.

4. Bishop, 67–68.

5. Emily Dickinson, "I cannot live with You," in *The Poems: Variorum Edition*, ed. R. W. Franklin (Cambridge, Mass.: Harvard University Press, 1998), 2: 674–676.

6. William Wordsworth, "Lines Written a Few Miles above Tintern Abbey, on Revisiting the Banks of the Wye during a Tour, July 13, 1798," *Lyrical Ballads, and Other Poems, 1797–1800*, ed. James Butler and Karen Green (Ithaca, N.Y.: Cornell University Press, 1992), 116–120.

7. Marjorie Levinson, *Wordsworth's Great Period Poems* (New York: Cambridge University Press, 1986), 37; Jerome McGann, *The Romantic Ideology* (Chicago: University of Chicago Press, 1983), 84, 85, 90.

8. John Keats, *The Letters*, ed. H. E. Rollins (Cambridge, Mass.: Harvard University Press, 1958), 1: 426, 301.

9. George Oppen, *New Collected Poems*, ed. Michael Davidson (New York: New Directions, 2002), 226.

10. D. W. Winnicott, *The Maturational Processes and the Facilitating Environment* (New York: International Universities Press, 1965), 150.

15

Jorie Graham Listening

WILLARD SPIEGELMAN

Any new creation by a major artist encourages—indeed forces—us to reconsider, realign, and reimagine all of her previous work. The 2002 publication of *Never* prompts many questions about Jorie Graham's ongoing negotiations with the world and with poetry itself. Her new poems exist along a spectrum from the difficult but comprehensible to the difficult and impenetrable. The poems continue and expand three of Graham's habitual stylistic tendencies. First, she favors long, convoluted, deeply subordinated sentences, often lacking distinct, parsible grammatical coordinates. Within any single poem, she repeats phrases, words, and motifs in a quasi-musical way. Second, there is the (annoying) habit of proliferating parentheses and brackets [it's often impossible to understand why she uses one marker instead of the other at any given moment], which suggest uncertainty, simultaneity, hallucination, or the equivalence of a painterly montage instead of a straight sequence. And third, Graham's—not entirely new—favorite parts of speech are gerunds and present participles, so that action seems never to begin or finish but always to be progressing and repeating itself. "The Turning" (from *The Errancy*, a previous book) in which an act of description becomes a *kind* of narrative, ends with the question: "Whose turn is it now?"[1] And we see here how Graham is playing not only with two senses of the word "turn" but also with the differences between the gerund and the simple noun. In the new book she poses another simple question: "Where does this *going /* go?" ("Philosopher's Stone," 9). The gerunds go wild in *Never*, much of which has seaside settings. Graham resists stasis, endings, and order in favor of "going," "turning," a world in motion. In her renderings of the lucent speckling of light upon water, of the "roiling" (a much used word), cresting and withdrawing, waves that she hears as well as watches, Graham has found a style apposite to her subject.

The opulent activity mimicked and produced within her poems comes often at the price of clarity. (Indeed, Adam Kirsch asks, sympathetically but sincerely, whether these poems are indeed "poems" or something else.)[2] Twenty years ago she entertained many of the same thematic preoccupations, but her sentences and her lines were shorter. Beginning with *The End of Beauty*, expansion, proliferation, and fracture took over. In the new poems, Graham typically starts with simplicity of articulation and notice, and then lets spin her metaphysical energies as she hurls her mind into the visible (or the audible) and its borders with the invisible (or the inaudible). More than half of the poems in *Never* have straightforward beginnings, whether simple sentences or mere phrases. Like Charles Wright, Pound, and Gary Snyder, Graham has adopted the habit of moving from phrases to clauses and of sometimes constructing lengthy phrases with no simple predicate. Here are some random openings:

I am beneath the tree. To the right the river is melting the young sun. ("Afterwards," 4)

It's like this. There are quantities. ("Philosopher's Stone," 6)

How old are you? ("Evolution," 21)

Those neck-pointing out full bodylength and calling outwards over the breaking waves. ("Gulls," 26)

Cluster of bird-chatter a knot at the center of a supreme unfolding. ("The Time Being," 44)

All day there had been clouds and the expectation of sun. ("Surf," 81)

The last of the lines cited above makes a deceptive nod in the direction of Elizabeth Bishop, whose steadiness of eye Graham professes to emulate, but whose modesty of means she seldom replicates. Like Bishop, Graham includes acts of self-correction in the very patterns of her observation. Graham moves from the seen to the unseen, gazing steadily like Bishop but then whipping off in a melodramatic frenzy of metaphysical speculation. Where Bishop is fastidious and self-effacing, Graham is explosive and rhapsodic. The two poets ask the same questions in different dialects: How is the natural world scripted? How can we reproduce nature's script in our own language? How might we model human language upon nature's ebb and flow, its waxing and waning? In our secular, post-Romantic age these questions constitute theological dilemmas, though they pertain less to matters of belief than to matters of approach. Four of her new poems are entitled "Prayer" (as in previous volumes Graham offers multiple takes on a single subject); others have religious titles ("Via Negativa," "Covenant") or subject matter ("The Taken-Down God"). More than a century after the death of God there is no one to answer her questions, many of which seem like poems directed outward into the void or into the inner depths. Like Bishop (in her early "Over 2000 Illustrations and a Complete Concordance"), Graham confronts the potential for religious experience only to "look and look [her] infant sight away." But *infans* (speechless)? Hardly.

The poems collected in *Never* find Graham moving away from the intertwined, multi-faceted narratives that gave substance to earlier poems such as "What the End Is For," "Fission," "From the New World," "The Phase After History," and "Manifest Destiny." (Two of the new poems, "The Taken-Down God," and "High Tide," retain the older narrative structure.) Because her major subject is our perceptual negotiations with the world, she keeps struggling to create or discover adequate aesthetic forms for her philosophical problems: how the world appears, how we register its appearance, and how it inhabits and expands our minds. Most significant in this regard is Graham's not entirely new but nevertheless pronounced and increasing attention to sound. Jorie Graham is listening. To what? To the outside world in general, to waves especially, and to birds in particular. *Never* heralds extensions as well as changes in Graham's style and methods, and moreover it signals a major reorganization of her repertoire of tropes, especially those of listening. Of twenty-seven poems in this book, only six (by my count) contain neither birds (visible and/or audible) nor major renderings of auditory phenomena.

From the start, more than two decades ago, Jorie Graham has been observing birds. *Never* provokes some interesting questions about poets' responses to birds; the answers to these questions may allow us to take the measure of this obdurate, knotty contemporary poet. Perhaps the most striking aspect of Graham's responses to a variety of birds (seabirds and land birds, American and European ones, single birds and flocks of them, named ones and unspecified ones) is the fact that only recently has hearing them become as poetically useful to her as looking at them. She has placed herself belatedly in the line of poets who listen. In her earlier volumes, infused with Derridean notions about writing and legibility, Graham *looked* at birds more frequently than she heard them, and she took them as figures of writing rather than as singers of wordless melody. The birds themselves served as visible traces of script in the sky or as the creators of that script. Graham made much of birds' feathers as pens. Because of her early exposure to, and interest in, the visual arts, Graham has always looked at the surround. What does the shift from sight to sound, or the frequent synaesthetic mingling of the two senses, say about Graham's poetic negotiations with and reconfigurations of the world?

The appeal of birds to poets needs little explaining. Both as metaphor—bird as idealized natural singer, unfreighted by language and consciousness—and as metonymy—bird as substitute for the soul and its wish for flight and freedom—members of the avian kingdom could sustain a poetic taxonomy equivalent to one devoted to flowers.[3] In the poetic continuum of the past two centuries that might go under the heading "Romanticism," birds have occupied a crucial position from Wordsworth's cuckoo, "a wandering voice," Shelley's invisible skylark and its "unpremeditated art," Keats's easy, "full-throated" nightingale, through the birds of Whitman, Hardy, Yeats, Eliot, Stevens, Frost, and Amy Clampitt.

There are many ways to trace the movements and changes in Graham's poetry since the appearance of *Hybrids of Plants and of Ghosts* in 1980. Her sentences have expanded. Often they are no longer even sentences. The lacunae, gaps, holes, and parenthetical and bracketed phrases suggesting simultaneity have also multiplied.[4] Clarity of diction, patience of observation, and an ordering of motifs have yielded to fracture, opacity, and impatience. And, for the purposes of this essay, looking has been supplemented by careful hearing (hearing of many things, not just birds) as another way of attending to the world's appearances and events.[5]

Listening and hearing constitute two aspects of one activity; the first is deliberate, the second (more often than not) accidental or superficial. In Graham's works, both play a part, as does human conversation, which requires either face-to-face confrontation or its simulacrum (on a telephone, for example), although it too may assume active or passive stances. Listening can occur from a point withdrawn, when one is hidden. John Stuart Mill famously defined lyric poetry as something we "overhear."[6] Even more than seeing, listening encourages or works from spots of hiding. It is a more surreptitious activity. Graham has always been partial to the kind of secrecies that allow her to place herself out of sight where she can oversee or overhear what goes on around her. What Ruskin said of himself in his autobiographical *Praeterita* would apply equally to Graham: "My entire delight was in observing without being myself noticed,— if I could have been invisible all the better."[7] She has always been, paradoxically, extravagant in thought, diction and poetic "performance," and reticent in presenting herself to the evidence of the material world that she takes in or absorbs. Her early claim ("The Lady and the Unicorn and Other Tapestries," *Erosion*) applies to her accumulated poetry of the past two decades: "If I have a faith it is something like this: this ordering of images / within an atmosphere that will receive them, hold them in solution, unsolved" (37). Like liquids dissolving or suspended in an emulsion, "unsolved" solutions require us to move back for a second look at the problems that initially provoked them. And these problems are all epistemological ones, pertaining to the location of the human subject—watching and listening—in the busy turbulence of her own thought and amid the external universe. In many ways Graham's work has amplified the conditions embodied in Stevens' Snow Man who "regard[s]" and "behold[s]" the external world, and then hears the sound of the wind, becoming a "listener" who (at poem's end) once again "beholds" the world's plenitude and emptiness. The marriage of the heard and the seen comes to occupy her energies more fully in her new poems.

In her earliest work Graham did not seem particularly interested in listening. Sounds appear, of course, but listening as an activity as arduous as looking develops only slowly. In *Hybrids* she briefly mentions songbirds ("Girl at the Piano"), a cricket ("Cross-Stitch") and trapped moths ("Harvest for Bergson"). In *Erosion* and *The End of Beauty* sound is one of several senses in "Scirocco," "In What Manner the Body is United with the Soule," "The Sense of an Ending," "Description," "Self-Portrait as Apollo and Daphne," and "What the End is For" (which details—inter alia—the buzzing and humming of Orpheus' detached head). By *Region of Unlikeness*, sound is matched with but subsidiary to sight in "Immobilism." The trapped juncos of "The Phase After History" are Graham's first important "Romantic" (i.e., heard but unseen) birds. Finally, in one of the poems entitled "Notes on the Reality of the Self" (*Materialism*), Graham listens to drum rolls and drum beats, but even here, luminousness rather than sound predominates. Or, rather, the synaesthesia that Graham increasingly practices overtakes and joins both senses: gleaming bushes, penetrated and animated by "thick insistent light" absorb every "molecule of sound" and "all the fulgid / instruments" become a "scintillant beast" (*M*, 10–11).

Graham mingles the senses dexterously as well as dangerously. "Ravel and Unravel" (*The End of Beauty*) begins with a reference to Penelope at her daily task of doing and undoing. This leads into a scene of the poet with her husband and daughter walking through a Western landscape in which (at poem's center) she hears the high-pitched mewing and hissing of two young eagles. Their cry mingles with that of the young child, but the poem ends, as it began, with the beautiful "view all around us" (*EB*, 70). Graham sandwiches the audible between slices of the visible. The poems immediately following this one also fail to isolate the heard from the seen. "Room Tone" begins with the parentheses and lacunae that become even more predominant in Graham's later work:

> Turn round (wind in the sycamore).
> Did you see that did you hear that (wind in the
> _____ _____ _____?) can you touch it,
> what *can* you touch? will you
> speak back to me,
> will you look up now, please? (*EB*, 73)

And the poem's title refers as much to the look of a room (in which two lovers meet) as to any human or non-human sound. Yet another poem whose title suggests sound, "Annunciation," begins indoors, with references to sounds outside, not coming clear at first and then being replaced by visual images of the mingling of body and soul.

In *Materialism* the relation between sight and sound becomes more intimate and intense. Sometimes one succeeds the other: "When the music ended she noticed the light" ("Invention of the Other," 131). "Event Horizon," a richly textured political poem, weaves details from Graham's domestic life (washing a dress, looking at the landscape, watching and hearing a pair of blue jays) with those of the Tienanmen Square uprising. Sight and sound are deeply intertwined. "Emergency" (*The Errancy*) actually begins with a listening that is almost spatialized and made tangible:

> Walking in the dark along the river's dark,
> I can hear its small wrestling-sound,
> its pasture of shutting and re-shutting pockets,
> its sideways-sound and long sleek zoneless mildly-enameled
> inherencies, but cannot *see*—
> not even alongside—so close night's motherings—into its celluloid
>   untellings—
> not even the slightest drifting gauzy bit of light,
> folding to ripple up
> the trancelike sugary vestibule
> of chains and chains and chains. (*Ey*, 95)

In the title poem of *Swarm*, Graham's most impenetrable, indecipherable, and generally troubled volume, listening assumes the crucial initiating as well as concluding position. In the Italian town of Todi, the speaker holds a telephone out of a small window to allow someone to "listen to the bells" before describing the visible scene. The tone of this poem is one of regret, almost of desperation, and it is sound—talking and listening—that stands in for a human relationship in disarray, and for the fact of physical separation. The poet extends the telephone in which she says she *has* her interlocutor, "you without eyes or arms or body now," and tells him to "listen to / the long ocean between us." Talking across a line, and using both speech and non-semantic sounds as means of confirming a personal connection, Graham seems coolly resigned to a dissolution: "this tiny geometric swarm of / openings sending to you // no parts of me you've touched, no places where you've // gone" (*S*, 57–58). This may very well be her saddest poem, a short proof of the urgent, unsettling, and ultimately unsatisfactory uses to which "far-sounding" i.e., telephonic, connections may be put.

Graham seems to have awakened to sound in her books from *Materialism* onward. "Red Umbrella Aubade" (*The Errancy*) begins near dawn with the poet hearing "one bloodshot / cardinal-call—bejangled clarity gripping firm" (*Ey*, 59). It is as though the persian-red of "For Mark Rothko" (*Hybrids*) has re-entered her sensory field as something heard rather than seen. The poet herself is uncertain about acts of listening, as she seems to be skeptical about the (perhaps adulterous) love affair detailed in these poems: "For you—for us—I know I should listen hard, / but to penetrate what? / my knowing to listen itself an aftermath of red" (*Ey*, 59). Red—the color of lust and embarrassment—has consequences for the ear.

In the same volume "The Turning" opens on an Umbrian village morning scene, in silence: "And more sun (no voices in it)." The whole book is filled with "aubades," and it is no wonder that sound comes to stand for awakening and announcements. Here, general animation erupts and a flock of birds lifts up:

>   now churchbells breaking up
>   in twos and threes
>   the flock
> which works across in
>   granular,
> forked, suddenly cacophonic
>   undulation
>   (though at the level
> of the inaudible) large differences of rustling, risings and lowerings,
>   swallowings of
>   silence where the wings
> en masse lift off—and then the other (indecipherable) new
>   silence where
>   wings aren't

>   used and the flock floats in
>   unison—
>   a flying-in-formation sound which
>   I can see across the wall (as if loud)—shrapnel of
>   blackness
>   against the brightnesses— (*Ey*, 104–105)

And so it goes. The dense thicket of Graham's syntax matches, of course, the density of her perceptions, and sight and sound mingle, as the birds she hears and sees go beyond even the "ambiguous undulations" of Wallace Stevens' pigeons ("Sunday Morning"); toward the end of the poem Graham in fact refers to "syncopated undulations of cooing." These birds turn and rise and become an "exfoliation of aural clottings where all wings open now to break / and pump—vapor of accreting inaudibles" (*Ey*, 105). As they get higher and higher they become both inaudible and indecipherable.

As with sound in general so with birds in particular, as both "The Turning" and "Red Umbrella Aubade" suggest. In early Graham they represent items in the visible field. In "Syntax" (*Hybrids*, 21), starlings are seen ("a regular syntax on wings"), not heard; in fact they catch singing bullfrogs. "For Mark Rothko" includes a persian-red cardinal as part of a color field. Hummingbirds and swallows ("Mind") are figures of human perception. Most notably, in "A Feather for Voltaire" a fallen feather is like a pen, and the bird's flight (as in Howard Nemerov's "The Blue Swallows") is like an alphabetic script:

>   The bird is an alphabet, it flies
>   above us, catch
>   as catch can,
>   a flock,
>   a travel plan.
>   Some never touch ground. (*H*, 66)

Like birds, both language and its meanings (propositions, innuendos, metaphors) evade us, try as we might to capture or control them. Graham's early poetry is devoted to figures for such efforts; her later, more swirling and expansive efforts represent in part the widening gyre in which her metaphysical claims, or the birds that figure them, fly away from us. Still later, in "Existence and Presence" (*M*, 142), Graham begins with details from several senses, before fixing her attention—hearing but primarily looking—upon a flock of birds. The first nine lines of this short poem depict the ways she thinks she feels her "thinking-self," against a natural backdrop of landscape and sound. The second nine lines balance the first half, which contains questions ("And how shall this soliloquy reverberate / over the hillside?" . . . "Who shall the listening be?"). Sight intervenes before subsiding into sound:

> A huntress ran across, near dusk—we saw the quiver
> like a small gleam on the back of a mossy knoll or maybe
> water between the far trees.
> An alphabet flew over, made liquid syntax for a while,
> diving and rising, forking, a caprice of clear meanings,
> right pauses, unwrapping the watching-temptation—
> then chopped and scattered, one last one chittering away,
> then silence, then the individual screeches of the nighthunters
> at dusk, the hollows sucked in around that cry.

The flock of unidentified alphabetic birds dips nibs into the air, creating perhaps only a tracery of meaning. The tentative myth-making efforts (Diana the huntress? "chittering" birds as relatives of Keats's twittering swallows in "To Autumn"?) proceed from the visual and then move away from it. Sound enters Graham's world slowly. She attunes her auditory senses hesitantly, indeed evasively.

This evasion proves unavoidable even in the visually alive "art" poems in *Erosion*, where one might expect the stasis inherent in ekphrasis to help the poet locate herself and her speculations within the confines of tight borders. What a painting depicts visually is verifiable and always present; it should therefore possess a solidity that sound, with its temporality, lacks, but for Graham, even the seen can elude our efforts to understand or grasp it. Thus, in "Massacio's Expulsion" (E, 66–69) she notices a large blue bird in the famous fresco in the Brancacci Chapel of Santa Maria del Carmine; she calls it a "Sharp-Shinned Hawk," which she has often seen "tearing into the woods / for which it's / too big." The problem is that no such bird exists in the picture. Instead, Graham has imaginatively enlarged upon a splotch of paint: "perhaps / it is a flaw // on the wall of this church, or age, / or merely the restlessness / of the brilliant / young painter." But from the available visible evidence she infers her predatory bird, "seeking a narrower / place," which she urges the fallen Adam and Eve to watch, in order that they (like her) might abandon whatever is open and "easily eloquent" in favor of what is closed and broken, or eroded. Human, i.e., fallen, Graham takes it upon herself to recommend to our first parents the virtues of choice, of narrowing. What she has suffered or inherited from them she throws back at them. Significantly, the imagined, reconstructed bird becomes the agency of communication between the viewer of the painting and the characters within it. The bird symbolizes a principle of narrowing and also one of expansion, since it comes from the capacious freedom of her own imagination. Like so many of Graham's poems about art, this one suggests echoes of Elizabeth Bishop's great "Poem" in *Geography III*, which relates the poet's encounter with a great uncle's small painting wherein daubs and squibs of paint become, recognizably, animals and birds.

When an entire poem revolves around a bird, we might expect something auditory to be used as inspiration or provocation, but in "Thinking" (*Ey*, 40–41), avian movement (not song) once again turns into a scripted sentence. Bird flight is visible, cursive, and even legible and interpretable. Sound is made secondary, via a simile: a crow "hung like a cough to a wire above me." The bird's materiality is compromised ("It was a version of a crow, untitled as such") and sound is, next, out of the question: "The soundless foamed." Like "Existence and Presence" the poem divides evenly into two parts (each of fifteen lines). The break occurs between a first half composed of what count as relatively short sentences in Graham's work, and a second half that is one swirling motion as the bird (which began the poem in a stationary pose, like Stevens' blackbird) takes flight, transforming himself into a Hopkinsesque falcon. Here is the bird's animation:

> eyeing all round, disqualifying, disqualifying
> all the bits within radius that hold no clue
> to whatever is sought, urgent but without hurry,
> me still by this hedge now, waiting for his black to blossom,
> then wing-thrash where he falls at first against the powerline,
> then updraft seized, gravity winnowed, the falling raggedly
> reversed, depth suddenly pursued, its invisibility ridged—bless him—
> until he is off, hinge by hinge, built of tiny wingtucks, filaments
> of flapped-back wind, until the thing (along whose spine
> his sentence of black talk, thrashing, wrinkling, dissipates—the history,
>   the wiring,
> shaking, with light—) is born.

The "thing" stands for both the idea of the bird in action and also the thought heralded by the "thinking" activity of the poem's title. Process becomes thing; action becomes event; doing becomes deed. And, equally important, the bird's "black talk" has become something visible, legible, another script for understanding the transformation of the present into the past, of perception into memory.

Birds are, in other words, examples of our transactions with the material world as well as symbols of our own yearning for freedom (from gravity, from speech, and from the world itself). Two poems in *The End of Beauty* stand out as relevant examples of Graham's sighting of birds. In "Vertigo" two lovers located on the edge of a cliff look down at the real world and its "flow." An unspecified bird drafts upward into view, a symbol of movement temporarily frozen in a downdraft—another version of Hopkins' "Windhover." Like Hopkins, Graham "stirs for a bird," but in a purely secular, or rather, philosophical way. The bird and its movements signify the accumulation of parts and whole, or stasis and movement, of freedom and captivity:

> the stages of flight, broken down, broken free,
> each wingflap folding, each splay of the feather-sets flattening
> for entry. . . . *Parts* she thought, *free* parts, watching the laws
> at work, *through which desire must course*
> seeking an ending, seeking a shape. Until the laws of flight and fall
>   increased.
> Until they made, all of an instant, a bird, a blue
> enchantment of properties no longer
> knowable. (*EB*, 66)

As with the blue blob of paint in "Massacio's Expulsion," the bird here masses into an identity and then gradually fades into an example or a proof of some higher law of both physics and metaphysics. And then the poet proceeds to remember another example of parts of something assembling into a unity; now it is "notes off the violin," rising free from an orchestral ensemble and then subsiding back into the mass of sound. Both examples—one visible, the other audible—provoke a musing on the human problem of singularity and togetherness, a problem Graham continues to investigate in poems with more overt erotic thematics.

Whereas "Vertigo" investigates the laws of nature with regard to freedom and departure, "Evening Prayer" likewise begins with the natural world and expands outward, but then takes the measure of gravity and its spiritual equivalences from a position much closer to earth. Starting with the sweet smell of newly mown grass, Graham creates a mower (like Keats's female "Autumn"?) who herself rises and turns freely in sun and wind. The first-person speaker, meanwhile, sees, walking home

> . . . the shadow of a bird, like a heart, like a scythe.
> I saw the shadow-wings cross through a wall.

Not the bird but its image, a symbol of will and energy, fighting against an updated urban scene of Keats's stubble-plains:

> But the bird, fistful of time and sinew, blue,
> dragged down over the cinderblock by light, lawed down and
> brushstroked down—how he went through, went
>   abstract,
> clean. Not hungry there and not afraid. (*EB*, 90)

Yet once more, Graham consigns her bird to an ambiguous position. Does she see *it*, or merely its shadow? Is it real or imagined, tangible or depicted, physical or abstract? The fact that its importance to her is entirely visual rather than musical suggests, like so much else in her earlier work, her own ineluctable preference of the eye to the ear.

In *Never* sound enters the equation more forcefully than ever before. In "The Taken-Down God," an Easter poem set in an Italian church, not only does the poet watch the preparations for a sculpted Christ's resurrection (i.e., the sculpture's re-positioning on the church wall), but she also listens to noises within and without. Now, even the "trapped-in light" within the chapel has its own "curious hum." The most important sound is the slightest; the poet is not supposed to be writing within the chapel, and her surreptitious activity is magnified: "My pen is / a bypath. It has come in from outside. It is colossal, the tiny sound it makes / as I insist in here" (*N*, 96). Whereas birds' feathers were figures for pens in her more conventional early work, now the pen itself has become an audible writing machine.

Probably no living American poet has as much hunger for speculation and for metaphysical questing as Graham. Her work is a welcome alternative to the intellectual, linguistic and emotional impoverishment of so much contemporary poetry. In her avidity she resembles Stevens; in her looking at the world she resembles Bishop, the late Amy Clampitt, and (one of Clampitt's and Bishop's favorite poets) Hopkins. But whereas patience is the virtue most associated with looking at the world, Graham's rare talent has resulted in *impatient* observing of both sights and sounds. Instead of the calm attention of Hopkins, Ruskin, and Darwin, the greatest of the Victorian lookers-at-the-surround, Graham offers swirling junkets of action, a mind and a world in perpetual motion. In "The Taken-Down God" Graham remarks "how deep the water of the watching is" and complements the action of her looking with the soft, insistent scratching of her forbidden writing, i.e., her own noise-making. Her noise is merely part of a symphony of sounds registered by her own listening, sounds that have an acutely visual effect.

"You do understand, don't you, by looking?" Graham asks over and over as a refrain in "Le Manteau de Pascal" (*The Errancy*), whose many other compelling repetitions act as a fugal stretto as well as a psychological gesture. Graham's compulsive looking and listening are allied to her ambivalent feeling that, on the one hand, she may be saved through her sensory activity or at least learn something from it, but that, on the other, looking—like language—is mediated by human consciousness and can never be other than partial. (She remains skeptical of the potential for resurrection on the day before Easter in "The Taken-Down God.") Similarly, sound—like sea, light, and air—can never be held but Graham aims her reach beyond what she can ever grasp. Wyatt's "Since in net I seek to hold the wind," the epigraph to *The Errancy*, might stand at the start of Graham's future *Collected Poems*. Whereas Bishop made "The Monument" (of wood) and a cabin on stilts ("The End of March") into objects for her descriptive energies and symbols of material reality, Graham prefers to draw nectar in a sieve.

At the same time, the sheer materiality of the world inspires the lush, almost tangible, densely syntactic thickets of Graham's poetry. Action—physical or mental—predominates so that all the poems seem to be written in the present tense (even when they are not). No other contemporary poet weaves so richly synaesthetic a fabric, or vibrates so excitedly between the seen and the heard. In "Where: The Person," seeing and hearing intertwine with touch as they do in Shelley's "Mont Blanc." Here, Graham witnesses "the hammer in the sun behind the fence" and, almost simultaneously, the way the "[w]ind silks the fronds" (*N*, 77). In "In/Silence" (see below) she identifies "[t]he song that falls upon the listener's *eye*" (*N*, 13). Like Whitman, Stevens, and Bishop, Graham loves to situate herself on a shoreline and to use the available sensory data as a goad to, and a reflection of, her metaphysical aspirations. These are also vocational ones. Like these other poets in the Romantic tradition who see evidence of natural writing in the world, and who listen attentively to the sounds of birds and wind, Graham challenges and measures herself with respect to her witnessing.

Listening is more problematic than seeing, if only because sound is temporal and more difficult to catch than light, harder to grasp than wind. In "The Complex Mechanism of the Break" (another poem whose very title signals the relationship of a natural phenomenon to an artistic one, in this case the breaks of waves and poetic lines), Graham begins with the visible, trying to describe the effect of waves waxing and waning. She seems to see and hear them ("ruffling front-thunder") simultaneously. Both the waves and the "real rows of low-flying pelicans" (*N*, 33) move and dissolve, two natural elements mirroring one another. In trying to see and to record the waves, Graham involves herself in acts of self-correction. Her stringing together of parenthetical phrases, both simultaneous and sequential in their effect, mimics the motion of the waves and also stands in for her greedy imaginative desire to rearrange linear time in order to make everything visible at once. She says straightforwardly: "The mind doesn't / want it to break—unease where the heart pushes out—the mind / wants only to keep it coming, yes, sun making the not-yet-breaking crest / so gold where the / pelicans turn as they glide—flapping then gliding—as long as possible without too much dropping" (*N*, 34). As usual her breathless, onrushing excitement sounds a sexual note. It is as though Molly Bloom had become an intellectual.

Graham has always looked hard at the world; now in mid-poem, she turns her attention from the visible to the audible. She listens hard. She asks her reader (or herself?) to "close your eyes" and then corrects herself, acknowledging the inevitable overlapping of the senses: "although it's only when you open them you hear the seven / kinds of / sound" (*N*, 34–35). (As with Empson's seven types of ambiguity, what is important is not so much the distinct kinds as the human effort to distinguish them. One is surprised not that it is done well but that it is done at all.) She has attended to "force" and now she measures it sonically, listening to "hiss-flattenings," "the pebbled wordlike pulling down and rolling up," through the "crash" of one wave hitting another, subsiding into the "lowering and sudden softening of all betweens," and then hearing "the first crash" yet once more. The conclusion of the poem—fifteen lines—begins and ends with parentheses; everything she hears, including a "momentary lull," is bracketed to give a sense of "betweenness." Like the ocean, the music of Graham's poetry ignores normal signatures of key and tempo; her most radical experiments may be those in which she both signals and eschews closure. Graham's earlier sensitivity to the visual world—whether painted or natural—is complemented and superseded by her musical sensitivity in poems like this. Her philosophical themes (shared in part with the late A. R. Ammons) are cause and effect, origin and destination, and the way things work temporally. By looking at waves and water she reproduces her obsession with middles, "betweens." Her hurly-burly, synaesthetic response to the world allows her to combine the philosopher's wonder with the painter's eye. And the listener's ear. Her true precursor here is Whitman, who like Graham abjures the polished, the finished. His analogy for his own verse is the ocean: "Its verses are the liquid, billowy waves, ever rising and falling, perhaps wild with storm, always moving, always alike in their nature as rolling waves, but hardly any two exactly alike in size or measure, never having the sense of something finished and fixed, always suggesting something beyond."[8]

Graham's sensitivity to an overwhelming, oceanic sense of sound has an additional point of origin in Whitman. In *Song of Myself*, Section 26, he proposes for himself what Graham actually accomplishes in "The Taken-Down God": "Now I will do nothing but listen, / To accrue what I hear into this song, to let sounds contribute toward it." But then the seigneurial cataloguer of American life, who hears "America singing" in his famous pronouncement, embarks upon an auditory journey whose path and whose end we could hardly predict. "I hear bravuras of birds," he begins, and supplements bird call with the "bustle of growing wheat," city noises, voices of young lovers, then builds toward musical sounds, first orchestral ones, then singing. He hears "the chorus . . . grand opera," then a tenor, and a soprano, whose voices against the orchestra produce an orgasmic experience at once deadly and life-affirming:

> The orchestra whirls me wider than Uranus flies,
> It wrenches such ardors from me I did not know I possess'd them,
> It sails me, I dab with bare feet, they are lick'd by the indolent waves,
> I am cut by bitter and angry hail, I lose my breath,
> Steep'd amid honey'd morphine, my windpipe throttled in fakes of death,
> At length let up again to feel the puzzle of puzzles,
> And that we call Being.

Although temporarily losing himself, Whitman cannot really be said to have found himself; he cagily refers only to feeling the puzzle, rather than the fact, of Being. Both Graham and Whitman admit of only temporary revelations, because their sensuous and mental engagements with the world can permit no stillness.

The marriage of the visible and the heard occupies her in "In/Silence," one of the few poems that pay attention to an ordinary songbird. When she announces "I looked today long and hard at a singing bird" (*N*, 12) she deliberately avoids saying at first whether the bird is of the "singing" variety or whether he is actively engaged in song at the moment of her looking. Such rich ambiguity might remind us of the commonplace paradox of pictures as silent poems, or ekphrastic poems as speaking pictures. (I think of Dryden's praise in "To Sir Godfrey Kneller": "At least thy Pictures look a Voice; and we / Imagine sounds, deceiv'd to that degree, / We think 'tis somewhat more than just to see.") Graham's songbird "looks a voice." Having begun by calling truth something one must repress and keep silent, she comes upon the unspecified small bird and watches him up close:

>   seeming
> to puff out and hold something within, something that
>   makes
> wind ruffle his exterior more—watched

> him lift and twist a beak sunlight made burnt-silver
> as he tossed it back—not so much to let
> anything *out* but more to carve and then to place firmly in the
> > listening space
> > around him
> a piece of inwardness . . . (*N*, 12)

Graham has encountered a cousin to the Romantic specimens that stand in for a poet's desires. Between the moments of silence and release the song falls upon the "listener's eye." The bird is visible (unlike Keats's nightingale and Shelley's skylark), until the moment when it ascends:

> lost in the going aloft with the as yet
> > unsung—then
> the betrayal (into the clear morning air)
> of the source of happiness into mere (sung) happiness. (*N*, 13)

Such troping of silence and song, containment and release, matches Graham's longtime interest in the visible manifestations of epiphany and evanescence—the kind of thing that she finds in seashore scenes. Now she has not only domesticated the trope but also expanded the sensuous skein of its articulation to include the audible. At the same time, she undermines our normal expectations. Rather than think of the bird—in flight and in song—as a synonym for freedom, she makes a subtler discrimination. As the bird hovers between silence and sound, Graham distinguishes the moment "before any dazzling release / of the unfree into the seeming free," which itself precedes the "overrun" of the (bird's) engine into "the truly free" (*N*, 13). Hence, I think, one way of understanding the odd title and its awkward back slash: the punctuation interrupts the intimacy of grammatical wholeness in the prepositional phrase. Two principles of observation and action—call them achievement or wholeness, and separation or momentariness—seem to exist simultaneously. It is as though a poetic line could be both end-stopped and enjambed.

The difficult compactness of this poem seems to force Graham into other forms of articulation within the same volume. For example, "The Time Being" consists of two separate parts, both subtitled "Todos Santos," the second of which has an additional label of place, "Palm Beach." Both parts of the poem deal with motifs of containment and exposure, as well as expulsion and "melting off," but the second part is entirely visual in its references, set as it is in a maritime scene. Part I, however, is predominantly auditory, beginning with a "cluster of bird-chatter," a "knot," which merges with a nearby sound from a thick rope, itself containing several parts. The simultaneity of sounds makes for chords. Graham relishes matching a visible knot with the richness of sounds in which "nothing can be singled out" (*N*, 44). The whole first section continues in an auditory mode: dog-bark, "clap of banana leaves," a car's engine, a woman calling out, a small boy tapping a glass jar, trucks driving near by, goat bells and cow bells. The virtual symphonic richness of sounds is unprecedented in Graham's poetry; it is as though she has finally opened her ears to the world as much as she had previously opened her eyes.

Whether watching and seeing, or hearing and listening, Graham is a poet who registers a world in motion. Nothing is ever still, and everything leaves a residue. The visible leaves its traces in ways that sound, except in the eternal roar of the waves, never can. In a poem titled "High Tide" Graham admits that once, after high tide, she "found a beachlong / scripting / of debris" (*N*, 102). Like Bishop's kite string in "The End of March," what Graham discovers inevitably reminds her, and her readers, of all efforts to penetrate the visible through to its origins and its meanings, to connect effect with cause. At the same time (I resort again to the distinction between nouns and gerunds) she is trying to distinguish between deeds and doings. A "scripting of debris" sounds like both a subjective and an objective genitive phrase: the debris *as* written evidence (a script written in debris) and as the direct object of the action of "scripting." No action seems completed in Graham's poetry; cessation or fulfillment would be equivalent to death. In his great autobiographical poem "Nutting" Wordsworth recounts a moment when, at the age of ten, he wandered into a hazel grove and ripped it apart in an act of rapacious, assertive masculinity. But before doing so he lolls about, taking his ease; he hears what he calls "the murmur and the murmuring sound" of nearby waters. I take this as a distinction between an abstraction and a present-tense activity, or between the Platonic idea of a thing and that same thing in a self-performance. That same distinction—between a thing in its "doneness" and in its "doing"—is very much at the heart of Graham's recent poetry. In "Exit Wound" she refers to "the blue between the branches / pulling upwards and away so that branches / become / *branching*" (*N*, 52). Much of the book generates questions about completion, about whether a thing is ever done. In her earlier "The Phase After History" (*Region of Unlikeness*) Graham embedded quotations from, and allusions to, *Macbeth*, the play that asks the equally Grahamian question about whether a thing is actually and thoroughly done "when 'tis done." Such queries are practical as well as philosophical and psychological. In *Never* Graham questions the efficacy of all action, and the ways in which we resist and also accept changes from within and without.

In *The Errancy*, Graham included a group of poems spoken by a series of "guardian angels," whom she identified as witnesses, unable to effect change. In *Never* it is the poet herself who wrestles not only with acts of perception but also with activities of control and the determination of destiny. The first poem ("Prayer") ends with her uncertainties about her power: "I could not choose words. I am free to go. / I cannot of course come back. Not to this. Never. / It is a ghost posed on my lips. Here: never" (*N*, 3). Such a ghost is like the bird about to sing in "In/Silence." The biographical background of these short declarations is probably the series of recent changes in Graham's life—a divorce, a physical move from the middle west to the east coast—but their function in the poem is to alert us, in a series of assertive renunciations, to affirmations still to come. "[N]ever anything but expectant": the waves and the tide in the book's final poem ("Relay Station," 107) are also a stand-in for the poet's own state of mind. In "Exit Wound" she distances herself from herself, referring (like Stevens) to "she," never to "I." (This self-objectification is another example of her legacy from Ruskin and his wish to remain invisible.) As she examines herself, she meditates on one of her habitual questions: "the problem as always was the problem of how / something could come out of nothing." At the end, recalling a previous condition she "felt as if she could / reconcile / this present to that one, and that the / thinking / wanted that so. And that it strived" (*N*, 56). The poet has determined to continue her movement, however ragged or rugged it might be, toward some degree of illumination. *Never* asks questions; it assays answers; it affirms and then withdraws its affirmations. The poet's mind and the activity of her poetic "thinking" resemble the waves she confronts and describes in acts of watching and hearing. Like the waves, they are endless in their glitter and in their music.

Notes

1. Jorie Graham, *The Errancy* (Hopewell, N.J.: Ecco Press, 1997), 106 (cited as *Ey*). Other Graham books cited here are *Hybrids of Plants and of Ghosts* (Princeton: Princeton University Press, 1980) (cited as *H*); *Erosion* (Princeton: Princeton University Press, 1987) (*E*); *The End of Beauty* (New York: Ecco Press, 1987) (*EB*); *Materialism* (Hopewell, N.J.: Ecco Press, 1993) (*M*); *Swarm* (New York: Ecco Press, 2000) (*S*); *Never* (New York: Ecco Press, 2002) (*N*).

2. See his stern but sympathetic review of *Swarm*, "The End of Beauty," *The New Republic*, 13 March 2000, 35–42. Kirsch observes that Graham's poetry "demands 'readings' even as it resists reading" (36), and that her willfulness results in lines that, when read and reconstructed, "sound merely like prose" (42). He cogently concludes: "the poet's work does not end with the opacity of the mind, it begins with it. As long as Jorie Graham asks her readers to fill in her blanks and solve for her X's, she has not realized, or even approached, poetry's greatest and truest possibilities" (42).

3. For a seminal discussion of the sense of hearing, see John Hollander, "The Poem in the Ear," in *Vision and Resonance: Two Senses of Poetic Form*, 2nd ed. (New Haven and London: Yale University Press, 1985), 3–43. Eleanor Cook, in "Birds in Paradise: Uses of Allusion in Milton, Keats, Whitman, Stevens and Ammons," *Studies in Romanticism* 26, no. 3 (Fall 1987): 421–443, elegantly follows a metaleptic line of birds, and allusions to other poets' birds through what the author calls "the history of a topos: birds in an earthly paradise as an image of voice for a poet. The topos includes matters of singing, flight, waking or sleeping, dreaming, death" (433). J. D. McClatchy's recent anthology, *On Wings of Song: Poems about Birds* (Alfred A. Knopf: New York, 2000) contains a wide selection of American and English poems about birds of every kind.

4. Thomas J. Otten, in "Jorie Graham's _____s," *PMLA*, 18, no. 2 (March 2003): 239–253, suggests that Graham's blanks are graphic representations of the lyric genre in their visualization of privacy and also of those contemporary materials like Formica, latex, and spray paint that are themselves mediating substances.

5. See my earlier essay (on Graham's volumes through *Materialism*) "Jorie Graham's 'New Way of Looking,'" *Salmagundi* 120 (Fall 1998): 244–275, for a discussion of renderings of sight and of acts of vision in her poems.

6. The whole question of who is speaking to whom is crucial to all of lyric poetry; in Graham's work the problem is heightened and would require a separate discussion of matters of voice and audience. In addition, listening to or overhearing human speech is a different enterprise from hearing natural or non-human sounds, especially in Graham's poetry, and would also require a separate, equally revealing, treatment.

7. From "The Col de la Faucille." Directly before this admission Ruskin quotes Emerson or Carlyle (he doesn't say which), who says that happiness arrives only when "we can think that here and there one is thinking of us, one is loving us." To which Ruskin responds, "*My times of happiness had always been when* nobody *was thinking of me.*"

8. Horace Traubel, *With Walt Whitman in Camden* (Boston: Small, Maynard, 1906), I: 414.

16

The Speaking Subject In/Me

Gender and Ethical Subjectivity in the Poetry of Jorie Graham

CYNTHIA HOGUE

In this essay, I propose to take a particular approach in relation to Jorie Graham's poetry. My point of departure is that ideologies of gender in the lyric—the notion that, as Rachel Blau DuPlessis asserts, historically "the genre poetry activates notable master plots, ideologies, and moves fundamentally inflected with gender relations"[1]—are among those Graham investigates rather extensively over the course of her remarkable career. Critics have turned incidental but not concerted analytical attention to this aspect of her work.[2] I situate the essay that follows in that critical gap. Sidelining gender in Graham's poetry implies that the material conditions of textual production have little bearing on her project. But to the contrary, connections a poem like "Concerning the Right to Life" draws—whose theme lies at the heart of Graham's oeuvre, "the material," and whose setting is an abortion clinic where there are protestors picketing outside—are central to the poem's concerns.

The poem opens with the speaker happening upon a huge rose, "tall as a man":

>   As I
> rounded the corner, the possible
> sprung from
>   possibility
>   into whipped red
> choice.[3]

Through this deft regendering of a traditional symbol of transient feminine beauty in the lyric, Graham implies that the rose, like the figure of Woman, has been a masculine thing all along. But the striking diction puzzles us. How are we to understand its shock, the "whipped red" compelled onward by enjambment to "choice"—as culinary or sensual s-m? Erotic or punishing? What is at stake in "form" (which she defines elsewhere as "*action* in language")[4]—whether the possible, "the *living*," may spring like the huge rose from amorphous possibility (*M*, 14–15; Graham's emphasis)—may have as much to do with *force* as with *choice*. Graham ravels rather than clarifies the terms of the debate.

The poem's structure works like an ever-widening spiral of implications, all connecting at the root to the concept of the rights of the individual, which is to say also to the rights of life-*forms*. Picket signs bearing the accusation *"the other / holocaust: don't kill / your children"* and screams by a "huge man" of "let the mother die but save the child" raise the question *Whose rights?* not *Who's right?* The historical past of the Holocaust intervenes in the language and consciousness of the personal present. As Helen Vendler contends about the poem "History," "history" in Graham's work "is not a two-dimensional remnant, like a photograph; it is an active force [i.e. in the present], like the delayed violence of [a] grenade."[5] In "Concerning the Right to Life," the Holocaust haunts alike the language of the protestors' cries of "*right to life*" (*M*, 17, 16; Graham's emphasis) and the speaker thinking, as she anxiously cools the forehead of her feverish child, that "there are realms where '*there is no choice*'" (*M*, 18; Graham's emphasis).[6] This eerie resonance draws attention to specificities of gender and ethnicity disappearing into the universalized concept of individual freedom. Thus, the poem compels us to ask whether the "will of the species" ought to outweigh a woman's "individual will,"[7] and, to whom does that "*immaculate spot* within— the freedom of / choice, illustrious / sleep, *bloody spot*" of (unformed) possibility inside the woman inherently belong (*M*, 16; emphasis added)?

Although Graham's purpose is not to adjudicate, the context in which she asks such questions genders the awareness the poem is tracking. The woman carrying the "punched-out spot / of blood which is *not her*" is neither *merely* a vessel bearing precious content, without value in and of herself, nor guilt-free (as the allusions to Lady Macbeth imply). One feels the dilemma of the woman within the context of choice, whereas there is no sympathy aroused by the imagery for the notion that the fate of the "red idea" within her should by rights be determined by the huge man screaming that she be let to die (*M*, 19). That "spot" is "immaculate," Graham suggests, because it is literally and figuratively as yet unformed—untouched—by all the ideological forces that would shape it, including gatekeepers to a woman's access to self-determination.

The fifth and final section of the poem makes this notion clear. The section splices in passages from the diary of Columbus's first journey to America, implying by juxtaposition that the mindset of the argument against "choice" comprises a dynamic similar to the colonizing mindset. In the fourth section, which I quote in full, Graham forges this gendered (and implicitly raced) connection:

> What is it, the spot inside Mary, the punched-out spot of
> blood which is *not her?*—
>   to whom does it belong?—immaculate
> garden—red idea; truth held *self-*
>   *evident*—
> through which the crowd can cross
>
>   and *take possession*
> *of the earth*—
>   So she is a shore, a *vulgar ocean* which round the *idea of*
>   *ocean*
> roils—
>
> (*M*, 19; Graham's emphasis)

The analogical yoking of ideas in this section enables Graham to probe the cultural connections among debates about individual rights (including the right to pursue *property*, the original right in Jefferson's Lockean formulation, eventually idealized as the right to pursue "happiness"); the abortion debate and women's rights (with evocations, in the issue of bodily self-possession, of both the Holocaust and Slavery); and the appropriative mentality in early Modern Europe which produced, among other events, the brutal colonization of America and the treatment of its original inhabitants.[8] The poem exposes how the feminine has been culturally construed as the empty space to cross to "*take possession*" of the "*not her*": by punning analogy, virgin territory.

As this poem indicates, cultural feminism is a social and intellectual movement that has influenced Graham,[9] and her method has as much to do with an ethical consciousness arrived at through embodied experience as with disembodied philosophical inquiry and aesthetics.[10] By insistently figuring the body into the poem thematically, and by contemplating the site of that figuration—in effect, refiguring the body[11]—Graham's work has scrutinized dominant structures of power, like gender ideologies, and subjectivities in the Symbolic that underpin Western thought as well as lyric tradition.

I'd like now to turn to other exemplary Graham poems in order to explore this thesis more deeply. An early poem in Graham's second collection *Erosion*,

"Two Paintings by Gustav Klimt," moves from a contemplation of a finished Klimt painting to regarding an unfinished painting of a woman whose body is, as the poem describes it,

> open at its point of
>   entry,
> rendered in graphic,
>   pornographic,
>
> detail—something like
>   a scream
> between her legs. Slowly,
>   feathery,
> he had begun to paint
>   a delicate
>
> garment (his trademark)
>   over this mouth
> of her body. (*E*, 62–63)

The body so insistently present in this poem refigures an aestheticized image of woman, a doubled, and—within a dominant visual economy—doubly objectified representation. That the poem has something to do with analyzing the currency of Woman in that symbolic economy is indicated by this mimetic doubling. As a figure of both excess and desire, she was about to be silenced by a beautiful cover up, which was never completed because of Klimt's untimely death. Like the uncompleted painting, the woman, rendered ironically in *too* complete detail, is exposed as "incomplete" herself.

As the transgendered allusion to another fin-de-siècle painting, Edvard Munch's *The Scream*, suggests, Graham has sketched here—"Slowly," in "feathery," "delicate" lines—a scene that revisits the notion of woman's uncanniness for the male subject, for whom Klimt stands in. Death interrupted Klimt before he had time to cover up the tracks of his ambivalence: both attracted and repulsed, he is caught between his desire to look and the injunction not to see. For her "port of entry" was also his—in its uncanny reverse, into the world—and thus to enter her scopically is both an invasion and return to safe harbor. Woman's sex in Western representation has been ambivalently both eroticized and repressed, because seeing nothing triggers the fear that there is *nothing to see*.[12]

But in Graham's poem, that horror of "nothing to see" is also reversed into the Stevensian fear of "seeing Nothing,"[13] the modern nihilism implied by the allusion to Munch's painting. This doubled, oppositional movement between fear and fascination thus highlights the framework structuring the woman's objectification. The associative connections Graham draws—among the "scream" between the woman's legs, the aggressive fear of castration, and the violation that is an aspect of the scopic drive—foreshadow the Holocaust (the future within the poem's frame but the past beyond it) through the coincidence of finished painting's title, *Buchenwald.*

Through its names and metaphors, the poem contemplates the fascist will to mastery that the "fabric" of beautiful "surface" and "story" hide. As Thomas Gardner astutely observes, "With this garment, we find ourselves in territory very close to Bishop's link between the eye's tapestry and colonialism."[14] The beautiful, pastoral "*buchen-wald*" of the nineteenth century in the poem casts forward to the twentieth-century horror of the Buchenwald concentration camp. Similarly, the aestheticized body of the woman contrasts with the graphically unaestheticizable bodies of those killed in the Holocaust, creating a "tension between the moral and the aesthetic and the aestheticizing of the moral," as Bonnie Costello argues.[15] The sculptured, precious style of this early poem (which has, as the last lines put it, "something to do / with pleasure") serves as formal sepulcher for the formless, the disembodied dead (which has something to do with the death drive).

The poems in Graham's next volume, *The End of Beauty*, often take as their investigative premise large, cultural issues, primarily the workings of power and its attendant forms (imperialism, colonialism, sexual and economic possession), subjects that continue to occupy her thinking up to and including her most recent collections. Graham contextualizes power by dramatizing specific instances, often coded as heterosexual. These dramatic scenes hover on the edge of potential, imaginative transformations of power, without spilling over into an imposed thematic resolution. Resisting the predictable structure of an age-old "plot" is often a crucial aspect of the form's relationship to theme, as critics have noted. "Imperialism," for example, opens generally by raising epistemological and ontological questions ("What I want to know . . . / is what it *is*, this life"), but then moves quickly into the details of a marital argument ("what is it *for* // this marriage"?). Hurling verbal "cruelties" (*EB*, 95), the partners manage with great effort to pull away from the "plot," with all its subplots of dominance and submission, although "It took all that we are / to keep the thing clear" (*EB*, 95).

Another poem that contemplates this "plot," "Self-Portrait as Apollo and Daphne," opens with an acknowledgment of women's complicity historically in maintaining the power differential of the heterosexual contract: "The truth is this [the pursuit] had been going on for a long time during which / they both wanted it to last" (*EB*, 30). It moves on, however, to the insights born of resistance: "she would not be the end towards which he was ceaselessly tending" (*EB*, 32). Graham dissects the structure of this masculinist plot and the feminine object it posits, analyzing the symbolic thinking that conforms to its strictures, opening the text to its possible transformation.[16]

Graham explores the theme of transformation through formal experiment, as the marked expansion of lines and poems between her second and third collections indicates. As she has remarked, "Shifts in my 'style' are a large part of [my] process."[17] Gone are the sculptured, exquisite structures of *Erosion*. *The End of Beauty* has put an end to their chiseled austerity. In its place is a Whitmanic expanse of both line and thought, often casting past the end of the line spatially through enjambment and indentation, a concrete formatting that will come to characterize Graham's mature style to varying degrees. Like the poems, the lines themselves now balance, poised, between the consummately wielded and near-overwhelmed.

Graham thereby acknowledges the difficulties that obstruct real transformation (and trans/formation of the real)—that identities have accrued around one's placement in the master plot (for example, that the feminine has been the often compliant object of the heroic quest). In "Self-Portrait as Apollo and Daphne," Daphne resolves not to "give shape to his hurry by being its destination," but after she steps out of that age-old story, "she would be who, / what?" (*EB*, 32–33). The poem poses no alternative identity for the very reason that it is complicating rather than settling the issue. The question the poem poses is whether that sudden openness, the fact that no alternative identity is given form within the space of the poem, indicates creative emptiness or existential void. Graham explores such a question in *The End of Beauty, Region of Unlikeness,* and *Materialism,* often specifically in terms of female subjectivity and heterosexual relations.

"Imperialism" opens with a marital disagreement and closes with a long, personal narrative, which resolves with the abjection of the mother, symbolically inaugurating the entry of the child in the poem into an awareness of cultural differences. During a trip to Calcutta, the speaker's mother wants her daughter to "*know the world,*" and tells her nine-year-old child to submerge herself in the Ganges River. The river is full of the matter humans produce in the process of living: people's laundry and dishes, people's bodies being washed, and the "ash and cartilage" of their cremated bodily remains, which are shaken into the river. After her baptism in the knowledge these teaming waters represent, the child is shocked awake—both to the phenomenological world, and to its inaccessibility to human frames of understanding, like that of utilitarianism—whether economic or aesthetic. What "imagery might / be of use," the adult speaker asks, and she continues in a punning fusion suggestive of the exploitative dangers of language: "What is the usery that's deep enough" to "touch" that reality (*EB*, 97)?

The speaker cannot answer such questions, for she has no memory of the trauma (and thus cannot re-member the facts). The past comes to her as literature rather than history. Afterwards, the "story" goes, the traumatized child could not be made to stop screaming, the reasons for which the adult speaker suggests was caused by the difference between the world and its representation, the gap between the truth *of* the real and *about* the real, which has been revealed to her.

When the distraught mother tries to hold and calm her daughter, she makes "it worse, / since her body (in particular) was / no longer relevant" (*EB*, 97):

> it became nothing to me after that, or something less,
>   because I saw what it was, her body, you see—a line
> brought round, all the way round, reader, a plot, a
>   shape, one of the finished things, one of the
>
> *beauties* (hear it click shut?) a thing
>
> completely narrowed down to love—
>
> (*EB*, 98–99)

The child sees that her mother's body is "one of the finished things," like a "plot" or a "story," which "narrowed" her existence down to one possibility for maternal identity and foreclosed the possibility of any others. For the daughter, the discovery of her mother's narrowed identity resolves what the poem suggests is a predictable plot of a particular gendered ideology imposed on women, and into which individual women disappear. Rejecting the mother as an object of identification, however idealized, and rejecting all that the mother symbolizes, the child has nothing with which to replace her, no alternative identity. There is no one and nothing to mirror her back to herself any longer in imaginary plenitude. The mother's abjected body has become an objectified "thing." The child, too, is abject.

The poem closes with these formally fraught lines figuring maternal loss, a kind of mother-in-pieces who disappears into her role as uncannily as Moore's paper nautilus:

> completely narrowed down to love—all arms, all arms extended in the
> > pulsing sticky heat, fan on, overhead on, all
> arms no face at all dear god, all arms—

(*EB*, 99)

Graham refrains from (re)unifying the abject subject, or from imposing the very "finished" shape with which the poem has taken formal issue.[18] As the poem's trajectory suggest, the child is posited in a less illusory subjectivity, which has just been revealed to her as divided (both from her mother, as mirror and mentor, and within herself). This emerging subject, although less secure (acknowledging her failure to touch the world with her words), is also more tolerant of alterity. The prosody of the last strophe—in its almost stuttering caesuras, and broken, typographically and thematically open-ended resolution—registers the choric (real) memory traces of the child's anxiety at this juncture. And in that hesitation, I suggest, the poem imaginatively construes an ethical subjectivity drawn from gendered experience.[19]

Scenes of exquisitely contemplated, feminine self-reflection—and more productively, of its failure—occur in some of Graham's most important poems in the volumes that follow *The End of Beauty*. In *Region of Unlikeness* and *Materialism*, there are a number of poems that contain literal mirror scenes, which function symbolically analogous to the Lacanian mirror stage, for they inaugurate the speaker as a young girl into the social contract.[20] The speaker in such poems (as either young girl or young woman) stands before a mirror, shocked by some event out of childish security—that sense of being one with herself—into a sense of self-alienation and difference. Nor does Graham proffer any compensatory reaffirmation of wholeness to cover over the rupture. Rather, she tracks it through the subject's sense of displacement, which is imaged literally as a di/vision before the mirror, thereby complicating and refiguring feminine narcissism, self-reflection and subjectivity.

In "Picnic," to take a specific example, the pre-pubescent speaker is placed in a scene suggestive of narcissistic plenitude, the expectations of which the poem shatters. On a picnic with family and friends, the girl wanders down to a pond and happens upon her "father with X," about to embark on an affair. She looks into the water and instead of seeing her face reflected back to her, she poses a question to the reader, which literally and metaphorically replaces the image of the speaker's face in the poem:

> Have you ever looked into standing water and seen it going very fast,
>> seen the breaks in the image where the suction shows,
> where the underneath is pointed and its tip shows through,
>> maybe something broken, maybe something spoked in there,
> your eyes weeds, mouth weeds,
>> no bed showing through, no pressure from some shore, no
>
> shore? I looked in there.
>
> (*RU*, 43)

The scene images the subject's inaugurating division through grammatical enactment and spatialized displacement. The subject's position and point of view are doubled through the shifts from apostrophe to first person. Perspective, too, is doubled and deepened: "I looked *in* there"; "The face stayed there" (*RU*, 44; emphasis added). What should be merely a reflective surface is revealed as having depth when the image hovering on the surface breaks up to expose what lies underneath, and then re-forms.

Later in the poem, there is a reflective scene between mother and daughter, whose dyadic relationship has been triangulated by the daughter's discovery of the dissemblance at the heart of her parents' marriage, the father's betrayal. The upset mother streaks make-up on her daughter's face, which has become the "the third / party" in the mirror, the "one face behind the other peering in":

> We painted that [face] alive,
> mother with her hands
>> fixing the outline clear—eyeholes, mouthhole—
> forcing the expression on.
>
> (*RU*, 44–45)

This face, "the only thing in the end of the day that seemed // believable," awakens in the young girl, shocked out of childish innocence, an awareness of the ethical and metaphysical bases (like "candor" and "freedom") on which fragile, human relations rest.

The poem ends on a subtle, Austenian note (via James): the women of privilege sitting around over drinks (and more drinks) in a beautiful garden speak of the marriage market—whether "The Princess // known as *Luciana*" should "marry the arms merchant named Rudi." Implicitly, as the names suggest, this would be a social marriage uniting national, economic, and class interests. Explicitly, the mother has taught her daughter to put her best face on, to make herself up—that is, to take her place in the masquerade of femininity. The pressure to take one's social place (for example, in the institution of marriage) skewers the symbolism of the poem's pastoral materialism, the note on which the poem closes (in which the leaves of spring are "taking up // place" [*RU*, 45]).

Other poems, like "From the New World" and "The Dream of the Unified Field," similarly complicate mirror scenes, which not only posit the daughter in the social realm, but also into a politicized, historicized, and gendered consciousness. As in "Imperialism" and "Picnic," Graham moves from cultural analysis in such poems to the imagined possibilities for a different subjectivity, one that is in process, less *self*-centered and more aware of others. Such moments, in which self-alienation is tentatively imaged as tolerated lead to new possibilities for a self among other selves in the world.

In "From the New World," the adult speaker, the author-surrogate named self-reflexively in the poem "Jorie," hears an unnamed survivor's eye-witness account, during the 1987 trial in Israel of the appalling Treblinka guard Ivan, of an unidentified girl who survived the gas chamber. She "came back out asking / for her mother," and whispered "*please*" as Ivan ordered her to be raped and sent back in (*RU*, 12, 15). It is hard to write out these facts (I mean critically as well), and part of the poem's struggle is to think through an event the horror of which renders it impossible to find language that might adequately contain and account for it. That is part of Graham's point: the aesthetic concerns (the "swerve into shapeliness") are "unmoored" by horrific details (*RU*, 12).

The figures in the poem seem to repeat each other's loss of identity. The adult "Jorie," mulling over the girl at Treblinka asking for her mother, is reminded of herself as a girl unsettled by her senile grandmother's failure to recognize her. The narrative of this event interrupts the narrative of the earlier event, a structural break that formally repeats the matrilinear disruption. The structural and associative equivalences between the two girls do not pose thematic equivalences, however, for the girl lost at Treblinka is lost to language, whereas "Jorie" is posited by division in language.[21]

When the speaker is misrecognized by her senile grandmother and steps into the bathroom, she stands before the mirror, but does not look to see herself mirrored reassuringly back to herself. The self-loss here is figurative, not literal as with the other girl, and the self-alienating moment opens her imaginatively to seeing others:

> Reader,
>   they were all in there, I didn't look up,
> they were all in there, the coiling and uncoiling
>   billions,
>
> the about-to-be-seized,
>   the about to be held down,
> . . .
> and the about-to-be stepping in,
>   one form at a time stepping in as if to stay clean,
> stepping over something to get into here,
>   something there on the floor now dissolving,
> not looking down but stepping up to clear it,
>
> and clearing it,
>   stepping in.
>
> (*RU*, 13)

This insistent, Whitmanic passage, structured as an apostrophe to the "Reader," opens imaginatively to a constantly renewing present as different readers occupy the place of being addressed. But for all the eloquence of apostrophe, the poem seems at a loss. It is repetitive in its articulations, again and again raising metaphysical issues, but not—in any but rhetorically illusory ways—the dead.

At the point at which the girl comes back out of the gas chamber saying "*please*,"

>   something begins, yes,
>   something new, something completely
> new, but what—there underneath the screaming—what?
>
> (*RU*, 16)

What indeed? The Holocaust victim's one whispered word, "*please*" (a wrenching pun on *pleas*) is the sign of some new "about-to-be" that has no name and no definition. The language in this passage is vague, echoing rather than articulating itself (*something / something, what / what?*). There is no likeness, no analogy, no other event to which the speaker can compare this one: "*like what*, I whisper, // *like* which is the last new world, *like, like*" (*RU*, 16; Graham's emphasis). The event can be imaginatively invoked, but there the text stalls: the speaker has been reduced to inarticulation.[22] The girl has come to an unnameable edge, which may be the possible emerging from possibility, but there's no illumination possible here. The noxious mindset that extinguishes her concretizes the atrocity of indifference to others.

By way of closing, I want to turn very briefly to Graham's recent work, and consider the significance of her more recent explorations of cultural, social, and psychological constructions of others, and the self among other selves. In a poem entitled "Ebbtide," for example, Graham denotes the divided subject as perceiving self, a receptive channel:

> I am a frequency, current flies through. One has
> >   to ride
> >   the spine.
> No peace [of mind] [of heart], among the other
> frequencies. How often and how hard are answerings. (*N*, 36)

Through the enjambed line breaks, spatial and graphic divisions, and mid-line thematic and typographic caesuras, form mimes the substantive tracking of division both within and outside what Graham calls in another poem "the speaking subject in / me" (*N*, 94).

Like the earlier poems discussed in these pages, there is much brooding on the nature of being in these later poems, but it has become less historically focused, more contemporary with current global concerns. Always a highly intertextual poet, Graham draws less from classical sources, more from popular culture. A poem entitled "The Taken-Down God," for instance (quoted above), is written with the awareness of the possibility of extinction, as the collaged quotation from an Italian newspaper story about the U.S.'s refusal to sign the Kyoto Accords suggests: "'Gli Stati Uniti rifiutano gli accordi di Kyoto—addio / al mondo—' [this serves as that which dates the *here*]. Weren't we here?" (*N*, 96; Graham's emphasis). There's no date here, and implicitly, no *here* here either, in which we could have been "here" (except that which is, like the shifter deictic that is its verbal sign, constantly shifting). "America: you witch: dreaming always of here from an // elsewhere, from a nowhere," a poem entitled "High Tide" impugns: "I'm looking through a wind that's like a wall for / a proper name: for identification: representation: // divine emptiness" (*N*, 104). The colons punctuate apparent specificities, which turn out to be the endless displacements of place itself, the irresolvable search for something with which to stabilize identity.

More hopefully, though, Graham ponders in that poem the possibilities inherent in "listening" to another person, who in the context of the poem is at its center, but specifically, as a homeless woman, is socially marginalized. Graham takes great care not to mark the other woman's liminal economic status as raced; rather, she is at pains emotionally to signify as well as respect the other's *humanity* (*N*, 101).²³ Seeing her in her sleeping bag on the street one November evening, the poem's speaker, an author-surrogate, approaches her:

>   If I get very close,
> I feel a wish between us like
> a silver thing. Sadness, yes, in our
> one gaze [at certain points as you
> approach it becomes one] [the ends of each long
>   separation
> knit]
>
> (*N*, 102–103)

As the isolation of "separation" indicates, the real social separation between the two women is typographically as well as thematically observed here.

Across that chasm, the speaker reaches to touch the other woman, to "knit" together the "ends" between them (to "get to a 'we,'" as Graham has put it elsewhere).²⁴ As she does so,

>   I fill
> with the sensation of having
> goodness—actual goodness?—fill with my
>   *thinking it good*
> out to the very edges of my hand—touching her cheek—feel love?
>
> (*N*, 103)

With its lunges and stops, enjambed half-meanings ("the sensation of having / goodness") and parenthetical caesuras, the passage restores the embodied affects that accompanied the gesture of the one woman—white ("with / listening," as "Estuary" slyly puts it [*N*, 59]), and privileged (she has, for example, health insurance and places to go where she is expected)—toward the other woman, destitute, aging and, as the poem makes clear, socially *othered*. The text acknowledges, in other words, that there are deep and permanent fissures that obstruct rather than facilitate any sense of "community."

That the body of the homeless woman in her sleeping bag on the street turns out instead to be a puppet underscores this awareness, causing the speaker to rethink stabilizing structures of identity, but does not change the nature of the speaker's gesture. As an empathic witness who earlier had listened to, heard, and seen the other woman in the fullness of her humanity, the speaker neither identifies with (sees herself) nor pities the homeless woman (the sadistic superiority with which *sympathy* is laced).[25] As such, the scene portrays something akin to the possibilities contained in the asymmetry of a Levinasian encounter with "the Other," the unreciprocal relation to another person that "reduces the ego."[26] The speaker has feelings of goodness and love, not because she sees herself as a good person doing a good deed (for she is not), and still less because she has in any way altered class and economic structures in which she thrives and the other woman languishes (for she does not).

What has transpired is more complex, more ambivalent. The speaker attends to the other woman, who is

>   talking all day to the forever-descending in-
>   visible,
> in the dome of listening, in hearing, in the invincible
> ministering: talking as if tasting of something on air [frost,
> host] and always rocking slightly back and forth—until one is finally
>   alongside her—
> walking by—

(*N*, 101)

Although Graham does not quote the woman's actual words, she portrays a "listening" and "hearing" subject who is "walking by." Part of the ethics with which this poem wrestles coalesces in that frank acknowledgment, implicating the speaker even as her ego has been "reduced" (as the "I" disappearing into a formalized "one" implies). The speaker has faced another person, refrained from displacing her with personal concerns, and in doing so, has arguably faced a face whose "destitution cries out for justice,"[27] which the speaker is powerless to proffer but can poetically represent.

Graham thinks through the poem with all the honesty that she can bring to bear on the encounter, and all the uncertainty that her method demands. As she has written recently of her poetic project:

> I would say I try, in my acts of composition, to experience subjectivity and objectivity at their most frayed and fruitful and morally freighted juncture. I try to do so as "honestly" as I can—as I believe that accurate representation of this juncture *is* possible, and that character is involved in approaching that border.

Character: good faith; generosity towards the world (when it comes to letting go of some ego, for example); admission of the *sensation* of defeat into the thinking process without having to turn immediately to defensive action (irony, for example).[28]

Graham's relationship to an ethics of representation in her most recent work has less to do with classical mimesis than with a postmodern process—minding the gaps, as it were. In "letting go of some ego" in her mature work, she has practiced a less studied style, weaving (through) the fray of the poem's choric texture—unraveling the linearity of lines, warping the poem's unifying devices. And as she has trained her formidable poetic intelligence on the ideology of dominance and all its manifestations in her work (*possession* and *empire*, more recently), her feminine speakers posit, like the ambitious humility of her poetic investigations, a divided subjectivity, which in its increasing capacity to hear others and tolerate difference, forges, we might say, *an Other* way.

Acknowledgments

I wish to thank Julie Vandivere for feedback crucial to revising this essay, Matt Peracovich for his assistance with research, and Thomas Gardner for generously sharing a forthcoming essay and an interview with Jorie Graham in manuscript with me.

Notes

1. Rachel Blau DuPlessis, "'Corpses of Poesy': Some Modern Poets and Some Gender Ideologies of Lyric," *Feminist Measures: Soundings in Poetry and Theory*, ed. Lynn Keller and Cristanne Miller (Ann Arbor: University of Michigan, 1994), 71.

2. By and large, critics have analyzed the "universal" aesthetic and thematic shifts in Graham's development. See, for example, Helen Vendler's "Jorie Graham: The Nameless and the Material," in *The Given and the Made: Strategies of Poetic Redefinition* (Cambridge, Mass.: Harvard University Press, 1995), 89–130, wherein Vendler asserts in passing that "since my topic is the material and its increasing claims on Graham, thematically, formally, and linguistically, I leave the question of genre (self-portraiture), and the question of gender (identities available to women) aside" (107). James Longenbach, in "Jorie Graham's Big Hunger," *Denver Quarterly* 31, no. 3 (Winter 1997): 97–118, discusses gender in Graham's work in astute terms, albeit briefly, since his focus is a useful and provocative analysis of the development of her stylistic methods in relation to her themes. Thomas Gardner, in *Regions of Unlikeness: Explaining Contemporary Poetry* (Lincoln: University of Nebraska Press, 1999), 168–213, is very aware of issues of gender and cultural critique in Graham's work, although his focus is the development of her Wittgensteinian approach to language and the limits of its representational capacity. Bonnie Costello, in "Art and Erosion," *Contemporary Literature* 33, no. 2 (Summer 1992): 373–395, tracks Graham's movement, from in her earliest collections, an affirmation of "the triumph of the beautiful" against history's erosion to an increased

attention in later volumes to "the tension between the moral and the aesthetic," 391, 393. Although focusing on the general issue of the possibilities for a poetics of "eloquence," Charles Altieri is perhaps the most direct in assessing the struggles of contemporary women poets:

> As a group women probably have the greatest stakes in winning a personal authority while at the same time shifting our sense of what constitutes that authority, and they have the greatest need for escaping the old plots while maintaining the capacity of non-rationalist modes of constructive activity to define possible models of value. *But I shall not focus here on that social context.* (46; emphasis added)

See Charles Altieri, "Jorie Graham and Ann Lauterbach: Towards a Contemporary Poetics of Eloquence," *Cream City Review* 12 (Summer 1988): 45–72.

For a trenchant analysis of "the criticism of poetry as inducing a perpetual affirmation of universalizing, rather than historical and situated modes of analysis" (37), see Rachel Blau DuPlessis, "Manifests," *diacritics* 26, no. 3–4 (Fall–Winter, 1996): 31–53.

3. Jorie Graham, *Materialism* (Hopewell, N.J.: Ecco Press, 1993), 14 (hereafter cited in text as *M*). Other texts cited are *Erosion* (Princeton: Princeton University Press, 1983) (*E*); *The End of Beauty* (New York: Ecco Press, 1987) (*EB*); *Region of Unlikeness* (New York: Ecco Press, 1991) (*RU*); *Never* (New York: Ecco Press, 2002) (*N*).

4. See Gardner, *Regions*, 216–217.

5. See Vendler, 99. She is speaking specifically of the poem entitled "History" from *Erosion*, but points out that this poem raises a topic that reappears in Graham's later volumes as well, "the denial, on the part of some skeptics (not to give them a worse name), of the reality of the Holocaust," 98.

6. The quotation from Graham's poem is embedded in my quotation from Gardner, *Regions*, 200.

7. Graham employs this binary in another context. See Gardner, *Regions*, 236.

8. For a discussion of the problems arising from this analogical method in Graham's work of this period, see Longenbach, "Jorie Graham's Big Hunger," 106–107.

9. Given how aptly the nuanced complexity of her poetry lends itself to a feminist approach, Graham seems to me clearly influenced by French feminist philosophy and cultural analysis in particular. (For instance, Hélène Cixous is cited in the notes to *Swarm*.) In addition, Graham has specifically articulated in an interview a symbolic, Jungian-inflected concern to "use poetry to reawaken the mother, the unconscious side," as she puts it. She notes that at this moment in our Western culture, "the way in which the female is ascendant [can be seen in] the desire for loss of hierarchies" and links this social desire to the figure of "the uroboric mother-archetype—neither terrible nor good, but both at once, unconscious" in Erich Neumann's *The History and Origin of Consciousness*. See Gardner, *Regions*, 222–223.

10. For a theoretical discussion of the relation between subjective identity, text, and world, see Teresa de Lauretis, *Alice Doesn't: Feminism, Semiotics, Cinema* (Bloomington: Indiana University Press, 1984), 158–186. By working closely through semiotic theory, de Lauretis considers the subjective and social aspects of meaning production by women and very specifically accounts for the relation of aesthetic practice to gendered experience. She postulates the relationship between the body, whose experience is determined by sexual difference, and

the semiotic subject, which not only is produced by but produces signs, and theorizes how an engendered subjectivity, a female subject, transforms the codes she employs.

11. Although the body in Graham's work is not always coded as feminine, the ubiquity of bodily presence in her work is arguably coded as feminized; thus, the constant critical move to disengender the body in her work is, in a sense, to remasculinize the text. For an analysis of the abjection of the feminine/feminized body from the philosophical text, what Elizabeth Grosz terms the "somatophobia" of Western philosophy, see Elizabeth Grosz, *Volatile Bodies: Toward a Corporeal Feminism* (Bloomington: Indiana University Press, 1994). For an essay arguing for a "bodily modernism" that incorporates and refigures the body, see Susan McCabe, "The '*Ballet Mécanique*' of Marianne Moore's Cinematic Modernism," *Mosaic* 33, no. 2 (June 2000): 67–86. Although I do not have the space here fully to argue the point, a productive approach to Graham's work might be to posit a "bodily postmodernism," given that ubiquity of not only bodily presence, but specifically of *women's* bodies in her oeuvre.

12. See Luce Irigaray, *This Sex Which Is Not One*, trans. Catherine Porter (Ithaca, N.Y.: Cornell University Press, 1986): "While [Woman's] body finds itself thus eroticized, and called to a double movement of exhibition and of chaste retreat in order to stimulate the drives of the 'subject,' her sexual organ represents *the horror of nothing to see*. . . . It is already evident in Greek statuary that this nothing-to-see has to be excluded, rejected, from such a scene of representation" (26; Irigaray's emphasis).

13. For an essay analyzing Graham's debt to Stevens, among other modernists, see Thomas Gardner, "Jorie Graham's *End of Beauty* and Modernist Process," *Southwest Review*, 88, nos. 2 and 3 (2003), 335–349.

14. Gardner, *Regions*, 24. For his astute postcolonial reading of Bishop's "Brazil, January 1, 1502," see *Regions*, 14–16.

15. Costello reads this poem as a "transformation in seeing from the nineteenth to the twentieth century, in which the idealization of the landscape is no longer possible and an unveiling of the moral horror beneath the masks of aestheticism is inevitable." But, she continues, "Graham's vision, and her view of art in particular, is too complex for this simple contrast. The beautiful holds its place" ("Art and Erosion," 393). For a psychoanalytic, historiographic discussion of the issues accompanying the act of representing the Holocaust (among other traumatic events) both in literature and in historic records (including eyewitness accounts), see Dominick LaCapra, *Writing History, Writing Trauma* (Baltimore, Md.: Johns Hopkins University Press, 2001).

16. Cf. Longenbach, who remarks (in a comment that caused me to wonder whether he had overlooked homosexual resistance to heterosexism) that "the plot of heterosexual desire cannot simply be evaded but must be more resolutely resisted from within" ("Big Hunger," 109).

17. See Jorie Graham, "Poetic Statement: At the Border," in *American Women Poets in the Twenty-First Century*, ed. Claudia Rankine and Juliana Spahr (Middletown, Conn.: Wesleyan University Press, 2002), 147.

18. Cf. Longenbach, who finds Graham's poems of this period lamenting "the ethical or political repercussions of aesthetic closure," while themselves "click[ing] shut" ("Big Hunger," 105).

19. I am specifically engaging the notion of "herethical" feminine subjectivity theorized by Julia Kristeva in "Women's Time" as well as *Revolution in Poetic Language* (which in theory can be posited by male as well as female speaking subjects, as Graham's poem arguably does). See my discussion of the possibilities for drawing from Kristeva's thinking a theory of ethical, female subjectivity in Cynthia Hogue, *Scheming Women: Poetry, Privilege, and the Politics of Subjectivity* (Albany: SUNY Press, 1995), 17–30. For a discussion of this theory as it applies to the poetry of Dickinson, Williams, and Graham, see Calvin Bedient, "Kristeva and Poetry as Shattered Signification," *Critical Inquiry* 16, no. 4 (Summer 1990), 807–829.

20. Kristeva builds on the notion that the subject in the Lacanian mirror stage is *already* constituted by division (between the self and its representation in the mirror), and that the discovery of this division posits the subject in language, i.e. the social contract. See Hogue, ibid.

21. I differ on this point with Longenbach, who contends, "But by drawing such a broad analogy between such bracingly different realms of human experience [i.e. the girl in Treblinka and "Jorie"], the poem itself seems tightly closed: it focuses our attention so sharply on the similarities of the narratives that it seems oddly unconcerned with their differences" ("Big Hunger," 105).

22. Also noting how the narrative is "unmoored" by the concentration camp victim's "agonized cry," Gardner suggests that "Graham makes a number of almost desperate attempts to find equivalents for the girl's pleading" (*Regions*, 190). My point is that Graham's point is that there *are* no equivalents.

23. Perhaps because of racial stereotypes that the poem's situation could too easily invoke (simply put, privileged white narrator/ black homeless woman), the poem is so subtly raced as arguably to be not raced at all, maintaining instead its focus on exploring an encounter between humans of any race. My thanks to Thomas Gardner and Brian Teare, both of whom read an earlier version of this essay in which I discussed the poem specifically—albeit obliquely—as raced. The questions they raised in two very helpful e-mail exchanges enabled me more accurately to nuance my reading of the text. In an e-mail to the author dated 9 March 2003, for example, Teare remarked,

> Graham is trying hard to keep [the poem] unmarked by race. On the one hand, I really can't read the description of the skin [of the homeless woman, i.e. "no light received or / fed back by / her skin," N, 100–101] clearly in terms of physical description . . . It could be dirty white skin; it could be ashy black skin; it could be malnourished coloration of either race. On the other hand, if one glosses the image in abstract terms, her skin is something that refuses exchange, in that it doesn't take in or give back— it embodies a kind of absence of participation in signification in that it will neither confirm nor negate the speaker's otherness, will not give back "light." It's interesting that, later, Graham claims the dialogue between the two of them is more of mind (or thought) than of heart or body. Often, I'm thinking, the language of Graham's descriptions of the physical world are meant to evoke the rhetoric at play in the world in and of the poem as much as any "real" thing. . . .

24. Graham describes the "social contract" and "the knowledge of a *we*" in terms of Emily Dickinson's and her own poetry, particularly in relation to the use of the lyric "I" and the

use of apostrophe. See Jorie Graham, "Jorie Graham Interview" in Thomas Gardner, *Emily Dickinson and Contemporary Writers*, forthcoming from Oxford University Press.

25. For an analysis of sympathy as sadistic, see Laura Hinton, *The Perverse Gaze of Sympathy: Sadomasochistic Sentiments from Clarissa to Rescue 911* (Albany, N.Y.: SUNY Press, 1999). On the importance of maintaining the crucial difference between witnessing and identification (which I am suggesting Graham does), see LaCapra, *Writing History*, esp. 47–48; on the differing methodologies of writing history and writing literature about traumatic events, including the differing approaches to those texts taken by literary critics and historians, see LaCapra's discussion of Cathy Caruth's work, esp. 106–107. On the "role of empathy and empathic unsettlement in the attentive secondary witness," which I am suggesting is the position Graham occupies, see LaCapra, 78–79.

26. For this reading, I have drawn on a discussion of Levinasian ethics in relation to literature by David P. Haney, "Aesthetics and Ethics in Gadamer, Levinas, and Romanticism: Problems of Phronesis and Techne" *PMLA* 114, no. 1 (January 1999): 32–45. Phrases from Levinas quoted from Haney, 40.

27. Levinas' phrase quoted from Haney, 41.

28. Graham, "Poetic Statement," 146.

17

"Tell Them *No*"

Jorie Graham's Poems of Adolescence

STEPHEN BURT

Despite or because of her European upbringing, by the time of her first *Selected Poems* Jorie Graham had written poems describing every phase of a modern American middle- or upper-class life: childhood ("Imperialism," "To the Reader"), courtship and married life ("What the End Is For." "Act III, sc. ii"), motherhood ("The Dream of the Unified Field," "The Tree of Knowledge"), old age ("At the Long Island Jewish Geriatric Home"). Her fourth book, *Region of Unlikeness* (1991), focused (as reviewers noted) on her biography; it began with one of several poems about her own adolescence—"Fission," portraying the poet at age twelve or thirteen. Another poem (also from *Region of Unlikeness*) depicts the public events of Graham's eighteenth year. Together with other poems which touch on her adolescence, this important pair of poems illuminates Graham's recurring concerns about temporality, history and the self's place in them; exposes a neglected aspect of her achievement; and shows how she (like any original poet) can put a preexisting cultural category—adolescence—at the service of her own style.

Graham's versions of lyric have always portrayed the self as a process, as something one has to discover or become. In "The Geese" (from her first book, *Hybrids of Plants and of Ghosts*) "the real / is crossing you, // your body an arrival / you know is false but can't outrun."[1] Here already Graham describes her sense that the body one knows as one's own is a false or incomplete representation of the self it holds. (We may associate that sense with adolescence, though this early poem never brings up that association.) *Erosion* portrays an incomplete self participating in stories about its own change:

> Who wouldn't want
>   to take
> into the self
>   something that burns
>
> or cuts, or wanders,
>   lost
> over the body? (*E*, 17)

The lines (as always in *Erosion*) avoid assimilation into any grammatical or rhythmic regularity smaller than a stanza, because they depict a self in motion, hungry, incomplete. The same poem ("The Age of Reason") later imagines

> desire hissing Tell me
>   your parts
> that I may understand
>   your body,
>
> your story. (*E*, 33)

The souls (selves, forms of consciousness) in *Erosion* sometimes display their hunger for bodies and stories capacious or powerful enough to contain them (at least temporarily). At other times those selves yearn for independence from constraints of time and space, of embodiment and biography—constraints which Graham would increasingly identify with instrumental reason, Western metaphysics, even (in the poem of that name) "Imperialism." "Salmon" recalls neo-Platonist tradition in identifying "light" with the disembodied soul:

>   What is the light
> at the end of the day, deep, reddish-gold, bathing the walls,
> the corridor, light that is no longer light, no longer clarifies,
> illuminates, antique, freed from the body of
> the air that carries it. What is it
> for the space of time
> where it is useless, merely
> beautiful? (*E*, 41)

These rapid lines (like all the stichic verse in *Erosion*) try hard to avoid all pattern, all predictability, as does the soul they represent. That soul, like "the light," seeks liberation from time and embodiment, but it can only defer and alter (never defeat or free itself permanently from) the narrative time and the physical facts that constrain it.

My last sentence describes the underlying "story" in many, perhaps most, of Graham's poems from *Erosion*, and in many of her later poems, too. Along with this truth about outcomes, Graham offers, as early as *Erosion*, a counter-truth about process: "there is no / entrance, / only entering"—embodiment and history, as they affect and constrain the speaking self, may look inescapable but can also remain unfinished. Graham represents that unfinished quality by a broad array of techniques, among them unstable, ametrical lines; gerunds; unfinished sentences; and (starting with *The End of Beauty*) her notorious _____s. The return of narrative constraint, historical time, or *story* within Graham's individual poems appears from *The End of Beauty* onward as the return of a (repressed or deferred) social context, of facts about society and history, or else as the return of biographical contexts, of facts about biology and the family. These returns have formal and grammatical equivalents in the deferred "ends" of clauses, lines and sentences, "seeking an ending, seeking a shape." (*EB*, 66) "What The End Is For" anomalously imagines the "end" of a love affair not as a final imposition of pattern but as that pattern's dissolution. Usually, though, the characters in *The End of Beauty*—especially in the "Self-Portrait" poems—want to inhabit narratives that have, as yet, no determinate shape, no "end." "Self-Portrait as Hurry and Delay," for example (like Stevens' "The Sail of Ulysses"), incarnates the lyric self as a Penelope who knows herself only so long as Ulysses *might* arrive but *has not* arrived. Graham shows Penelope "wanting to go on living // beginning always beginning the ending," hence living in an "immaculate present-tense" (*DUF*, 83, 81).

These ways of viewing Graham's first three books (derived partly from Helen Vendler's powerful readings) will not surprise any reader who knows those books well. I rehearse them here partly in order to show how the questions that Graham's poetry advances (questions Graham's readers ordinarily view either within the domain of lyric alone, or in the related domains of Continental philosophy) have other, more homely analogues in American and European thinking about how individuals grow up, change, and learn to live in the world. The state of being in which we discover or decide who we are—in which we learn that those discoveries await us, that they have not yet been made—is the state of being Graham's poetry often identifies with the self in lyric (the self just prior to its final fixing in narrative). For much of contemporary America (and some of Europe), these terms also describe adolescence, the portion of an individual's life in which she learns what her body is and can do, settles (but has not *already settled*) on one concept of herself, and decides where she wants her life to go. The analogy between the self of lyric (as Graham conceives it) and the self of adolescence (as twentieth-century Anglophone culture defined it) enters Graham's work in *Region of Unlikeness*; that analogy drives that book's strongest poems, in particular "Fission" and "The Hiding Place," on which the rest of this essay will dwell.

The first poem in the book after Graham's collage "Foreword," "Fission" takes place in a movie theatre in Italy in November 1963, when Graham (born in 1950) would likely have been thirteen years old. As the poem begins, the young poet watches the famous scene in Stanley Kubrick's *Lolita* in which both James Mason as Humbert Humbert, and the viewers, first encounter the title character (played by Sue Lyon): Lyon looks back at Humbert (and at us) through her iconic sunglasses, from her pose on a lawn. The young Graham then watches as "a man" announces that President Kennedy has been shot; the house lights come up and the theatre's skylight opens. While the film continues (silently, and in daylight) Graham considers her own imbrication in historical time, in biological puberty, and in moment-by-moment experience.

"Fission" considers the putatively stopped time of lyric along with the moment-by-moment time created by cinematic experience (in which a succession of individual frames creates the illusion of a continuous picture).[2] It takes up the time of narrative, in which stories move from beginning to end, and the (slightly) larger scale of biography, in which one life moves from birth to death. It juxtaposes all these kinds of time with the more public time-scales of historical and cultural change. And it does so in order to explore potential analogies among them.[3] Is the poet's discovery that she has one body and no other, that her life story will be the story of that mortal body, like the discovery that Kennedy has been shot? Can the one have prompted the other? Does the poet's discovery of a new verbal form resemble the adolescent discovery that one's body has changed, is changing? Might that analogy itself depend on contingencies in social, cultural, even political history? In order to show how Graham answers all these questions (her answer to each turns out to be *yes*) we will have to move slowly through that one poem.

Vendler writes that in "the autobiographical poems of *Region of Unlikeness* . . . memory oscillates . . . between a past moment . . . and the same past moment revived as a present-tense moment."[4] In "Fission," this double focus invites readers to compare the two people involved in the memory (Graham-the-adult-poet and Graham-at-13), asking to what extent those people differ. Yet the poem begins not with temporal but with spatial comparisons: "real electric light upon the full-sized / screen / on which the greater-than-life-size girl appears" (*RU*, 3).

"Tell Them *No*": Jorie Graham's Poems of Adolescence

Recalling Graham's earlier self presentation as the "girl" who "appears" at the end of "To the Reader," Sue Lyon's Lolita looks "full-sized" (like an adult) but also "greater-than-life-size," both physically larger (since she's on a movie screen) and more developed than a real "girl" at Lolita's age might be. (Hostile film critics singled out Lyon's "well-built" Lolita as too developed, or too old; the *New York Times* thought her "a good seventeen.")[5] This Lolita not only accepts a spectator's gaze but looks back; to become the object of a sexualized gaze seems to Graham here the cost of becoming an agent of any kind—one is seen sexually or else "never . . . seen." Lyon's / Lolita's alluring "glance is let loose into the auditorium" as a sign of her entry into the movie and into the public world; that glance seems to have "stopped" a man "in his tracks."

This stopped moment of interlocking gazes (Humbert's at Lolita, Lyon's at the audience and "the man," Graham's and ours at Lyon) creates a moment of initiation, of firstness, much like the moments Graham depicts in earlier poems—the moment, for example, in "San Sepolcro" "before / the birth of god" (*E*, 2) As in "San Sepolcro," Graham will depict our understanding of such an encounter as a journey away from it: we understand innocence, or initiation, only after the fact, from a position of experience. But where "San Sepolcro" (like the painting it describes) depicted the moment just before a birth, "Fission" (like the frames of film it describes) begins at the moment just before a fall:

> as the houselights come on—midscene—
> not quite killing the picture which keeps flowing beneath,
>
> a man comes running down the aisle
> asking for our attention—
> Ladies and Gentlemen.
> I watch the houselights lap against the other light—the tunnel
> of image-making dots licking the white sheet awake—
> a man, a girl, her desperate mother—daisies growing in the corner — (3–4)

The moment those lines chronicle, in which our and Graham's experience of time gets decoupled from that of the people on film, becomes the paradigmatic fall into experience, the "fission" (separation), which the rest of the poem will explore. (After "being / outmaneuvered" [3], eleven of the next twelve line breaks occur at grammatical pauses, as if to enforce the sense of a separation, a halt.) Since *Lolita* is a film (and a book) devoted to moments of fall, of innocence lost, Graham can depict such a fall (or separation, "fission") at once in herself (as she stands in the theatre), in the crowd (as they realize that Kennedy has been shot), and on screen (as Dolores approaches her encounter with Humbert). "Like the movie heroine," writes Laurence Goldstein, "Graham's spectator . . . is now abandoned to a fate rushing towards her with the single-mindedness of Humbert himself."[6] Graham's next lines show her increasing distance from the action onscreen, describing it in greater, slower detail: we scrutinize

> thighs like receipts slapped down on a
> > slim silver tray,
>
> her eyes as she lowers the heart-shaped shades,
> > as the glance glides over what used to be the open,
> the free,
> > as the glance moves, pianissimo, over the glint of day,
> over the sprinkler, the mother's voice shrieking like a grappling
> > hook,
> the grass blades aflame with being-seen, here on the out-
> > skirts. . . . (4)

These Chandleresque metaphors (and even the pun on "skirts") identify Dolores/Lyon as ready to be "corrupted," ready to meet the gaze of her desirer. She looks back because she is ready to be looked at: "her sun-barred shoulders . . . accompany / her neck, her face, the / looking-up" (5). As the film fades, "the theater's skylight is opened and noon slides in," Lyon appears at once to grow up and to become less visible (to spectators generally as to Graham in particular). In ever-lengthening lines, her incipient story gives way to an absence of story; events simply pile up in apparent simultaneity:

> a grave of possible shapes called *likeness*—see it?—something
> > scrawling up there that could be skin or daylight or even
>
> the expressway now that he's gotten her to leave with him—
> > (it happened rather fast) (do you recall)—
>
> the man up front screaming the President's been shot, waving
> > his hat, slamming one hand flat
> over the open
> > to somehow get
> our attention,
>
> in Dallas, behind him the scorcher—whites, grays,
> > laying themselves across his face—

> him like a beggar in front of us, holding his hat—
>   I don't recall what I did,
> I don't recall what the right thing to do would be,
>   I wanted someone to love.... (5–6)

The Kennedy assassination wrecks not just the confidence of Americans but the progress of Kubrick's film, and by extension the progress of American girls (like Lyon onscreen, like Graham below it) through time on their way to becoming women, finding "someone to love."

Given her descriptions of the film up to this point, we might *expect* the young Graham to hope the story would resume: to rejoin in imagination the story about growing-up which Lyon's character seemed about to tell. But such a story (as we know, as the adult Graham knows) has a tragic, or at least a traumatic, ending, an ending the poem appears to extend from Dolores Haze to all young women: though the story of female adolescence begins, perhaps, with allure and promise, that story, that experience, can seem in retrospect like a gradual loss. The next line becomes a turning point for Graham's poem—the first time she uses past tense to describe herself, and one of only two places where a new sentence coincides with the start of a stanza. In that line Graham seeks not a way to *resume* the story of becoming a woman, but (like Daphne in "Self-Portrait as Apollo and Daphne") a way to avoid stories, and narrative time, entirely. Graham then projects that search onto the Dolores Haze of the film:

> There is a way she lay down on that lawn
> to begin with,
>   in the heart of the sprinklers,
> before the mother's call,
>   before the man's shadow laid itself down,
>
> there is a way to not yet be wanted,
>
>   there is a way to lie there at twenty-four frames
> per second—no faster— (6)

Wanting to resist incorporation into the stream of history, and wanting to resist her own bodily development (as we will see later), Graham projects those desires onto the character now fading from view onscreen: Lyon's Lolita wants (Graham imagines) to exist in the static time of those first frames depicting a motionless subject, and not at the faster

>   speed of plot,
> not at the speed of desire—
>
> *the road out—expressway—hotels—motels—*
> no telling what we'll have to see next,
>   no telling what all we'll have to want next
> (right past the stunned rows of houses),
>   no telling what on earth we'll have to marry marry marry. . . . (6)

"Marry marry marry" echoes Sylvia Plath's "The Applicant": "My boy, it's your last resort. / Will you marry it, marry it, marry it."[7] The apparent allusion to Plath (very rare in Graham) reminds us to look here for Plath's frequent concerns: what would Fifties, or early Sixties, femininity do to the young women who embraced it? What "plot," what "desire," would it make young women accept, and what other story, if any, might those women inhabit instead?

Now this way of thinking about time and narrative, looking and "being-seen"—initial fascination with its allure, followed by discovery of its dangers and a wish to withdraw or postpone—describes (a) Graham's thirteen-year-old self as "Fission" depicts her; (b) the adult Graham of *Region* and of *The End of Beauty*, and many of her mythological alter egos (Daphne, Penelope, Saint Teresa, Eurydice); and (c) girls or female adolescents generally, as depicted by a battery of thinkers and analysts. Simone de Beauvoir in *The Second Sex* (to pick one influential example) asked

> why adolescence is for a woman so difficult and decisive a moment. Up to this time she has been an autonomous individual: now she must renounce her sovereignty. Not only is she torn, like her brothers, though more painfully, between the past and the future, but in addition a conflict breaks out between her original claim to be subject, active free, and, on the other hand, her erotic urges and the social pressures to accept herself as passive object.[8]

Beauvoir adds, in what might be a gloss on Graham's lines:

> The young girl feels that her body is getting away from her, it is no longer the straightforward expression of her individuality; it becomes foreign to her and at the same time she becomes for others a thing: on the street men follow her with their eyes and comment on her anatomy. She would like to be invisible; it frightens her to become flesh and to show her flesh.[9]

The "young girl" for Beauvoir wants "to be a child no longer, but she does not accept becoming an adult"; hence she occupies "a position of continual denial," which serves as "the key to most of her behavior; she does not accept the destiny assigned to her by nature and by society; and yet she does not repudiate it completely." Instead, Beauvoir's typical girl "limits herself to a flight from reality or a symbolic struggle against it."[10] Just such a symbolic struggle appears, in "Fission," twice: in Lyon's Dolores (as the young Graham viewed her) and in the young Graham as the older poet remembers her.

"Fission" thus derives its remarkable power in part from the analogy between Graham's general resistance to teleology, narrative, closure, and Western history (on the one hand) and girls' resistance to womanhood (on the other). The poem suggests not only an analogy but a homology (a shared source): what if the resistance to narrative time Graham so often depicts derives from a resistance to ways of "being-seen," to ways of becoming a woman? These suggestions make "Fission" not just one of Graham's most affecting poems but one of her most effectively feminist. Graham returns (as several recent feminist writers have asked women to return) to an immediately pre-sexual moment as a source of power, a chance to resist being told "what to want next."[11]

That return also looks like a withdrawal from the situations the film depicts—a withdrawal, in turn, for which Graham (once a film student herself) solicits useful analogues in film theory. Laura Mulvey famously discovered the Lacanian mirror phase in the condition of cinema-viewing, with its "extreme contrast between the darkness in the auditorium . . . and the brilliance on the screen": for Mulvey, in cinema as in Lacan "the image recognized is conceived as the reflected body of the self, but its misrecognition as superior" ("larger-than-life-size," Graham says) "projects the body outside itself as an ideal ego."[12] One need not accept Mulvey's account of cinema generally to see that she describes a process of identification much like the one depicted in Graham's poem. Barbara Creed adds (quoting Teresa de Lauretis) "that the female spectator is always involved in a 'double identification' in which she identifies with both the passive object (woman, body, landscape) and the active subject positions (the look of the male and the camera)."[13] Graham depicts not only this double identification (with camera, with spectators, with Lyon) but something like the anti-patriarchal resistance to "the screen illusion" which Mulvey recommended as a feminist project.[14] Graham fuses both the identification, and the resistance, into a poem depicting her own entry into adolescent self-consciousness: the end of the poem will explore the limits which that resistance finds.

We might name Graham's next experience not fission but fusion: "three lights" (skylight, house lights, movie-projector light) interrupt her reverie by "merging" across her person: "the image licked my small body from the front, the story playing // all over my face my / forwardness" (6). Having imagined herself as Lolita resisting the motion of plot, she now seems doomed to inhabit that plot, moving ahead into history and womanhood, already caressed, obscenely, by filmic light. After this fusion, however, comes the titular fission: the lights start to come apart, illuminating Graham's body as something less than a unified image:

> they flared up around my body unable to
>
> merge into each other
>   over my likeness,
> slamming down one side of me, unquenchable—here static
>
>   there flaming—
> sifting grays into other grays—
>   mixing the split second into the long haul—
> flanking me—undressing something there where my
>   body is
> though not my body—
>   where they play on the field of my willingness,
>
> where they kiss and brood, filtering each other to no avail,
>   all over my solo
> appearance (7)

The journalist and social researcher Emily White compares girls' adolescence to "a psychological morning, disorienting in its brightness"; "the girl who develops [physically] ahead of time," White adds, "feels like she is being pulled forward, suddenly thrust into the harsh light of the world's gaze."[15] Graham's lines evoke just such feelings, and just such comparisons. Here, again, the play of the lights on Graham's body figures the dilemma of female adolescence generally as de Beauvoir and others see it: whether to act in order to become a passive object of men's desires, or whether, instead, to eschew action (thereby becoming all the more passive, perhaps more desirable). Graham ties these concerns about female development over weeks, months, years to her continuing poetic concerns about how we experience time in minutes, moments, seconds: her lyric strategies for exploring, stretching out, dissecting time can therefore come to represent her own (and other characters') resistance to the limiting, sexist "story" of feminine development.

Sharon Cameron has suggested that lyric poetry as a genre works to remove particular moments from time: "the contradiction between social and personal time," she writes, "is the lyric's generating impulse."[16] Graham can imagine herself as exempt from time, from history, and from womanly becoming for the held space of the lyric poem, but she cannot end the poem without subordinating her own (remembered) consciousness once again to the threatening, even malevolent "road out" towards womanhood, learnt passivity, and (in the poem's political-historical dimension) the turbulent late 1960s. To reenter the social world—to spend "the dollar bill / in my hand"—would be to make a "choice," and "choice" is "the thing that wrecks the sensuous here the glorious here— / that wrecks the beauty" (9) of lyric exemption from time.

The moment of learning about this assassination, of course, marked an entry into history, or an awakening to public history, for many boys and girls of Graham's generation: "Fission" perhaps represents (among many other projects) Graham's demonstration that despite her unusual international background she is, after all, an American Baby Boomer. The memoirist Richard Rodriguez (born in 1944) has written that for his "generation, the baby-boom generation," "prolonged adolescence became the point of us." He continues: "Adolescence is the source of our national unity. American storytellers do better with the beginning of a story than with the conclusion. We do not know how to mark the end of adolescence."[17] Having contemplated and rejected "choice," Graham's poem mirrors many of her generation's stories of adolescence in refusing any kind of conclusive or satisfying end. It concludes instead on a dash, on a held breath, on extended contemplation

> of the layers of the
>   real: what is, what also is, what might be that is,
> what could have been that is, what
>   might have been that is, what I say that is,
> what the words say that is,
>   what you imagine the words say that is—Don't move, don't
>
> wreck the shroud, don't move— (8)

The poem finally valorizes its moments of refusal: Graham imagines withholding her consent from the story her culture wants her to start telling about her body, her social being, and her era. That withholding, more than any other experience here, links the adult Graham who speaks the poem to the younger Graham the poem depicts. And in valorizing such refusals, Graham places herself in the company not of the philosophers and poets to whom she's most often compared (Eliot, Heidegger, Stevens) but in the "negationist" company of post-1968 rebels in music and in visual art: of the Situationists, even (if we believe Greil Marcus) of punk rockers, seeking "images of possibility or negation that can speak beyond their time."[18]

Graham's sometime "negationism" (Marcus' term), her drive to resist closure, history, and "implied endings," should be less surprising than it is: after all, Graham was a '68 rebel herself.[19] Graham attended the Sorbonne in 1968 (aged 17 or 18) along with protest leader Daniel Cohn-Bendit; she was arrested twice during the Paris upheaval, and then (according to Robert Casper's profile) "expelled for taking part in student protests."[20] Those protests and their associated philosophy inform Graham's work in ways few readers explore. The sociologist Deena Weinstein writes that while "children are taught to have ideas of what they would like to 'be' when they grow up," "adolescents have the privilege and torment of raising the question of whether they want to be anything that society holds out for them."[21] Such questions—and the refusals which serve as their answers—informed both the protests of May 1968 and the poem from *Region* which recalls them, "The Hiding Place."

"The Hiding Place" resembles "Fission" in telling a story about a turning point in public history; in describing a crowded, dark place from which the young Graham emerges into shocking light; and in making that emergence stand for a transition in her life course. Once again, Graham identifies a valuable, even a heroic, resistance (to narrative, and to authority) with the stage she feels she has left behind. Where that stage had (in "Fission") a mute and phantasmatic representative (the "larger-than-life" Lyon/Lolita), here youth and resistance acquire an articulate, defiant spokesman, "a certain leader":

> I found his face above an open streetfire.
> *No* he said, tell them *no concessions.*
> His voice above the fire as if there were no fire—
>
> language floating everywhere above the sleeping bodies;
>   and crates of fruit donated in secret;
>   and torn sheets (for tear gas) tossed down from shuttered windows;
>   and bread; and blankets; stolen from the firehouse. (19)

The array of "sleeping bodies" suggests Whitman's "The Sleepers," in which the poet (like Graham's student leader) moves "from bedside to bedside," from battlefield corpses to cradles, "close with the other sleepers each in turn."[22] That Whitmanesque leader (whose name Graham may never have known) represents and unifies the dispossessed Parisians of the poem. Graham then cuts with

"Tell Them *No*": Jorie Graham's Poems of Adolescence 269

cinematic abruptness to her time in jail: "In the cell we were so crowded no one could sit or lean. / People peed on each other," and guards beat a "girl in her eighth month" of pregnancy (19). These scenes of heroism and horror (like the unrolling film at the start of "Fission") introduce the longer, more personal part of the poem: "I remember the cell vividly / but is it from a photograph?"

> Do I see it from inside now—his hands, her face—or
> is it from the news account?
>   The strangest part of getting out again was *streets*.
> The light running down them.
>   Everything spilling whenever the wall breaks.
> And the air—thick with dwellings—the air filled—doubled—
>   as if the open
>
> had been made to render—
>   The open squeezed for space until the hollows spill out,
> story upon story of them
>   starting to light up as I walked out.
> How thick was the empty meant to be?
>   What were we finding in the air? (20)

As usual in Graham, a change of mind and subject arrives with a change of line length, pace and frequency of enjambment: shorter and more often enjambed than those in the first six stanzas, these lines shift our attention from *what happened* to Graham to *how it felt to be the person around whom these things had happened*—in other words, from story to the non-narrative, doubled, reflective temporality of meditative lyric.

Just as in "Fission," Graham looks back on her younger self at a moment immediately after trauma, and as in "Fission" she imagines what it would mean *not* to have reentered the stream of history, narrative, maturity, in a public, agreed-upon world. Newly released from jail, Graham feels she does not belong (in a repeated pun) to any of the "stories" around her—a foreigner and a defeated student rebel, she has neither a home nor a clear course of action, and in this she stands for all the defeated young radicals of 1968, not so much for their political programs (which she describes vaguely as "claims") but for their mood: "Was I meant to get up again? I was inside. The century clicked by." Public history has slipped back into its ordinary, adult-driven course: "They made agreements we all returned to work. / The government fell but then it was all right again." Graham ends not in that tone of flat dejection but on the exhilarating student leader, a hero of imagination resisting what Stevens named "the pressure of reality"—what Graham, or Marcus, might call the pressure of history.[23] At the end of the poem, we see, not the "helicopters" or "the government" but

> The man above the fire, listening to my question,
>
> the red wool shirt he wore: where is it? who has it?
> He looked straight back into the century: no concessions.
> I took the message back.
> The look in his eyes—shoving out—into the open—
> expressionless with thought:
>
> *no*—tell them *no*— (21)

The man who responds to the state's demands, who "looked back" at "the century," meets a public gaze with confidence almost as Lyon's Lolita in "Fission" had done; both recall Beauvoir's description of the teenage girl's "continual denial," and both take in the plots of their respective poems an action Graham reflects in her style, her grammar and even her punctuation. "The Hiding Place," like "Fission," ends on an em-dash, avoiding (in print) the visible symbol of closure as it avoids (aloud) the tone of voice which might make closure seem apt.

That refusal of (grammatical, narrative, or conceptual) closure becomes fundamental to the way Graham turns her ideas into poems, and to the use these particular poems make of adolescence. "The way the sentence operates," Graham told Thomas Gardner, "became connected, for me, with notions like ending-dependence and eschatological thinking," with "manifest destiny, westward expansion."[24] To end a poem like "Fission" or "The Hiding Place" without ending its final sentence is to leave readers without "the sense of an ending," and to leave the characters in that poem in the irresolution for which they have wished. The student, the girl, in these poems of adolescence wish "to postpone closure" in their own life courses just as the poems "postpone closure" in their grammatical elaborations.[25]

"The Hiding Place" thus recaps in the explicitly political (and French) context of Graham's eighteenth year many of the ideas, and some of the techniques, which mark, in "Fission," her thirteenth year. Once again Graham wants to celebrate a youthful figure who appears momentarily able to stop adults' public time, and once again the poem both valorizes that resistance and shows that it could not last. Nor are "The Hiding Place" and "Fission" alone in that regard: other poems in *Region* focus on defining moments of adolescence in Graham's life—learning to wear makeup, and discovering her father's affair ("Picnic"); a sexual encounter, perhaps Graham's first ("The Region of Unlikeness"). And the resistance to time and teleology, the mobilization of long lines, enjambments, and grammar on behalf of such resistance, which together characterized "Fission" and "The Hiding Place" also informs those other poems. In the title poem, for example, an early fall into sexual experience ("the speaker / thirteen") becomes a prompt to self-consciousness about time, a source of solidarity with other women, and (conjecturally) a reason the adult Graham writes as she does:

> The window is open, it is raining, then it has just
>   ceased. What is the purpose of poetry, friend?
> And you, are you one of those girls? (37)

Readers of *The End of Beauty* noted how its series of "self-portraits" divided Graham into pursuer and pursued, the (male) agent who wants to finish a story and the (female) object who wants to escape it. Compared to their counterparts in *The End of Beauty*, both "Fission" and "The Hiding Place" appear to take sides: were she to rewrite "Fission" in that earlier style, Graham would have to call the poems "Self-Portrait as Lolita and Humbert," or "Self-Portrait as Girl and Man Shouting." In the event—in "Fission" as in "The Hiding Place" and in "The Region of Unlikeness"—Graham sides with the young people (and with the women), with the figures who say "no," who "resist closure."[26] The doubleness in these autobiographical poems comes not from self-division within one moment, but (as both Gardner and Vendler note) from the temporal divide between the young Graham of the moment remembered and the older Graham who considers the memory. The older and the younger Graham agree, however, in seeking and dramatizing a refusal, a postponement, of narrative, closure, and instrumental reason.

That quest looks different once we see it as undertaken in the name of youth, in proto-feminist resistance to womanhood, or in sympathy with a student revolt. Graham's resistance to "history," in this context, might even recall earlier social thinkers' characterizations of adolescence as such: "Youth," Erik Erikson claimed in 1963, resents "any suggestion that it may be hopelessly determined by what went before in life histories or in history. Psychosocially speaking, this would mean that irreversible childhood identifications would deprive an individual of an identity of his own." Erikson famously defined adolescence as a "moratorium" in which young people did not have to settle definitively on any one role.[27] James Longenbach has critiqued Graham's "dream of openness" in *Region* as politically (or even ontologically) unrealistic; Longenbach suggests that Graham's more recent poetry views the avoidance of narrative closure more reasonably, as a mere postponement of "patterns and laws."[28] We might say that Graham's poems of adolescence in *Region* make that concession already: to stand outside history, to avoid shape and story, to avoid the passage of time itself and the development of the body, appear in these poems as linked and finally unachievable wishes—wishes also inseparable from the young person's wish never to fully grow up.

Graham does not make concepts of adolescence central to her most recent poems (though she does depict young people within them: see, for example, "The Dream of the Unified Field," from *Materialism*, or "Untitled Two" from *The Errancy*). Where Graham does use those concepts in *Region*, her concerns (some of them rightly called feminist concerns) and her techniques make those concepts stand for the more abstract, philosophical and phenomenological concerns which mark her poetry more generally. Graham's poems about herself at thirteen and at eighteen not only help us to read the sometimes forbiddingly abstract investigations in other, larger poems but to also to find original poetic forms for historical versions of adolescence (the Fifties teen, the Sixties student rebel)—versions explored before and since by other poets, but not with such sustained attention to temporality, nor in such originally extended, inwardly attentive modes.

Notes

1. Jorie Graham, *Hybrids of Plants and of Ghosts* (Princeton, N.J.: Princeton University Press, 1980), 38–39 (hereafter cited as *HPG*). Other Graham texts cited here are *Erosion* (Princeton, N.J.: Princeton University Press, 1983) (*E*); *The End of Beauty* (New York: Ecco Press, 1987) (*EB*); *Region of Unlikeness* (New York: Ecco Press, 1991) (*RU*).

2. Helen Vendler writes that Graham's *End of Beauty* poems appropriate "the rhythms of cinematography—this moment, then that moment," and that their "model for this use of the long line seems to be the cinematic freeze-frame." *Soul Says* (Cambridge, Mass.: Harvard University Press, 1995), 241; *The Breaking of Style: Hopkins, Heaney, Graham* (Cambridge, Mass.: Harvard University Press, 1995), 80. For another reading of "Fission," focused on philosophical skepticism, see Thomas Gardner, *Regions of Unlikeness: Explaining Contemporary Poetry* (Lincoln: University of Nebraska Press, 1999), 188–190.

3. Laurence Goldstein's earlier discussion—likely the first extended reading of this poem—also pursues these analogies but reaches far more optimistic conclusions: for him, "the poet's revenge" on these cultural systems "is to create a secondary world of enduring power" (perhaps analogous to the medium of film itself). See Goldstein, *The American Poet at the Movies* (Ann Arbor: University of Michigan Press, 1994), 235.

4. Helen Vendler, "Indigo, Cyanine, Beryl," *London Review of Books*, 23 Jan. 2003, 13–16, 14.

5. David Hughes, *The Complete Kubrick* (London: Virgin, 2000), 99; quoting Norman Kagan, *The Cinema of Stanley Kubrick* (New York: Holt, Rinehart and Winston, 1972), 99.

6. Goldstein, *American Poet*, 235.

7. Sylvia Plath, *Collected Poems*, ed. Ted Hughes (London: Faber & Faber, 1981), 222.

8. Simone de Beauvoir, *The Second Sex*, trans. H. M. Parshley (New York: Alfred A. Knopf, 1953), 314.

9. Beauvoir, 288.

10. Beauvoir, 314.

11. See, for example, the work of Carol Gilligan—or the iconography of the 1990s Riot Grrrl movement. For an especially powerful fictive instance, see Lorrie Moore's novella *Who Will Run the Frog Hospital?* (New York: Warner, 1995), whose heroine tries "to learn the meaning of myself good god whatever that was" and instead discovers a girlhood solidarity which her retrospective narration insistently celebrates (46). On feminist resistance to "being seen" and its consequences for visual art, see also Peggy Phelan's *Unmarked* (London: Routledge, 1993), chs. 1 and 3; my thanks to Laura Engel for the reference.

12. Laura Mulvey, "Visual Pleasure and Narrative Cinema," in *The Film Studies Reader*, ed. Joanne Holloway, Peter Hutchings and Mark Jancovich (London: Arnold, 2000), 238–248, 241.

13. Barbara Creed, in *The Sexual Subject: A Screen Reader in Sexuality* (London: Routledge, 1992), 224.

14. Mulvey, "Visual Pleasure," 248.

15. Emily White, *Fast Girls: Teenage Tribes and the Myth of the Slut* (New York: Scribner, 2002), 24, 51.

16. Sharon Cameron, *Lyric Time: Dickinson and the Limits of Genre* (Baltimore, Md.: Johns Hopkins University Press, 1979), 206.

17. Richard Rodriguez, "The Invention of Adolescence," afterword to Lauren Greenfield, *Fast Forward: Growing Up in the Shadow of Hollywood*, ed. Greenfield and Leah Painter Roberts (New York: Alfred A. Knopf/ Melcher Media, 1997), 124–126, 125, 126.

18. Greil Marcus, *The Dustbin of History* (Cambridge, Mass.: Harvard University Press, 1995), 141.

19. Greil Marcus, *Lipstick Traces: A Secret History of the Twentieth Century* (Cambridge, Mass.: Harvard University Press, 1989) (passim); Gardner, *Regions*, 214.

20. Robert Casper, "About Jorie Graham: A Profile," *Ploughshares* 27, no. 4 (Winter 2001–02), http://www.pshares.org/issues/article.cfm?prmarticleID=7400 (accessed Oct. 30, 2003).

21. Deena Weinstein, "Rock: Youth and Its Music," in *If It's Too Loud You're Too Old: Adolescents and Their Music*, ed. Jonathan Epstein (New York: Garland, 1994), 3–23, 10.

22. Walt Whitman, *The Complete Poems*, ed. Francis Murphy, (New York: Penguin, 1975), 441.

23. Wallace Stevens, *Collected Poetry and Prose*, ed. Frank Kermode and Joan Richardson (New York: Library of America, 1997), 656.

24. Gardner, *Regions*, 218.

25. Gardner, *Regions*, 219.

26. Gardner, *Regions*, 221.

27. Erik Erikson, "Youth: Fidelity and Diversity," in *The Challenge of Youth*, ed. Erik Erikson (New York: Anchor Books, 1965), 1–29, 14–15. For this idea in twentieth-century fiction, see especially Patricia Meyer Spacks, *The Adolescent Idea: Myths of Youth and the Adult Imagination* (New York: Basic Books, 1982), without which this essay could not have been written.

28. James Longenbach, *Modern Poetry after Modernism* (New York: Oxford University Press, 1997), 170–171.

18

Toward a Jorie Graham Lexicon

CALVIN BEDIENT

beauty—

five takes:

1. The end of beauty is the inherent sublimity of the present: "Here it is, *here*, the end of beauty, the present" ("The Lovers," *The End of Beauty*). For Jorie Graham, as for Jean-François Lyotard, the new sublime is the Now, as unpresentable and inhuman: Augustine on time plus Heisenberg on indeterminacy. (Of Newman's canvases, Lyotard writes: "The message 'speaks' of nothing; it emanates from no one."[1]) What can "trap it"? This look? This thought? "The suck of shapelessness" ("Untitled," *Region of Unlikeness*)? No, no, no. "You have to leave her be / if all you have to touch her with / is form," Jorie Graham writes in straining-to-push-you-back iambs ("Noli Me Tangere," *The End of Beauty*).
2. Beauty is a fear of not existing. Lyotard: "Existing is to be awoken from the nothingness of disaffection by something sensible over there. An affective cloud lifts at that moment and deploys its nuance for a moment" (*Postmodern Fables*[2]).
3. Beauty, like plotline, is "digressive" ("Noli Me Tangere"). In contrast, the real of the Now is as instantaneous as it is untotalizable.
4. On the other hand, beauty ends in itself ("a line / brought round . . . , reader, a plot, a / shape, one of the finished things, one of the / *beauties* (hear it click shut?) a thing / completely narrowed down to love" ("Imperialism," *The End of Beauty*), whereas the sublime, an acid thrown on outline, is unlovable.

5. In *Swarm*—Jorie Graham's essay at "submission to . . . untouchable authority" ("Is not the desire now to lose all personal will?")—beauty is conceived, though only in the hesitation of "as if," as *force* (the force conceptualized by modern physics) felt in its narrowing passage through us: "time and submission and event / as we turn the page and meaning follows / as if beauty flowed through us as if we were a gap / in the page . . . without reality" ("Underneath (Eurydice)"). Beauty is the merciful form of the sublime, but not so merciful as to fail to annihilate us. Where beauty is, we are not; not real; only the beauty is real. In contrast, the sublime has no location at all, no *where*. We cannot locate our own frequency in relation to its cosmic hiss.

Jorie Graham's vision, like Rilke's, like Monet's, trembles with the cosmic gulps and displacements of quantum physics:

I am a frequency, current flies through. One has
                      to ride
                      the spine
No peace [of mind] [of heart], among the other
frequencies.

("Ebbtide," *Never*)

Beauty can hardly hold a candle to such raging vibration. As Lyotard states (and overstates), "the economy of the beautiful [is] appalling in view of the 'reality of the real,' that is, death and pain" (this may be a reductive definition of the real); and although "the beautiful gives positive pleasure . . . there is another sort of pleasure, linked to a passion stronger than satisfaction, which is pain and the approach of death." Now, Jorie Graham does not write *beautifully*—nothing so self-satisfied and slight. ("Ride / the spine"! This is too true to be beautiful.) Her phrases have a prose-like intentness on seeing ahead ("up, further out"). They reject the narcissism and self-regarding *retard* of lyrical eloquence. What she conveys, always, is that "Too much is asked." And, as Longinus noted, "too much" is the hallmark of the sublime.

    Why should the shut thing not be true enough
anymore?
    (*Open up open open* the stillness shrieked.)

("Picnic," *Region of Unlikeness*)

body—

The body "cannot / follow, cannot love" ("Vertigo")? On the contrary, it is the fertile soil of the beautiful: "But the wall / of the flesh / opens endlessly, / its vanishing point so deep / and receding // we have yet to find it, / to have it / stop us. So he cut / deeper, / graduating slowly / from the symbolic / to the beautiful." ("At Luca Signorelli's Resurrection of the Body," *Erosion*).

Precisely for that reason, Jorie Graham leaves the body falling behind, *just* behind, as thought takes over from the senses. Thought: a will to truth-by-analysis. "Next door the roses flow. / Blood in the hand that reaches for them flows"—thus she x-rays. Her writing is powered forward (as distinct from impulsive): "O stubborn appetite: *I*, then *I*, / loping through the poem. Shall I do that again?" ("Woods," *Never*). A Jorie Graham poem is both reluctantly and relentlessly thoughtful ("Why do we *think*? What is the thinking for?")

The heart of the Grahamian body is in its stomach. When this poet says "Dear," is really a gesture of love or politeness disguising a yelp, a gesture of appeasement? "Dear history of this visible world, scuffling / at the edges of you is / no edge, no whereabout," etc.

The body is less a tamping down (though it *is* that) than the forked basis of looking *up*: "a pronged cry or a tuning fork / this body of which I // am the core, looking up, tamping the dark with / my looking up, / or is it *airing* up. . . [?]" A body-on-tiptoe, then. Less sensual (though it *is* so) than an effort to clear out "the starry dizziness / rammed into the eyepits" ("The Break of Day," *Materialism*). "The pain of my eyes is piercing" ("Underneath [with Chorus]," *Swarm*).

The body is baggage in the effort to reach the absolute ("Bottom is there but depth conceals it," goes a brilliant line in "Middle Distance," also in *Swarm*). Partly because of it, the "invisible" is too close (while being too far) to be anything but a more-than-Newman-like blank, like your face when you have no mirror in which to see it: "Eyes closed I touch my face. / My hand hovers like the very question of my face / over my face" ("Evolution I," *Never*).

Should we not pity this temporary bit of smudge on the universal vibrations? "My body, my tiny piece of / the century" ("The Dream of The Unified Field," *Materialism*). Half opportunity for a connection, half its preclusion. Lovers— "How can they cross over and the difference between them swell with / existence?" ("Manifest Destiny"). Reader—do you have senses available to reinforce my own, "do you taste / salt now if / I say to you the air is *salt*. . . ?" ("Young Maples in Wind," *Materialism*).

At any rate,

dear reader—

"Stay with me. / Can we make this a *thinking*, here, this determination / between us to co- / exist" ("The Break of Day"). *Thinking*: "stringent self-analysis— / a tyranny of utter self-reflexiveness." "A deep fissure / the days suck round." A "nearness to the invisible" ("Opulence").

Only Whitman has made more of the ploy of addressing the reader in the big wind-wet and blow of the pronoun "you." How seductively he reached across the democratic loneliness to the stranger across the way. The greater the loneliness, the sweeter the promise—and American loneliness, circa 1855, was a continental one, even cosmic, with great slabs of blue skyshell on its head. What a call, then, for the famous imputed hospitality, indeed the infinite readiness for intimacy, of the anonymous "you."

Whitman eroticized the Reader as his lover and a lover *with* him of Democratic Flesh (cosmicized flesh)—beginning (why not?) with Whitman's sweet own. It was partly a bachelor's make-out fantasy, partly a replacement of the I-Thou intimacies of religion (the *other* religions). Whoever you are holding me now in hand, you touch me into realness, I thank you. It is in a different, philosophically *mined* atmosphere that Jorie Graham revives the trope of the even-now listening reader (a trope so near to being literal that it has every excuse and, even in the primitive sense, *charm*; as it traffics in a virtual fast-forward/fast-reverse). Her reader ("dear-are-you-there") is the uncertain *other* mind in the age of phenomenological loneliness: a new kind of loneliness, cosmic, too, *but always already equivocally in your debt, objects, to which I come with my tin can of thought and its gun-slinger measuring notches, hoping to get a little real by thinking about being.*

This ontological loneliness of the mind (Nietzsche, Husserl, Sartre, and others have written of it) was already historically tired by the time Jorie Graham came to it, but neither outlived nor outthought, and she brought and still brings to it a purpose and passion part ethical obligation to, part ferocious hunger for, the truth, also part ambition. She took it up as a way of being necessary to the age, and she is.

Imagine this, imagine that, she characteristically instructs both herself and the reader (and already so in her first book, *Hybrids of Plants and of Ghosts*). Imagine your way, even, into the dreamed-of seamlessness of being, like "these men along the lush / green banks," these fishermen, "trying to slip in / and pass // for the natural world" ("Reading Plato" *Erosion*). But here, of course, the word "trying" doesn't even let the imagination cheat. Jorie Graham is terrible with conscience. (No writer who isn't so is worth reading anymore.)

Jorie Graham focuses on the pathos of the mind as such. But also (if this is an also) on the mind's persistence, its reliance on itself. The tension in her work springs from the contest (and, in what is beyond unraveling, the cooperation) between analysis and creativity—between grammar and style. Michel Serres illuminates the opposition:

> Clarity is paid for . . . with sterility, invention and speed with confusion and obscurity. . . . The grammarian to the stylist, Get out of here, confused and irrational mind. The stylist [:] . . . wily, prudent, rigorous, . . . you advance one-half a millimeter per century. During this time, inattentive, courageous, intuitive, I create meaning . . . about life, the world, the tragic, knowledge even, love, neighborly relations. . . . . I make language live at the price of clarity. You clarify language at the cost of life" (*The Troubadour of Knowledge*)[3]

The analyst in Jorie Graham keeps in check the tempting and terrible capacity of words to martyr themselves in an ecstasy of irrationality. She is formidable, this internal analyst—as powerful as any powerful creative will (and Jorie Graham has this power, as well) could face. Entertainment? Gladiatorial.

In her latest book, *Never*, her eighth, she is still worrying the scab of mentality (in fact, her work has been obsessed from the first with just a few essential problems), still conscious of being nothing more (or less) than conscious, conscious of the mere "swagger of dwelling in place, in voice" ("Woods"). Once again she is after us, dear Poet that she is, to shore up, dear Reader that we are, our common awkward hesitant self-betrayed inconsequential perishing and persistent inwardness. Not just to think with her, but see, feel, hunger. And hope, even, to be a *thinker interrupted*: "One turns / to speak. / One wishes so one could be interrupted" ("Prayer [Am I still in the near distance]").

One recourse is to look to shape? "Look: acceptance has a shape," she instructs in "Evolution 1." Shape, then, is an acceptance—but essentially an acceptance of itself. In any case, in her typically rather long poems Graham herself doesn't head directly for economy of shape; she's too aware—oh, the curse of awareness!—that "The words [are] leaping . . . over their own / staying . . . / my clutch of / words / swaying and stemming from my / saying, no / echo. No stopping on the temporarily exposed and drying rock / out there" ("Gulls"). She must keep writing and writing, so as to exhaust a need to demonstrate to herself a certain power to pound on the rock, wash over it with an abundance of words. To bear down and bear on.

Which is where we—the dear friends—come in. To be, after all, her words' echo (if indeed the words are hers: "The" words, in any case).

Can we comfort the poet in her lonely, heroic endeavor, that of trying, trying exhaustively and exhaustingly to find "enough," and never really *having* it, not with the mind, especially not with the mind, that "wound of meaning" ("Dusk Shore Prayer")? "The reader is tired. / I am so very tired" ("That Greater Than Which Nothing," *The Errancy*); nonetheless, dear well-meaning futility, at whom my words gaze "straight up" (a Whitmanic trope), words "filled with ultimate fatigue," it comforts me for all my life is worth that

> slowly in the listener the prisoners emerge:
> slowly in you reader they stand like madmen facing into the wind:
> nowhere is there any trace of blood
> spilled in the service of kings, or love, or for the sake of honor,
> or for some other reason.
>
> ("Gulls," *Never*)

"We live. We speak at the horizon" ("Prayer [Am I still in the near distance]"). We single out objects. Perhaps we see "fishermen . . . from the back as they / disappear through the palms" ("The Time Being"). But, really, "Nothing can be singled out." (Again, from "Kyoto," still in *Never*. "Nothing is partial. One must know partiality.") Phenomenological knowledge consists only of "almost-knowables" in the stream of *world without end*. (In "Solitude," the line "Speaking subject: world without end" has a section to itself, because naming what is radically insurmountable). How bear this impure ontological solitude? (Husserl argued that the mind itself is ontological, but *regional*, for ontology is divided into regions.) Can a poet who is a prey to her own clamoring *and* altruistic openness to the world at least not hope for a few trustworthy listeners? Really, it is the world itself that Jorie Graham would have listen, just as she herself (as if showing it how) listens to its bird calls. There is no ultimacy of speaking because there is no ultimacy of listening. The Reader is not dear, really. Nor, alas, fond of her as we may be, is the Poet, as such. Just ask her. She will tell you how loveless it is to be a mental castaway.

Pathos. Never, never to be removed. "We exist Meet me." "Are you listening?" "Dear sentence. . . . I feel scribbled-in. Something inattentive has barely / written me in." "What should the poem do?" "Come, come, the trouble will not stop, pay attention."

A measure of theatrics, then, in place of the final goods: "What do you think I've been about all this long time, / half-crazed, pen-in-hand, looking up, looking back down, taking it down, taking it *all* down." "You've read enough now." "Look I push the book off my desk / into the flood."

the glance—

"The glance? braiding and braiding the many promises of vision." Or (?) "The glance, however exiled, wanting nonetheless only to come full term / into the absolute orphanhood" ("That Greater Than Which Nothing").

history—

Child of metaphysics though he was, Whitman was yet so taken with the horizon of the entities that he wanted the moment of history to be prolonged indefinitely. For him, the interlocutor is not a thou, but a you. He is you, reader. Here in the always already ecstatic state of being (Phillipe Lacoue-Labarthe says that to the question "What is man?" the answer, today, is that man is always already the subject, thrown into being), we withstand the invasion of totality by a sensuous, amorous dalliance with phenomena. So, then, we have a story: history is a You becoming a Thou as surely and as slowly as possible. (Levinas, in *Totality and Infinity*: "as a stage the separated being traverses on the way of its return to its metaphysical source, a moment of a history that will be concluded by union, metaphysics would be an Odyssey, and its disquietude nostalgia."[4])

Since Emerson, American poetry has been a romance with phenomena—loving, driven, querulous at times (Frost), destined. Things in space, or rather the feelings about and the metaphysical implications of things in space, have been its focus and genius. It sprang out of a rebel country in which history drew a chit on the future, and where the antithesis of history, namely the Now, was correspondingly tremendous. It is still tremendous, but history has in the meantime become the Crisis of History and since the 1950s the two great protagonists of the human adventure have lost much of their following. Jorie Graham has responded to this dilemma with more comprehension and with a more nearly constant and lacerated openness than other American poets have done. (Of course, there are European counterparts: Geoffrey Hill, Paul Celan, Inger Christensen. . . .) This is her work's principle significance.

What Ortega y Gasset called the *modern theme*—vitality, immediacy, flesh, joy, spontaneous immanence—was practically an American discovery, is already full-blown in Whitman, though present also at the beginnings of English romanticism, loudest in Blake, of course, and quietest and sweetest in the elegiac "To Autumn." It tumbles Emerson, Melville, Thoreau, and Whitman into the same river of metamorphosis. They meant to keep up with what Emerson called "the central flowing forces." Holding that "ecstasy will be found normal, or only an example on a higher plane of the same gentle gravitation by which stones fall and rivers run," Emerson knew or said he knew "the Now to be eternal," and

"Being" a "vast affirmative." He rejected as blasphemous the thought that the world is "two"—"Me and It."[5] Whitman commanded the moment in American culture when the Me, Phenomena, and History could be seen as tributaries to the same ecstasy, surpassing Emerson through his gusto and more groaning delirious grounding. (Pound tried to repeat it, in changed terms, but the result was cacophonous, and finally apologetic.) Gertrude Stein marks the moment when the phenomenological field was still "all the long way to be in that length which makes no more [and no less] of some cuckoo. . . . It is so cheerful and the breath which is not all of a response is used some more,"[6] but at the cost of reducing history to a succession of essentially untroubled re-compositions. And Jorie Graham, as said, tackles the moment when not only has history become unbearable but American poetry has encountered the impossible in the phenomenological: impasses of consciousness and a subjective and transubjective real increasingly impossible to define.

So for Jorie Graham, neither of Whitman's twin passions—for history and for phenomena—has survived intact. When she started out (which was not so very long ago), history had long since become humanity's all but open and shut case against itself ("Elsewhere a people now is being forced / from home"). How dangerous and disastrous human nature is! Of course, what Blanchot called "the writing of disaster" is more centrally and obsessively the subject of Carolyn Forché's "Europeanized" poetry, in whose work the "American" question of Being becomes correspondingly occluded by smoke and screams. Jorie Graham's obsession lies on the contrary, apparently nonhistorical side of the pair of yoked crises (a side that nonetheless has behind it the pressure of Western history and philosophy, in particular the actual and intellectual capitalism and imperialism of the Enlightenment). Nonetheless, for her the two great categories of experience are inseparable, and steeped in the same general experience of betrayed promise. The earth no longer comes out entirely beautiful from the smoking syllables (Vallejo).

Again, it is in this exemplary and (as it were) sacrificial assumption of both the historical and the philosophical burden of the present that Jorie Graham's work establishes its significance—both its moment and its stature (her methods and intelligence having stood up to the nonetheless impossible challenge, the writing so brilliantly lit yet so strenuous and adventurous, neither over- nor under-controlled, the lines alive in their breakings, and if often more discursive than poetry needs to be, perhaps not more discursive than the big project of *her* poetry needs to be). In "History" (in *Region of Unlikeness*) the poet says that

>   what I wanted was to have looked up at the only
>   right time, the intended time,
>   punctual,
>   the millisecond I was bred to look up into, click, no
>   half-tone, no orchard of
>   possibilities,
>
>   up into the eyes of my own
>   fate, not the world's.

But the world's fate and her own are effectively the same, insofar as any two such incommensurates can be so. The very logic of the passage argues for their identity. What else could explain the "intended time"? ("Up into the eyes": how she wants to be looked at, this poet whose own gaze never quits.)

History is no longer "a *whole story*"; is only a "cold current." Of course, it has specific aims; in fact, its vice is "to feel the end's insistence / (on war for instance)" ("Probity," *Swarm*). This poet whose own will can on occasion be problematical with respect to her material (straining, as in the allegorical overreaching of "The Phase After History," out of big-minded and big-hearted ambition) is nonetheless primed to detect imperialism (witness "Where definition first comes upon us empire"). History is will in excess of "justice"—a word she cites occasionally and certainly fathoms, but leaves inert, as rhetoric; it is will in excess of inquiry. Her own *poetic* will inquires in order to come into (and in neither sense before) being, not to possess it: "We write. We would like to live somewhere." For all its spectacular determination and self-dramatization, it's too famished to be imperialistic. No "empire" can be founded in the reciprocal threatened loss of both the object and the subject.

Even if Heidegger called being "the disclosive appropriating Event," he meant by that its becoming apparent, not its becoming property. As "eminent potentiality," it cannot be property. It is a "clearing,"[7] a word Jorie Graham adopts from him:

>   and the clearing
>   itself
>   is entered—look: there is no one way to go—
>   light floods a bit, one feels a center, all directions shine from it,
>   [is a center sought?] . . .
>
>   ("By the Way," *Never*)

Being is the openness of subjectivity, untotalizable, not subject to accumulation: "For the summer of the clearing is long / once you enter the first person." If it can be "said," it is only in many ways. It is not a "story," whether a masternarrative or petite, a *conte*. It is, rather, "the clearing where / the spine of the picked-clean story shines" ("Ebbtide," *Never*).

the invisible (underneath, something, something else, the x, the absolute)—

The unrepresentable Jewish deity has been superceded, or reinterpreted, as invisible vibrancy—as Nietzschean force, a continual excess of something dynamic over form, something self-explosive, non-self-identical). "There is a god here but it is not shaped. / Is moving around us" ("Underneath [Always]," *Swarm*). By contrast, I myself "am held to myself by force. / No voyage home / over blossoming's broad back. / Forced down instead into the stalk" ("Underneath [Calypso]"). In fact, almost everything we know "is choked into the forced / *becoming visible* . . . guards of the / imprisoned prisoner" ("Little Requiem," *The Errancy*).

The invisible, the *x*, the "something" (alternatively, the "something else"), the "underneath," thus indifferently pushes us both up and down on ourselves. Like the Spinozan "underneath" cause, it "exists entirely in its own movement, the infinite productivity and dynamism that alone make it what it is" (I quote from Warren Montag's preface to *The New Spinoza*). It is "What carries universal law as meaning secreted within / itself" ("Miscellaneous Weights and Measures," *The Errancy*). *Deus sive natura*, in Spinoza's famous definition in the preface to *Ethics IV*: God, that is, nature. It is "metamorphosis" such as Emerson, as the author of "Brahma," would understand it—not warm and Whitmanic, but featureless: "unincarnate— / tireless dimensions— / metamorphic yet unpliant" ("That Greater Than Which Nothing"). Taking, however, when pulled our way, the form of desire ("the . . . inalienable / welding of matter to / desire" ["Miscellaneous Weights and Measures"]).

The force cannot be seen, anymore than "Being" can; in fact, it is the cause and huge background of Being, the latter only as wide as subjectivity is. In "Opulence," Jorie Graham bears down on the birth-process of an amaryllis with a vengeance, determined to detect the immanent cause. Overheated and overwritten, the poem flails at its subject, as it makes audible, kinetic, appetitive, and pulsing—"bits of *clench, jolt, fray* and a*ssuage*— / bits of *gnaw* and *pulse* and, even, *ruse*"—the "something from underneath" that coaxes "the packed buds up." (Coax" and "packed buds" are cuts from Roethke's "Cuttings," but the force that drives this amaryllis through its green fuse would have shattered his father's greenhouses.) It may be the only poem in which Jorie Graham forces the force to disclose itself; its fever brings out by contrast the poise (if desperate poise) of her characteristic work.

The five hundred B-52s "fully loaded fully manned pointed in all the directions / running every minute / of every day" in Grand Forks, North Dakota, as splendidly evoked in "What the End is For" (in *The End of Beauty*), make even "watching . . . an anachronism." They are the visible and audible equivalent of invisible force. Try talking over the noise! They blot, as the falling darkness does (and perhaps something in us *wants* to be "shapes the shapelessness was taking back"), the supposed reality of individuation. At the powerful close of the poem, even Orpheus's head, always already torn off and drifting, can be heard singing only "until the sound of the cataracts grows."

Julia Kristeva's contention that a woman's being (her psychical bisexuality) "never adheres to the illusion of being" comes close to catching Jorie Graham's poetry by its skirts, and, yes, Kristeva has in mind the girl's perception that "she is not the phallus" and her consequent "disappointment with regard to the symbolic link."[8] Jorie Graham keeps trying to love "the small hole inside I'm supposed to love," but it's a *black* hole, in which (again) uncreation reigns. Is hers then a woman's version of the metaphysics of Being, stemming from what Kristeva names a female "paroxysmal . . . ambition bordering on martyrology"? If so, the whole age is feminine, its sublimity masochistic, its secret pleasure the pornography of the void. Lyotard has argued as much, and we have but to recall Celan's sublime of destitution, *o einer, o keiner, o Niemand, o du,* and reflect on why for poets it is so compelling and so *popular*.

The invisible is the terrible. Is us. Is too much to be us. Is too much for us. "What is it cannot be judged? / What is it / is corporeal but still concealed? . . . We are *in a drama*" ("The Break of Day," *Materialism*). Jorie Graham, dramatist of the thinking of the invisible.

now (here)—

The "Now," that great American subject, is an ecstatic unconcealment; or would be so if . . . if it were more than a theory? "The ecstatic relationship," Heidegger said, "cannot be represented. As soon as I represent it, I have two objects, and I am outside the ecstatic relationship." So the poet of the Now tries to present what cannot be represented:

> The path of thought also now too bright
>
> So that its edges cut
>
> So that I'm writing this in the cold
>
> keeping the parts from finding the whole again
>
> ("*from* The Reformation Journal [2]," *Swarm*)

The poet emulates the "substantial polyvocity of being" by "reproposing its viscosity," Umberto Eco notes in *Kant and the Platypus: Essays on Language and Cognition;* but the only real evidence for Being is its own, which is "luminous."[9] To try to *say* Being darkens its luminosity ("the world is all that is displaced," Michael Palmer says, punning, of course, on Wiggenstein's statement that the world is all that is the case, and Jorie Graham speaks of "the stump interpretation" and comments, in "The Taken-Down God" in *Never,* on "this constant incompletion as it tries to *be* (softly as possible) over this page"; hence the appeal, even to her, though as a poet she doesn't often *work* the silence, of silence: "how neatly silence describes the thing" ("Underneath [Eurydice]"). Again, "I've listened where the words and the minutes would touch," she says, but there was "slippage" ("Noli Me Tangere," *The End of Beauty*).

One of Jorie Graham's urges is to say that something "is"—is *in time* (even in the sense of *to rescue*)—despite time's instant self-dissolution. Augustine reeled with the question; Walter Pater was famously poignant on it; and Jorie Graham worries it obsessively, when she is not courting its opposite, the "horror" of uncreation (see, in particular, "Miscellaneous Weights and Measures"). Why? Because she feels overcome by *Sorge* (Care)—feels assigned by destiny to save the phenomena and subjectivity (the two regions of being) in one and the same breath: "A curtain rose. I felt an obligation. / I tried to feel the thing that blossoms in me . . . / the whole world intelligently lit / up there in front of me" ("Untitled One," *The Errancy*). Past, present, and future phenomena: "In the 'then,'" writes Werner Brock in his commentary on Heidegger's *Existence and Being,* "the Care speaks in 'anticipation' . . . ; in the 'now,' in the mode of 'rendering present'; in the 'at that time' in the mode of 'bearing in mind,' in relating to the past."[10] The past: "Remember . . . / The bright brief hatchlings buzzing the pane. / Remember . . . / brief strips of sunshine playing the dirt. / . . . Oh brilliant drowning" ("The Lovers," *Swarm*). Again, "One cannot keep all of it. What is enough / of it. And *keep*—I am being swept away—what is *keep*? A waking good" ("Evolution," *Never*). The present: "One must see the cowbird spread its tail—just so—and / shut it again, clean, just / after landing. One must know" ("Kyoto"). The future: "what there is to be thought: love: / begin with the world: let it be small enough" ("Afterwards," *Never*).

So this poet who leaves the door ajar so that "uncreated substance . . . can show up anytime" ("It is the law in her dress of things we want let in. / It is the world made strange again / we want invited in") is nonetheless also up early to look— she's as hungry to see and hear everything as she is one who waits "blindly for / uncreated substance," for "the other sceneless thing, . . . / where there is no subject" ("Miscellaneous Weights and Measures"). Such is her vacillation and hesitation between the near and the far side of Being.

One of the ways Jorie Graham differs from Gertrude Stein (who was to *her* age what Jorie Graham is to her own, namely indexical, a definitive philosophical presence in poetry) is in not trusting *even in theory* to what Husserl called *intuition* (immediate and direct knowledge). "Does it seem to you, too, stranger, that something died? / Something we could call the great *thereness* of being." ("Untitled," *Region of Unlikeness*). ("Thereness" is here, as for Heidegger, that into which our existence has been thrown.) Always Jorie Graham has to *think* about the here and now even while imagining herself in them, and so she cannot unlock what is plenipotentiary. ("When do I say   yes / And it become again a form of joy?" ["5/3/98," *Swarm*].) For only immediate perception could conceivably be adequate. Gertrude Stein theorized and anticipated this adequacy all but endlessly: "the full service is in the height of a rich thick sandy sticky silence. There is no dispute when there is harmony. All the date is in the place." Again: "Soon to have an eye, soon to have plenty of them," etc.[11] Always the upbeat note. By contrast, here, from "Covenant" in *Never* is Jorie Graham on the insufficiency (yet so tormentingly more than that) of the "me" and the "here" and the "now":

> At peak: the mesmerization of here, this me here, this me
> passing now.
> So as to leave *what* behind?
> . . . .
> And to have it come so close and yet not *know* it:
> . . . .
> how the instant is very wide and bright and we cannot
>   ever
> get away with it—the instant—what holds the "know"

And later: "the covenant: yes: that there be plenitude, yes, / but only as the simultaneous emptying—of the before, where it came / from—and of the after (the eager place to which it so / 'eagerly' goes)" ("The Covenant," *Never*). Too, in "Chaos," in *Region of Unlikeness*, the poet remarks on "the sensation of lateness pulling up out of // the sensation of there not being / enough."

In Jorie Graham, then, one longing—she says it is "The longing"—"is to be pure" ("Prayer")—purely here, purely now. In *Poetry as Experience*, Lacoue-Labarthe says that "the immediacy of the god . . . is—as tragedy attests—man's death, or plunge into turmoil,"[12] and this is one explanation of the longing (just hear, again, in fascination, the roar of those five-hundred B-52s). But (in this section) let us put a happy face upon it and bring back the word *plenipotentiary*, an overflowing plenitude of the sense of being. The reality, of course, is to be, instead, transitive and, as it were, serial, instead, "frame after frame of nowhere // turning into the living past" ("Breakdancing," *The End of Beauty*). So (and I quote from "Imperialism" in the same volume),

> What I want to know, dear are-you-there,
> is what it *is*, this life a shadow and a dust-road have,
>   the shape constantly laying herself down over the sparkling dust
> she cannot own—
>   What can they touch of one another, and what is it *for*. . . .

( ), [ ] (parentheses, brackets)—

Except in *Swarm*, her hair shirt volume, Jorie Graham is discursive. She does not cut and reappear *over here*, laughing at rational connectivity's slow and infuriatingly sane feet of gravity. Not exactly; but her signature use of frequent parentheses (she starts them buzzing like plucked taut strings on the page), and in *Never* of brackets as well, is a prairie I mean practice of asides, of goings-underneath, if still within layers of sober reflection. They advertise that thinking is equipped for all directions, at least by way of exceptions and qualifications; thinking is an angle artist ("She tried every angle. [. . .] [. . .]," etc.—"Estuary," *Never*). Just as modernist painters alternately broke up the plane of flat space and reduced sprung and cubic space to flatness, so Jorie Graham multiplies, scatters, and tilts lines of thought, even as she keeps the progress of *thinking* subservient to grammar (else would it still be thinking? And if there is not *thought* of the sublime aporia of being, what is there? Nothing but psychosis, as Hegel and Nietzsche suspected and as Lacan obsessively theorized in splats of dissatisfied paragraphs?)

point of view—

"The points-of-view are dead, they come and go," they are fugitive oyster spits in relation to "the great *thereness* of being," to the "something else" that has always already started to pool (again) all around them ("Untitled," *Region of Unlikeness*). Niche perspectives, as Nietzsche called them. Fragmentary in relation to the unimaginable whole, which they yet seek to seize, hold down, bite clean. Always the outline must be amended by the invisible (see "I Watched a Snake"), or else one can never become "blossomfree," as Jorie Graham puts it in "The Lovers"—dire and angelic with absoluteness. The *new absolute*: the impossible totality of all directions and perspectives.

"The world is a desperate element." Both the point of view and its unpresentable opposite are untenable: the first "dead," the second unlivable. Where to turn? "The glance reaching her shoreline" in "Orpheus and Eurydice" wants "only to be recalled" and wants "only to be taken in"—pure ambivalence. In the framework of the (meta)physical realm of Force, cognition and perception are place-holdings where there is no place.

Gertrude Stein, together with Virginia Woolf, the *other* modern English-language writer preoccupied with the vicissitudes and ontological status of the point of view, was also poised to be devastating toward it, as in: "There is no use in a pencil, there is no use in any direction of succeeding in experience" ("England"). But her perspective on perspective includes an exit-clause, which is identical with Heidegger's notion that "success" on the pathways of experience consists in continuing on the way: "Experience means *eundo assequi*, to obtain something along the way, to attain something by going on a way" (Lacoue-Labarthe, *Poetry as Experience*, 98). So conducted, "there is not one single objection," in Gertrude Stein's words, to the mental life: "The wholesale cloth is not handled with a sprinkler [not addressed everywhere at once, as with a sprinkler], it is so handled that when there is no obligation there is every inducement it is so handled that pathways are mended [by continuing along them], it is so handled that there is a single sound [the auditory equivalent of the invisible, an impossible singularity, here posited as self-presentable, much as in Jorie Graham's description in 'Studies in Secrecy' of 'the chittering of manyness' at the 'suction-point' of the unseen, a chittering 'made to / clot / into a thrumming singleness']."[13] Though lucid, Gertrude Stein does not *suffer* the aporia of the part/whole problem. Jorie Graham almost always has the harder mind, even if she is unnervingly *intent* on having it.

story (plot, outline)

1. "Brittleness, shapeliness . . . meaning . . . the ticket . . . the idiom in you, the why" ("Soul Says").
2. A cover-up for nowhere, notime, nohow. "Oh it has vibrancy, she thought, this emptiness, this intake just / prior to / the start of a story, the mind . . . feeling it like a sickness this wanting / to snag, catch hold, begin" ("Vertigo," *The End of Beauty*). "Are you still waiting for the true story? (God's laughter)" ("Underneath [9]," *Swarm*). Representation is exile: "Exile   Angle of vision. / So steep   the representation . . . / Centuries lean up into its weave, shudder, go out" ("The Veil," *Swarm*). Story's come-along means, starting up from "always and everywhere" ("Little Requiem"), can't get us to "the sharp edge that we seek . . . / the true roughness," the thing "glittering with exaggeration— / dazzling the still philosophies" ("Willow in Spring Wind"). And yet, dear are-you-there, dear restless Ulysses, "How else to keep you" ("Underneath [Calypso]," *Swarm*).

3. Consolation. "I who used to be inconsolable (and the world // wild around me) can stand here now. . . . one must grow . . . consolable. Listen: / the x ['Now: *feel the creature, the x*'] gnaws, making stories . . . whole long stories which are its gentle gnawing" ("History").
4. Broadly used, a term for anything not chaotic and indescribable. No, even chaos may be part of the story. But "the apparent *strengths* of the story" (emphasis added) are "well-drawn," like the "fields and, closer-up, a saucer-magnolia / where one bud, today, has just begun to rip / into view" ("Which but for Vacancy," *The Errancy*). Even the grass tips conceive "their paraphrase of wind" ("Oblivion Aubade"), and the willow drags "its alphabet of buds all along the gravelly walk" ("Willow in Spring Wind: A Showing"). The world is mad with the potential for story. But, again, it means nothing. What is a story? A fiction. "Far into the cave of seem" ("Flood").

thinking—

1. Earnest, sincere: "the *thinking* she so laid / down hard, the gesture that of the practiced / plasterer spreading the thin gesso / on the church wall" ("Estuary," *Never*).
2. Squaring: "there, she / thought, / is my thought before me. Like a planted / thing in its pot. Not quite in nature / yet still alive / and—most crucially—self-evident" ("Exit Wound," *Never*).
3. Devout: "When I 'think,' it is near the future, just this / side of it. / Something I can't conceive of without saying *you*" ("Via Negativa," *Never*). A "you," possibly, of vain incantation, or the temptation to tame the Other, which "threatens to . . . cast us down from the height of its appearance" (*The Seminar of Jacques Lacan, Book VII*).[14]
4. Failing. Its Western flair/flare on the wane, "the captains gone but some of us / who saw the plan drawn out / still here—who saw the thinking clot-up in the bodies of the greater men" ("The Guardian Angel of the Private Life," *The Errancy*).
5. Corrosive; moving off. Secret ally of the "something else." "My sweet mind shouldering / so willingly the impossible / as if craning forward to see round / some bend" ("Probity," *Swarm*). Yeats: "man's life is thought, / And he, despite his terror, cannot cease / Ravening through century after century, / Ravening, raging, and uprooting that he may come / Into the desolation of reality" ("Meru").

waiting—

to exist. "As if it really / were possible to exist, and exist, never to be pulled back / in, given and given never to be received." "Having waited a long time and /

still having / to wait" ("The Dream of the Unified Field"). Now wakeful, now narcoleptic (as splendidly imagined in "nights ripen and fall off / into our flesh / narcotic the waiting" ("Underneath [Eurydice]").

Gertrude Stein: "patience . . . all the whole way is uplifted with that."[15] Jorie Graham: "married to hurry / and grim song" ("Of Forced Sightes and Trusty Ferefulness," *The End of Beauty*).

"Waiting is different from patience, friend" ("Picnic," *Region of Unlikeness*).

Notes

1. Jean-François Lyotard, "Newman: The Instant," in *The Lyotard Reader*, ed. Andrew Benjamin (Oxford: Basil Blackwell, 1989), 242.

2. Jean-François Lyotard, "Anima Minima," in *Postmodern Fables*, trans. Georges Van Den Abbeele (Minneapolis: University of Minnesota Press, 1997), 243.

3. Michel Serres, *The Troubadour of Knowledge*, trans. Sheila Faria Glaser with William Paulson (Ann Arbor: University of Michigan Press, 1997), 78.

4. Emmanuel Levinas, *Totality and Infinity*, trans. Alphonso Lingis (Pittsburgh, Pa.: Duquesne University Press, 1969), 102.

5. Ralph Waldo Emerson, "Inspiration" in *Letters and Social Aims* (Boston: Houghton, Mifflin, 1904), 275; "Composition," in *The Collected Works of Ralph Waldo Emerson*, vol. 2, *Essays: First Series* (Cambridge, Mass.: Harvard University Press, 1979), 70.

6. Gertrude Stein, "England," in *Geography and Plays* (Madison: University of Wisconsin Press, 1993), 85.

7. Martin Heidegger, *Zollikon Seminars: Protocols, Conversations, Letters*, ed. Medard Boss, trans. Franz Mayr and Richard Askay (Evanston, Ill.: Northwestern University Press, 2001), 178.

8. Julia Kristeva, *The Sense and Non-sense of Revolt: The Powers and Limits of Psychoanalysis*, trans. Jeanine Herman (New York: Columbia University Press, 2000), 100.

9. Umberto Eco, *Kant and the Platypus: Essays in Language and Cognition*, trans. Alastair McEwen (New York: Harcourt Brace, 1999), 34.

10. Martin Heidegger, *Existence and Being*, introduction and analysis by Werner Brock (Chicago: Gateway, 1949), 98.

11. Stein, "England," 85.

12. Phillipe Lacoue-Labarthe, *Poetry as Experience*, trans. Andrea Tarrowski (Stanford Calif.: Stanford University Press), 77.

13. Stein, "England," 93.

14. Jacques Lacan, *The Seminar of Jacques Lacan, Book VII: The Ethics of Psychoanalysis 1959–1960*, trans. Dennis Porter (New York: Norton, 1986), 56.

15. Stein, "England," 85.

Contributors

CALVIN BEDIENT, a Professor of English at UCLA, is the author of several books of criticism, including *He Do the Police in Different Voices:* The Waste Land *and Its Protagonist* and *In the Heart's Last Kingdom: Robert Penn Warren's Major Poetry*. He has also published two books of poetry: *Candy Necklace* and *The Violence of the Morning*.

STEPHEN BURT teaches at Macalester College in St Paul, Minn. His work includes a book of poems, *Popular Music*; a critical study, *Randall Jarrell and His Age*; and poems, reviews, and articles for various journals in Britain and America, among them *ALH, Boston Review, Colorado Review, Modern Philology, PN Review, Poetry Review* (UK), and the *Yale Review*. Due out in 2005 is his edition of Randall Jarrell's lectures on W. H. Auden, and in 2006 a book of poems, *Parallel Play*.

BONNIE COSTELLO is Professor of English at Boston University and Director of the College of Arts and Sciences Honors Program. She is the author of many articles and books on modern and contemporary poetry, most recently *Shifting Ground: Reinventing Landscape in Modern American Poetry*. She is currently at work on *Planets on Tables*, a study of still life and lyric poetry, and of their representation of intimate space in times of public upheaval.

ELISABETH FROST is the author of *The Feminist Avant-Garde in American Poetry*. She has published poetry in such journals as *The Denver Quarterly, Poetry, The Yale Review*, and others. She has held grants from the Rockefeller

Foundation-Bellagio Center, the MacDowell Colony for the Arts, and the Constance Saltonstall Foundation. She is Associate Professor of English and Director of Poets Out Loud at Fordham University.

FORREST GANDER is the author of numerous books including *Science & Steepleflower* and *Torn Awake*, both from New Directions. His most recent translations are *No Shelter: Selected Poems of Pura Lopez Colome* and (with Kent Johnson) *Immanent Visitor: Selected Poems of Jaime Saenz*. He is a Professor of Comparative Literature and Literary Arts at Brown University.

THOMAS GARDNER is the author of two books of criticism: *Discovering Ourselves in Whitman: The Contemporary American Long Poem* and *Regions of Unlikeness: Explaining Contemporary Poetry*. He has edited three special issues of *Contemporary Literature* on poetry of the seventies, eighties and nineties. He is Professor of English at Virginia Tech.

BRIAN HENRY is the author of three books of poetry, most recently *Graft*, and editor of *On James Tate*. His fourth book of poetry, *Quarantine*, won the 2003 Alice Fay di Castagnola Award from the Poetry Society of America. His criticism has appeared in numerous publications around the world, including the *TLS*, *New York Times Book Review*, *The Yale Review*, *The Kenyon Review*, *Jacket*, *Boston Review*, and *The Georgia Review*, as well as in various scholarly books. He edits *Verse* and is Associate Professor of English at the University of Georgia.

CYNTHIA HOGUE'S criticism includes *Scheming Women: Poetry, Privilege, and the Politics of Subjectivity* and the co-edited *We Who Love to Be Astonished: Experimental Women's Writing and Performance Poetics*. Her collections of poetry include *Flux* and *The Incognito Body*, her fourth. She directed the Stadler Center for Poetry and taught English at Bucknell University for eight years. She is currently the Maxine and Jonathan Marshall Chair in Modern and Contemporary Poetry at Arizona State University.

JOANNA KLINK is the author of *They Are Sleeping* (University of Georgia Press, 2000). She is working on a second book of poems, *Circadian*, and a book on Paul Celan called *You*. She teaches in the M.F.A. Program at the University of Montana.

JAMES LONGENBACH is the author of two books of poems, *Fleet River* and *Threshold*, as well as several books of literary criticism, including *Modern*

Poetry after Modernism and *The Resistance to Poetry*. He is the Joseph H. Gilmore Professor of English at the University of Rochester.

THOMAS J. OTTEN teaches English at Boston University. He has completed a book-length study of Henry James and materialism, sections of which have appeared in *American Literature* and *Yale Journal of Criticism*.

ANNE SHIFRER is an Associate Professor at Utah State University. Most of her scholarly work has been in the area of modern and contemporary poetry by women. She has written essays on Marianne Moore, Elizabeth Bishop, P. K. Page, H.D., Laura Riding, and Eavan Boland. She is currently at work on a book-length project about lyric subjectivity in relation to depression and postmodern conceptions of self.

WILLARD SPIEGELMAN is Hughes Professor of English and Editor-in-Chief of the *Southwest Review*, at Southern Methodist University. His forthcoming works include *How Poets See the World: The Art of Description in Poetry* (Oxford), and *Love, Amy: The Selected Letters of Amy Clampitt* (Columbia).

HELEN VENDLER is the Porter University Professor at Harvard University. She is the author of books on Yeats, Stevens, Keats, Herbert, Shakespeare, and Heaney. Her book, *Poets Thinking*, was published by the Harvard University Press in 2004. In 2005, *Invisible Listeners* will appear from Princeton University Press.

STEPHEN YENSER'S book of poems *The Fire in All Things* received the Walt Whitman Award from the Academy of American Poets. The author of three critical books and co-editor of James Merrill's work (the third volume is Merrill's *Collected Prose*), he is Professor of English and Director of Creative Writing at UCLA.

Index of Graham's Works

"2/18/97," 162, 177
"5/3/98," 287

"Act III, Sc. 2," 257
"Afterwards," 215, 220, 286
"Against Eloquence," 80, 109
"The Age of Reason," 88, 118–20, 121, 162, 258
"Annunciation," 224
"Annunciation with a Bullet in It," 35, 203n.7
"At Luca Signorelli's Resurrection of the Body," 25–27, 45–46, 48, 87–88, 116–17, 120, 144n.15, 277
"At the Exhumed Body of Santa Chiara, Assisi," 15, 24, 26
"At the Long Island Jewish Geriatric Home," 196, 257

"Breakdancing," 288
"The Break of Day," 36, 104, 190, 277, 278, 285
"By the Way," 283

"Chaos," 287
"The Complex Mechanism of the Break," 231

"Concerning the Right to Life," 35, 95, 101n.12, 141, 238–40
"Covenant," 221, 287
"Cross-Stitch," 223

"Daphne," 154
"Description," 223
"The Dream of the Unified Field," 41, 52–54, 95–98, 104, 157, 174–75, 186, 247, 257, 272, 277, 291
The Dream of the Unified Field, 8, 98, 170, 257
"Dusk Shore Prayer," 171, 280

Earth Took of Earth, 189
"Easter Morning Aubade," 110
"Ebbtide," 171, 179, 249, 276, 284
"Emergency," 80, 105, 224
The End of Beauty, 4, 5, 32, 34, 40, 47–52, 60, 61, 69, 85–88, 90–94, 100, 103, 104, 111, 121–29, 148, 162, 163, 172, 173, 175, 184, 185, 202n.1, 202n.3, 220, 223, 229–30, 242–45, 259, 264, 271
"The End of Progress Aubade (Eurydice to Orpheus)," 110
"Erosion," 14, 114
Erosion, 4, 5, 8–9, 13–33, 44–47, 52, 60–69, 72, 85–88, 90, 91, 93, 100, 103, 115–22,

Erosion (continued)
    144n.15, 162, 172–73, 184, 223, 227–28, 240, 243, 257–59
"The Errancy," 78, 79, 106, 108, 111, 176
The Errancy, 4–5, 11n.3, 75–81, 105–12, 161, 164, 192, 193, 194, 198, 206–7, 236, 272
"Eschatological Prayer," 47
"Estuary," 171, 288, 290
"Eurydice on History," 154, 155
"Evening Prayer," 229–30
"Event Horizon," 199, 224
"Evolution (1)," 171, 220, 277, 279
"Evolution (2)," 171, 286
"Existence and Presence," 41, 226–27, 228
"Exit Wound," 235, 236, 290

"A Feather for Voltaire," 226
"Fission," 11, 69–73, 88, 130–31, 186, 192, 199, 221, 257, 260–68, 269, 270, 271
"Flood," 105, 290
"Foreword" *(Region of Unlikeness)*, 129, 260
"For Mark Rothko," 186, 194–95, 225, 226
"For One Must Want / To Shut the Other's Gaze," 164, 209–10, 211, 213, 214
"From the New World," 88, 89, 97–98, 131–32, 195–99, 202n.6, 221, 247–49
"*from* The Reformation Journal (1)," 148–49, 165
"*from* The Reformation Journal (2)," 178, 285
"Fuse," 152

"The Geese," 156, 257
"Girl at the Piano," 223
"The Guardian Angel of Not Feeling," 79
"The Guardian Angel of Self-Knowledge," 78
"The Guardian Angel of the Little Utopia," 109
"The Guardian Angel of the Private Life," 79, 106, 290
"The Guardian Angel of the Swarm," 106, 191
"Gulls," 171, 215–17, 220, 279, 280

"Harvest for Bergson," 223
"The Hiding Place," 260, 268–70, 271
"High Tide," 171, 182, 203n.7, 239, 253n.5
"History" *(Region of Unlikeness)*, 282–83, 290
"How the Body Fits on the Cross," 105, 109
"The Hurrying-Home Aubade," 106, 110
Hybrids of Plants and of Ghosts, 13, 156, 222, 223, 257, 278

"Immobilism," 223
"Imperialism," 90, 93, 128–29, 242, 243–45, 247, 257, 258, 275, 288
"In / Silence," 231, 233–34, 236
"Interview: Jorie Graham" (Ann Snodgrass), 61–62
"Interview with Jorie Graham" (Thomas Gardner), 60–61, 67, 68, 84, 85, 90, 101n.15, 139, 239, 270
"In the Hotel," 36, 104
"In the Pasture," 107
"Introduction: *Earth Took of Earth*," 100, 101n.12
"Introduction: *The Best American Poetry 1990*," 113
"Invention of the Other," 34, 224
"In What Manner the Body is United with the Soule," 15, 16–18, 31, 223
"I Watched a Snake," 288

"Kimono," 15, 22–23, 116–17, 120, 144n.15
"Kyoto," 180–81, 280, 286

"The Lady and the Unicorn and Other Tapestries," 15, 20–21, 28, 222
"Le Manteau de Pascal," 78, 80, 156, 157, 158, 161, 207–8, 231
"Little Requiem," 80, 106, 284, 289
"The Lovers" *(The End of Beauty)*, 194, 195, 199, 275, 288
"The Lovers" *(Swarm)*, 286

"Manifest Destiny" *(Materialism)*, 143, 221, 277

"Manifest Destiny" *(Region of Unlikeness)*, 95, 132
"Manteau," 80, 105, 106
"Masaccio's Expulsion," 25, 27–29, 227–28, 229
Materialism, 4, 5, 9, 34–37, 38–41, 52–54, 75, 82–83, 86, 90, 91, 93, 94–98, 103, 104, 105–6, 138–43, 157, 172, 174–75, 198, 201, 203n.8, 224, 225, 243, 245, 272
"Middle Distance," 164, 277
"Mind," 226
"Miscellaneous Weights and Measures," 110, 284, 286
"Mist," 14, 15–16

Never, 5, 7, 8, 170–84, 214–17, 219–22, 230–36, 279, 288
"Noli Me Tangere," 47, 275, 286
"Notes on the Reality of the Self" (sequence), 95, 96, 104, 106, 174
"Notes on the Reality of the Self (1)," 40, 94
"Notes on the Reality of the Self (2)," 83, 94–95, 223
"Notes on the Reality of the Self (3)," 38–39

"Oblivion Aubade," 106, 290
"Of the Ever-Changing Agitation in the Air," 107, 111
"Of Forced Sightes and Trusty Ferefulness," 93, 291
"Opulence," 44, 104, 278, 284
"Orpheus and Eurydice," 124–25, 130, 288–89

"Patience," 120–21, 130
"The Phase After History," 88, 136–37, 153, 157, 221, 223, 235, 283
"Philosopher's Stone," 219, 220
"Picnic," 133–35, 173–74, 245–47, 271, 276, 291
"Pleasure," 3, 6
"Poetic Statement: At the Border," 3, 6, 243, 251–52

"Pollock and Canvas," 48, 49, 50–52, 165, 195
"Prayer (1)" *(Never)*, 236, 287
"Prayer (2)" *(Never)*, 279, 280
"Prayer *(after Hölderlin)*," 167
"Probity," 151, 159, 167–68, 283, 290

"Ravel and Unravel," 223
"Reading Plato," 14, 16, 278
"Recovered from the Storm," 80, 83–84, 85, 87, 94, 95, 98–99, 107, 108
"Red Umbrella Aubade," 106, 110, 225, 226
"The Region of Unlikeness," 132–33, 271
Region of Unlikeness, 4, 5, 11, 34, 40, 52, 60, 61, 69–73, 86–90, 93, 94, 95, 100, 103, 129–37, 144n.17, 148, 153, 172, 173–74, 185, 223, 243, 245, 257, 260, 264, 270, 271, 272
"Relativity: A Quartet," 41, 141–42
"Relay Station," 236
"Room Tone," 61, 195, 223–224

"Salmon," 258–59
"San Sepolcro," 23–24, 26, 62, 115–16, 144n.15, 261
"The Scanning," 76–78, 80, 105, 106
"Scirocco," 44–45, 117–18, 172–73, 223
"Sea-Blue Aubade," 106
"Self-Portrait as Apollo and Daphne," 49, 91–92, 125–26, 138, 223, 242–43, 263
"Self-Portrait as Both Parties," 49, 123–24
"Self-Portrait as Demeter and Persephone," 49, 92–93, 127–28
"Self-Portrait as Hurry and Delay," 49, 91, 92, 126–27, 259
"Self-Portrait as the Gesture between Them," 49, 91, 92, 122–23, 202n.3
"The Sense of an Ending," 87, 88, 223
"Solitude," 280
"Some Notes on Silence," 3, 69, 113, 167
"So Sure of Nowhere Buying Times to Come," 106
"Soul Says," 90, 289

"Spelled from the Shadows Aubade," 110, 193
"Steering Wheel," 36
"Still Life with Window and Fish," 15, 18–19
"The Strangers," 106
"Studies in Secrecy," 106, 289
"Subjectivity," 34, 35, 41, 139–41
"Surf," 171, 220
"The Surface," 41, 104
"The Swarm," 210–11, 224–25
Swarm, 7, 9, 11n.3, 147–55, 156–69, 176–78, 206, 208–14, 217, 236n.2, 253n.9, 276, 288
"Syntax," 226

"The Taken-Down God," 181–82, 221, 230, 231, 233, 249, 286
"That Greater Than Which Nothing," 280, 281, 284
"Thinking," 107–8, 228
"The Time Being," 220, 234–35, 280
"To a Friend Going Blind," 15, 19–20, 27
"To the Reader," 187–90, 191, 192, 257, 261
"The Tree of Knowledge," 86, 257
"Try On," 153, 157, 161
"The Turning," 54–58, 105, 219, 225–26
"Two Paintings by Gustav Klimt," 29–32, 63–67, 69, 70, 121, 145n.21, 241

"Underneath (1)," 153, 211–12, 216
"Underneath (3)," 165, 177–78

"Underneath (8)," 151–52, 157
"Underneath (9)," 151, 152, 155, 162, 289
"Underneath (13)," 165–67, 178
"Underneath (Always)," 151, 154, 284
"Underneath (Calypso)," 154, 284, 289
"Underneath (Eurydice)," 276, 286, 291
"Underneath (Uplands)," 154
"Underneath (With Chorus)," 277
"Untitled" (*Region of Unlikeness*), 187, 275, 287, 288
"Untitled One," 106, 286
"Untitled Two," 78, 106, 206–7, 208, 272
"Updraft," 46–47, 48

"The Veil" (*The End of Beauty*), 104
"The Veil" (*Swarm*), 289
"Vertigo," 47–48, 104, 229, 277, 289
"Via Negativa," 221, 290
"The Visible World," 41

"The Way Things Work," 103
"What the End Is For," 89, 90, 203n.7, 221, 223, 257, 259, 285
"Where: The Person," 231
"Which but for Vacancy," 290
"Who Watches from the Dark Porch," 135–36
"Willow in Spring Wind: A Showing," 78, 107, 289, 290
"Woods," 277, 279

"Young Maples in Wind," 104, 141, 277

Index of Names

Adorno, Theodor, 196, 197, 198
Aeschylus, *Agamemnon*, 152
Altieri, Charles, 89, 145n.24, 253n.2
Ammons, A. R., 180, 232; *Glare*, 190
Ashbery, John, 49, 52, 85, 86, 100, 107, 112
Audubon, John James, 35, 106
Augustine, 130, 138, 148, 149, 279, 286
Austen, Jane, 246

Bacon, Francis, 34, 35–36, 39, 106
Baer, Ulrich, 196–97
Bahti, Timothy, 201
Baudrillard, Jean, 72
Bedient, Calvin, 9–10, 145n.24, 202n.1, 255n.19
Benjamin, Walter, 34, 40, 106
Bernstein, Charles, 99, 101n.15
Berryman, John, 42, 99; *Homage to Mistress Bradstreet*, 149
Bible, 43; I Corinthians, 153; Isaiah, 130, 142; Job, 142; Psalms, 142; *Revelation*, 130
Bidart, Frank, *Desire*, 147
Bishop, Elizabeth, 23, 84, 99, 101n.15, 116, 138–39, 161, 184, 220, 230, 231, 242; "Brazil, January 1, 1502," 92, 119, 254n.14; "Cape Breton," 126, 207–8, 213, 214; "The End of March," 231, 235; "In the Waiting Room," 72; "The Monument," 231; "Over 2000 Illustrations and a Complete Concordance," 221; "Poem," 228
Blake, William, 281
Blanchot, Maurice, 282
Bloom, Harold, 62, 187
Brecht, Bertolt, 138
Bridges, Robert, 102
Brock, Werner, 286
Büchner, Georg, *Woyzeck*, 88
Burt, Stephen, 11

Cameron, Sharon, 201, 266–67
Carlyle, Thomas, 237n.7
Caruth, Cathy, 256n.25
Casper, Robert, 268
Cavell, Stanley, 114, 118, 119, 120, 122, 128, 140
Celan, Paul, 197, 201, 202n.6, 281, 285
Christ, 15, 80, 183
Christensen, Inger, 281
Cixous, Hélène, 253n.9
Clampitt, Amy, 84, 222, 230
Clark, Kenneth, 62
Clark, T. J., 189
Cohn-Bendit, Daniel, 268

Index of Names

Coleridge, Samuel Taylor, 75, 84
Columbus, Christopher, 35, 53–54, 97, 98, 101n.12, 239
Comini, Alessandra, 29, 33n.5, 65
Cook, Eleanor, 237n.3
Costello, Bonnie, 8–9, 11n.3, 60, 62–63, 69, 85–86, 144n.15, 202n.1, 242, 252–53n.2, 254n.15
Crane, Hart, 75
Creed, Barbara, 265
Croll, Morris, 99
Culler, Jonathan, 201
Cummings, E. E., 42

Dante, 34, 184
Darwin, Charles, 171, 230
da Vinci, Leonardo, 39
de Beauvoir, Simone, 264–65, 266, 270
de Lauretis, Teresa, 253n.10, 265
Deleuze, Gilles, 191
della Francesca, Piero. *See* Piero della Francesca
de Man, Paul, 201
Demanjuk, John, 89
Derrida, Jacques, 221
Dickinson, Emily, 3, 9, 58, 75, 79, 103, 149, 150–51, 255nn.19 24; "I cannot live with You—," 149–50, 151, 209, 212
Dryden, John, "To Sir Godfrey Kneller," 233
Duncan, Robert, "A Poem Beginning with a Line by Pindar," 189
DuPlessis, Rachel Blau, 238, 253n.2

Eagleton, Terry, 100n.7
Eco, Umberto, 286
Eder, Richard, 159–60
Edwards, Jonathan, 40, 138
Eliot, George, 40
Eliot, T. S., 84, 87, 90, 157, 222, 267; "Burnt Norton," 151; *Four Quartets*, 147; *The Waste Land*, 50, 75, 84, 85, 147, 152, 160
Emerson, Ralph Waldo, 40, 98, 99, 237n.7, 281–82; "Brahma," 284

Empson, William, 232
Erikson, Erik, 271

Felman, Shoshana, 202n.6
Forché, Carolyn, 40, 282
Freud, Sigmund, 31, 207, 214, 217
Fried, Michael, 195
Frost, Elisabeth, 7
Frost, Robert, 84, 87, 190, 222, 281
Fumerton, Patricia, 203n.10

Gander, Forrest, 4–5
Gardner, Thomas, 6–7, 60–61, 67, 68, 84, 85, 90, 101n.15, 139, 202n.1, 239, 242, 252n.2, 253nn.6 7 9, 254nn.13 14, 255n.22, 256n.24, 270, 271, 272n.2
Giddens, Anthony, 199–200, 201
Gilligan, Carol, 273n.11
Ginsberg, Allen, "Kaddish," 58
Goldstein, Laurence, 262, 272n.2
Goya, Francisco de, 60
Gregerson, Linda, 111
Grossman, Allen, 100n.2
Grosz, Elizabeth, 254n.11

Halliday, Mark, 100n.2
Haman, Phillipe, 192
Haney, David, 256n.26
Hardy, Thomas, 222
Hartley, Marsden, 32n.2
Hartman, Geoffrey, 193
Hass, Robert, 116, 126
Heaney, Seamus, 42; *North*, 44
Hegel, G. W. F., 288
Heidegger, Martin, 130, 267, 283, 285, 286, 287, 289
Heinsenberg, Werner, 275
Henry, Brian, 5
Herbert, George, 79, 80, 152
Herzog, Werner, 88, 118
Hill, Geoffrey, 281
Hinton, Laura, 256n.25
Hogue, Cynthia, 10, 255nn.19, 20
Hölderlin, Friedrich, 148, 201

Index of Names

Hollander, John, 99, 237n.3
Hopkins, Gerard Manley, 42–44, 102, 104, 161, 230; "Spelt from Sibyl's Leaves," 43; "The Windhover," 228, 229; "The Wreck of the Deutschland,' 43
Howard, Richard, 84
Husserl, Edmund, 82–83, 278, 280, 287

Irigaray, Luce, 254n.12

James, Henry, 246
Jarman, Mark, 100n.6
Jefferson, Thomas, 240
Jones, David: *The Anathemata*, 147, 163; *The Sleeping Lord*, 163
Jung, Carl, 253n.9
Justice, Donald, "Poem," 189

Kagan, Norman, 273n.5
Keats, John, 28, 43, 51, 117, 161, 214, 222, 234; "To Autumn," 227, 229–30
Kennedy, John, 70, 72, 73, 130, 176, 193, 260, 261, 263
Kirsch, Adam, 11n.3, 159–60, 220, 236n.2
Klimt, Gustav, 15, 29–31, 33n.5, 63–67, 69, 70, 138, 241
Klink, Joanna, 6, 8
Krauss, Karl, 33n.6
Kristeva, Julia, 7, 47, 255nn.19 20, 285
Kubrick, Stanley, 69, 130, 192–93, 260, 263

Lacan, Jacques, 245, 255n.20, 265, 288, 290
LaCapra, Dominick, 254n.15, 256n.25
Lacoue-Labarthe, Philippe, 197, 202–3n.6, 281, 287, 289
Leibniz, Gottfried Wilhelm von, 191–92
Leonardo da Vinci, 39
Levinas, Emmanuel, 251, 256n.26, 281
Levinson, Marjorie, 214
Lewalski, Barbara, 202n.2
Lewis, David, 190
Lewis, Stephanie, 190
Locke, John, 240

Longenbach, James, 5, 7, 145nn.18 22 27, 202n.1, 252n.2, 253n.8, 254nn.16 18, 255n.21, 271–72
Longinus, 276
Louis, Morris, 194
Lowell, Robert: *Land of Unlikeness*, 90; *Life Studies*, 86
Lyon, Sue, 260–63, 265, 268, 270
Lyotard, Jean-François, 200, 201, 203n.9, 275, 276, 285

Macpherson, James, 43
Magritte, René, 79, 189, 202n.4
Mallarmé, Stéphane, 57
Marcus, Greil, 268, 270
Marx, Karl, 34, 190–91, 200
Masaccio, 15, 27, 60, 62
Mason, James, 260
McCabe, Susan, 254n.11
McClatchy, J. D., 237n.3
McGann, Jerome, 89, 214
Melville, Herman, 281; *Moby-Dick*, 38, 39, 40
Merrill, James, 84–85; *The Changing Light at Sandover*, 85, 99; "Overdue Pilgrimage to Nova Scotia," 85
Michelangelo, 155
Mill, John Stuart, 222
Milton, John, 52, 192, 202nn.2 3; *Paradise Lost*, 186–87
Monet, Claude, 276
Montag, Warren, 284
Moore, Lorrie, 273n.11
Moore, Marianne, 38, 52, 58, 85, 244
Mulvey, Laura, 71, 73, 265
Munch, Edvard, 241–42
Munro, Alice, 72

Nabokov, Vladimir, 69
Nancy, Jean-Luc, 38
Nemerov, Howard, "The Blue Swallows," 226
Neumann, Erich, 253n.9
Newman, Barnett, 275, 277

Nietzsche, Friedrich, 278, 284, 288
Noland, Carrie, 203n.10

Oakeshott, Michael, 138
Olitski, Jules, 195
Oppen, George, 75, 215
Ortega y Gasset, José, 281
Otten, Thomas J., 10, 237n.4
Ovid, 138

Paglia, Camille, 72
Palattella, John, 101n.15
Palmer, Michael, 163, 286; *Sun*, 147
Parmigianino, 49
Pascal, Blaise, 79–80
Pater, Walter, 286
Phelan, Peggy, 273n.11
Piero della Francesca, 15, 23, 60, 62, 110
Pinsky, Robert, 84, 99
Plath, Sylvia, "The Applicant," 264, 273n.7
Plato, 16, 34, 39, 106, 170, 235
Poirier, Richard, 190
Pollock, Jackson, 48, 50–51, 60–61, 67, 70, 195
Pound, Ezra, 84, 90, 120, 149, 220, 282; *The Cantos*, 85, 147, 154; "Canto II," 189; "Canto XCII," 154
Puttenham, George, 149

Rich, Adrienne, "The Burning of Paper instead of Children," 190
Rilke, Rainer Maria, 40, 75, 111, 276
Rodriguez, Richard, 267
Roethke, Theodore, "Cuttings," 284
Ronell, Avital, 202–3n.6
Rothko, Mark, 194, 195
Ruskin, John, 222, 230, 236, 237n.7

Sartre, Jean Paul, 278
Scarry, Elaine, 203n.10
Schell, Jonathan, 68
Serres, Michel, 279
Shakespeare, William, 201; *King Lear*, 154; *Macbeth*, 235

Shelley, Percy Bysshe, 58, 93, 222, 234; "Mont Blanc," 231
Shifrer, Anne, 9
Signorelli, Luca, 15, 25–27, 45, 48, 60, 87, 116–18, 122
Snodgrass, Ann, 61–62
Snyder, Gary, 220
Spacks, Patricia Myer, 274n.27
Spiegelman, Willard, 8, 12n.8, 237n.5
Spinoza, Baruch, 284
Stein, Gertrude, 9, 282, 287, 289, 291
Stevens, Wallace, 3, 6, 44, 52, 55, 75, 77, 84, 90, 98, 99, 104, 107, 157, 178, 179, 201, 222, 228, 230, 231, 236, 241, 254n.13, 267, 270; "The Auroras of Autumn," 159; "Esthétique du Mal," 156; "The Man with the Blue Guitar," 53; "The Noble Rider and the Sound of Words," 168; "Notes toward a Supreme Fiction," 54–55; "Peter Quince at the Clavier," 24; "Prologues to What Is Possible," 44; "The Sail of Ulysses," 259; "The Snow Man," 190, 223; "Sunday Morning," 226; "Thirteen Ways of Looking at a Blackbird," 107; "The Weeping Burgher," 43; "The Well Dressed Man with a Beard," 107

Taylor, Charles, 199
Teare, Brian, 255n.23
Thoreau, Henry David, 114, 140, 281
Tiffany, Daniel, 191, 202n.5
Todorov, Tzvetan, 101n.12

Ungaretti, Giuseppe, 177

Vallejo, César, 282
Vasari, Giorgio, 26–27, 33n.4
Vaughan, Henry, "Distraction," 109
Vendler, Helen, 4, 5–6, 7, 68–69, 86, 89, 94, 103, 144n.16, 145nn.23 28 29, 146n.31, 163, 202n.1, 239, 252n.2, 253n.5, 259, 260, 271, 272n.2
Vermeer, Johannes, 49, 170

Index of Names

Weinstein, Deena, 268
White, Emily, 266
Whitman, Walt, 9, 34, 43, 44, 52, 58, 90, 102, 103, 139, 178, 222, 231, 232, 243, 248, 278, 280, 281–82, 284, 286; "As I Ebb'd with the Ocean of Life," 183; "Crossing Brooklyn Ferry," 139, 143, 175, 200, 203n.8; "Of the Terrible Doubt of Appearances," 44; "The Sleepers," 268; *Song of Myself*, 232–33
Wilbur, Richard, 84, 99, 100
Williams, C. K., 104
Williams, William Carlos, 45, 84, 156, 255n.19; "To Elsie," 189
Winnicott, D. W., 217
Wittgenstein, Ludwig, 6, 34, 39, 106, 114, 138, 252n.2

Woolf, Virginia, 289
Wordsworth, William, 52, 193, 214, 222; "The Idiot Boy," 202n.6; "Nutting," 235; "Tintern Abbey," 213–14
Wright, Charles, 103, 104, 112, 220; *Halflife*, 102, 105; *Quarter Notes*, 102, 105
Wyatt, Thomas, 105, 231

Yeats, W. B., 82, 184, 222; "Meru," 290; "A Prayer for My Daughter," 85; "The Second Coming," 85
Yenser, Stephen, 9

Zeno, 49
Zetterling, Mai, 75

CONTEMPORARY NORTH AMERICAN POETRY

Jorie Graham: Essays on the Poetry
EDITED BY THOMAS GARDNER

Paracritical Hinge: Essays, Talks, Notes, Interviews
NATHANIEL MACKEY

DATE DUE

GAYLORD PRINTED IN U.S.A.